The Eucharist
The discussion on the Eucharist by the Faith and Order Commission of the World Council of Churches Lausanne 1927 - Lima 1982.

European University Studies

Europäische Hochschulschriften
Publications Universitaires Européennes

Series XXIII
Theology

Reihe XXIII   Série XXIII

Theologie
Théologie

Vol./Bd. 370

PETER LANG
Frankfurt am Main · Bern · New York · Paris

Polycarp Chuma Ibebuike

The Eucharist

The discussion on the Eucharist
by the Faith and Order Commission
of the World Council of Churches
Lausanne 1927 – Lima 1982

PETER LANG
Frankfurt am Main · Bern · New York · Paris

CIP-Titelaufnahme der Deutschen Bibliothek

Ibebuike, Polycarp Chuma:

The Eucharist : the discussion on the Eucharist by the Faith and Order Commission of the World Council of Churches Lausanne 1927 - Lima 1982 / Polycarp Chuma Ibebuike. - Frankfurt am Main ; Bern ; New York ; Paris : Lang, 1989
(Europäische Hochschulschriften : Reihe 23, Theologie ; Bd. 370)
Zugl.: Frankfurt (Main), Phil.-Theol. Hochsch. St. Georgen, Diss., 1988
ISBN 3-631-42119-2

NE: Europäische Hochschulschriften / 23

ISSN 0721-3409
ISBN 3-631-42119-2

© Verlag Peter Lang GmbH, Frankfurt am Main 1989
Alle Rechte vorbehalten.

Printed in Germany 1   3 4 5 6 7

I

TABLE OF CONTENTS

		PAGE
Abbreviations		VII

Foreword

Introduction 1

Chapter One: Lausanne 1927 6

1.1	The Beginnings.	6
1.1.1	The Episcopal Church of America	6
1.2	The origin of Faith and Order	13
1.2.1	The North American Preparatory Conference	17
1.2.2	The Geneva preliminary conference 1920	18
1.2.3	The world conference at Lausanne 1927	25
1.2.3.1	The method of, and proceeding at Lausanne conference	25
1.3	Papers presented by the Confessions on: The Nature of the Church	32
1.3.1	The Orthodox Church	32
1.3.2	Congregational, Lutheran, Methodist.	34
1.3.3	The Report of Section III on The Nature of the Church	40
1.3.4	Assessment.	41
1.4	Papers presented by the Confessions on: The Sacraments.	46
1.4.1	The Orthodox Church.	46
1.4.2	Congregational	48
1.4.3	The Evangelical Lutheran	53
1.4.4	Report of Section VI	57
1.4.5	Assessment.	58

Chapter Two: Edinburgh To Montreal

2.1	Lausanne to Edinburgh	61
2.2	Edinburgh 1937	64
2.2.1	Report of Section III.	66
2.2.1.1	Authority of the sacraments	66
2.2.1.2	The nature of sacraments	67
2.2.1.3	Number of sacraments	68
2.2.1.4	Validity of sacraments	69
2.2.1.5	The Euchrarist	71
2.2.1.6	Intercommunion	73

Page

2.3	Formation of World Council of Churches. Faith and Order as a component part	75
2.3.1	The Committee of Thiry-five	77
2.3.2	Resolution of Life and Work at Oxford	79
2.3.2	Resolution of Faith and Order at Edinburgh	79
2.3.4	The Committee of Fourteen	81
2.3.5	Amsterdam 1948	83
2.4.	Lund 1952	87
2.4.1	Report of Section IV on: ways of Worship	90
2.4.2	Report of Section V on: Inter-communion.	93
2.4.3	Communion at ecumnical gatherings	97
2.5	Montreal 1963: Report of section IV on: The Eucharist.	99
2.6	Developments in the Roman Catholic Church: The Second Vatican Council	102
2.6.1	Dogmatic Constitution on the Church	103
2.6.2	Decree on Ecumenism.	106
2.6.3	Other related texts on ecumenim	116
Chapter Three: Aarhus To Accra.		
3.1	Aarhus: Report of Committee III..	124
3.2	Thoughts on a study of the eucharist.	126
3.2.1	The historical method...	127
3.2.2	The diversity of liturgies in the ancient church...	130
3.2.3	Maranatha	132
3.2.4	Eucharist and Agape	133
3.2.5	Apostolic office and the eucharist...	134
3.3	Consultation at Grandchamp 1965. Notes on the Lord's Supper	137
3.3.1	Anamnesis and epiclesis	137
3.3.2	Nuptial communion and fraternal communion	140
3.3.3	The Supper as the revelation of the limits and fullness of the church...	144
3.3.4	Living bread and sacrifice	146
3.3.5	Prayer and its fulfilment	153
3.3.6	Mass and Eucharist	154
3.3.7	Report of the Cunsultation	156
3.4	Bristol 1967: The holy Eucharist	162

		PAGE
3.4.1	The anamnetic and epikletic character of the eucharist	162
3.4.2	the catholic character of the eucharist	164
3.4.3	Eucharist and Agape	166
3.4.4	Report of Section II	168
3.5	Louvain 1971	170
3.5.1	Beyond Intercommunion	171
3.6	Accra 1974: The Eucharist	184
3.6.1	Preamble	184
3.6.2	The institution of the eucharist	185
3.6.3	The meaning of the eucharist	186
3.6.3.1	Thanksgiving to the Father	186
3.6.3.2	Anamnesis or Memorial of Christ	187
3.6.3.3.	Invocation and gift of the Spirit	188
3.6.3.4	Communion within the Body of Christ	190
3.6.4	Implications of the eucharist	191
3.6.5	The elements of the eucharist	192
3.6.6	Recommendations	193
3.6.7	Evaluation	195

Chapter Four: Ecumenical Eucharistic Statements.

4.0	Introduction	201
4.1	The Arnoldshain Theses 1957	203
4.1.1	Assessment	207
4.2	Angican/Roman Catholic: The Windsor Statement 1971	211
4.2.1	Historical background	211
4.2.2	Windsor Statement 1971	212
4.2.2.1	The mystery of the eucharist	213
4.2.2.2	The eucharist and sacrifice of Christ	214
4.2.2.3	The presence of Christ	214
4.2.3	The Elucidation 1979	219
4.2.4	Assessment	222
4.3	Group of Les dombes	226
4.3.1	Doctrinal agreement on the eucharist	227
4.3.1.1	The Eucharist: The Lord's Supper	227
4.3.1.2	The Eucharist: Act of thanksgiving to the Father	228
4.3.1.3	The Eucharist: Memorial of Christ	228
4.3.1.4	The Eucharist: Gift of the Spirit	230
4.3.1.5	The sacramental presence of Christ	231

		Page
4.3.1.6	The Eucharist: Communion in the Body of Christ	232
4.3.1.7	The Eucharist: A mission in the world	233
4.3.1.8	The Eucharist: Banquet of the kingdom	234
4.3.1.9	The presidency of the eucharist	
4.3.2	Pastoral agreement: The meaning of the eucharist	236
4.3.3	Assessment	239
4.4	Lutheran/Roman Catholic: The Eucharist 1978	242
4.4.1	Historical background	242
4.4.2	The legacy of Christ according to the scripture	243
4.4.2.1	Mystery of faith	244
4.4.2.2	Through, with an in Christ	245
4.4.2.3	In the unity of the Holy Spirit	249
4.4.2.4	Glorifiation of the Father	251
4.4.2.5	For the life of the world	256
4.4.2.6	With a view to the future glory	257
4.4.3	Common Tasks.	259
4.4.3.1	Eucharistic presence	259
4.4.3.2	Eucharistic sacrifice	262
4.4.3.3	Eucharistic communion	266
4.4.3.4	Eucharistic ministry	268
4.4.3.5	Eucharistic fellowship	269
4.4.3.6	Liturgical form	271
4.5	Orthodox/Roman Catholic: Historical background	273
4.5.1	The mystery of the Church and the eucharist in the light of the mystery of the Holy Trinitiy	276
4.5.1.1	Part I	277
4.5.1.2	Part II	281
4.5.1.3	Part III	286
4.5.1.4	Evaluation	289
Chapter	Five: Roman Catholic View-Points	309
5.1	Pope Paul VI: Mysterium Fidei - historical background	311
5.1.2	The mystery of faith	316
5.1.3	The eucharistic real presence	318
5.1.4	Opinions	322
5.1.5	Eucharistic sacrifice	338
5.1.6	Eucharistic worship	344
5.1.7	Summary	348
5.2	The New Order of Mass	349
5.2.1	Preliminary history	350
5.2.2	The structure of the Mass	354
5.2.3	The Liturgy of the Word	355

		Page
5.2.4	The Liturgy of the eucharist	357
5.3	Exkurs: anamnesis	364
5.3.1	Old Testament	365
5.3.2	New Testament	369
5.4	Intercommunion (communicatio in Sacris)..	373
5.4.1	A brief history of S.P.C.U.	373
5.4.2	The Eumenical Directory, May 1967	376
5.4.3	Cases of admission to communion in the Catholic Church, June 1972.	379
5.4.3.1	The Eucharist and the mystery of the church	379
5.4.3.2	The Eucharist as spiritual food	381
5.4.4	General principles governing admission to communion	382
5.4.5	Differences in view of the principles between members of the Oriental Churches and Other Christians.	384
5.4.6	Authority that decides particular cases	385
5.4.7	Evaluation	386
Chapter Six:	Bangalore To Lima	
6.1	Recapitulation	393
6.1.2	Bangalore to Lima	394
6.2	The Eucharist: Lima convergence Text	399
6.2.1	The institution of the eucharist	399
6.2.2	The meaning of the eucharist	400
6.2.2.1	The eucharist as thanksgiving to the Father	401
6.2.2.2	The eucharist as anamnesis or memorial	402
6.2.2.3	The eucharist as invocation of the Spirit	407
6.2.2.4	The eucharist as commuion of the faithful	409
6.2.2.5	The eucharist as meal of the kingdom	412
6.2.3	The celebration of the eucharist	413
6.2.4	Evaluation	415
6.3	The Lima Eucharistic Liturgy	431
6.3.1	Origin	431
6.3.2	The structure	432
6.3.3	Liturgy of entrance	433
6.3.4	Liturgy of the Word	434
6.3.5	Liturgy of the Eucharist	435
6.3.6	Evaluation	439

		Page
6.4	The response of the Churches	444
6.4.1	Romanian Orthodox Church	447
6.4.2	Church of England	453
6.4.3	Evangelical Lutheran Church in Bavaria	461
6.4.4	Netherlands Reformed Church and reformed Churches in the Netherlands	466
6.4.5	American Baptist Churches in the U.S.A.	468
6.4.6	Evangelical Church of Westphalia	471
6.4.7	The Roman Catholic Church	477
6.4.8	Evaluation	490
	Conclusion	501
	Bibliography	509

ABBREVIATIONS

AAS	- Acta Apostolicae Sedis.
acc.	- according to.
A.G.	- Ad Gentes.
ARIC	- Anglican Roman Catholic International Commission
BEM	- Baptism, Eucharist and Minstry.
C.D.	- Christus Domini.
cf.	- confer.
DS.	- Densinger.Schönmetzer.
D.V.	- Dei Verbum.
ed/eds	- edited, editor / editors.
EKD	- Evangelische Kirche Deutschlands.
FO	- Faith and Order Papers.
G.I.	- General Instruction.
hrsg.	- Herausgegeben,
ibid.	- Ibidem.
IMC	- International Missionary Council.
IS	- Information Service.
JWG	- Joint Working Group.
KNA	- Katholische Nachrichten Agentur.
KuD	- Kerygma und Dogma.
Life and Work	- The universal Christian Council for life and work.
L.G.	- Lumen Gentium.
No.	- Number.
O.E.	- Orientalium Ecclesiarum.
op.cit.	- opus citatum.
O.P.	- Optatam Totius.
ÖR	- Ökumenische Rundschau.
P.O.	- Presbyterorum Ordnis.
p/pp.	- page/pages.
S.C.	- Sacrosanctum Concilium.
SPCU	- Secretariat for the Promotion of Christian Unity.
ThPh	- Theologie und Philosophie.
TQT	- Theologische Quartalschrift Tübingen.
U.R.	- Unitas Redintergratio.
USA	- United States of America.
VELKD	- Vereinigte Evangelische Lutherische Kirche Deutschlands
vol.	- Volume
WCC	- World Council of Churches.
Y.M.C.A.	- Young Men's Christian Association.
Y.W.C.A.	- Young Women's Christian Association.
ZKtH	- Zeitschrift für Katholische Theologie.

The abbreviations for the biblical references are the same as found in the Jerusalem Bible, Standard Version, London, Darton, Longman and Todd, 1966, pp. x-xi.

ABBREVIATIONS

AAS	– Acta Apostolicae Sedis
acc.	– according to
ACC	– AC Centre
ARIC	– Anglican-Roman Catholic International Commission
BEM	– Baptism, Eucharist and Ministry
CD	– Christus Dominus
cf.	– confer
D	– Denzinger-Schönmetzer
D.V.	– Dei Verbum
ed./eds.	– edition/edition & editors
EKD	– Evangelische Kirche Deutschlands
G.I.	– General Instruction
hrsg.	– herausgegeben
ibid.	– ibidem
IMC	– International Missionary Council
IS	– Information Service
JWG	– Joint Working Group
KNA	– Katholische Nachrichten Agentur
LuG	– Leitgedanken und Gebet
L&W	– Life and Work – The Universal Christian Council for life and work
L.G.	– Lumen Gentium
No.	– Number
O.E.	– Orientalium Ecclesiarum
op.cit.	– opus citatum
O.R.	– Osservatore Romano
ÖR	– Ökumenische Rundschau
P.O.	– Presbyterorum Ordinis
p/pp	– page/pages
S.C.	– Sacrosanctum Concilium
SPCU	– Secretariat for the Promotion of Christian Unity
T&Ph	– Theologie und Philosophie
TQU	– Theologische Quartalschrift Tübingen
UiR	– Unitas in Christus
USA	– United States of America
VELKD	– Vereinigte Evangelisch-Lutherische Kirche Deutschlands
vol.	– Volume
WCC	– World Council of Churches
Y.M.C.A.	– Young Men's Christian Association
Y.W.C.A.	– Young Women's Christian Association
ZKTh	– Zeitschrift für Katholische Theologie

The abbreviations for the Biblical references are the same as found in the Jerusalem Bible, Standard version, London, Darton, Longman and Todd, 1966, pp. x-xi.

FOREWORD

After I have concluded and defended my dissertation, I learnt that a similar topic was handled by one Gerhard Karl Schäfer at the Evangelical Faculty of Theology of the University of Tübingen. (Eucharistie im ökumenischen Kontext. Zur Diskussion um das Herrenmahl in Glauben und Kirchenverfassung von Lausanne 1927 bis Lima 1982, Göttingen, Vandenhoeck u. Ruprecht, 1988).

I was happy that I did not know of this work and I carried out my research in my own way.

The two works are similar in the sense that both covered the Faith and Order discussion on the eucharist starting from Lausanne 1927 to Lima 1982. But each of us went his own way in presenting the historical-dogmatic work. The two works differ from each other in so far as I incorporated into my work some bilateral discussions on the eucharist as is evident in chapter four. Another outstanding difference can be noted in chapter five of my work, where I treated the Catholic teaching on the eucharist based on Pope Paul VI's encyclical: Mysterium Fidei, her stand on the issue of communicatio in sacris and her eucharistic liturgy. One other conspicuous difference touches the response of the churches of which a selected few was presented in my work.

One may feel free to say that the two works compliment each other; the one was written in German and the other in English. Again the work is handled by two theologians of different backgrounds, one Protestant, the other Catholic.

ACKNOWLEDGEMENTS

In the light of St. Paul`s exhortation to the
Colossians to "Always be thankful", (Col. 3:15), I
wish to record my thanks and gratitude here to a
number of people who assisted me in various ways
during the period I was writing this work.

My heart-felt thanks and gratitude go to my
Moderator Prof. Dr. Werner Löser, who inspired me
to take up this topic that touches the heart of
the Ecumenical movement today. His kindness,
sympathy and encouragements during our discussion
sessions sustained me not a little to march on
till the end. May the good Lord continue to guide
and bless him in his teaching apostolate.

My indeptedness goes to Prof. Dr. Ludwig
Bertsch, the then Rector of the faculty, who is
also the Co-Referent to my dissertation. He was a
source of consolation and encouragement in moments
of difficulties. It is the Lord who in his
infinite goodness that can best reward him. I
thank very specially as well all the professors
at Hochschule St. Georgen.

I thank the chief librarian at the WCC centre
in Geneva, A. J. van der Bent and his colleagues
for making the library accessible to me. Frau
Hannelore Pohlenz and her co-workers at the
Ecumenical centre in Frankfurt deserve my hearty
thanks and Dr. G. Miczka and his co-workers as
well of the library of St. Georgen in Frankfurt.

I thank my bishop, Most Rev. G.O. Ochiagha, the
Catholic bishop of Orlu, Nigeria, who sent me to
Federal Republic of germany to study. His constant

letters to find out my situation, his eventual
visit to see things for himself and his assurance
of prayers are signs of solidarity which went a
long way to sustain me.

I hereby express my special thanks to the
Bishop of Limburg, Most Rev. F. Kamphaus, for his
invitation to study in Germany and for shouldering
part of my financial burdens. May the good Lord
bless him and all those placed under his pastoral
care.

I very sincerely thank Missio-Wissenschaftliche
Institute Aachen for the scholarship.

My special and filial respect go to my parents,
Boniface and Cecilia Ibebuike. They brought me up
in the Christian faith and to this upbringing I
pledge to hold very tenaciously.

I will not forget to thank my colleague, Rev.
S.I. Okechukwu, whose comradeship became a source
of mutual encouragement that sustained us throughout these years of sojourn in Europe. May I use
this forum to thank all those who in any way
rendered me help during my studies.

Finally, I thank our Father in Heaven, who made
all these things to be possible. To Him be honour,
praise and glory now and for ever.

Frankfurt, 31 May 1988   P.C. Ibebuike

INTRODUCTION.

Our topic has to do with the theological
discussion on the eucharist by the Faith and
Order Commission of the World Council of
Churhces. This did not take place just in one
session or within one year but lasted for fifty-
five years. In handling it a historical appraoch
to the Faith and Order Movement was incorporated.
The Faith and Order Movement itself was born as a
result of the peplexity provoked by the exclusion
from the agenda of matters concerning faith and
order of the Edinburgh International Missionary
Conference in 1910. Bishop Brent of the Episcopal
Church of America, before he left home after the
conference gave a hint to some of his friends
that he would call upon his Church to arrange a
similar conference where matters concerning faith
and order would be discussed.

Because of the role of the Episcopal Church to
initiate the Faith and Order Movement, we
undertook a brief history of this Church to
highlight her previous moves towards the unity of
the Church. This was handled in the first chapter
along with the history of the origin of the Faith
and Order Movement, which culminated at the first
World Conference of Faith and Order at Lausanne
in 1927. We presented a selection of the papers
by different confessions on the Nature of the
Church, and on the Sacraments. The topic on the
sacraments is directly related to our subject
matter here, the paper on "The Nature of the
Church", was incorporated because of the
ecclesiological importance to the overall quest

for the unity of the church. The reports of the
section groups on the two topics are presented and
the result reflects the differences that exist
among the churches.

The second chapter covered the range between the
Second World Conference at Edinburgh 1937, and
the Fourth at Montreal in 1963. The conference at
Edinburgh saw not only the discussion on the
sacraments including the eucharist but also on
intercommunion and a resolution on the formation
of the WCC. The stages towards the formation of
the WCC were outlined. The WCC was finally
constituted at Amsterdam in 1948 with Faith and
Order as its component part. The conference at
Lund brought an end to the method of "comparative
ecclesiology", which has been in vogue. The new
method consists in going back to the common
sources, namely: the scriptures, tradition, the
Fathers of the church, the ancient councils and
synods to varify a common statement of the
conference. While the conference at Lund tackled
the topics "ways of worship and intercommunion",
at Montreal the eucharist was discussed. All
along the Catholic Church was not involved in
this ecumenical movement. It has been the preoccupation of the Protestant Churches and some
Orthodox Churches. The Second Vatican Council
opened the way to the Catholics to participate in
the movement. The close of chapter two saw
recorded the developments brought about by the
Council towards the ecumenical movement.

The eucharist was taken up as a study project by
the Faith and Order Commission in 1965, in

accordance with the specifications worked out in
1964 at Aarhus by the Commission. Two papers that
stimulated the discussion were presented. The
study project then went through the plenary
meetings of the Commission at Bristol, 1967,
Louvain 1971, and Accra 1974. The Accra text was
sent to the churches and their reactions were
sought in the manner of response. All these are
found in the third chapter.

The Roman Catholic Church brought with her into
the ecumenical movement a new accent in the area
of bilateral dialogue between her and other
Churches. The Faith and Order Commission which
organized the multilateral dialogue, took
advantage of the results of the bilaterals on the
common topics like the eucharist. It co-ordinated
the results of the bilaterals and noted that the
two types of dialogues compliment each other. On
account of this, we devoted the fourth chapter
mainly to selected bilateral dialogues on the
eucharist, understood here as an extension of the
discussion by the Commission on Faith and Order
on the eucharist.

It is a well known fact that the schism of 1054
was between the east and the west, that is,
between the Orthodox Church and the Catholic
Church; and that the Reformation in the 16
century was directed against the Catholic Church.
The controversy on the question of the
eucharistic sacrifice, the real presence of
Christ and eucharistic worship since the
Refomation is still with us today. The Roman
Catholic Church is affected on both sides. In the

fifth chapter the eucharistic teaching of the
Roman Catholic Church based on Pope Paul VI's
encyclical, Mysterium Fidei, was presented. This
will help the reader to understand the stand of
the Catholic Church on the controverted issues as
they re-appear in the dialogues both bilateral
and multi-lateral. In addition we presented the
ecucharistic liturgy of the Catholic Church in
vogue since 1969 and finally the stand of the
Catholic Church on eucharistic hospitality.

The response of the Churches to the Accra text
indicate that the eucharistic text has to be
revised. In chapter six, we continued the study
project on the eucharist after Accra. This time
it went through Bangalore 1978, to Lima 1982. At
Lima the fifty-five year long discussion on the
eucharist was said to have reached a matured
stage to be sent to the churches for their
responses. The eucharistic Lima text was
published alongside with the texts on baptism and
ministry as a convergence text. A selection of
the responses of the churches are presented and
analyzed. In this selection we represented the
responses of the major churches and confessions.

METHOD.

Our topic is both historical and dogmatical
work. It is historical in the sense that the
plenary meetings of the Faith and Order Commission
did not just take place on one day. The discussion
lasted for fifty-five years, and this at an inter-
val of at least four years. These stages are
historically traced and the development and progress of the dogmatic discussion were vividly
recorded. The hisotrical background to certain
sub-headings are undertaken both for clarity and
in favour of my would-be-readers back home in
Nigeria.
At every stage of the discussion, the
Commissison issued a report. In this work each
report of the Commission at the corresponding
stage is presented, criticized and evaluated
under the dogmatic view-points. This method has
the advantage of helping the reader to evaluate
without much difficulty, the amount of progress
made at each stage and at the same time to have a
broad view on the overall issues. On account of
this method and for the fact that much was drawn
from the original sources, the outcome looks like
a collage (image from images). This result becomes
profitable not only to the professional theologian
but also to the non professional. In effect both
can make meaningful contributions in the process
of the reception of the eucharistic document.
The aim of the ecumenial movement is directed
towards the goal of visible unity of the Christian
churches and in one eucharistic fellowship and
common life in Christ that the world may believe.
The eucharistic dialogue is designated to clear
the misunderstandings and differences among the
churches on the controverted issues and thus open
the way to eucharistic communion for the churches.
The Lima eucharistic convergence text is a compendium of this effort, and this work reflects it
comprehensively.

CHAPTER ONE.

LAUSANNE 1927

1.1 T H E B E G I N N I N G S.

Before we delve into the eucharistic discussion
by the Faith and Order at the Lausanne
Conference, we would like to give a historical
background to the origin of the Faith and Order
Movement. It was the Episcopal Church of America
that initiated the Movement. On account of this,
we shall first of all highlight a few facts in
the life and polity of the Episcopal Church of
America, and certain moves it made towards the
unity of the church; then we shall say something
about the origin of the Faith and Order Movement
before presenting part of what happened at the
First World Conference on Faith and Order at
Lausanne in 1927.

1.1.1 THE EPISCOPAL CHURCH OF AMERICA.

The idea of a World Conference on Faith and
Order was the brain child of Bishop Charles Brent,
the then bishop of the Philippines. He was a delegate from the Episcopal Church of America to the
Missionary Conference in Edinburgh, 1910. The detailed history of the Episcopal Church of America
is not within the scope of this essay but I want
to bring out certain moves made by this church
towards christian unity in the late 19th century,

which I think prepared the ground for the initial break through within this church to undertake the preparation for a world conference on Faith and Order, which took place at Lausanne 1927.

The Prostestant Episcopal Church of America is the Anglican church in the United States of America. It won its autonomy and became independent from the Church of England since 1789 but remained an integral part of the Anglican Communion of Churches and joined in kinship of faith, government and worship to the English mother church.[1] The ecclesiastical system of government in the Episcopal church includes parish or local congregations, dioceses, provinces and the General Convention. The diocese, consisting of a number of parishes, is governed by a bishop; and the diocesan convention, which is held annually is presided over by the bishop and is composed of both priests and laity. The highest governing body is the General Convention. It meets every three years and consists of two Houses: the House of Bishops and the House of Deputies. The House of Bishops is made up of all bishops as members, while the House of Deputies is composed of delegates, consisting of equal number of priests and laymen elected from each diocese. The National Council, with the presiding bishop of the House of Bishops as its head, carries on the national work of the church between sessions of the General Convention.

---

1. cf. The New Catholic Encyclopedia, vol. V, New York, London, Sydney, McGraw-Hill, 1967, p. 487.

The Episcopal Church holds to the Apostles' and
Nicene creeds as doctrinal symbols. At its General Convention in 1801 it accepted with some
modifications the Thirty-Nine Articles of the
Church of England as a general statement of doctrine, but adherence to them as a creed is not
demanded. This liberal attitude was made clear in
the forward to the Book of Common Prayer, for it
states: "It is a most invaluable part of that
blessed 'liberty wherewith Christ hath made us
free', that in his worship different forms and
usages may without offence be allowed, provided
the substance of the Faith be kept entire; and
that, in every Church, what cannot be clearly
determined to belong to Doctrine must be referred
to Discipline; and therefore, by common consent
and authority may be altered, abridged, enlarged,
amended, or otherwise disposed of, as may seem
most convenient for the edification of the
people, 'according to the various exigency of
times and occasions.'"[2]

In the first half of the 19th century, when
certain people in America were crusading for a
united church of America, the Episcopalians developed their own variation towards christian unity. The Reverend Thomas Hubbard Vail of Hartford,
Connecticut, in 1841 came up with the idea of a
comprehensive church. His idea was to start with
a church which has a "comprehensive programme"
and as the other churches join what is imperfect
in it would be perfected. In his opinion he says:

---

2. cf. Book of Common Prayers, p.V.

"Instead of endeavouring to strike out an entirely new system of ecclesiastical unity, the
proper and only feasible course is to select, for
the purpose of uniting within it, some system
already established, and which realizes most
nearly the idea of a Comprehensive Church, and if
it be not in every respect perfect, to improve
it, if it will allow improvement, into perfection."[3] There is no doubt that for Vail, the
existing system was found in his own Episcopalian
church, for he felt that "It may be, there is
such a system amongst us - a system whose structure is capable of any modification, and in whose
organisation are instrumentalities by which it
may be shaped into any form which the majority of
christians in our country may desire. We believe
there is such a system among us."[4] The Rev. Vail
was insistent that it was his church which could
provide the system when he writes: "The Episcopal
church offers the comprehensive programme for
unity, for it includes within itself all the
points of church life which the other denominations hold essential, as well as its own individual excellences e.g. the three fold ministry."[5]

---

3. Yoder D.H., Christian Unity in Nineteenth-
   Century America; in: Rouse Ruth and Neill S.C,
   (ed.), A History of the Ecumenical Movement
   1517-1948, London, S.P.C.K., 1954, p. 248.
4. ibid.
5. ibid.

The proposals made by Vail proved too vague for
application, and it was left to other minds to
work in more practical and specific ways to awa-
ken the church to its newly-conceived mission.

At the General Convention of 1853, Dr. Willian
Augustus Muhlenberg led a group of presbyters in
addressing the House of Bishops, the now famous
"Muhlenberg Memorial". The Memorial requested the
assembled bishops to set up "some ecclesiastical
system, broader and more comprehensive than that
which you now administer, surrounding and including the Prostestant Episcopal Church as it now
is, leaving that church untouched, identical with
that church in all its great principles, yet providing for as much freedom in opinion, discipline, and worship as is compatible with the
essential Faith and Order of the Gospel."[6] In the
opinion of Yoder D. Herbert, "The principal immediate result of the Memorial was the appointment
in 1856 of a committee to renew the correspondence with the Church of Sweden, which has elap-
sed since colonial days."[7]

Another advocate for christian unity among the
Episcopalians in the late 19th century, and perhaps the most influential, was William Reed
Huntington. In his book - The Church Idea - An
Essay Toward Unity published in 1870, he set forth
a minimum list of "essentials" of Anglicanism
upon which other groups could unite. As formulated in 1870, this pioneer union proposal include:

---

6. Yoder D.H., op. cit., p. 249.
7. ibid.

"1. the Holy Scriptures as the Word of God;

2. the primitive Creeds as the rule of faith;

3. the two Sacraments ordained by Christ himself;

4. the historic episcopate as the keystone of governmental unity."[8] This is known as Huntington's Quadrilateral, which later made history.

The General Convention of 1886 in Chicago finally adopted Huntington's Quadrilateral as the four-point basis to be used in future Episcopalian proposals for christian unity. The committee of the House of Bishops reported inter alia: "We do hereby affirm that the Christian unity now so earnestly disired by the memorials can be restored only by the return of christian communions to the principles of unity exemplified by the undivided Catholic church during the first ages of its existence; which principles we believe to be the substantial deposit of Christian Faith and Order committed by Christ and his Apostles to the Church into the end of the world, and therefore incapable of compromise or surrender by those who have been ordained to be its stewards and trustees for the common and equal benefit of all men. As inherent parts of this sacred deposit, and therefore as essential to the restoration of unity among the divided branches of christendom, we account the following to wit:

1. The Holy Scriptures of the Old and New Testament as the revealed Word of God.

---

8. ibid, p. 250

2. The Nicene Creed as the sufficient statement
of the christian Faith.

3. The two sacraments-Baptism and the Supper of
the Lord ministered with unfailing use of
Christ's word of institution and of elements
ordained by him.

4. The Historic Episcopate, locally adapted in
the methods of its administration of the very
needs of the nations and peoples called of God
into the unity of His Church."[9]

A commission was set up from the House of
Deputies with a mandate, using the "Chicago
Quadrilateral" - as it is now called - as the
basis for discussion on christian unity with
other churches. This Chicago Quadrilateral, was
slightly modified by the Lambeth Conference of
1888 and was thus named the "Lambeth
Quadrilateral", a very important ecumenical
statement for the Anglican Communion.

---

9. cf. Journal of the General Convention 1886, p.
   80. quoted here acc. to: Epting K.C., Ein
   Gespräch beginnt, Zürich Theologischer Verlag,
   1972, p. 16.

1.2 THE ORIGIN OF FAITH AND ORDER.

The origin of the proposal to hold a World Conference on Faith and Order[10] is associated with the World Missionary Conference, in Edinburgh, 1910.

This conference should be understood as an important event in the Protestant church history and one of the basis of ecumenical events of our time. As a missionary conference it set out to discuss the problems facing the church and how to solve them. To make it possible for many Protestant communions to attend the conference the organising committee in its constitution among other things said that "no expression of opinion should be sought from the conference on any matter

---

10. "Das Begriffspaar "Faith and Order" erschien zum ersten Mal in dem Einigungsprogramm der Episkopalkirche in Amerika von 1886. "Faith" meint den Glaubensinhalt im Unterschied zur Glaubensfunktion (belief) oder zur Formulierung eines Glaubensbekenntnisses (creed). "Order" meint im anglikanischen Sprachgebrauch die Fragen nach der Kirche, des geistlichen Amtes und der Sakramente. "Order ist der Inbegriff der festen Formen göttlicher Einsetzung, die zum Wesen der Kirche gehören". cf. Frieling Reinhard, Die Bewegung für Glauben und Kirchenverfassung 1910-1937, Vandenhoeck & Ruprecht, Göttingen, 1970, pp. 19-20
"That pair of words "Faith and Order" was used for the first time in the programme of unity of the Episcopal Church of America in 1886. Faith denotes the content of belief in contrast to belief in its functional dimension and in contrast to the creed. "Order" is used by the Anglicans to indicate matters concerning the church, ministry and sacraments. "Order is the essence of all kinds of divine institution, which belong to the nature of the church."" (Translation is mine).

involving any ecclesiastical or doctrinal question on which those taking part in the conference differed among themselves."[11] This clause made it possible for the Anglican church and other High churchmen to send delegates to the conference. In a joint letter addressed to the Society for Preaching the Gospel (Church of England), which has already rejected the invitation to attend the Edinburgh conference, bishop Charles Gore and bishop Talbot said that they had been given assurances by the executive officers, that the conference "proceeds upon the principle of entire mutual respect between christian denominations, and has definitely pledged itself that questions affecting the differences of Doctrine and Order between the Christian bodies shall not be brought before the conference for discussion or resolution."[12]

To this conference was bishop Charles Brent a delegate. He was a member of the Protestant Episcopal Church of America, and then a missionary bishop of the Philippines. The question of not discussing issues about Faith and Order was one of his perplexities and also a subject of meditation during the conference. In his address, a day before the close of the conference, he said inter alia: "During these days a new vision has been unfolded to us. But whenever God gives a vision He also points to some new responsibility, and you and I, when we leave this assembly, will go

---

11. World Missionary Conference vo. 9. 1910, p.8.
12. Tatlow Tissington, the World Conference on Faith and Order, in: Rouse Ruth and Neill S.C., (ed.), A History of Ecumenical Movement 1517-1948, London, S.P.C.K., 1954, p.406.

away with some fresh duties to perform, and perhaps as we have thought of the new responsibilities that this conference has suggested to us, we
have been somewhat troubled, because already our
load is heavy."[13] The new vision for bishop Brent
was certainly the vision of the united church,
and one of the new responsibilities was to initiate a world conference on Faith and Order. He
told some of his friends in Edinburgh about his
resolution to call upon his own church to take
the lead in preparing another world conference to
deal with those matters of Faith and Order that
had been excluded in Edinburgh.

Bishop Brent utilized the opportunity he was
looking for during the General Convention of the
Episcopal Church in October 1910. The General
Convention took place in Cincinnati on 19th October. The day before the Convention, the bishop
addressed a mass meeting of the delegates from
both Houses of the Convention and told about the
Edinburgh conference, the need for unity that was
revealed there, and about his conviction that the
time had come to examine differences frankly in a
world conference on Faith and Order. An influential layman, Robert Gardiner, suggested that
steps should be taken to secure some definite
action by the Convention. It was the Rev. W.T.
Manning, later bishop of New York, on 19th October, who proposed a resolution which was passed
unanimously by both Houses:
"That a Joint Commission be appointed to bring
about a conference for the consideration of

---

13. World Missionary Conference vol.9, 1910,
    p.330.

questions touching Faith and Order, and that all
Christian Communions throughout the world which
confess our Lord Jesus Christ as God and Saviour
be asked to unite with us in arranging for and
conducting such a conference."[14] The commission
was duly appointed comprising seven bishops,
seven priests and seven laymen. It elected the
bishop of Chicago, C.P. Anderson as president and
Mr. Robert Gardiner as secretary. While it was
Bishop Brent who conceived the idea of the conference on faith and order, it was upon Gardiner
that most of the work fell.

At the time the Protestant Episcopal church
was holding its General Convention, two other
Protestant churches were holding theirs as well.
The National Convention of the Disciples of
Christ on 18. October 1910 passed a resolution
and created a commission for Christian Union.
This was realized through the indefatigable
effort of Rev. Peter Ainslie. The National Council of Congregational Churches in the United
States of America, on the very same day and quite
independently, appointed a special commission to
consider any overture which might be made "in
view of the possibility of fraternal discussion
of church unity suggested by the Lambeth Conference of Bishops in 1908."[15]

These resolutions were seen as a happy coinci-
dence. The commission of the Episcopal Church
appointed a committee on Plan and Scope. The
committee held frequent meetings and examined
suggestions of what its general plan should be,

---

14. Tatlow Tissington, op.cit., p.407
15. op.cit., p.408

before it subsequently "advised the commission to
ask the prayers of all christian people for the
movement; to secure the appointment of independent but cooperating Commissions of all the churches of the world; to bring such Commissions into
conference, and through an Executive appointed by
them to work out plans for a World Conference on
Faith and Order."[16]

1.2.1 THE NORTH AMERICAN PREPARATORY CONFERENCE.

The American Commissions of Faith and Order
Movement met from 4-6 January 1916 in Garden
City, Long Island. Inevitably Faith and Order
work in Europe and other parts of the world came
almost completly to an end, because of the First
World War. It was at the instance of the commission of the Protestant Episcopal church that this
meeting convened. Sixty-three delegates attended,
representing fifteen churches. The secretary, Mr.
Gardiner remarked that the idea of the world
conference was in many cases misunderstood. That
people could not differentiate between unity and
uniformity or unity, federation or cooperation.
The conference showed that it was aware of where
it was steering the boat judging from the topics
which it decided should be handled by the world
conference. The subjects decided are:

1. The church, its nature and functions;
2. The Catholic Creeds, as the safeguards of the
   faith of the church;

---

16. ibid.

3. Grace and Sacraments in general;
4. The Ministry, its nature and functions;
5. Practical questions connected with the missionary and other administrative functions of the
   church.[17]

In January 1917, the second meeting of the
commissions was held in Garden City, with fifty
delegates in attendance. The aim of this meeting
was to detach the organisation of the movement
from the hands of the Protestant Episcopal
church. Although new leaders were chosen, they
could not operate until after the Geneva Preliminary Conference of 1920.

1.2.2. THE GENEVA PRELIMINARY CONFERENCE, 1920.

When the war ended, the Episcopal church -
Commission lost no time in despatching a deputation to visit Europe and the near East. The duty
of the deputation was to talk about the planned
world conference on faith and order to the churches and to get their support. The move was
greatly rewarded as many churches promised to
send delegates to the conference. This commission
later decided to invite all cooperating commit-
tees and commissions to send three delegates each
to Geneva in order to decide what subjects should
be prepared for the world conference.

That meeting assembled on 12-20 August at
Athénée in Geneva. The 133 delegates came from
about forty countries representing eighty chur-

---

17. Tatlow Tissington, op.cit., p.414.

ches, "including all the great families or groups
of Trinitarian Churches, except the church of
Rome which had declined to participate."[18] Bishop
Brent of the Episcopal church of America was
elected as chairman. In his opening speech, he
told the delegates that this movement originated
from his vision at the world missionary conference in Edinburgh and the subsequent resolution
of his church to set up a commission to bring
about a conference for the consideration of questions touching faith and order. The purpose was
to bring about an outward and evident unity of
the church of God. He went further and told the
delegates why they had gathered: "The purpose of
this present conference is to prepare for the
World Conference which is our ultimate goal. We
must discuss and arrange for organisation, determine what topics should occupy our attention when
we meet and adopt measures which will best further our purpose. It is possible that there will
be not one conference, but many conferences. We
must remember that what we are undertaking is the
most colosal thing that men could set their hand
to, and as I have said before, if it were not for
the fact that we know it is in accordance with
God's will we would not dare to undertake it."[19]

The first days were devoted to hearing speeches from representatives of churches on their
idea of the unity of the church in general. When
the conference progressed methodologically, Bishop Gore, (Anglican), and Dr. Bartlet (Congregational), were asked to give talks on "the meaning

---

18. Faith and Order Pamphlets No. 33, p.2.
19. op. cit., p.22.

of the Church and what we mean by unity." Then
there followed detailed discussion. Another topic
that engaged the conference was "what is the
place of the Bible and a Creed in relation to
reunion?" All the resolutions made were referred
to the business committee. Before the conference
dispersed it appointed a Continuation Committee
consisting of forty persons and charged them
among other things: "...with the duty of carrying
on the work of preparation for the World Conference or Conferences on Faith and Order, correspondence and co-operation with the Commissions of
various communions, fixing the time and place of
a conference, and performing all such other duties as may be necessary to arrange for the Conference."[20]

The Continuation Committee met on the 19th of
August and elected Bishop Brent as its chairman
and Mr. R. Gardiner as secretary. This committee
appointed a 'Subject Committee', whose duty was
to select the topics for discussion and to draw
the programme for the World Conference. The
committee under its chairman, the then bishop of
Bombay, proceeded immediately to frame questions
concerning the "faith of the reunited Church",
which were circulated for purposes of information.
The continuation committee had two other outstanding meetings before the World Conference;
one in Stockholm in 1925, the other in Berne
1926. In Stockholm, the committee named Lausanne
as the venue of the World Conference, chose the
date, determined the duration and the number of
delegates that would be expected. The committee

---

20. Faith and Order Pamphlets, No. 33, p.73.

also drew up the programme interposing it with
the seven topics selected. The problem which
emanated from it was solved and ratified in Berne
1926.

As was its custom, the Subject Committee sent
out questions to the churches concerning two
sacraments, baptism and eucharist, wanting to
know whether differences in practice would be
accomodated in the reunited church. From the
answers it received, it issued a statement in the
name of the subject committee. Below is the summary of their statement on the eucharist.

In the preamble the committee said that what
was necessary for the reunited church concerning
the eucharist for all those who take part in it
was the readiness to do what the Lord did and
commanded, and also the readiness to receive what
he would wish to give. It went further to point
out what was generally agreed upon from the answers it received, namely:

1. that the eucharist is the memorial celebration
   of the death of the Lord;
2. The Lord is (in faith) present in it in his
   whole saving power.
3. that the believer receives from Him spiritual
   food and through his bond with the Lord is
   renewed and strengthened;
4. that through this renewal and strengthening of
   his membership with the Lord, he renews and
   strengthens that unity with other members of
   His Body.[21]

---

21. Sasse H., Die Weltkonferenz für Glauben und
    Kirchenverfassung, Lausanne 3-21 August 1927,
    Im Furche-Verlag, Berlin, 1929, pp.82-83

Generally bread and wine are recognized as the
sign of the sacrament. For the consecration of
the bread and wine the words of institution must
be said during the service. There were different
opinions about the Real presence and the sacrificial character of the eucharist on one hand and
the relationship between the minister of this
sacrament and the validity and effectiveness of
the rite on the other. The committee hoped that
when different teachings are probed and discussed
in the atmosphere of tolerance, then agreement
could be reached on the question of the presence
of the Lord in the eucharist. The committee received from many people the question: "who was the
lawful minister of this sacrament?" One group of
the questioners represent the idea that only a
priest ordained by a lawful bishop can preside
over the eucharist; the other group which opposed
this idea because it has no ordained minister
maintained from the argument a posteriori, that
they experience the grace of God when they celebrate the eucharist. The committee gave its
opinion thus:

1. that the members are convinced that the power
   and grace from this sacrament come from God
   not from men and that men are only God's instrument;
2. that the minister of this sacrament acts not
   on his behalf but for the community and the
   church;
3. that the minister should be ordained to receive the mandate, in order to act for God and
   to represent the whole church before God.
4. that the validity of the sacrament should not

be called into question when it is presided
over by one who is not ordained; that the
matter should not be a pre-condition for the
unity of the church, but that it is necessary
to win over the recognition of the ministry.
5. that some believe on the general priesthood of
christians, and therefore maintain that one
who does not receive ordination but is chosen
by a church can preside over the eucharist.[22]

After the meeting of the continuation committee in Stockholm in 1925, a rumour had gained
wide currency to the effect that "a programme had
been decided upon which would restrict the freedom of the conference, in that decisions were
being made for it in advance."[23] When the continuation committee met at Stockholm from 15-18
August 1925, only 15 members were present under
the chairmanship of Bishop Brent. One of the purposes of this meeting was to draw up the programme
for the World conference. The seven topics to be
discussed were confirmed. Resolutions on the
first topic - The call for Unity - and the
seventh, - the continuation of the work of the
conference - were drawn up which would be put
before the conference for a vote.[24] This idea of
formulating resolutions before hand and the fact
that only a few members were present in the committee meeting gave occasion for suspicion and
complaints. The Germans proposed a supplementary
topic - The Church's message to the world: the
Gospel. From the United States, Professor

---

22. op. cit., p.83.
23. Tatlow Tissington, op. cit., p.419
24. cf. Frieling Reinhard, op. cit., p.54

F.J. Hall (Episcopal Church) in a letter he
circulated, criticized sharply the programme that
was already drawn. When the continuation
committee met in Berne 1926, Dr. Scherer (United
Lutheran Church of America), relied on that
letter and demanded in the name of his church
that they be given more opportunity to err their
views, so that the movement would not be
dominated by the idea of the Anglicans and of the
English speaking Free churches.[25] Bishop Cannon
(Methodist) proposed a resolution which saved the
continuation committee from the danger of
compromise in matters concerning faith and a pre-
emted programme for the unity of the church.[26] On
this account the continuation committee passed a
resolution: "in view of the serious misunderstandings which have arisen and which are likely
to arise in the future", which rendered obsolete
the programme drawn up in Stockholm and insisted
that "the official programme of the conference
should contain only the statement of times and
places of meeting... the subjects to be discussed
and the names of the speakers... and that all
resolutions to the contrary should be re-
scinded."[27] The topic suggested by the Germans was
accepted and included in the final list which read
as follows:

1. The call to unity.
2. The church's message to the world: the Gospel.
3. The nature of the church
4. The church's common confession of faith.

---

25. ibid, p.56.
26. ibid.
27. ibid.

5. The church's ministry.
6. The sacraments.
7. The unity of christendom and the relation
   thereto of existing churches.[28]

It was this list of topics that the First World
Conference on Faith and Order discussed in Lausanne, 1927.

1.2.3   THE WORLD CONFERENCE AT LAUSANNE 1927.

1.2.3.1 METHOD OF PROCEEDINGS IN LAUSANNE
        CONFERENCE

On August, 1927, at the University of Lausanne, a total number of about 439 delegates
representing 108 churches assembled for the First
World Conference on Faith and Order. After the
opening service in the Cathedral, the conference
began its work by electing Bishop Brent as President and Dr. A.E. Garvie was appointed deputy
chairman. The first four successive days were
devoted to hearing papers expounded by representatives from different confessions, of course from
the point of view of their own church. Each
speech was followed by a general discussion.
After four days the conference divided into four
sections of about equal size for three days of
simultaneous discussion of the first four subjects. Then the conference came together to discuss the first draft of the report prepared by
each section. A similar plan was followed for the

---

28. cf. Tatlow Tissington, op.cit., p.420.

second half of the agenda, and by 20 August six
reports had been accepted for transmission to the
churches.[29]

Until the third World Conference in Lund 1952,
the first two conferences in Lausanne and Edinburgh, as regards the manner in which the papers
were presented has been described as "comparative
ecclesiology". That corresponds with the intention of the Episcopal Church of America, which
initiated the movement in 1910. In the resolution
proposed by Rev. W.T. Manning, he said among
other things that "...the conference is for the
definite purpose of consideration those things in
which we differ, in the hope that a better understanding of divergent views of faith and order
will result in a deepened desire for reunion and
in official action on the part of the separated
communions themselves."[30] This principle was
maintained throughout the conference in Lausanne
and as if to crown it all the preamble to the
reports sent to the churches after the conference
portrays the same idea for they wrote: "...its
object is to register the apparent level of
fundamental agreements within the conference and
the grave points of disagreements remaining."[31]
The conference sought ways and means not only of
understanding one another but also for the future, how to get at more agreements in order to
make the movement grow. This spirit was expressed

29. ibid, p.421
30. cf. Frieling Reinhard, op.cit., p.21.
31. Bate H.N. (ed.), Faith and Order Proceedings
    of the World Conference Lausanne, August 3-
    21, 1927 Garden City, New York, 1928, p.59.
    Further quotations as: Faith and Order,
    Lausanne 1927.

by W.A. Browns in his remarks before the report
was given on - The nature of the church. For he
said: "If we had to choose between rhetoric and
love, we felt it our duty every time to let
rhetoric go. I trust that the purists in the
conference will bear this in mind when they study
the construction of some of our sentences. To the
eye of the rhetorician they may seem clumsy and
ineffective, but for us they have proved bridges
by which we have walked across the rivers of our
division to the fertile valleys of spiritual
unity."[32]

The Rules of Procedure for the conference were
eleven in number. The section seven is concerned
with the method of adopting section reports. It
stated that "no statement shall be declared to be
adopted by the conference unless it be accepted
either unanimously or 'nemine contradicente'.[33]
The conference could determine what other steps
it could take when a statement could not gain
acceptance by the stipulated rule. Bishop Gore
recognized that the suggested rule would preclude
the adoption of any statement by the conference
upon which the conference was not completely unanimous. What he sought for was that some "words
(be) inserted which would prevent statements
approved merely by a large majority of the conference from being regarded as receiving its
approval."[34] The question was discussed at length
and finally the Section seven of the Rules was

32. op.cit., p.225.
33. op.cit., p.41.
34. ibid, p.42.

referred to the Arrangements Committee for re-
drafting. The redrafted and adopted section seven
read thus:

"When reports from the sections have been made
to the full conference, if alterations in them
are proposed, the Conference may refer them to a
Drafting Committe for consideration and report.
In any such report any differences remaining
shall be clearly indicated, as well as the agreement reached. No statement shall be declared to
be accepted by the Conference unless it be accepted either unanimously or nemine contradicente."[35]

To some delegates at the conference the aim of
the conference was not quite clear. Some thought
that the conference aimed at working out a plan
for a united church before it dispersed. Bishop
Brent had oft restated that: "this Conference was
not called to provide a sufficient basis for
unity in its first inception, "But rather" a
conference in which both agreements and disagreements were to be carefully noted."[36] According to
Tatlow "These misconceptions of the aim were at
least partly responsible for a marked feature of
the later part of the conference - a series of
declarations of their position by the members of
different communions."[37]

On the morning of 17 August, on behalf of the
Evangelical Lutherans, a declaration was read in
German, French and English, signed by Lutheran
leaders from France, Norway, Latvia, the United
States, Germany and Sweden. They expressed their

35. Faith and Order, Lausanne 1927, p.197.
36. op.cit., p.387.
37. Tatlow Tissington, op.cit., p.423.

profound conviction of the need for unity, and
their whole-hearted sympathy with the aims and
spirit of the conference, and also their desire
that no final vote should be taken on the
propositions formulated there. They should be
regarded as material for further consideration.
It was also their opinion that these material
should be referred to a commission representative
of various churches which should be charged with
the duty of carefully examining the propositions
and to set forth the points of agreement and
difference in doctrine and to refer them to commissions of different communions.[38] "There can be
little doubt", said Tatlow "that behind this
cautious attitude towards pronouncements lay the
feeling among the Lutherans and other Continen-
tals that difficulties of language and use of
Anglo-Saxon methods of procedure unfamiliar to
them had prevented them from making their due
contribution to the discussions, and made them
hesitate to assume responsibility for the decisions reached."[39]

The next morning, 18 August, Archbishop Ger-
manos read a declaration on behalf of the Orthodox Churches. Their declaration stated that they
had "taken part in every meeting held here for
the purpose of promoting closer brotherhood and
fellowship between the representatives of the
different Churches and for the general good and
welfare of the whole body of Christians."[40] They

---

38. cf. Faith and Order, Lausanne 1927, p.374.
39. Tatlow Tissinton, op.cit., p.423.
40. Faith and Order, Lausanne 1927, p.383.

regret "that the basis assumed for the foundation
of the Reports which are to be submitted to the
vote of the Conference, are inconsistent with the
principles of the Orthodox Church."[41] It went
further to specify the differences which separate
them from other members of the conference and
added to these inconsistencies "we cannot enter-
tain the idea of a reunion which is confined to a
few common points of verbal statement."[42] The
declaration stated categorically that the Orthodox representatives "must refrain from agreeing
to any Reports other than that upon the Message
of the Chruch, which we accept and are ready to
vote upon", and what they could most do was "to
enter into co-operation with other Churches in
the social and moral sphere on a basis of christian love."[43] Tatlow traced the origin of this
declaration to the continuous meetings held by
the representatives of the Orthodox Churches in
the course of the conference and the fact that
they failed to present a united front regarding
the section reports which were presented for
acceptance "owing to there being both conserva-
tive and progressive groups among them."[44]

These two declarations gave rise to other
statements from groups and individuals each ex-
pounding the position for which it represents.
Particular among them were a group of Reformed
churches in Europe, and the Society of Friends.[45]

---

41. ibid,
42. ibid, p.385.
43. ibid.
44. Tatlow Tissington, op.cit., p.424.
45. cf, Faith and Order, Lausanne 1927, pp.395;
    409-413

By the end of the conference the assembly had
unanimously adopted a statement on "The call to
unity", prepared by the officers of the conference and the chairmen and secretaries of the six
sections. The full conference had also received
"nemine contradicente", the reports of sections
II-IV and referred the report of section VII to
the Continuation Committee.

We shall now address ourself to the papers
delivered on "The Nature of the Church" and "The
Sacraments".

1.3 PAPERS PRESENTED BY THE CONFESSIONS ON: THE
     NATURE OF THE CHURCH

At his opening remarks at the presentation of
the first version of the report of Section III,
W. A. Brown spoke of three main groups represented in their section whose convictions and traditions needed to be considered. The first group
could be named "catholic" to which the Orthodox,
the Anglicans and the Old Catholics belong. The
next is congregational in polity and it includes
the Congregationalists and the third was named as
the intermediate group. We begin with the first
group.

1.3.1 THE ORTHODOX. (Chrysostom/Alivisatos).

This address was presented by Prof. H.S. Ali-
visatos on behalf of Archbishop Chrysostom.
    In his address Chrysostom maintained that the
church was divinely instituted for the salvation
of the faithful. The church was founded by
Christ, who determined also its laws, means and
ordinances on which it was built. It was to the
apostles chosen by Christ, who had the onus to
establish the church everywhere in the world.
This church is visible and invisible because of
its divine and human nature. He argued that "this
twofold nature of the church seen and unseen, can
be inferred from the Bible and the Fathers, which
teach us to regard the Church as symbolising the
two natures, divine and human, in the Person of

the Lord, whose work the Church continues."[46]
Adducing proofs from the scripture and from the
Fathers he showed that the church founded by
Christ as a visible community is infallible. The
aim of the church "is the sanctification of men
and the building up of the Kingdom of God, that
is to say, the uniting of man with God, who is
the fountain of life and blessedness."[47] This
church of Christ is one and looking at it externally "this unity is not affected by the use of
varying languages in worship, nor by the external
varieties of organisation in local Churches."[48]
Religious Communion severed from it either by
heresy or schism, looses its membership, and this
does not affect the unity of the church. He went
further to say that "the church is one in her
internal life, and this unity is based upon the
one Christ, who, abiding with her, gives life to
her through the Holy Spirit, uniting the faithful, the members of the one body, with Himself as
its Head."[49] The church is also Holy because her
body is holy and the Holy Spirit works in her.
The church is catholic because it "knows no local
limitations. It is ecumenical and worldwide, as
that kingdom of God which Jesus proclaimed
..though scattered over the world, it existed as
one whole through the identity of its faith in
our Lord Jesus Christ."[50] He emphasized the catholicity of the local church, which could be
identified with "the Church which possesses the

---

46. Faith and Order, Lausanne 1927, p.108.
47. ibid, p.110.
48. op.cit., p.110.
49. ibid.
50. ibid. pp.112-113.

true and right faith."[51] The church is also apostolic and for any church to have a rightful
claim to this apostolicity "it must keep unspot-
ted the apostolic doctrine and tradition exactly
as these existed in the time of the Apostles",[52]
and this apostolicity is maintained "through the
divinely-constituted Hierarchy, and so alone,
this church is connected by unbroken succession
with the Apostles and keeps the deposit committed
unto it by them."[53]

Concluding, the Archbishop said that their
view of the nature of the church corresponds to
what was held in the ancient and undivided
church. For him all christian bodies could be
united on the basis he outlined if only they
would avoid what he called "the extravagances of
Romanism" and "the extremes of the theories most
opposed to Romanism." What these meant he did not
elaborate.

1.3.2 CONGREGATIONAL (Rev. S. Parkes Cadman).

The Rev. Cadman set forth to say that his duty
was to trace in barest outline the genesis and
development of the church as God's living organism for the world's redemption. He went on to
say that "the christian Church is the most characteristic creation of our common faith" and
that her chief glory consists of "regenerated
souls who are the living stones built into her

---

51. ibid.
52. ibid.
53. ibid.

spiritual fabric."[54] He spoke of the significance
of different confessions and communions, which he
said should be recognized "as indispensable parts
of organic whole in the kingdom of the Holy
Spirit", and that "all are branches of the one
Vine."[55] The ideals of the church survived all
the turbulent periods and thrived in the hearts
of many. He declared: "The conception of the
Church as for ever one, holy and indivisible,
God's new creation in Christ Jesus her Lord, has
survived the perilous patronage of the great and
noble. It still thrives in many hearts unwithered
by the glare of sectional prejudice or national
arrogance."[56]

He said that the church did not start as an
institution. "Her institutional forms first found
shape in distinct isolated assemblies, attracted
by their common life in Christ, and related on to
another by the personal influence and authority
of His Apostles and their messengers."[57]
The threefold order of ministry developed after
the apostles which he recalled was invoked by St.
Cyprian, was "not in behalf of subsequent theories of apostolic succession or sacerdotal prero-
gative, but for the unity of the Church and the
defence of her doctrinal purity."[58]

Talking briefly on the problems of the church
which led to the Reformation in Europe he concluded it with the concept of the church pro-
minent among the Congregationalists in the 17

54. Faith an Order, Lausanne 1927, p.115.
55. ibid.
56. ibid.
57. ibid.
58. ibid.

36

century and in his own words: "The Church universal is not a visible organisation, but the sum
total of all faithful souls who group themselves
in fellowship fashioned for their needs and
convictions, and who obey what they hold to be
the precedents of Holy Scripture."[59]

On his vision about the reunited church he
spoke about freedom and equality and was convinced that "believers of every persuasion are
one organism animated by a common religious life,
knit together by the unity of one spiritual discipline, and held by the tie of a united hope."[60]
The model of equality which he advocated was
exemplified in the reorganisation of the British
Commonwealth of Nations, "upon the basis of abso-
lutely free and equal self-governing states,
between which there is no question of superior or
inferior status, though all gladly recognise in
the Motherland the primus inter pares."[61] In the
thinking of the Congregationalists therefore,
"The Church is best united by flexible ties,
unhampered by onerous restrictions, and having
the pliablity of life as against the rigidity of
uniformity, combined with hearty acknowledgement
of the historic past."[62] He goes on to say that
no historic or local communion has hitherto borne
an exclusive witness to the saving truths of God.

He went further to talk about the criterion of
the true church which he says "is not conformity
to type, but effectiveness in fulfilling the will
of her Lord, and therefore that organisation need

59. ibid, p.122.
60. ibid.
61. ibid.
62. ibid.

not be of a single type."[63] Next he spoke about
the gulf between freedom and authority in the
church and called for their harmonization and
questioned why not: "The very nature of the
church and of her ordinances imply an order which
begins and ends with freedom, passing from that
freedom which obeys lawful authority to the larger freedom to which such obedience leads."[64] He
described the church as "the extension of her
Lord's Incarnation" which "must always be the
companion of earthly circumstances." He argued
against using the past events in the church to
judge the present insisting that much of the past
should not be cared for "except as it enables us
to see our way through that which is happening
now." He went further to show his pragmatic ideas
and portrayed his doubts when he said: "But I
know no theory of the Church, her doctrines, her
ministry, or her sacraments, which contains their
measureless significance for the transmission of
God's saving grace."[65] He concluded by saying
that "our finest conceptions of the church are
therefore tentative and predictive rather than
absolute and final."

Having summarized the addresses of Chrysostom
and Cadman as representing the first and second
groups as was classified by W.A. Brown, we now
come to the third. This group which he called the
"intermediate group", comprises the Lutherans,
the Presbyterians and Reformed, the Methodists
and the Evangelical Churches of Germany. In
actual fact this group as such did not exist for

---

63. ibid.
64. ibid.
65. op.cit., p.126.

there was no homogeneous concept of the church
among them. But here and there, were statements
about the nature of the church stemming from the
Reformation period. We mention some of them in
brief.

Prof. Ménégoz (Lutheran), rejected certain
views of the nature of the church expressed by
the Orthodox. He said: "Certainly we are at one
in rejecting two views of the nature of the
Church: that which identifies a particular ecclesiastical organisation with the kingdom of God,
and that which makes a radical division between
the visible and the invisible Church."[66] He then
went on to describe the church as: "The totality
of the various denominations claiming the name of
Jesus Christ, being the sphere in which the divine "Pneuma" breathes, as the agent of human
redemption: or briefly, the Church is the "Body
of Christ" animated by the Holy Spirit."[67]

The Rev. H.B. Workmann (Methodist), who spoke
about the static and dynamic concepts of the
church, but preferred the dynamic, described the
church as: "a living organism with a life comparable to that of any retardation, only grander,
richer, fuller, for it is an organism instinct
with the divine life and with an oversoul in
which we find the workings of the Holy Spirit
Himself."[68] In the opinion of Prof. Siegmund
Schultze, "the church is the highest thing with
which our earthly knowledge brings us into
contact. It is closely knit-up with Jesus Chirst:

---

66. op.cit., p.139.
67. ibid, p.139.
68. ibid, p.143.

it is the mystical Body of Christ."[69] This body
of Christ implies plurality of members ruled by
the Spirit. The church being destined for all men
is universal, and because the revelation of God
is committed to it, it is holy, and thus "its
continuity, from the Apostles whom Jesus sent
out, to our own day, is an essential mark of the
Church."[70] In conclusion he reiterates that the
church of Christ in this age is a suffering not a
triumphant body. The resurrection he said must be
preceded by the cross.

The next description of the church came from
H.J. Wotherspoon (Presbyterian), as "a company of
poor sinners gathered at the foot of the cross
and seeking to offer themselves to the will of
God."[71]

Prof. Otto Schmitz (Evangelical), saw some
contrasts in the nature of the church and recommended faith as the only instrument for dis-
cernment. He said that: "The New Testament presents us with the vision of a Church which is
more than an idea, invisible in itself but sym-
bolically represented in acutal Churches; with a
divine sphere of salvation, energising in this
world with the powers of the world to come and
yet essentially contrasted with this world. Faith
requires us to discern this Church in the organised Churches."[72]

---

69. ibid, p.147.
70. ibid.
71. ibid, p.157
72. ibid, p.158

1.3.3 THE REPORT OF SECTION III ON THE NATURE OF THE CHURCH

The Report[73] of section III is presented in the following order: First the agreements reached by the delegates were put down in five paragraphs; next come the disagreements followed by explanatory notes. The agreements are:

1. God founded the Church, Christ is the head of the church, the Holy Spirit its continuing life.
2. The New Testament metaphors are retained for those who believe in Christ as: the Body of Christ, the Temple of God, the People of the New Covenant.
3. The Church functions as God's chosen instrument by which Christ, through the Holy Spirit, reconciles men to God through faith.
4. The attributes of the church are: one, holy, catholic and apostolic.
5. Six characteristics of the church by which it can be known by men.
   a. Holy Scripture.
   b. Profession of faith in God.
   c. Preaching of the gospel to every creature.
   d. The observance of the sacraments.
   e. Ministry for pastoral office, preaching of the word and the administration of sacraments.
   f. spirituality and holiness.

---

73. cf., Faith and Order, Lausanne 1927, pp.463-466.

The differences in opinion concern:

1. Relationship between Scripture and Tradition.
2. The nature of the visible and invisible church.
3. The significance of the divisions in the church, past and present.

1.3.4 ASSESSMENT.

From the report of section III, one can observe that the ideas of the "catholic" group often prevailed over the Denominational. Just from the first paragraph of the report it was stated that "The church of the living God is constituted by His own will, not by the will or consent or beliefs of men whether as individuals or as societies."[74] Human beings play an instrumental role in the hands of God. This agreement demolished the submission of Cadman who maintained that the christian church is the most characteristic creation of our common faith. A definitive blow was dealt to the idealistic concept of the church held by the Congregationalist and the historical understanding of the church held by the Orthodox prevailed. This is evident in the fifth paragraph of the report, where it is stated that there are certain characteristics which the church on earth posseses, and through which it can be known since the days of the apostles. The basic dogmatic difference between the two groups in this report lies in the fact that

---

74. ibid., p.463.

one group maintains a trinitarian concept in the
salvation history identifying the church with the
kingdom of God, and emphasizes Tradition as regards the nature and structure of the church. The
other is pneumatic in character and directs its
attention to the believers, differentiating between the Holy Spirit and apostolic Tradition, as
well as between the church and the kingdom of
God.[75] For the latter the origin and continuity
of the church lies in the gospel of Jesus.

The report attempted to summarize the different positions in a general explanation when it
talks about, 'the divine institution of the
church'; 'the fellowship of those who believe in
God'; and about 'God's chosen instrument'. It
maintained in the second paragraph the New Testament metaphors for the church, the consensus
secured earlier by the Subject Committee.

The statement of paragraph three is trinitarian in nature pointing towards eschatology:
"The Church is God's chosen instrument by which
Christ, through the Holy Spirit, reconciles men
to God through faith..until His Kingdom come in
glory."[76]

The factors of unity were outlined in paragraph four and these are the four attributes of
the church contained in the Nicene Creed, viz,
one, holy, catholic and apostolic. This brought
to light once more that the unity of the church
sought by one group is through the complex unity
in faith and institution while for the other it
is a pneumatic unity. For the first group, the

75. cf., Frieling Reinhard, op.cit., p.104.
76. Faith and Order, Lausanne 1927, pp.463-464.

elements of the apostolicity of the church are
the apostolic doctrine and Tradition, with the
apostolic succession; and for the other, it is
the preservation of the apostolic faith contained
in the gospel.

The established differences brought out by the
report, first concerned the interpretation of the
word of God, for it said: "Some hold that this
interpretation is given through the tradition;
others through the immediate witness of the
Spirit to the heart and conscience of believers;
others through both combined."[77] From this difference of opinion comes what was acceptable to the
delegates but however could not narrow the difference. The report put it thus: "The possession
and acknowledgement of the Word of God as given
in Holy Scripture and interpreted by the Holy
Spirit to the Church and to the individual."[78]

The second basic difference established in the
report concerned "the nature of the church visible and the church invisible, their relation to
each other, and the number of those who are included in it". In the first paragraph of the
notes relating this problem, the different opinions were that: "Some hold that the invisible
Church is wholly in heaven; others include in it
all true believers on earth, whether contained in
any organisation or not."[79] This concerns in a
sense the conception of St. Augustine "coetus
electorum", carried through by western theology
which the Orthodox is not used to. But this idea
was foremost in the speech of Bishop Gore during

---

77. ibid, p.465.
78. ibid, p.464.
79. ibid, p.465.

the section report.[80]

The other paragraphs of the remarks do not speak about visible and invisible church but about the permanent structure or otherwise of the church; whether the only true church is identifiable with one particular church, and whether one particular form of ministry is necessary for the good of the church. It goes on to say that:

Some hold that the visible expression of the church was determined by Christ Himself and is therefore unchangeable; others that the one Church under the guidance of the Holy Spirit may express itself in varying forms.

Some hold that one or other of the existing churches is the only true church; others that the church as we have described it is to be found in some or all of the existing communions taken together.

Some, while recognising other christian bodies as churches, are persuaded that in the providence of God and by the teaching of history a particular form of ministry has been shown to be necessary to the best welfare of the church; others hold that no one form of organisation is inherently preferable; still others, that no organisation is necessary.[81]

---

80. "Most of us probably hold that the number of those who are being saved in the world today is not completely included in any branch of the church, or in all together, but that they are known to God, and the existence of such disciples whom the church has not known how to win is made known to men through the fruits of the Spirit in their lives." cf., Faith and Order, Lausanne 1927, p.422.
81. op.cit., p.465.

The significance of the divisions in the
church past and present was differently evaluated.
One group's view was "that no division of christendom has ever come to pass with out sin", yet
the other "that the divisions were the inevitable
outcome of different gifts of the Spirit and
different understandings of truth", and finally
that God has advanced His cause in the world, in
spite of and even through these divisions.[82]

The debate about the nature of the church was
bipolar. The one group represented "Orthodox-
Catholic" concept of the church; the other represented the Protestant. One is trinitarian and
identifies the church with the kingdom of God and
holds Tradition for the nature and structure of
the church. The other was pneumatic and laid
emphasis on the individual believers and differentiates between the Holy Spirit and apostolic
Tradition. There is no doubt that their different
ecclesiologies will manifest itself as we consider the next topic on the sacraments.

---

82. ibid.

1.4   PAPERS PRESENTED BY THE CONFESSIONS ON:
        THE SACRAMENTS.

1.4.1   THE ORTHODOX. (BISHOP NICHOLAI).

The bishop went straight to the subject matter
and said that the sacraments which are also
called mysteries in the East are seven in number
in the church namely:
"Baptism, Confirmation, Eucharist, Penance, Ordination, (cheirotonia), Marriage and Extreme
Unction."[83] He said also that each sacrament
hides itself in 'a mysterious and miraculous
action of the Holy Spirit'. Although the christian does not know how the Holy Spirit works in
the sacrament, he believes that the Spirit works
in and through it.

Through the sacrament of Baptism, the soul is
cleansed from sin, becomes an adopted son of God
and is incoporated into the army of Christ. Baptism which is also called new birth was commanded
by the Lord, the bishop explained. He showed that
baptism is indispensable quoting Cyril of Alexandria: "Whosoever be unbaptized cannot be saved,
except the martyrs, who even without water (but
by the blood) receive the Kingdom."[84]

In the sacrament of Confirmation the baptized
receive the gifts or powers of the Holy Spirit.
Quoting from the scriptures he showed that Confirmation was ordained and instituted through the
practice of the Apostles.[85]

About the Eucharist he said that at the moment

---

83. Faith and Order, Lausanne 1927, p.286.
84. ibid.
85. cf, (Acts 8, 15-17; 19, 1-6; 2Cor1, 20-22).

of the priest's invocation, "God the Holy Spirit
descends on the bread and wine which have been
set forth and sanctified and transubstantiates
them into Christ's body and blood. (not transforms them but transubstantiates them; for the
substance is changed while the form of bread and
wine remains to our eyes unchanged)." [86] He called
the eucharist 'a mystery of the perpetual love of
God through sacrifice'. In the eucharist, Christ
is our real food, and this fact characteristi-
cally differentiates this sacrament from the
others. "So great is the love of God that in this
mystery the Lord gives us not only His gifts, as
in other mysteries, but Himself." [87]

Through the sacrament of Penance man receives
forgiveness of his sins committed after baptism.
The bishop then went further to show the order in
which it works: "Sin being repented of, confessed
and forgiven, man gets the liberty to enter again
the house of his Father." [88]

In the sacrament of Ordination of priests, the
Holy Spirit gives the special grace of orders to
the priest "through the act of laying-on of the
hands of the Apostles and their successors upon
the head of those who have been found worthy." [89]

Through the sacrament of Marriage, man and
woman are united as husband and wife "for the
special purpose of the growth of the church of
God according to God's commandment and for the
mutual help of husband and wife in the work of
their salvation." [90]

---

86. Faith and Order, Lausanne 1927, p.287.
87. ibid.
88. ibid.
89. ibid, pp. 287-288.
90. ibid.

In the sacrament of Extreme Unction, (the Anointing of the sick), the bishop said that "the Holy Spirit comes to man's life in its last emergency and heals the sick."[91] Through this sacrament therefore, health is restored and sins are remitted.

The bishop saw in the seven sacraments, the seven different workings of the Holy Spirit which correspond to the living situation of the individual and of the church community. To apply the question of more or less important to the sacraments, should not arise, for according to the bishop: "Throughout its whole past, down to our times, the church has gathered a rich experience of the effective workings of God the Holy Spirit in all these seven Mysteries."[92] In conclusion the bishop sounded a note of caution to those who might think that baptism and eucharist are the only sacraments and asked them to pray to God for light, so that he may reveal to them the truth as he had always revealed to the saints.

1.4.2 THE CONGREGATIONALIST (Prof. J.V. Bartlet).

He set forth to discuss only two sacraments namely, baptism and the eucharist, which he said have "clear New Testament authority." He noted that the diversities in the conception of the sacraments among the churches constitute a crucial problem especially in the eucharist. "This is the case particularly with the sacrament of

---

91. ibid.
92. ibid. p.289.

the Lord's Supper, that Holy Communion in which
inner unity ought to find its most typically
Christian expression, but which has in fact become the great dividing line and barrier to
fuller fellowship."[93] He went further to trace
the origin of these diversities, and identified
them with the different approaches to the Scriptures between 'Catholics' and 'Evangelicals'.
According to him 'catholics' are "those who view
'the mind of Christ' primarily through the meaning
put on His teaching and that of the apostolic
writers by the Ancient Church of the Greek and
Latin Fathers; by 'Evangelicals', those who rely
more on direct study of the New Testament read in
its own light and usage - made the more clear by
a comparative study of the Old Testament writings, as illustrative of the forms of thought in
which Biblical revelation is couched."[94]

In discussing Baptism, he started from John
the Baptist, who called for moral repentance on
prohetic lines and as the condition of readiness
for the kingdom of God. John realised from the
beginning the provisional nature of his work and
looked forward to the coming of the one mightier
than he. "But John realised the merely provisional nature of his own work: the positive inspiration needful to achieve the great change to a new
level of life, one really divine in quality,
would come as a baptism with something of more
transforming power than water, what he called
'fire'."[95] On Pentecost day and during the
Apostolic Age, he observed that: "Christian

93. Faith and Order, Lausanne 1927, p.291.
94. ibid.
95. ibid, p.294.

Baptism was essentially baptism or drenching with 'Holy Spirit', as a fact of human experience, both for the recipient and for onlookers, but a fact in which God as Holy Spirit was manifest as immediate agent."[96] Water was simply a symbol which was sometime added after the Spirit-baptism as was evident in the case of Cornelius and his friends. He described baptism as "the purification of the heart by fath", and through it the baptized receives the "Divine Seal", begins to associate himself with Christ and with his visible Body the church. This 'Divine Seal' he called "Confirmation in the original sense."

Prof. Barlet observed that primitive baptism moved wholly in the sphere of religious experience and moral personality in the case of those capable of personal faith. This was quite different in the case of children, who by their christian birth-right are 'holy' within the sphere of the covenant. This thought was dominant in Hebraism, he maintained, and leaned on it to support infant baptism saying: "According to this deep sense of family solidarity, and of the wider solidarity of 'the family of faith' as the psycological atmosphere of the child's awakening consciousness, it was also the natural thing that the symbol of the parents' religious relation should be administered even to the infant children of believers."[97] This concept or usage was accountable for the absence of controversy over the issue in the apostolic age. The controversy over infant baptism arose when the prevailing menta-

---

96. ibid, p.294.
97. ibid, p.295.

lity of the church changed decidedly to one, non
Hebraic and Hellenistic in sacramental conception. He therefore urged the Baptists to recognize infant baptism as the first stage of the
full rite, since some churches regard membership
in the church as incomplete until Confirmation.

He applied historical method on his approach
to the eucharist. He maintained that whatever
associations to the eucharist that could not be
verified in the historical context of its setting
should not be treated as having the direct authority of Jesus. In instituting this sacrament,
Jesus' desire was to bring home to his disciples
what has been central to his ministry, and that
is, the redemptive significance of his coming
death. Then taking advantage of the paschal season, when the people were filled with the idea of
redemption through the blood of an innocent lamb,
Jesus made use of it in a prophetic manner: "to
suggest by this most acceptable approach, that
Isreal's final salvation will come through the
breaking of His own body and the shedding of His
own blood 'for many'."[98] The idea that is represented by this saying according to Prof. Barlet
is found in the declaration of St. Paul which
says that in celebrating this sacrament, it is
the Lord's death that is proclaimed. He remarked
that in the words of the institution the copulate
was missing and thus: "the words simply attach to
the familiar ritual a new and special symbolism,
a prophetic objective lesson of what was soon to
be, but was not yet, objective fact."[99] For Bartlet

---

98. ibid, pp.296-297.
99. ibid.

the words of institution are "prophetico-symbo-
lic", and the valid meaning of this sacrament as
it is explained in the Anglican Prayer Book of
1552, which states: "Take and eat this is in
remembrance that Christ died for thee, and feed
on Him in thy heart by faith with thanksgiving."[100] He named some biblical symbolisms that
are associated with the eucharist, namely: 'the
unity of the church as sharing in the one loaf';
'Christ as the bread of life to the soul'; and
'the association of the church's self oblation
with the supreme example of the principle in the
person of the head'. (The last is not actually in
the N.T.).

Speaking about the sacrificial character of
the eucharist, he associates it with the notion
of the self-giving of the church, which he describes as "the church's one recurring 'sacrifice', was a specialised symbolic or of the
general christian 'living sacrifice' of oneself
body and soul, in 'spiritual service', in virtue
of the priesthood of the believers."[101] He said
that there was no mention of "propitiation for
sins" in the eucharistic sacrifice in the ante-
Nicene church, what was paramount then was the
idea of "the sacrifice of praise". He dismissed
the doctrine of the real presence of Christ's
body and blood in the elements, maitaining that
"it is a pure accretion of a non-Hebraic and
subpersonal order. It came in originally to satisfy the Hellenistic mentality in its craving
after a quasi-physical 'food of immortality' for

---

100. ibid.
101. ibid, p.298,

the corruptible human body."[102]

He concluded with an appeal to "Catholics" and
"Evangelicals" to allow inter-communion, despite
their different conceptions and usages, which he
said, "do not cancel the unity of underlying idea
as apprehended in personal experience. Thus in
the Holy Communion of the Lord's Supper there is
experienced by both a special spiritual union
between Christ and His own, in death to sin and
new life unto God."[103]

1.4.3 THE EVANGELICAL-LUTHERAN (Dr. Schoell).

Dr. Schoell began by pointing out areas of
agreement reached among the churches regarding
the sacraments. One such agreement is on the
necessity of both word and sacrament for the
foundation and maintenance of the christian life.
Because of this, he pointed out, that some emphasize the preaching of the word, others the use of
sacraments. Sacraments are divine institution and
they are concerned with divine means of grace.
Finally only those who desire to receive the
sacrament obtain the benefit. That is to say,
that God's grace is offered to us in the sacrament, but it is not imposed on us.

Discussing the differences that arise in the
conception of sacraments, Dr. Schoell associates
them closely with, first, the understanding of
divine grace and secondly with the divergent
views in the conception of the nature of God

---

102. ibid.
103. ibid, p.299

Himself. About the divergent views in the conception of God, one is metaphysical the other, ethical. The first emphasizes the supernatural
essence of God, the other His loving purpose and
will. Applying these to the sacraments he said
that: "From the standpoint of the first group the
sacrament is the penetration of the divine
essence into the human nature, enabling the christian to participate in the divine nature. From
the standpoint of the other group the sacrament
is the proof of divine love, witnessed to by
signs and ritual, which gives the christian assurance of forgiveness and of sonship with God."[104]

Refusing to show his preference regarding the
manner of baptism, and avoiding to discuss the
question of infant baptism, Dr. Schoell stressed
the necessity of baptism which he said must be
performed in the name of the Father, the Son and
the Holy Spirit. He regarded baptism as a means
of admission into the community of Christ and of
christians. He observed that there is divergent
of opinions between the two groups mentioned
above in regarding baptism as re-birth. For the
first group "Baptism is the beginning of a
genuine re-birth, of a transformation of the
human nature into the divine nature", and for the
second group baptism is regarded "as a token of
God's will that a child of man is to be transformed into a child of God, and he will only
acknowledge it as the beginning of a re-birth to
the extent that the divine will for salvation is
accepted by the baptized person through faith,
either at the moment of Baptism, or subsequently

---

104. op.cit., p.310.

during his life."[105]

Dr. Schoell called the eucharist "a feast of
remembrance for the sacrificial death of Christ,
not in the sense of a mere memorial of the fact
and circumstances of His death, but as a Eucharist, as a thanksgiving for all that our Lord won
for us by the sacrifice of His body and the shedding of His blood."[106] He further described the
eucharist as a real union with the Lord, the head
of the church and finally as a feast "which binds
the disciples of the Lord together in a communion
of love". The differences that arise, he attributed to the divergency in conceptions of the two
groups already mentioned. As for the first group,
he said, that "it is of vital moment to declare
that the elements are the actual vehicles of a
physical and super-physical salvation; and for
them it becomes an essential condition for true
communion that the elements should be consecrated
in the prescribed form by a priest who has been
validly ordained in that capacity."[107] This group
associates intimately with the idea of the sacramental sacrifice with reverence for the consecrated elements, and for the effect of the sacrament
it holds it to be a union of spirit and body with
Christ. About the other group he said: "For them
the symbolic betokening of the gift which Christ
offers us of His body and His blood is a means
whereby faith may be fortified, the sticken conscience may be consoled, and the assurance of sin
forgiven and life made holier may be obtained.[108]

---

105. ibid, p.311.
106. ibid, pp.311-312.
107. ibid.
108. ibid, p.315.

Dr. Schoell took note of the magnitude of the differences and rejoiced over what was commonly held by both groups.

There were actually seven speakers on this topic; the three considered above, treated the matter in such a way that all the groups were represented. Mention will be made of two other speakers because of their peculiarities.

Dr. Ashworth (Baptist), said that sacraments are called ordinances by his church. He discussed only baptism and the eucharist. He said inter alia that: "Baptists practise the baptism of believers only, and employ the New Testament mode of immersion, and maintain the simplicity of the Lord's Supper as it was first instituted."[109] In Holy Communion, he maintains that the believer meets his saviour in 'mystical fellowship', and meets his brother christians "upon the highest plane upon which human fellowship is possible".

The Rev. H.M. Hughes (Methodist), raised specifically the issue of intercommunion. He called it a "thorny issue" and deplored the fact that "the sacrament of the Holy Communion, which ought to be the trysting-place of all the redeemed, has unhappily become the centre of our disunity."[110] In order to achieve his proposal, he threw away dogma and history and recommended brotherly love.

---

109. ibid.
110. ibid, pp.319-320

1.4.4 REPORT OF SECTION VI.

The Report[111] was carefully composed and it
began with sacrament in general, then baptism and
finally the eucharist. The difference were then
outlined at the end of the report. Here therefore
is the summary of the report.

1. The purpose of the report is to show that
   there is a common approach to and appreciation
   of the sacraments despite the difference in
   conception and interpretation.
2. The significance and value of the sacraments
   for the life of the church were underlined.
3. The divine institution of the sacraments was
   generally acknowledged.
4. Sacraments are means of grace and have an
   outward sign and cover inward grace.
5. There was no agreement on the number of sacraments.
6. Through baptism christians become one body.
7. The Lord is present in the eucharist, and we
   have fellowship with God in Jesus Christ.

The eucharist is the church's most sacred act
of worship. In the eucharist, the Lord's death is
commemorated. The eucharist is a sacrifice of
praise and thanksgiving, and an act of solemn
self-oblation. The divergent views are:

1. The mode and manner of the presence of Christ
   in the Eucharist.

---

111. cf. Faith and Order, Lausanne 1927, pp.472-
     473.

2. The conception of the commemoration and the sacrifice.
3. The relationship between the elements and the grace conferred.
4. The relation between the minister of the sacraments and the validity and efficacy of the rite.

1.4.5 ASSESSMENT.

The divergent conceptions about the sacraments and the question of grace since the Reformation, appeared prominently in the various papers presented under section VI. All the schools of thought were represented, and the speakers only adjusted themselves properly according to the spirit of the conference and avoided polemics. The report showed that the section did not delve into discussing the different conceptions about the sacraments rather it went on to say that "the purpose is to show that there may be a common approach to and appreciation of sacraments on the part of those who may otherwise differ in conception and interpretation."[112] Agreement was reached on the general principles of sacrament in general and the report stressed the fact that "in the sacraments there is an outward sign and an inward grace, and that the sacraments are means of grace through which God works invisibly in us."[113] The report did not limit God's channel of conferring grace to the soul to sacraments alone;

---

112. op., cit., p.472.
113. ibid.

it maintained that "we recognise also that in the gifts of His grace God is not limited by His own sacraments." The number of sacraments was never discussed. The report only indicated that some held the sacraments to be seven in number, while others regarded only Baptism and the Eucharist as sacraments. It seemed that a compromise was quickly reached with the Orthodox and the section concentrated on the two sacraments only.

Frieling was of the opinion that because the Orthodox placed on report that "the sacraments are of divine appointment and that the Church ought thankfully to observe them as divine gifts", satisfied them and helped to keep the section discussion in progress.[114]

The question of the validity of the sacraments in relation to the minister was among the differences noted down. It was not discussed probably becuase section V of the conference dealth with the Ministry of the Church.

Apart from certain agreements reached on the eucharist, no attempt was made to handle any one issue where there existed divergent views. An exception was the problem of intercommunion raised by W.A. Brown during the first reading of the report. He suggested that it be put to the churches:

a) whether in the future conferences, there would be the possibility of a common or a simultaneous Eucharistic service.
b) whether it would be possible to admit to communion members of other churches in a place

---

114. Frieling Reinhard, op.cit., p.121.

where no other possibility exists.
c) whether intercommunion would be possible among
the young churches.

The discussion that followed showed among
other things the unpreparedness of the section to
delve into areas where opinions deeply vary. This
was clear in the opinion of Bishop Gore who said
that "they raised controversial questions which
went beyond anything that the Conference could
adequately consider."[115] This problem about intercommunion was partially handled in Edinburgh
Conference in 1937, by the commission on "The
Church's unity in Life and Worship." It came up
once again in Lund, 1952 and also in Montreal
under Communion Services at ecumenical gatherings, as we shall later see.

Among the divergent views outlined in the
report included the question of how the Lord is
present in the Eucharist, and what is meant by
commemoration and the sacrificial character of
the eucharist. It is conspicuos from this therefore that the toothing problems about the eucharist which would engage, the Faith and Order
Commission later, were present from the very
beginning at the conference in Lausanne, 1927.
Reviewing the sacraments, the sixth subject in
the conference at Lausanne, is necessary here
because it was there that the discussion on the
eucharist had its basis before it was later handled as a study project by the Faith and Order
Commission of the World Council of Churches.

---

115. Faith and Order, Lausanne 1927, p.394.

CHAPTER TWO.

EDINBURGH TO MONTREAL.

2.1 LAUSANNE TO EDINBURGH.

Before the Lausanne Conference dispersed in
1927, a Continuation Committee of about one hund-
red members was appointed, with Bishop Brent as
chairman. Among some of its duties were the su-
pervision of the circulation of the Conference
Report to the Churches and the reception of their
replies; to decide when another World Conference
should be summoned and to make arrangements for
it.[1] In 1929, the Continuation Committe formed
a Theological Committee under the chairmanship of
Bishop Headlam (Anglican). The first subject
handled by this committee was the "Doctrine of
Grace". At its meeting in England in 1931, the
Continuation Committee decided that the Second
World Conference on Faith and Order should hold
in 1937 and in December of the same year letters
of invitation were sent to the churches. The
Theological Committee produced its report on the
Doctrine of Grace and was commissioned to go on
to study the Eucharist. This new assignment was
not carried out, due to the world economic reces-
sion of the 1930's. Tissington Tatlow described
how the economic situation affected the Faith and
Order Movement thus:

---

1. cf, Hodgson L. (ed)., The Second World
   Conference on Faith and Order, 1937, London,
   S.C.M., 1938, p.5. Further quotations as:
   Faith and Order Conference, Edinburgh, 1937.

"The financial slump after the boom which
followed the First World War, the effect of which
was felt especially in the United States, necessitated drastic retrenchment on the part of
the Continuation Committee. It held no meetings
in 1932 and 1933, its Geneva office was closed,
and Mr. Brown (secretary) offered his resigna-
tion, which was accepted with regret, for his
services had proved of considerable value".[2]

When the economic situation improved, the
Continuation Committee resumed its interrupted
sessions in 1934 with a meeting at Hertenstein,
Switzerland. The Churches were beginning to look
forward with the expectation of the Second World
Conference and the Committee spent some time
discussing the programme for it. This meeting
appointed two other commissions and charged them
with new subjects, "The Church and the World",
and "The Church's Unity in Life and Worship", to
work side by side with the Theological Committee,
which could not work on the Eucharist, which
rather set to work on the "Ministry and the Sacraments".

The 1935 meeting of the Continuation Committee
was held at Hindsgaul, Denmark. It was there that
the decision to hold the Second World Conference
at Edinburgh was taken and the programme was
also finalised.[3] In 1936 the Continuation

2. Tissington Tatlow, The World Conference on
   Faith and Order in: Rouse & Neill C.S. (ed),
   A History of the Ecumenical Movement 1517-
   1948, London, S.P.C.K., 1954, p.428.
3. Faith and Order Conference, Edinburgh 1937,
   p.10. cf. also, Frieling R., Die Bewegung
   für Glauben und Kirchenverfassung 1920-1937,
   Göttingen, 1970, p.178.

Committee met again in Clarens, Switzerland and
received interim reports on the work of the
Commissions.[4] At Clarens Prof. Henri Clavier of
Montpellier was appointed a travelling secretary
in preparation for the Edinburgh Conference. In
his double trips of 1936 and 1937, he visited
mainly some European countries and the Middle
East. His visits awakened interest of the churches visited in the Faith and Order Movement and
these churches in turn sent delegates to Edinburgh Conference. Tissington said of the Professor:

"Clavier prepared carefully beforehand by
correspondence for his visits. Largely as a result, he was able to see the more important
church leaders in the countries visited and to
address gatherings of people called to meet
him...and it was due to his devoted work that
many churches in Europe and in the Middle East
were represented, which apart from his efforts
would not have had anyone at Edinburgh".[5]

The Continuation Committee did not meet again
before the Edinburgh Conference, besides its
executive which met near Paris in February 1937
and finally at Edinburgh on the eve of the conference.

---

4. Faith and Order, op.cit., p.11.
5. Tissington Tatlow, op.cit., p.430.

2.2 EDINBURGH 1937.

The second World Conference on Faith and Order
assembled at Edinburgh on 3. August 1937. There
were altogether 504 persons, including the delegates, their alternates and members of the Continuation Committee.[6] The assembly elected as her
president, the Archbishop of York, William Temple
(Anglican). The president paid tribute to some
deceased members of the Movement, in his opening
speech. Among them was its first president,
Bishop Brent, others were Archbishop Söderblom,
Dr. Deissmann and Dr. Zoellner. The Conference
met without a delegation from the German Evangelical Church, passports having been refused them
by the German Government, - "sign of the growing
strength and intolerance of the National Socia-
list Movement".[7] The president expressed his
feelings about the absence of the German delegates and how it would affect the conference thus:

"That we should meet to discuss the themes
before us without the aid of a delegation from
the German Evangelical Church is to labour under
a heavy handicap. We deeply regret the absence
of our German friends,...and we pray that we may
follow their example of faithfulness and enduran-
ce."[8]

On the method that should be adopted for the
general discussion on the topics and their subsequent reports, the president suggested something
different from the method adopted in Lausanne. He

---

6. Tissington Tatlow, op.cit., p.431.
7. ibid.
8. Faith and Order Conference, Edingburgh 1937,
    pp.29-30

said: "Instead of starting with general discussion in the full conference, we are proposing
to refer the Reports of our Commissions at once
to the sections which will discuss them and present to us their findings upon them. This is made
possible by the fact that the Commissions have
been so thorough in their preparatory work".[9]

The chairman of the sections were chosen from
the floor, men who had no hand in preparing the
papers that were discussed. This was in conso-
nance with the decision of the executive
committee on the eve of the assembly, for "the
committee realised that as the conference consisted of delegates officially appointed by their
churches to discuss together certain subjects, it
must be given every opportunity to take charge of
its own business and conduct it in its own
way".[10]
Satisfied with the work of these men and the
sections in producing the reports and also with
the principle adopted, Hodgson wrote:
"No little part of the value of the conference
Report is due to their self-sacrificing labours.
Its significance cannot be fully grasped unless
it is realised that it represents the genuine
work of the conference itself, composed under the
leadership of chairmen chosen "from the floor""[11]
The subjects tackled by the sections were:

1. The Grace of our Lord Jesus Christ.
2. The Church of Christ and the Word of God.

---

9. ibid, p.62.
10. Faith and Order Conference, Edinburgh, 1937,
    p.13.
11. idem, p.14.

3. The Church of Christ: Ministry and Sacraments.
4. The Church's Unity in Life and Worship.

In practice each of the four sections carried
on its work by further grouping of its members.
This sectional work lasted for ten days, when the
whole conference assembled in full session to
receive and discuss the section reports serially.

2.2.1   REPORT OF SECTION III.
          THE CHURCH OF CHRIST: MINISTRY AND
          SACRAMENTS.

2.2.1.1   AUTHORITY OF THE SACRAMENTS.

The Report set forth to say that: "We are
agreed that in all sacramental doctrine and practice the supreme authority is our Lord Jesus
Christ Himself". It is on the evidence of the New
Testament that the Churches based their belief
and doctrine on the sacraments and accept them as
instituted by Christ. Among these "Baptism and
the Lord's Supper occupied from the beginning a
central position in the Church's common life, and
take their origin from what was said and done by
Jesus during His life on earth".[12]
The sacraments are Christ's gift to his Church,
and this Church is not a static society rather a
"living and growing organism and communion, gui-
ded by the Holy Spirit into all truth". It is by
the guidance of the Holy Spirit that the Church

12. Faith and Order Conference, Edinburgh 1937,
    p.239.

in her faith in the risen Lord interprets the
Scripture to every age as the living word of God,
and exercises her stewardship over the sacraments. The report concluded with a rather controversial point when it said:

"All Church tradition regarding the sacraments
ought to be controlled and tested by Scripture".[13] Controversial because, the Orthodox and
some others would wish to add: "all these sacraments can be founded upon Holy Scripture as completed, explained, interpreted and understood in
the Holy Tradition by the guidance of the Holy
Spirit residing in the Church".[14] And Anglican
members observed that "The Church of England,
while recognising the authority of the Church to
decree rites and ceremonies, forbids it to ordain
anything contrary to the Scriptures, but limits
the necessity of Scripture sanction to articles
of faith in things necessary to salvation".[15]

2.2.1.2   THE NATURE OF THE SACRAMENTS.

The Report further stated that "the sacraments
are given by Christ to the Church as outward and
visible signs of His invisible grace. They are
not bare symbols, but pledges and seals of grace,
and means whereby it is received."[16] Faith is a
necessary condition for the effectual reception
of grace, for according to the Report "Grace is
bestowed in the sacraments within the fellowship

---

13. ibid, p.240.
14. ibid.
15. ibid.
16. ibid, p.240.

of the Church by the personal action of Christ upon the believers."[17] The Report noted that God's gracious acts are not limited to the sacraments. The Orthodox delegates and some others took exception to this proposition, owing to the fact that some may fail to benefit from the sacraments due to contempt or culpable negligence of them," since sacraments are divinely instituted means of grace generally necessary for salvation." In the report it was also stated that the minister of the sacraments is only an instrument for "it is our Lord Jesus Christ who through the Holy Spirit accomplishes every sacrament." The sacraments are no personal property of the minister, but he administers them as the minister of the Church. Agreement was not reached regarding the obligation of the sacraments and the questions whether and in what way they are to be deemed necessary for salvation.

2.2.1.3 NUMBER OF SACRAMENTS.

As was the case in Lausanne so also in Edinburgh, there was no agreement on the number of sacraments. While the Orthodox Churches, the Catholics and the Old Catholic Church hold that there are seven sacraments, the Protestants accept only two, namely, Baptism and the Eucharist. The Anglican Church, as stated in the report "has never strictly defined the number of sacraments, but gives a pre-eminent position to Baptism and the Lord's Supper as alone 'generally

---

17. ibid.

necessary to salvation'"[18] The Society of
Friends and Salvation Army observe no sacraments
in the usual sense of the term. The report attributed the disparity to the various definitions
and conceptions of sacrament, by different churches, for "In most of the Protestant Churches
there are such solemn religious acts as correspond more or less closely with some or all of the
five other sacraments which are taught by the
Roman, Orthodox, Old Catholic, and other Churches."[19] The report did not regard the problem of
the number of sacraments to be insurmountable but
rather remarked that "The divergence between the
practice of the Society of Friends and the Salvation Army on the one hand, and that of other
Churches on the other, admittedly presents serious difficulties."[20]

2.2.1.4 VALIDITY OF SACRAMENTS.[21]

The report opened with a general statement
that: "We agree that the sacraments practised by
any christian church which believes itself to be
observing what Christ appointed for His Church
are means of grace to those who partake of them
with faith." It went further to identify the use
of the term "valid", which may attimes be con-
fusing; "it is sometimes used synonymously with
'efficatious', so that the term 'invalid' would

---

18. ibid, p.241.
19. ibid.
20. ibid.
21. Quotations from: Faith and Order Conference,
    Edinburgh 1937, pp. 241-243.

imply that a sacrament has no spiritual value and
is not a means of grace.

(b) It is sometimes used to imply that the sacrament has been correctly performed. Having identified the problem, the report went further to
advise the Churches that in the name of christian
truth and charity, they should not judge the
sacraments practised by others as invalid and if
they would want to do that, it begged them to
state clearly the grounds on which they would
pass their judgment. A special difficulty of
union in agreement stems from those churches
which hold the validity of Holy Orders as an
indispensable condition for the validity of the
other sacraments. Some others although they hold
that an ordained minister is the proper minister
of the Eucharist, do not hold ordination to be
instituted by Christ. Yet others while they hold
that ordination is a sacrament do not hold it to
be essential for the validity of other sacraments. The report maintained that "every sacrament should be so ordered that all may recognize
in it an act performed on behalf of the universal
church". Concluding it said: "there is need of an
ordained ministry recognised by all to act on
behalf of the universal Church in the administration of the sacraments".*

---

* Note- "As regards the validity of sacraments
the Orthodox delegates would like to confine
themselves to the following statement: According
to the Orthodox doctrine valid sacraments are
only those which are (1) administered by a ca-
nonically ordained and instituted minister and
(2) rightly performed according to the sacramental order of the Church". cf. Faith and Order
Conference, Edinburgh 1937, p. 243

2.2.1.5 THE EUCHARIST.

The conference was in agreement that: "Christ
is truly present in the Eucharist", but differed
in how the presence of Christ is manifested or
realized. Any attempt to define this presence is
bound to be limited, and such attempt to find a
definition and to impose it on the church, was
attributed to be the cause of disunity in the
past. In the words of the report it was stated
that: "Every precise definition of the presence
is bound to be a limiting thing, and the attempt
to formulate such definitions and to impose them
on the church has itself been the cause of disunity in the past."[22] And what is important according to the report is that "We should celebrate the Eucharist with unfailing use of bread
and wine, and of prayer, and of the words of
institution, and with agreement as to essential
and spiritual meaning."[23]

The sacrificial character of the eucharist has
always been a point of disagreement. The root
cause of the disagreement lies on the divergent
concept of sacrifice. Here the report states: "If
sacrifice is understood as it was by our Lord and
His followers and in the early church, it includes, not His death only, but the obedience of His
earthly ministry, and His risen and ascended
life, in which He still does His Fathers will and
ever liveth to make intercession for us. Such a
sacrifice can never be repeated, but is proclaimed and set forth in the eucharistic action

_____

22. ibid, p. 244.
23. ibid.

of the whole church when we come to God in Christ at the Eucharist or Lord's Supper".[24] The report went further to say that the secret of joining in that sacrifice is for the worship and service of God. In this sacrifice each one of us makes the 'corporate act of self-oblation' his own, not simply for the ceremony but as an act of doing God's will. The conference also believed that "the eucharist is a supreme moment of prayer, because the Lord is the celebrant or minister for us at every celebration, and it is in His prayers for God's gifts and for us all that we join".[25] It went on to say that according to the accounts of the institution of the Eucharist in the New Testament that "His prayer is itself a giving of thanks; so that the Lord's Supper is both a ver-bum visibile of the divine grace, and the supreme thanksgiving (eucharistia) of the people of God."[26] In this celebration we are throughout in the realm of the Spirit; and 'it is through the Holy Spirit that the blessing and the gift are given'. The presence which the report declines to define, is said to be a spiritual presence. It then concludes by relating the Eucharist to "the historical fact of the Incarnation in the power of the Holy Spirit" and from there we move on to enjoy the fortaste of the 'spiritual reality of the coming of the Lord and the life of the Hea-venly city."

There was no significant progress made at Edinburgh on the Eucharist. The theological commission could not handle the topic when it was

---

24. ibid.
25. ibid, p.244.
26. ibid.

proposed due to the financial problem of that
time. In its report on "Ministry and Sacraments",
section III restated mainly, where it touched on
the eucharist, the report from Lausanne, but was
more systematic in its presentation. There was an
attempt to discuss the sacrificial character of
the eucharist but this was given up and the section satisfied itself with general statement that
there is a sacrificial element in the eucharist.

2.2.1.6 INTERCOMMUNION.

In Edinburgh, "intercommunion" was not a subject of its own. It was briefly treated as a sub-
heading by section IV, which handled the topic:
"The Churches' Unity in Life and Worship". The
section regarded intercommunion as an aspect and
necessary part of church unity and defined it as
"the fullest expression of a mutual recognition
between two or more churches."[27] Such recognition
could be manifested in the exchange of membership
and ministrations. This definition could also
simply imply that "all concerned are true churches, or true branches of the one Church". Nar-
rowing down the different connotations of the
word intercommunion, the report said that in its
fullest sense it means "a relation between two
or more churches in which the communion of each
is open to all members of the other at all times." This could be distinguished from relations
in which one church admits members of the other
church to communion without a reciprocal gesture

_____

27. ibid, p.251.

from the other and further from the occasional
admittance of members of other churches by a
church whose normal rule could exclude them. The
report finally gave an advice that the precise
definition of the term, intercommunion should be
given whenever it is used in the discussion about
the unity of the church.

A commission was later appointed to handle the
topic in detail and this commission submitted its
report at the Conference in Lund, 1952.

2.3. FORMATION OF WORLD COUNCIL OF CHRUCHES:
FAITH AND ORDER AS A COMPONENT PART.

Side by side with Faith and Order as an ecumenical movement, grew also the Universal Council
for Practical Christianity better known as Life
and Work, whose founder was Archbishop Söderblom,
the then Primate of the Church of Sweden. Each
movement concerned itself with what its name
pointed at. Life and Work had its First World
Conference at Stockholm in 1925, while Faith and
Order held hers at Lausanne in 1927. The second
World Conference for both movements was held in
1937, Life and Work at Oxford and Faith and Order
at Edinburgh. There were yet other international
movements, viz, I.M.C., Y.M.C.A., Y.W.C.A. Each
had its objectives and endeavoured to execute
them. Since the Stockholm and Lausanne conferences, there had been calls for a council of
churches. The call became stronger in the 1930's.
As W.A. Visser't Hooft put it:

"The idea of a World Council of Chruches was
in the air, but so long as there were in existence several different and independent ecumenical bodies it seemed impossible of realization."[28] The two bodies most directly concerned
for these calls were Faith and Order and Life and
Work, for these had in many countries the closest
relationship to the churches, and sometimes the
same persons held influential posts in both.

_____

28. Visser't Hooft W.A., The Genesis of the World
Council of Churches, in: Rouse Ruth and Neill
Stephen (ed), A History of the Ecumenical
Movement 1517-1948, London, S.P.C.K., 1954,
p.698.

There were suggestions that the two movements
should unite and the chief inducements for this
proposal have been:

"that the two movements or conferences in
carrying out their commissions, as received from
the churches, have learned that they have many
interest and purposes in common and are closely
related. It has also been learned that in the
appeal to the churches for continued interest and
support the question is often naturally asked why
there should be two world movements when the lay
mind does not understand and appreciate their
distinctive functions."[29] There was also the
fact that Life and Work in the effort to carry
out its work was becoming more theological and
Faith and Order in the same vein was becoming
more practical. Another factor that necessitated
the union of these two bodies was the situation
in the 1930's concerning the relationship between
the church and the state. On the side of the
church, she sought for a sense of solidarity, as
Visser't Hooft observed:

"The new situation which arose for the church
as a result of the emergence of totalitarian
doctrines reinforced the conclusion that the
ecumenical task must be conceived as a single
whole."[30]

At their separate sessions held in August at
Chamby and in September, 1936, at Clarens, in
successive weeks, the Universal Council for Life
and Work, and the Continuation Committee of the

29. Hodgson L. (ed), The Second World Conference
    on Faith and Order, Edinburgh 1937, London,
    S.C.M., 1938, p.270.
30. Visser't Hooft W.A., op. cit., p.700.

World Conference on Faith and Order passed resolutions recommending the appointment of a
committee to review the work of ecumenical co-
operation since the Stockholm and Lausanne conferences, and to report to the Oxford and Edinburgh Conferences regarding the future policy,
organisation and work of the ecumenical movement.
This committee consisted, as it was agreed, of
persons who held posts of responsibility in the
Churches and provisions were made for women and
youth representatives as well as for some officers of other ecumenical movements. This group
designated for this purpose, constituted the
committee known as the "Committee of thirty-
five".

2.3.1 THE COMMITTEE OF THIRTY-FIVE.

The thirty-five members of the committee met
at Westfield College in London on 8-10 July 1937.
As a result of their deliberations, the committee
made a unanimous recommendation which the two
World Conferences at Oxford and Edinburgh should
adopt as proposals for the foundation of a World
Council of Churches. For the sake of making
easier the more effective action of the christian
church in the modern world, each conference was
asked to approve the union of Life and Work and
Faith and Order, in which the representative of
the Churches should cater for interests of each
movement. Each conference was requested to
approve the memorandum adopted by the committee
of thirty-five, which read: "The new organisation
which is proposed shall have no power to legis-

late for the churches or to commit them to action
without their consent; but if it is to be effective, it must deserve and win the respect of the
churches in such measure that the people of greatest influence in the life of the churches may be
willing to give time and thought to its work.
Further, the witness which the church in the
modern world is called to give is such that in
certain spheres the predominant voice in the
utterance of it must be that of lay people holding posts of responsibility and influence in the
secular world. For both these reasons, a first-
class intelligence staff is indispensable in
order that material for discussion and action may
be adequately prepared."[31]

The committee also proposed that the new council would enter into relationship with other
ecumenical bodies, so that the life in them might
derive stability and true perspective from the
churches. Each conference was asked to approve
the establishment of a World Council of Churches,
which would function through a general assembly
of representatives of the churches; a central
committee, a commission for the further study of
Life and Work subjects and a commission for the
further study of Faith and Order subject. Pending
the formation of the world council, each
conference was required to carry on its activities
through its staff. To work out the details and to
bring the council into existence, each conference
was required to appoint seven members to form a
committee.

---

31. Visser't Hooft W.A., The Genesis and
    Formation of the World Council of Churches,
    Geneva, W,C.C., 1982, p.104.

2.3.2 RESOLUTION OF LIFE AND WORK AT OXFORD.

At its conference in Oxford, Life and Work referred the proposals of the Committee of Thirty-
five to the regional meetings and this provided
an opportunity for full discussion. William A.
Brown worked hard to secure the approval from the
United States' delegates while Marc Boegner did
the same on the European side, and reported unanimous acceptance of the proposals. When the
motion to approve the proposals of the Committee
of Thirty-five was put to the floor of the assembly, the conference approved it with only two
dissenting voices.[32] The conference then ordered
the executive committee to name the seven delegates and their alternates. The delegates were
given the mandate to effect any amendment in
their discussion with their counterpart from
Faith and Order and to implement the plans for
the World Council of Churches.[33]

2.3.3 RESOLUTION OF FAITH AND ORDER AT EDINBURGH

The proposal of the Committee of Thirty-five
were first referred to a special committee of
sixty members representative of the conference
with Dr. Ross Stevenson as chairman. This was
done in order to secure that the proposals were

---

32. cf., Visser't Hooft W.A., op. cit., p. 43.
33. cf., Kirche und Welt in Ökumenischer Sicht.
    Bericht der Weltkirchenkonferenz von Oxford
    über Kirche, Volk und Staat. Hrsg. von:
    Forschungsabteilung des Ökomenischen Rates
    für Praktisches Christentum, Schweiz: Huber &
    Co, 1938, p.274.

thoroughly examined and the considered judgement
of the conference obtained. This committee later
submited its report. It recommended that the
conference should: "give a sympathetic welcome to
the general plan without committing itself to
details and should commend it to the favourable
consideration of the churches."[34] The report,
further recommended, that the continuation
committee of the conference should be instructed
to approve the completed plan only if a number of
guarantees were incorporated, namely, "That the
World Council's Commission on Faith and Order
shall in the first instance, be the continuation
committee appointed by this conference. In any
further appointment made by the council to membership of the Commission on Faith and Order, the
persons appointed shall always be members of the
churches which fall within the terms of the Faith
and Order invitation as addressed to 'all christian bodies throughout the world which accept
our Lord Jesus Christ as God and Saviour'."[35]
Other guarantees were that the work of Faith and
Order should be carried out under a theological
secretariat; that the world council should consist of official representatives of participating
churches; and that the state of the council
should be provisional until the first general
assembly. The report recommended the appointment
of the seven members who would co-operate with
its counterpart appointed by Life and Work at
Oxford. These seven were given the mandate to
complete the detailed plans for the world coun-

34. Hodgson L., op. cit., p.271.
35. ibid, pp.271-272

cil; to submit the completed plans to the continuation committee and after its approval to con-
vene the world council. The motion was tabled to
approve the report of the special committee and
it carried with one dissient voice.

After the committee of Fourteen had finished
its work, which was the drawing up of the draft
constitution of the World Council of Churches,
the Faith and Order component did submit the work
to its continuation committee in 1938 at Clarens.
It was at Clarens therefore that Faith and Order
gave her final approval to the union with Life
and Work to form the proposed World Council of
Churches.

2.3.4 THE COMMITTEE OF FOURTEEN.

The committee of Fourteen consisted of seven
members each appointed by the conferences at
Oxford and Edinburgh in 1937. The task of the
committee was to form the World Council of Churches. The committee invited reprensentative group
of churches to help in drawing up the draft constitution, for the purpose of gainful co-operation of the churches. The meeting of the
committee with the church leaders took place at
Utrecht in May 1938. The plan elaborated by the
committee of thirty five was used as the starting
point, and three problems were discussed in greater detail namely, the authority of the council,
its doctrinal basis and the manner of selecting
reprentatives for the assembly and for the central committee. On the question of the authority
of the council the meeting agreed that: "The

World Council shall offer counsel and provide
opportunity for united action in matters as one
or more of them may commit to it. It shall have
authority to call regional and world conferences
on specific subjects as occasion may require. The
World Council shall not legislate for the churches; nor shall it act for them in any manner
except as indicated above or as may hereafter be
specified by the constituent Churches."[36] The
chairman, Archbishop Temple, clarified the matter
further in his explanatory memorandum on the
proposed constitution, he wrote: "The world
council is not a federation as commonly understood and its Assembly and central committee will
have no constitutional authority over its constituent churches. Any authority that it may have
will consist in the weight which it carries with
the churches by its wisdom."[37] The doctrinal
basis for the council generated a prolonged argument but at the end the meeting agreed to the
statement that: "The Council stands on faith in
our Lord Jesus Christ as God and Saviour. As its
brevity shows, the basis is an affirmation of the
Christian faith of the participating churches,
and not a credal test to judge churches or persons. It is an affirmation of the Incarnation and
the Atonement. The council desires to be a
fellowship of those churches which accept these
truths. But it does not concern itself with the
manner in which the churches interpret them. It
will therefore be the responsibility of each
particular church to decide whether it can colla-

---

36. Visser't Hooft W.A., op. cit., p.49.
37. ibid.

borate on this basis."[38] The debate on the manner
of representations did not yield its final result
at Utrecht. The recommendation which was adopted
by the assembly stated that the seats in the
Assembly were to be allocated by the Central
Committee and the membership of the Central
Committee was to be distributed among the member
churches by the Assembly.

For interim arrangements, a provisional
committee for the World Council was set up comprising the committee of Fourteen and their
alternates, and three members each appointed by
the Administrative Committee of Life and Work and
the Continuation Committee of Faith and Order.
This committee was headed by Arshbishop Temple
and W.A. Visser't Hooft was its general secretary. The provisional committee set to work immediately. At its meeting in Germain January 1939,
a provisional date for the first assembly was
billed for August 1941. Hence letters of invitation were sent out to the churches embodying also
the draft constitution at Utrecht. As it turned
out the Second World war broke out in September
1939, and the first assembly could take place
only after the war, and in Amsterdam 1948.

2.3.5 AMSTERDAM 1948.

On the 22 of August 1948, 351 delegates from 135
denominations in 44 countries, assembled for the
formation of the World Council of Churches. On 23
August during the first plenary session, Pastor

---

38. ibid, p.50.

Marc Boegner submitted the resolution to constitute the World Council of Churches in the name of
the Committee of Fourteen and the Provisional
committee in these words: "That the first Assembly of the World Council of Churches be declared
to be and is hereby constituted, in accordance
with the Constitution drafted at Utrecht in 1938
and approved by the churches; that the Assembly
consists of those persons who have been appointed
as the official delegates of the churches adhering to the Council; and that the formation of
the World Council of Churches be declared to be
and is hereby completed."[39] The resolution was
adopted nemine contradicente in a wave of app-
lause. Thus the vision and endeavours of ten long
years of formation was completed. The joy of this
success was reflected also in the message to the
churches by the assembly where it was said: "We
bless God our Father, and our Lord Jesus Christ,
who gathers together in one the children of God
that are scattered abroad. He has brought us here
together at Amsterdam. We are one in acknowledging Him as our God and Saviour. We are divided
from one another not only in matters of faith,
order and tradition, but also by pride of nation,
class and race. But Christ has made us His own,
and He is not divided. In seeking Him we find one
another. Here at Amsterdam we have committed
ourselves afresh to him, and have covenanted with
one another in constituting this World Council of
Churches."[40]

---

39. Visser't Hooft W.A. (ed), The First Assembly
    of the World Council of Churches. London,
    S.C.M., 1949, p.28.
40. Visser't Hooft W.A., op. cit., The First
    Assembly of the World Council of Churches, p.9

The functions of the Council include: "To carry on the work of the two world movements for Faith and Order and Life and Work. To facilitate common action by the Churches. To promote co-operation in study. To promote the growth of ecumenical consciousness in the member churches. To establish relations with denominational fe-derations of world-wide scope and with other ecumenical movements. To call world conferences on specific subjects as occasion may require. To support the churches in their task of evange-lism."[41]

The Council draws her members from the chur-ches which agree with "the basis upon which the council had been formed", and which fulfil four other criteria, namely: "Autonomy, that is to say that a church is responsbile to no other church for the conduct of its own life. The se-cond was stability and the third was size, while the fourth was the relationship to other chur-ches."[42]

At the first assembly of the World Council of Churches, the official report stated that: "all confessional families except the Roman Catholics were represented."[43] This means precisely that the Roman Catholic Church is not a member of the World Council of Churches. She has rather estab-lished friendly ties with the Council. In 1961, she sent for the first time official observers to

---

41. op. cit., pp.197-198
42. Visser't Hooft W.A., op. cit., The Genesis and Formation of the World Council of Churches, p.62.
43. Visser't Hooft W.A., op. cit., The Genesis and Formation of the World Council of Churches, p.63.

the general Assembly of the World Council of
Churches in New Delhi. A Joint Working Group was
established between the Vatican and the W.C.C. in
1965 as the official organ of co-operation. Since
1968, some Catholic theologians work as full
members in Faith and Order Commission of the
World Council of Churches.

The Orthodox Churches of the four ancient
Patriachates of Alexandria, Anthioch, Constan-
tinople and Jerusalem, were all foundation mem-
bers of the W.C.C., as well as the Church of
Greece and the Orthodox Church in the United
States of America.[44] The Orthodox Churches of
Eastern Europe became members in 1961.

It was at the General Assembly in New Delhi
1961, that the International Missionary Council
became part of the World Council of Churches.
From the 1982 statistics, membership of the World
Council of Churches comprises 303 member churches, 29 union churches, from about 100 countries, with a total number of 400 million believers.[45]

---

44. ibid, p.64.
45. Krüger H., (Hrsg.), Ökumene Lexikon, Frank-
    furt/Main, Verlag Otto Lembeck und Josef
    Knecht, 1983, p.899.

2.4   LUND 1952

The period between Edinburgh and Lund witnessed some developments in the ecumenical movement. One of the most outstanding events was the
formation of the World Council of Churches in
1948, which was the union of Faith and Order and
Life and Work. There were also some theological
progress in the Faith and Order Commission. The
Edinburgh Continuation Committee in 1939,
appointed three theological commissions on three
study subjects namely, "The nature of the church",
"Ways of Worship", and "Intercommunion", and urged
them to submit their reports to the next world
conference. The reports of the commissions formed
the topics for discussion at the conference at
Lund. In effect, the conference of Faith and Order
at Lund is its first World Conference as Faith and
Order Commission of the World Council of Churches.

The Third World conference on Faith and Order
recorded a milestone in its history by the aboli-
tion of "comparative ecclesiology", and replaced
it with "christocentric ecclesiology". This came
out clearly in the report of section II, on
"Christ and his Church". There was no attempt to
record agreements and disagreements on the issue,
rather it sought to initiate a theological basis
of the biblical teaching about the relation between Christ and the Church. This advance could be
attributed to the effect of different speeches
made at the opening of the conference by different personalities that piloted the affairs of
Faith and Order Commission. Among them, the
appeal made by Rev. O.S. Tomkins, the conference
secretary, is of great significance, for he said:

"I would suggest, this covenant relationship
brings us to the end of what I would call a mere
comparative eccesiology. It was an essential and
pioneer task of Faith and Order to enable the
churches simply to explain themselves to one
another...if we seek too much to explain our
differences by comparative statement of our beliefs about the church we are tempted by the same
process to justify them. Our various 'confessional positions' tend to become embattled ramparts
which we are determined to defend rather than
confessions of faith under which we march out to
witness to a common Lord."[46] This new spirit
permeated the conference so that in its message
to the Churches, the conference wrote: "We have
seen clearly that we can make no real advances
towards unity if we only compare our several
conceptions of the nature of the church and the
traditions in which they are embodied. But once
again it has been proved true that as we seek to
draw closer to Christ we come closer to another.
We need, therefore, to penetrate behind our divisions to a deeper and richer understanding of the
mystery of the God-given union of Christ with his
church."[47]

In writing its report on "Christ and his
Church", section II, began it with a preamble
saying: "We believe in Jesus Christ our Lord, who
loved the church and gave himself for it, and has
brought the church into an abiding union with

---

46. Tomkins O.S. (ed), The Third World Conference
    on Faith and Order Lund 1952, London, S.C.M.,
    1953, pp.165-166.
47. op. cit., p.15.

himself. Because we believe in Jesus Christ we
believe also in the Church as the Body of
Christ."[48] It went on to say that with faith in
Jesus Christ, the powers of sin and death, which
he has overcome through his suffering, death and
resurrection, can no longer dominate us. Through
his atonement for man's sin, Christ has reconciled man with God, so that man may live in union
with him. As the king of the new People of God,
Jesus is the chief cornerstone, in which the
whole building, fitly framed together, grow up
into a holy temple in the Lord. Jesus is the head
of the Church, his Body, and "through His Spirit,
Jesus Christ Himself is present in his Church.
Christ lives in His Church and the Church lives
in Christ."[49] The christians as members of the
Body of Christ are made one with him in the
fellowship of his life. That Christ is at the
centre of his church is further brought out by
the report when it said that: "what has happened
to Christ uniquely in His-once-for-all death and
resurrection on our behalf, happens also to the
church in its way as His Body. As the Church is
made a partaker in the crucified Body of Christ,
so also it is given to be partaker in the risen
Body of the same Lord."[50] Speaking of the nature
and mission of the church, the report says that,
through his word and Spirit, Jesus calls his
church from the world, sends it into the world to
be both the salt of the earth and the light of
the world. The Church participates in Christ's
ministry of reconciliation, proclaims the gospel

---

48. ibid, p.17.
49. ibid.
50. ibid, p.18.

of salvation to all the nations and through its
witness, Jesus is at work among men as Saviour.
Looking hopefully to the consumation of all
things in Jesus, the report says: "At the end of
its pilgrimage Jesus Christ, the crucified and
risen, will come again to meet his Church in
order to complete his work of redemption and
judgment. Out of all peoples and ages he will
gather his own who look for his appearing and for
a new earth, and he will consumate the union
between Christ and his Church in the eternal
kingdom of God."[51]

2.4.1 REPORT OF SECTION IV ON: WAYS OF WORSHIP

The Continuation Committee of the Edinburgh
Conference appointed a theological commission in
1939 to study the topic "Ways of worship". The
report was submitted at the World Conference in
Lund and section IV studied it and reported to
the conference.

The section IV, studied the work of the
commission, and presented its report by outlining
what it called agreements, then the unsolved
problems and finally made its recommendations.
The reports stated: "We worship one God, Father,
Son and Holy Spirit, the triune God, by whose
spirit all true worship is inspired and unto whom
all christian worship is offered".[52] It recognized that in the encounter with God, it is the
Lord who takes the initiative by his gift of

---

51. ibid, p.20
52. Tomkins O.S. op. cit., p.39.

faith to man. By men's response to this gift from
God, they understand that they "could not have
been seeking God, had He not already found them,
and that the faith by which they responded was
itself God's gift to them." This response as
expressed in worship involves adoration, intercession, supplication, thanksgiving, words and
sacraments. Through the preaching of the word and
the administration of the sacraments, God offers
man his grace, imparts saving knowledge of Himself and draws man into communion with himself.

Using the "sacrificial language" in discussing
the Eucharist had seemed all along a taboo, so to
say, in the ecumenical circle and in this report
the section came out with its new understanding
when it said: "We record in thankfulness that we
have reached in our discussions a measure of
understanding, which none of us could ever have
anticipated, on the problem of the sacrificial
element in Holy Communion. The mystery of the
love of God, which we celebrate at the Lord's
Table, surpasses human expression. But in our
attempts to describe that mystery we have the
warrant of the Holy Scripture for using sacrificial language."[53] The report further descibed the
sacrifice of atonement made by Christ on Calvary
in these words: "Our Lord Jesus Christ in all his
life on earth and chiefly in his death and resurrection has overcome the powers of darkness. In
his one perfect and sufficient sacrifice on Calvary he offered perfect obedience to the Father
in atonement for the sin of the whole world. This
was an act of expiation made once and for all and

---

53. Tomkins O.S., op. cit., p.42.

is unrepeatable. In His risen and ascended life
He ever makes intercession for us."[54] Here our
response in worship consists in praise, prayer,
thanksgiving and offering of ourselves in faith
and obedience to the Father in the name of
Christ. In treating the difficulty which concerns
the relationship between our earthly worship and
the eternal intercession of Christ in heaven, the
report agreed that it touches an "element of
mystery."

Recording their differences, the report says
that: "Some of us believe that in the Lord's
Supper, where they enter into communion with the
crucified and risen Lord, they only offer a sacrifice of praise and thanksgiving and obedient
service as a response in faith to the benefits
the Lord gives us. Others would like to insist,
however, that in the Holy Eucharist the Lord
Jesus Christ as our Great High Priest unites the
oblation made by his body, the Church, with his
own sacrifices, and so takes up her adoration
into the sanctus of the company of heaven."[55] Some
others were of the opinion that although the
discussion centred only on the sacrificial aspect
of the Eucharist, that the main problem concerns
the real presence of Christ in the eucharist.
This re-echoes what the theological commission
said, that "The mode of the Real Presence of
Christ in eucharistic worship is the main
question in debate."[56]

---

54. ibid.
55. ibid, pp.42-43.
56. cf. Edward P. Haymann E, Maxwell W.D. (ed)
    Ways of Worship, London, S.C.M., 1951, p.25.

2.4.2 REPORT OF SECTION V ON: INTERCOMMUNION.

The subject matter, Intercommunion, was briefly treated in Edinburgh and was said to be a
necessary aspect towards church unity. The Edinburgh continuation committee in 1939 appointed a
theological commission to study the matter in
depth and report to the world conference. The
commission stated what the problem was all about
in its report to the conference at Lund in these
words: "Our problems concerning intercommunion
arise in a christendom divided into a number of
"chruches", which are not simply the local congregations of the one church, but denominations
related to one another somewhat after the manner
of sovereign independent states, themselves sometimes divided geographically into fellow-members
of an Anglican, Lutheran, Methodist, Presbyterian
or other family. Were this not so, were we really
one church, there would be no need of the prefix
inter. We should simply all be in communion with
one another. The word inter-communion presupposes
different churches, which may or may not be in
communion with one another."[57]

The section V, which handled the issue at Lund
recalled the call made at Edinburgh regarding
making specific definitions while discussing
intercommunion. In effect seven alternative definitions were outlined and explained. The first is
what it called

Full Communion: this obtains among churches which
have doctrinal agreement or which belong to the

---

57. Baille D., Marsh J., (ed), Intercommunion,
London, S.C.M., 1952, p.18.

same confessional family, and their ministers
freely officiate in either church, and the members communicate at the altars of each. The second it called, Intercommunion and Intercelebration: this involves churches which are not of the
same confessional family, but by agreement, they
receive communion at each others altar and the
ministers have the freedom to officiate at each
others church. The third it simply called Intercommunion: again this involves two churches which
by agreement allow their members to communicate
at the altars of each. The next is Open Communion: this obtains where a church extends her
invitation to members of other churches who are
present at her eucharistic celebrations to receive communion. The fifth is Mutual Open Communion: this obtains where two or more churches in
principle invite each others members to communion
and the invitees are free to accept the invitation, and this does not necessarily involve
intercelebration. The next is Limited Open Communion: this is described as the admission of
members of other churches not in full communion
with the host church, to holy communion in cases
of emergency or in other special circumstances.
Finally the report talked about Closed Communion:
this also obtains where a church limits participation in the Lord's Supper to its own members.

The report further said that the adequate
ordering of the Lord's Table in his name is entrusted to the church. The church has the duty to
warn her members not to eat or drink unworthily at
the Lord's Table. Because of the division in the
church, the ordering of the Lord's Table is carried out by the different churches, and each has

a grave responsibility before God in its administration particularly when it comes to withhol-
ding the communion from any of God's people. To
admit one to this sacrament, baptism, some instruction, profession of faith and confirmation
are among the things required. The report made it
clear that the Table belongs to the Lord and he
gives himself to us in the sacrament of the eucharist, and it went further to decry the divisive situation which prevents full communion, as
it said: "When we are unable to share together in
the Lord's Supper the pain and scandal of our
divisions is most severely felt because we seek
the one Lord, and know that we should be able to
partake as brethren in the family of God at one
Table."[58] The section report affirmed its recognition in the administration of the Eucharist
in the divided churches "when controlled by the
words of institution, as real means of grace
through which Christ gives himself to those who
in faith receive the appointed elements of bread
and wine."[59] The report recorded its agreement on
the Eucharist in these words: "The dominical
sacrament of Christ's Body and Blood, controlled
by the words of institution, with the use of the
appointed elements of bread and wine, is: a) a
memorial of Christ's incarnation and earthly
ministry, of his death and resurrection; b) a
sacrament in which he is truly present to give
himself to us, uniting us to himself, to his
eternal sacrifice, and to one another; and c)
eschatologically, an anticipation of our fellow-

---

58. Tomkins O.S., op. cit., p.53.
59. ibid.

ship with Christ in his eternal kingdom."[60]

There were differences of opinion regarding
the responsibility of a church in her refusal to
admit members of other churches to communion and
also of forbidding her members from partaking in
the communion of others. Some argued that a
fundamental unity exists among the members of the
World Council of Churches, as to justify or require joint participation at the Lord's Supper.
Others, without questioning the reality of the
unity so far attained, believe that fellowship in
the sacrament rightly exists only where there is
fuller doctrinal agreement, a mutually acceptable
ministry or organic unity in the life of the
church. At this juncture the report stated that
for the Orthodox Church, receiving the eucharist
is possible only between those who are members of
the Orthodox Church.

The report then called on the churches to re-
examine their ways of ordering and administering
the Eucharist, as regards the basic requirements
from the communicants, which will pave the way
for closer agreement and help towards intercommunion. It also called for attention to be given
to the theology, practice of, and relationship
between baptism and eucharist. A call was also
made to the churches that practice Limited Open
Communion, to re-examine their practice. And the
churches which practice Mutual Open Communion,
were asked to seriously examine the objections to
the practice urged on the grounds of doctrine and
order. The report lamented the lack of a larger
measure of agreement.

---

60. ibid, pp.53-54

2.4.3 COMMUNION AT ECUMENICAL GATHERINGS.

The problem of intercommunion is felt at
ecumenical gatherings most. Here the report noted
that for the participants at such gatherings
"their life and worship together are not complete
unless they can have the fellowship of the Lord's
Table." Eventhough a conference which gathers in
the name of Christ may be regarded as a temporary
and local expression of the church, yet it claims
neither the right to ordain, nor to authorize its
own ministry to celebrate the eucharist. The
report then observed that: "when all members are
not able to meet at the Lord's Table, no service
which is held can be regarded as the communion
service of the conference."[61]

In the face of such difficult situation the
section made the following recommendations: That
a penitential service should precede the
celebration of the eucharist. This service should
in its character bring about repentance on the
fact of the divisions in the church. That
communion services should be held at different
times to make it possible for the delegates to
receive communion without violating their
conscience or being disloyal to their tradition.
There should be occasion for open communion
services, irrespective of the place where the
conference is holding, that is, whether in urban
or remote area, and the invitation to receive
communion should be issued by the local church or
churches which sanction such services. Invitation
should always be extended to those who would not

61. Tomkins O.S., op. cit., p.58.

receive communion to be present as worshippers.
The report said that these recommendations do not
solve the practical problems which arise from the
unreconciled divergences in the doctrine of the
church and called the Faith and Order Commission
to undertake further study on the subject. A
further study was undertaken and section IV, of
the World Conference at Montreal 1963, reported
on it. Their report was sent to the central
committee of the World Council of Churches which
then issued the final resolution. The resolution
embodied only slight changes from the report we
have just considered above from Lund.

2.5 MONTREAL 1963.

REPORT OF SECTION IV, ON: THE EUCHARIST.

The section IV handled the topic "Worship and
the oneness of Christ's Church", and treated the
eucharist as part of sub-heading II. It said that
in the eucharist we proclaim and celebrate a
memorial of the saving acts of God, and that what
God did in the incarnation, life, death, resurrection and ascension of Christ, he does not do
again. In other words, that these events are
unique and cannot be repeated, extended or continued. This memorial which we celebrate in the
eucharist is not simply a recall of the past
events, rather "God makes them present through
the Holy Spirit who takes of the things of Christ
and declares them to us, thus making us participants in Christ."[62] Amid disagreements and great
desire for full statements on the eucharist the
report was able to say from a unanimous vote
that: "The Lord's Supper, a gift of God to his
Church, is a sacrament of the presence of the
crucified and glorified Christ until he come, and
a means whereby the sacrifice of the cross, which
we proclaim, is operative within the Church."[63]
It also said that in the Lord's Supper, the unity
of the members of Christ's Body is sustained.
With Christ who is the High Priest and Intercessor, we offer our praise, thanksgiving and
intercession to the Father in the power of the
Holy Spirit. This sacrifice made with contrite

---

62. Rodger P.C. and Visher L. (ed), The Fourth
    World Conference on Faith and Order, Montreal
    1963, London, S.C.M., 1964, p.73.
63. ibid.

hearts is a living and holy sacrifice which must
be expressed daily in our lives. Thus in this
eucharistic sacrifice we are "united to our Lord,
and to the Church triumphant, and in fellowship
with the whole church on earth, we are renewed in
the covenant sealed by the blood of Christ... we
also anticipate the marriage-supper of the Lamb
in the Kingdom of God."[64]

To articulate the liturgical procedure in
celebrating the eucharist, two major parts were
called to mind. One it called "A service of the
Word" and the other "A service of the sacrament."
The service of the word includes, reading and
preaching the word of God, and interecessory
prayers for the church and the world. The service
of the sacrament includes, the action of taking
bread and wine; 'blessing God for creation and
redemption', invocation of the Holy Spirit, reci-
ting the words of institution, thanksgiving prayer, the Lord's prayer and finally the breaking
of the bread and the distribution of wine. The
report apologetically said: "This list of liturgical items is not meant to exclude reference
during the service to many other important theological themes such as the expression of contrition; the declaration of forgiveness of sins; the
affirmation of faith in credal forms; the announcement of the Lord's coming; and the self-dedica-
tion of the faithful to God."[65]

This report was made in the setting of worship, although some statements were made about
the eucharist. This section IV, while discussing

---

64. ibid, p.74.
65. ibid.

the issue of eucharist in ecumenical gatherings, recommended to the Faith and Order Commission, to devote some attention in the future to the study of the Eucharist. The first consultation on the subject was held in 1965, and we shall discuss that in the next chapter.

2.6 DEVELOPMENTS IN THE ROMAN CATHOLIC CHURCH. THE SECOND VATICAN COUNCIL.

When Pope John XXIII on 25 January 1959 announced that he would convoke an Ecumenical Council for the universal church, the announcement stunned Roman Catholics and perplexed other christians. Series of questions were asked: "Was this a papal attempt to reunite all christians in the fashion of the Councils of Lyons (1274) and of Florence (1438-1442) - a common table at which "reunion formulae" could and would be forged?"[66] The Pope contemplated a council that would be of service "not only for the spiritual good and joy of the christian people but also an invitation to the separated communities to seek again that unity for which many souls are longing in these days throughout the world."[67] The Pope later specified that only bishops in communion with the See of Rome would gather to discuss these pressing topics which concern "the development of the Catholic faith, the revival of christian standards of living, and the bringing of ecclesiastical discipline into closer accord with the needs and conditions of our times."[68]

In his opening speech at the Second Vatican Council, 11 October 1962, the Pope made it clear that the Council has not assembled to condemn but even in the face of tackling error, its approach

---

66. cf. Stranky F., and Sheerin J.B., (ed.), Doing the Truth in Charity, New York, Paulist Press, 1982, p.5.
67. A.A.S. 51 (1959), p.69, quoted according to: Stranky F. Sheerin J.B., op. cit., p.5
68. A.A.S. 51 (1959), p.511, op. cit., p.5.

its pastoral. "The Church has always opposed
these errors. Nowadays, however, the Spouse of
Christ prefers to make use of the medicine of
mercy rather than that of severity. She considers
that she meets the needs of the present day by
demonstrating the validity of her teaching rather
than by condemnations."[69] From the onset the
Council pointed clearly at where it is going -
renewal- so that in their message to Humanity at
the beginning of the Council, the Council Fathers
said inter alia: "In this assembly under the guidance of the Holy Spirit, we wish to inquire how
we ought to renew ourselves, so that we may be
found increasingly faithful to the gospel of
Christ. We shall take pains so to present to the
men of this age God's truth in its intergrity and
purity that they may understand it and gladly
assent to it."[70]

The Council promulgated altogether sixteen documents. New developments were recorded in relationship between Catholics and other christians
in the Decree on Ecumensim and in other related
texts of the Council's documents, and to this
area we now turn our attention.

2.6.1 DOGMATIC CONSTITUTION ON THE CHURCH (LUMEN GENTIUM)

The entire Constitution on the Church is not
our interest here, but those momentuos sayings
therein on ecumenism. What comes to mind imme-

---

69. Abbort W.M., the Documents of Vatican II,
    London Geoffrey Chapman, 1966, p.716.
70. Abbott W.M., op. cit., pp.3-4.

diately therefore, is the recognition of the
"ecclesial elements" outside the structure of the
Catholic Church. In L.G.7, the Constitution
speaks about the church as the body of Christ,
and baptism as the means of incorporation into
that body. At the beginning of number 8, the way
is prepared for a new view. Speaking of the uniqueness of the church, the Council does not simply say that the one church willed by Christ is
identical with the church governed by the Roman
Pontiff. Rather it says: "This Church, constituted and organised in the world as a society,
subsists in the Catholic Church, which is governed by the successor of Peter and by the bishops
in union with that successor", and it adds immediately "although many elements of sanctification
and of truth can be found outside her visible
structure. These elements, however, as gifts,
properly belonging to the church of Christ
possess an inner dynamism toward Catholic
Unity."[71] Further clarification on these elements
of sanctification are given in number fifteen,
where it says: "The church recognises that in many
ways she is linked with those who, being baptized,
are honoured with the name of christian, though
they do not profess the faith in its entirety or
do not preserve unity of communion with the
successor of Peter. For there are many who honour
sacred Scripture, taking it as a norm of belief
and of action, and who show a true religious

---

71. All the quotations of the Vat. II documents
    are taken from Abbott W.M., The Documents of
    Vatican II, London, Geoffrey Chapman, 1966;
    according to their Latin names and numbers.
    L.G. No. 8.

zeal. They lovingly believe in God the Father and Saviour. They also recognise and receive other sacraments within their own churches or ecclesiastical communities. Many of them rejoice in the episcopate, celebrate the Holy Eucharist, and cultivate devotion toward the Virgin Mother of God. They also share with us in prayer and other spiritual benefits."[72] While treating the Church as the People of God, the Council fathers did not lose sight of all the baptized who are not in communion with the See of Rome. They are accorded recognition in these words: "All men are called to be part of this Catholic unity of the People of God, a unity which is harbinger of the universal peace it promotes. And there belong to it or are related to it in various ways, the Catholic faithful as well as all who believe in Christ, and indeed the whole of mankind. For all men are called to salvation by the grace of God."[73] On the devotion to the Blessed Virgin Mary in the church the Constitution while recommending that the veneration of images of Christ, the Blessed Virgin, and the saints be observed, warned against "falsity of exaggeration" on the one hand and "the excess of narrow-mindedness" on the other. The theologians were instructed to "painstakinly guard against any word or deed which could lead separated brethren or anyone else into error regarding the doctrine of the Church", and the faithful were reminded that "true devotion consists neither in fruitless and passing emotion, nor in a certain vain credulity."[74]

---

72. L.G. No. 15.
73. L.G. No. 13.
74. L.G. No. 67

The Constitution then rejoices with the separated
brethren of the East, "who with ardent emotion
and devout mind concour in reverencing the Mother
of God, ever Virgin."[75]

2.6.2 DECREE ON ECUMENISM
   (UNITAS REDINTEGRATIO).

The Decree on Ecumenism, promulgated on 21
November 1964, specifies the Catholic Church's
manner of approach to the ecumenical movement.
The Catholic Church had in the past refrained
from joining the 'ecumenical movement' started by
the Protestant Churches, and had either warned or
forbidden Catholics from taking part in the movement. This ecumenical movement brought about the
development of the World Council of Churches, the
growth of national and world-wide groupings of
Protestant churches and the mergers of churches.
The Decree on Ecumenism marks an end to the former attitude and spelt out how the Catholics
should go forward to work for the unity of the
Church.

The Decree has three chapters. The first
chapter in brief is about what the church believes, which it takes with to the dialogue with
other churches. The second chapter outlines how
the principles could be put into practice and
finally the third chapter outlines the basis for
the dialogue first with the Eastern Churches and
secondly with the Protestant Churches of the
West.

---

75. L.G. No. 69.

The brief introduction to the Decree states
among other things that one of the chief concerns
of the Second Vatican Council is to promote the
restoration of unity among christians. The Church
established by Christ the Lord is one and unique,
but many communions present their convictions
about the message of Christ in diverse ways as if
Christ himself were divided. And taking cognizan-
ce of the ecumenical movement among those "who
invoke the Triune God and confess Jesus as Lord
and saviour", the council wishes to set forth for
all the Catholics, certain helps and methods by
which they can respond to the ecumenical movement.

First the document began with the facts of our
faith. God revealed his love to man through the
incarnation. Christ before his death on the cross
prayed for the unity of those who believe, instituted the sacrament of the Eucharist, which signifies and brings about the unity of the Church.
After his glorification, he sent the Holy Spirit
on those he called and gathered into the New
Covenant, which comprises the Church. To establish the Church everywhere, Christ also entrusted
the task of preaching, ruling and sanctifying to
the college of the twelve apostles, among whom
Peter was chosen as head. Christ remains the chief
shepherd and the cornerstone. The continuity of
this work is assured "through the faithful preaching of the gospel by the apostles and their
successors - the bishops with Peter's successor
at their head - through their administration of
the sacraments, and through their loving exercise
of authority, that Jesus Christ wishes His people
to increase under the influence of the Holy

Spirit. Thereby too, He perfects His people's
fellowship in unity: in the confession of one
faith, in the common celebration of divine
worship, and in the fraternal harmony of the
family of God."[76] The Decree sees the role of the
Church as minister of the gospel of peace to
mankind, as she makes her pilgrim way to the
fatherland above, as "the sacred mystery of the
unity of the Church, in Christ through Christ,
with the Holy Spirit energizing a variety of
functions. The highest exemplar and source of this
mystery is the unity in the Trinity of Persons, of
one God, the Father, and the Son in the Holy
Spirit."[77]

Speaking of the divisions in the church, the
Decree says that "men of both sides were to
blame" and declared that those presently born in
these communities separated from the Catholic
Church, cannot be imputed the sin of separation.
Since they are instilled with Christ's faith,
they are accepted by the Catholic Church as
brothers. The difference in doctrine, in discipline or concerning the structure of the church,
which the ecumenical movement is striving to
overcome, are serious obstacles to ecclesiastical
communion. But all those justified by faith
through baptism are incorporated into Christ. The
ecclesial elements found outside the structure of
the Catholic Church according to the decree are
"the written word of God; the life of grace;
faith, hope, and charity, along with other inte-
rior gifts of the Holy Spirit and visible

---

76. U.R. No. 2.
77. U.R. No. 2.

elements. All of these, which come from Christ
and lead back to Him, belong by right to the one
Church of Christ."[78] Despite the defects which
the separated churches suffer, the decree maintains that they are not deprived of the "significance and importance in the mystery of salvation." One thing remains clear and that is "our
separated brethren, whether considered as individuals or as communities and churches, are not
blessed with that unity which Jesus Christ wished
to bestow on all those whom He has regenerated
and vivified into one body and newness of life
that unity which the holy Scriptures and the
revered tradition of the Church proclaim. For it
is through Christ's Catholic Church alone, which
is the all embracing means of salvation, that the
fullness of the means of salvation can be obtained."[79]

The decree then exhorts all Catholics to recognise the signs of the time and to participate
skillfully in the work of ecumenism. It described
the ecumenical work as "those activities and
enterprises which, according to various needs of
the church and opportune occasions, are started
and organized for the forstering of unity among
christians."[80] It condemned polemics and ex-
tolled dialogue between competent experts from
different churches and communities. The end result of these activities supervised by the bishops will be the gradual overcome of obstacles
and the eventual common celebration of the
eucharist into that unity of the one and only

---

78. U.R. No. 3.
79. ibid.
80. U.R.No. 4.

Church. That the work of ecumenism among catholics may be effective, the decree called for a renewal in the Catholic household itself. It urged for preservation of unity in essentials and called for the reign of charity in all things. Catholics should acknowledge and esteem the truly christian endowments from our common heritage found among the separated brethren.

The second chapter of the decree outlines the practical methods which catholics should follow in the work of ecumenism. It was made clear that the concern for restoring unity pertains to the whole church, the faithful and the clergy alike, and therefore calls for the church's renewal which consists in fidelity to her own calling. For ecumenism to worth its name, the decree calls for a change of heart, "For it is from newness of attitudes, from self-denial and unstinted love, that yearnings for unity take their rise and grow toward maturity."[81] This change of heart could be manifested in prayer, humility and in being gentle in the service of others. Recognising that both parties in the separation have sinned against unity, it begged pardon of God and of our separated brethren. Although Catholics have the custom of praying for unity, the decree now asks them to join in such prayers with the separated brethren. Indiscriminate common worship as means for the restoration of christian unity is forbidden, for "such worship depends chiefly on two principles: it should signify the unity of the Church; it should provide a sharing in the means of grace. The fact that it should signify unity

---

81. U.R. No. 7.

generally rules out common worship. Yet the gaining of a needed grace sometimes commends it."[82]
To understand the general outlook of the separated brethren, the decree recommends study, which
should be pursued with fidelity to truth and in a
spirit of good will. Catholics should understand
the distinctive doctrines of the separated brethren, as well as their history, spiritual and
liturgical life, their religious psychology and
cultural background. All this will be of immense
help to the theological discussion, which should
be among competent experts from both sides in an
atmosphere of equality. The document directs that
instruction in sacred theology and other branches
of knowledge should be presented from an ecumenical point of view but warned against approxima-
ting the truth in these words: "The manner and
order in which catholic belief is expressed
should in no way become an obstacle to dialogue
with our brethren. It is, of course, essential
that doctrine be clearly presented in its entirety. Nothing is so foreign to the spirit of ecumenism as a false conciliatory approach which
harms the purity of Catholic doctrine and obscures its assured genuine meaning."[83] The Catholic experts who would be engaged in dialogue
with the separated brethren are reminded that
"when comparing doctrines, they should remember
that in Catholic teaching there exists an order
or "hierarchy" of truths, since they vary in
their relationship to the foundation of the

82. U.R. No. 8.
83. U.R. No. 11.

christian faith."[84] All catholics are called to
cooperate with their separated brethren in social
matters as these would contribute to just appreciation of the human dignity, the promotion of
peace and the application of the gospel principles
to social life. The decree also called all christians to profess their faith before the whole
world "in God, one in three, in the incarnate Son
of God, our Redeemer and Lord."

In chapter three, the special position of the
Eastern Churches was first handled. The decree
recalled that for several centuries ago the Churches of the East and West parted, and that in
whatever disagreements in belief and discipline
that arose, "the Roman See acted by common consent". It noted significantly how the local churches of the East flourish and recognises the
Partriachal Churches as holding the first place
among them, for these claim their origins from
the apostles themselves. The West has drawn from
the treasury of the East in areas of liturgy,
spiritual tradition and jurisprudence and called
to mind the fact that the trinitarian dogma, the
dogma of the Incarnation were defined in the
Ecumenical Councils held in the East. It then
made this important observation that: "the heritage handed down by the apostles was received in
different forms and ways, so that from the very
beginnings of the church it has had a varied
development in various places, thanks to a similar variety of natural gifts and conditions of
life. Added to external causes, and to mutual
failures in understanding and charity, all these

---

84. ibid.

circumstances set the stage for separation."[85]
Hence for a meaningful dialogue to be carried out
between the Eastern Churches and the Catholic
Church one has to take into consideration the
origin and growth of the churches in the East and
their relationship with the Catholic Church before the separation. Remarking that the Eastern
Churches possess true sacraments the decree
speaks of their close relationship with the Catholic Church in these words: "Although these
Churches are separated from us, they possess true
sacraments, above all-by apostolic succession
the priesthood and the Eucharist, whereby they are
still joined to us in a very close relationship.
Therefore given suitable circumstances and the
approval of church authority, some worship in
common is not merely possible but is recommended."[86] Aware that from the earliest times the
Eastern churches followed their own disciplines,
the decree stresses unity in diversity.[87] This
legitimate variety applies also in the method of
theological investigations which are formulated
differently in the East and West, and should be
seen as commplimentary rather than conflicting
with each other. To realize the desired unity the
Council called the various organisations and
parishes to prayer and looks forward to fraternal
dialogue on matters of doctrine and on pressing
pastoral problems.

On the Churches and ecclesial communities in
the West, the decree says that they, "are bound

---

85. U.R. No. 14.
86. U.R. No. 15.
87. cf. U.R. No. 16.

to the Catholic Church by a special affinity and
close relationship in view of the long span of
earlier centuries when the christian people lived
in ecclesiastical communion."[88] Their complex
nature lies in the fact that: "in origin, teaching, and spiritual practice, these churches and
ecclesial communities differ not only from us but
also among themselves to a considerable degree."[89] There are notable differences between
the separated brethren themselves on the one hand
and the Catholic church on the other, in the
areas not only of historical, sociological, psychological and cultural nature but especially in
the interpretation of the revealed truth. To come
to grips with these differences, the decree opts
for ecumenical dialogue and went on to suggest
what would serve as basis and motivation for such
dialogue. Those who are to engage in dialogue
with the Catholic church are those who have their
basis as "those christians who openly confess
Jesus Christ as God and Lord and as the sole
Mediator between God and man unto the glory of
the one God, Father, Son, and Holy Spirit."[90]
Different views exist between them and the Catholic Church on christology, the work of redemption, the mystery and ministry of the church and
the role of Mary in the work of salvation. These
in effect form the basis for the dialogue. Further differences exist in determining the relationship between the Scriptures and the church.
The decree points out that the separated brethren

---

88. U.R. No. 19.
89. ibid.
90. U.R. No. 20 (This is similar to the basis of
    admission into the W.C.C.)

lacked that fullness of unity which should flow
from baptism and because they lack the sacrament
of Orders, they have not preserved the genuine
and total reality of the Eucharistic mystery.[91]
Because of this, the Lord's Supper the other
sacraments and the church's worship and ministry
are recommended as subjects for dialogue. In
moral matters there are many christians who do
not understand the gospel as catholics do, hence
the decree called for ecumenical dialogue on the
application of the gospel to moral questions.

The Council after outlining the circumstances
and principles within which ecumenical activities
can operate, warned against superficiality or
imprudent zeal which can impede progress and
prays that "the initiatives of the sons of the
Catholic Church, joined with those of the separated brethren, go forward without obstructing the
ways of divine Providence and without prejudging
the future inspiration of the Holy Spirit."[92] It
is aware that the task of reconciling all christians in the unity of one and only Church of
Christ transcends human energies and abilities
and reposes hope entirely on the prayer of Christ
for the Church.

---

91. cf. U.R. No. 22.
92. U.R. No. 24.

2.6.3 OTHER RELATED VAT. II TEXTS TO ECUMENISM. DECREE ON EASTERN CATHOLIC CHURCHES.

In the decree on the Eastern Catholic Churches provisions were made for their relationship with the brethren from the separated churches in accordance with the decree on Ecumenism. They were enjoined to keep to the principles outlined in the decree on Ecumenism, namely, that of prayer, fidelity to ancient traditions, mutual knowledge and regard for objects and attitudes. What is demanded of any brother from the separated Eastern churches who wishes to join himself to the Catholic unity is a simple profession of faith. This holds also for the clerics, and they can thereafter exercise the orders which they have received. Common worship as a means of restoring unity is forbidden, for it "would damage the unity of the church or involve formal acceptance for falsehood or the danger of deviation in the faith, of scandal, or of indifferentism."[93] In order to remove obstacles on the way for those seeking salvation in view of special circumstances of time, place and personage, the decree says that the "sacrament of penance, the Eucharist and the anointing of the sick" may be granted to separated Eastern christians, who on their own accord with good dispositions asked for them.[94] Catholics may in similar situations and when access to a catholic priest is physically or morally impossible, ask for these sacraments from the ministers of those churches that possess valid

---

93. Orientalium Ecclesiarum (O.E.) No. 26.
94. ibid.

sacraments. The same conditions just mentioned above may warrant a catholic to join the separated Eastern brethren in sacred functions. Provisions are made for mutual consultations among the ordinaries of both churches, so that they may govern relations between christians by timely and effective rules and regulations.

The decree on the Pastoral office of Bishops called upon the bishops to approach people seeking and fostering dialogue with them. Such dialogue whose ulterior motive is for salvation should be characterised by its clarity of speech and humility so that truth may be joined to charity. In exercising their pastoral office the bishops were charged "to deal lovingly with the separated brethren, urging the faithful also to conduct themselves with great kindness and charity in their regard, and fostering ecumenism as it is understood by the church."[95]

While the decree on Priestly Formation demands that seminarians should be led to understand the churches and ecclesial communities separated from the Roman, Apostolic See, so that they can contribute to the restoration of christian unity;[96] the decree on the Ministry and life of Priest asks the priests to be mindful of the Council's directives on ecumenism and therefore should not forget their brothers who do not enjoy full ecclesiastical communion with the Catholic Church.[97]

The decree on the Church's Missionary Activity

---

95. Christus Dominus No. 16.
96. cf. Optatam Totius, No. 16.
97. cf. Presbyterorum Ordinis, No. 9.

took note of the difference that exists in missionary activity among nations, pastoral activity
among the faithful and the different methods to
restore unity among christians. These differences
led the Council to lament the division among
christians in these words: "The division among
christians damages the most holy cause of preaching the gospel to every creature and blocks the
way to the faith of many."[98] The decree therefore
called on all the baptized to be gathered into
one flock, to be able to bear witness to Christ
before the nations. As part of their christian
witness the faithful are asked to take their part
in the strivings of various christian communities
and non christian religions, in waging war
against famine, ignorance and disease. In general
the laity may collaborate with other groups in
social and technical projects as well as in cultural and religious ones. Even the neophytes
should be nurtured in ecumenical spirit, so that
they may consider that the brethren who believe
in Christ and are baptized are sharers with the
people of God in many riches.[99] The men of letters and research in institutes and universities,
who promote knowledge of peoples and religions,
are required to "cooperate in brotherly spirit
with other christians, with non-christians, and
with members of international organisations,
having always before their eyes the fact that
"the building up of the earthly city should have
its foundation in the Lord, and should be directed toward Him"".[100] In planning missionary

---

98. Ad Gentes, No. 6.
99. cf. Ad Gentes, No. 15.
100. Ad Gentes, No. 41.

activity the decree calls for cooperation between
the congregation for the Propagation of Faith and
the Secretariat for Promoting Christian Unity, in
searching out ways and means for bringing about
and directing fraternal cooperation with other
christian communities so that the scandal of
division may be removed.[101]

The Pastoral constitution on the Church in the
modern world (Gaudium et Spes), says that the
church can contribute greatly towards making the
family of man and its history more human through
her members. In this context therefore "the Catholic Church gladly holds in high esteem the things
which other christian churches or ecclesial communities have done or are doing cooperatively by
way of achieving this goal."[102] The document went
further to call the catholics to cooperate actively in the international community with the
separated brethren, with whom they profess together the gospel of love, in the world-wide
promotion of justice for the poor and in showing
them the charity of Christ.[103] Mindful of the fact
that the bond which unites are mightier than
anything which divides, and the very fact that
the Catholics with their separated brethren are
linked in their profession of the Father, Son and
Holy Spirit and also by the bond of charity, the
constitution calls all to work for the unity of
christians which is awaited by many.[104]

The dogmatic constitution on divine Revelation, aware that the sacred scriptures should

---

101. cf. Ad Gentes, No. 29.
102. Gaudium et Spes, No. 40.
103. cf. Gaudium et Spes, No. 90.
104. cf. Gaudium et Spes, No. 92.

be provided for all the christians, called for
joint translation of the scripture from the original text, for the use of all. The text says
"...and if, given the opportunity and the approval of church authority, these translations are
produced in cooperation with the separated
brethren as well, all christians will be able to
use them."[105]

The Second Vatican Council recorded a significant development in ecumenical movement in respect of the decree on Ecumenism and in the other
related texts of the Council. The ecumenical
movement as it is known today developed outside
the catholic church, whose participation it
lacked. The decree on Ecumenism marks a new era
in the relation of the churches with one another.
The Council does not equate the one Church of
Christ with the Roman Catholic Church, rather it
says: "This Church constituted and organized in
the world as a society, subsists in the Catholic
Church, which is governed by the successor of
Peter and by the bishops in union with that successor."[106] Thus the way was paved to say that
many elements of salvation and truth can be found
outside the visible structure of the Catholic
Church. And the decree on Ecumenism also said
that the sacred actions of the christian religion
performed by the separated brethren" can truly
engender a life of grace, and can be rightly
described as capable of providing access to the
community of salvation."[107]

---

105. Dei Verbum, No. 22.
106. L.G. No. 8
107. U.R. No. 3

This way of speaking about the separated brethren or ecclesial community is a new development. When one reads these documents of the Second Vatican Council side by side with the papal
encyclicals of Leo XIII "Satis Cognitum" of 1896
and "Mortalium animos", 1912 of Pius XI, one
cannot but appreciate the cordiality and frank-
ness of the Council Fathers in speaking about the
separated brethren and according them some recognition. These encyclicals did not only equate the
Roman Catholic church as the one Church founded
by Christ, but also said that those who did not
belong to it live in area of darkness and corrup-
tion.[108] No wonder then McCrea Cavert, a Protestant, in his Response to the decree on Ecumenism
wrote inter alia "The Decree's recognition of the
"truly christian endowments" which are to be
found among the non-Roman bodies is crucial. The
ecumenical dialogue is lifted to a new level when
it is acknowledged that they "have by no means
been deprived of significance and importance in
the mystery of salvation" and that the work of
God's grace in them could result in "a more ample
realization of the very mystery of Christ and the
church. The assumption that the Holy Spirit is at
work in "ecclesial communities" outside the Roman
Catholic Church is very different from the previous way of treating non-Roman christians merely
as individuals and ignoring their corporate life
and structure."[109] The Catholic Church neverthe-

---

108. cf. A.A.S. 28 (1895-1896) 617 ff; quoted
     acc. Löser W. (Hrsg.), Das Einheits- und
     Ökumenismusverständnis, in: Die Kirchen der
     Welt, Band XX, Frankfurt/Main, E.V., 1986,
     p.323.
109. Abbott W.M., op. cit., p.367.

less maintains according to Vat. II, to be the
Church of Christ, but does not exclude the other
christian communities to be churches.

What is clear is that through the Vat. II, a
new understanding has developed but there is no
break with the past as regards the unity of the
church. As W. Löser rightly put it: "Das neue
Verständnis ist das Ergebnis der Weiterentwick-
lung des früheren. Neue Akzente sind gesetzt
worden. Von einem Bruch zwischen dem früheren und
dem gegenwärtigen Einheitskonzept kann jedoch
nicht die Rede sein."[110]

The decree on Ecumensimn took the bull on the
horns by admitting guilt and said that men of
both sides were to blame for the sin of separation, and went further to ask for pardon of God
and of the separated brethren. It maintained that
Christ the Lord founded one Church, and the division "openly contradicts the will of Christ,
provides a stumbling block to the world and in-
flicts damage on the most holy cause of proclaiming the good news to every creature."[111] The
spirit of renewal ran through the documents of
the Council in humility and the Council demonstrates its eagerness to reunion by encouraging
ecumenical dialogue and stipulating principles
that would make it operative. Some steps have
already been taken by the church to impliment her
recommendations. She has jointly established a

---

110. Löser W., op. cit., p.335.
     "The new understanding is the result of the
     further development of the former one. New
     accents are set. There is no question of a
     grief between the former and the later
     concept of unity." (Translation is mine).
111. U.R. No. 1.

body with the World Council of Churches known as the: Joint Working Group, for the purpose of dialogue and other areas of cooperation between the two bodies. Since 1968, some catholic theologians take active part in the activities of the Faith and Order Commission of the World Council of Churches. And we shall see later that she has engaged in dialogue with different churches and ecclesial communities. The church realises that the task of reconciling the christians is not an easy task and has therefore called for a change of heart and for prayer while reposing her hope in the prayer of Christ himself for the Church, "that all may be one."

Index to other related texts to ecumenism.
LUMEN GENTIUM: Nos. 8, 13, 15, 67, 69.
ORIENTALIUM ECCLESIARUM: Nos. 24, 25, 26, 27, 28, 29.
CHRISTUS DOMINI: Nos. 13, 16.
PERFECTAE CARITATIS: Nos. 2.
OPTATAM TOTIUS: No. 16.
PRESBYTERORUM ORDINIS: No. 9.
APOSTOLICAM ACTUOSITATEM: no. 27.
GRAVISSIMUM EDUCATIONIS: Nos. 1, 11.
AD GENTES: Nos. 6, 12, 15, 16, 29, 36, 41.
GAUDIUM ET SPES: Nos. 40, 90, 92
DEI VERBUM: No. 22.

CHAPTER THREE.

AARHUS TO ACCRA.

3.1 AARHUS: REPORT OF COMMITTEE III.

Among the resolutions of the section IV of the
Fourth World Conference on Faith and Order in
Montreal 1963, was that "The Faith and Order
Commission might well in the years ahead devote
to the sacrament of Holy Communion the attention
recently devoted to Baptism. Such attention would
require deocumentation of the eucharistic teaching and practice, including the liturgy of the
individual churches and would include careful
study of recent suggestions for concelebration
and Agape-meal."[1] At the meeting of the commission and its working committee in Aarhus, 1964,
Committee III was assigned to study the Montreal's resolution and to report to the plenary
assembly. The committee produced a guideline for
the new study project which was later adopted by
the Plenum.

In its report, the committee arranged the
study of the eucharist under seven chapters.
While the first chapter was to be concerned with
the relevant biblical texts, the second was to
deal on the ancient liturgies and its later developments in which the eucharist had been celebrated. It was also to tackle the relationship between Agape and the Eucharist. In the rest of the
schema, the eucharist as a sacrament was to be

---

1. Rodger P.C., Visher L. (ed), The Fourth World
   Conference on Faith and Order, London, SCM,
   1964, p.78.

studied to include the presence of Christ in the
eucharist; the eucharist as a sacrifice and the
role of the Holy Spirit when the sacrament is
celebrated. Others concern: the transforming
power of the eucharist; the eucharist and the
church and finally the eucharist and unity.

The committee recommended that the study
should benefit from the best theological resour-
ces that are available and as is fitting in an
ecumenical study, the interest of the churches
should be engaged in its progress. The results
should be communicated to the churches in the
most useful form. Then it called for a single
report to be produced on completion of the study.
To make the study workable and in order to produce result as early as possible the committee
further recommended that: "The conduct of the
study be in the hands of a small ecumenical
commission, assisted by the secretariat; this
commission to be set up with the minimum of de-
lay, by invitation of the staff and with the
approval of the Working Committee."[2] The committee finally recommended that a study guide
should be prepared by one or more writers who
should be responsible to the commission. This
part of the recommendation provoked the two papers which we shall immediately consider.

---

2. Minutes of the Meeting of the Commission and
   Working Committee 1964 Aarhus, Denmark. F.O.
   No. 44, p.56.

3.2 THOUGHTS ON A STUDY OF THE EUCHARIST.
(L. VISCHER).*

This paper was intended to stimulate thoughts
on the study project, the Eucharist. The author,
in the preamble to his paper pointed out that the
division of christendom stares us in the face by
the fact that christians are not in the position
to celebrate the eucharist together, the meal
which was instituted by Christ as a sign of
fellowship. He noted how painful this experience
is felt by those who are engaged in ecumenical
movement. He is of the opinion that to describe
the problem as is evident in some ecumenical
literatures, may turn up to be a substitute for
its solution. He then declared: "We must rather
turn all our powers to the problem itself and
attempt to come to a solution." The fact that
will not make the matter look hopeless is that we
have unity in Christ, and this fact could be made
real.

The question is, how do we proceed in this
apparent contradiction? The contradiction is that
although we have unity in Christ, yet we are
separated at his table. The author himself went
ahead to suggest a starting point and said: "When
we acknowledge that in Christ we are also bound
together with the members of other churches, we
learn indeed to view their celebration of the
Eucharist with other eyes. We understand that
Christ is also present with them. We no longer

---

* Lukas Vischer is a Minister in the Reformed
Church. Executive Director of Faith and Order
from 1966-1979. His paper is documented as:
FO/64:25.

judge their action in the first place from the
view-point of error, falsification and invali-
dity, but begin with the assumption that the Holy
Spirit is also at work and brings fruit among
them."[3] To be able therefore to take one another
seriously, we must confront one another on the
reference to the unity given to us in Christ,
otherwise no real conversation will take place
but only an ecumenically-clothed attack, maintains the author.

He arranged the paper under five sub-headings,
starting with the historical method which he said
would help break down the walls of separation.

3.2.1   THE HISTORICAL METHOD.

The historical method, the author maintained,
will no doubt bring us to such questions as how
did Christ institute the eucharist; the meaning
he gave to it, and how the eucharist which we
celebrate today arose from the action established
by Christ. The churches were convinced of the
action instituted by Christ and the correct exe-
cution of his command. The critical historical
method in the opinion of the author undermines
this self-evidence. This can be demonstrated from
some problems connected with the eucharist. The
first that comes to mind is the different forms
of words which Jesus used at the Last Supper as
was handed down by the gospels and St. Paul.
Another example is the question about when the
Lord Jesus did celebrate the Last Supper with his

---

3. FO/64:25, p.1.

disciples. Did he celebrate it before the feast
of Passover or on the day of the Passover itself?
The New Testament witnesses differ from each
other in their accounts. While John is obviously
of the opinion that the Jews had not celebrated
the Passover meal as Jesus was tried and killed,
the Synoptic writers affirm however that the
final meal took place at the same time as the
Jewish Passover meals. Here the author's opinion
is that the difference has some importance. He
went on to say: "The question of the date is
indeed of secondary importance and we could put
aside the question of differences if they only
involved the date of the meal and of Jesus'
death. They are, however, also important in the
interpreation of the action instituted by Christ.
Was the meal a common meal and only later interpreted as a Passover meal? Or did Jesus consciously submit himself to the liturgy of the
feast of the Passover and give it a new content?"[4] The different ways in which answers are
given to these questions underline the different
understanding of the eucharist. An example is
that those who follow the statement of John use
leavened bread in the eucharistic celebration
(Orthodox, Reformed Churches and some other Evangelical Churches), while those who decide for the
Synoptics prefer unleavened bread (Roman Catholic
Church, Anglicans and Lutherans).

The historical method has to look into the
form which the eucharist took in the early
Church. It has to deal with the difficult question of whether the disciples of Jesus began

---

4. op. cit., FO/64:25, p.4.

to celebrate the eucharist of the Lord's resurrection because they had his command and wanted
to fulfil it; or whether they came to celebrate
the memory of the Lord in a sacred meal for other
reasons; and to what extent the sacrificial meals
influenced the origin of the eucharist. About the
way the early Church celebrated the eucharist, we
hear that: "They went as a body to the Temple
every day but met in their houses for the breaking of bread; they shared their food gladly and
generously."[5] It is here clear that the eucharist
was connected with a real meal. Some more questions could still be asked: In what way are the
memory of the Lord and the meal connected; are
they woven together in such a way that they formed a whole; or are they only related in a loose
way; and for which reasons did they finally come
to celebrate the eucharist without a full meal?

The beginning of this development was clear in
St. Paul. With the Corinthians in mind, he under-
scored the sacred character of the celebration
and held the view that the full meal should not
take place in the congregation, but in the
homes.[6]

These examples no doubt have exposed the situation in which we have become involved through
the historical-critical method. What is important
in view of the ecumenical movement should be the
very fact that the eucharistic celebration had a
gradual development. Having this in mind the
author asked whether the conclusion should not
lead to accepting that the eucharist could not be

---

5. cf. Acts 2:46.
6. cf. 1Cor 11:22.

understood in only one form, even in the present
age. He then advised that the discussion on the
eucharist proceed on a new basis bearing in mind
the diversity which the New Testament itself
occasioned.

3.2.2 THE DIVERSITY OF LITURGIES IN THE ANCIENT CHURCH.

The celebration of the eucharist developed in
the ancient Church and the liturgical action
became fixed in an ever-increasing degree. This
is reponsible for the similarity of the liturgies
that came down to us. The fixed liturgy made it
impossible for the basic elements of the eucharistic services of worship to be varied at will.
Despite all this, there is evidence of considerable differences in the liturgy. This is responsible for variations in structure and formulations even where the same elements appear. However, he noted that the different liturgies stood
beside one another without coming into conflict.
The author cited the words of institution to
illustrate the similarities. In the first case,
all liturgies contained as self-evident the report of the institution. These liturgies as a
whole hold the tradition of Matthew and above all
the tradition of Paul. The report of the institution is handled with freedom, with the result
that some formulations are longer than others.
It is in the meaning and position of epiclesis
that important differences occured among the
liturgies of the ancient Church. Normally, the
report of the institution ends with the charge to

repeat the meal in the memory of Christ. This is
followed by the anamnesis, that is, a short text
which takes up this charge and affirms the will
to comply with it. In most liturgies this is
followed by the epiclesis, the petition that God
will send the Holy Spirit upon the gifts and
change bread and wine into the body and blood of
Christ. The formulation of the prayers is not the
same everywhere. In some other liturgies the
epiclesis appears in another position. In Egyptian liturgies, the epiclesis appears before the
words of institution and after the anamnesis. It
is clear that epiclesis receives a somewhat different meaning when it stands between the offering of the gift and the words of institution. In
this investigation two types of liturgies as
concerned epiclesis in the ancient Church is
noted and that is to say: "Liturgies in which the
prayer for the work of the Holy Spirit forms the
middle-point after the anamnesis, and liturgies
in which the idea of the offering of the gifts
receives central importance. The second type is
represented pre-eminently by the liturgies of the
West."[7] The author noted that the liturgies of
the ancient church exhibit numerous differences
within an overarching basic unity and that "these
differences, however, did not at the beginning
lead to separation. The consciousness of the
unity and solidarity given in Christ was so
strong that they could be allowed to stand beside
one another. They only became factors of separation after this consciousness of unity was lost
and the separation had become a fact for other

---

7. op. cit., FO/64:25, p.7.

reasons. Only then was the strong distinction made between the worship forms of the 'East'and of the 'West'."[8] The question then is, whether the liturgy today cannot be developed further according to the situation of our time.

3.2.3 MARANATHA.

Here the author recalled how the ancient congregation lived in great expectation of the Lord, Maranatha, come Lord, was their prayer. The final time began with the exaltation of Christ at the right hand of God. The congregation experienced the powers of the kingdom through their faith in the risen Lord, and as the Holy Spirit worked in their hearts, they lived already in the new world. The celebration of the eucharist should therefore be understood in this context for "it is an eschatological festival of joy, born of the consciousness that the exalted Lord is already present and directed toward the promise that he will come again as victor and submit all things under him."[9] It was Christ himself who gave this understanding to his disciples at the Last Supper, when he said: "because, I tell you, I shall not eat it again until it is fulfilled in the kingdom of God."[10] At a point in history the eschatological dimension seemed to be lost sight of but later was recovered. Today the emphasis on the eschatological dimension is of great importance for the ecumenical movement, because "it

8. ibid.
9. op. cit., FO/64:25, p.8.
10. cf. Lk.22:16

directs the view of the separated churches ahead
to the Lord who 'will gather his kingdom from the
four winds'. It lets us understand the Eucharist
as the meal of expectation, and strengthens us in
the consciousness that we belong to a pilgrim
people which must again and again start out anew
in order to move towards its Lord."[11]

3.2.4 EUCHARIST AND AGAPE.

About the relationship between the eucharist
and agape the author is of the opinion that the
eucharist could have been connected with a regular meal in early times. The case of the Corinthians was cited as an example, and when abuses
crept in, Paul did not hesitate to criticize the
community, in order to restore the proper sense
and place of the eucharist. He noted that from
Paul's narration of the institution which he
passed on to the Corinthians, it appears to presuppose a regular meal. This idea of the eucharist presupposing a meal is evident in Didache:
"After the meal you shall thus give thanks."[12]
The Apostolic Constitution of Hippolyt also described the agape meals. In each case the agape
meal comes before the celebration of the eucharist. It is certain that with the passage of
time, the eucharist came to be celebrated without
a common meal. Then the relation between the
Eucharist and Agape becomes more difficult to
determine. Certainly the problem of their rela-

---

11. op. cit., FO/64:25, p.9.
12. cf. Didache 9-10

tionship becomes difficult to solve and some
questions come up naturally to be asked: "Did
they originally form a whole and only develop
into the different rites with the passage of
time? Or did they arise from different origins
and only later become combined? Did the Eucharist
arise from the Last Supper while the Agape represents the continuation of fellowship which the
Lord had with his disciples at meals..?"[13]

Eventhough these questions cannot be answered
with certainty, the author is of the opinion that
"the sources allow us to recognize clearly that
the Eucharist was understood as a meal much more
than today." He noted that in almost all the
churches today, the eucharist has lost the character of the meal. He further said that the
eucharist has been separated from the care of the
poor as was the case in the ancient times, however adding that "it has become a sacred event in
which one is indeed reminded of his responsibility for his neighbour, but which is not connected as directly with works of love as in the
ancient Church."[14] He finally suggested that
agape could be taken up again as the worship-form
for special congregation like house-fellowships.

3.2.5 APOSTOLIC OFFICE AND THE EUCHARIST.

The author once more observed that when the problem of the eucharist is discussed among the
separated churches, the issue of determining the

---

13. op. cit., FO/64:25, p.10.
14. op. cit., p.11.

minister of this sacrament prevents reaching an
agreement. This fact suggests that the following
questions be asked: "What importance does the
apostolic office have for the Eucharist? Who
should preside over the celebration of the Eucharist? Must such a person stand in the apostolic
succession? Or is it enough that he is called and
ordained by his church?"[15] The New Testament
gives no information about these questions and
when occasionally considerations are made on the
basis of biblical statements, one must be clear
that these have to do - historically seen - with
pure supposition. Even if the New Testament does
not give answers to the questions, the author
maintains that it was known already at an early
date that the bishop presided over the eucharistic celebration. This is evident in the prayers handed down in the Didache which were spoken
by the bishop and the emphasis made by Ignatius
of Antioch that the eucharist could not be without a bishop. He argues further that the connection between a bishop standing in apostolic succession and his eligibility as the rightful president at the eucharistic celebration is not
found in the earliest sources. And according to
him "It shows that the apostolic succession, as
presupposition for the valid celebration of the
Eucharist, may not be viewed in isolation. It
stands in the Church which has preserved the
apostolic truth is in a position to celebrate the
Eucharist. The presence of the bishop is the
visible sign that the celebration takes place in
the true fellowship."[16] He went on to say that

---

15. ibid.
16. op. cit., FO/64:25, p12.

the struggle for the unity of the church contri-
butes essentially to the emphasis laid on the
necessity of apostolic succession.It became a
criterion which was easy to apply, so that when
someone took over the direction of a church without standing in the apostolic succession, he
placed himself outside the true church. Apostolic
succession was a sign of unity of the church. The
criteria of succession, he noted, played an important role in the struggle with heretical,
schismatic and secterian groups in the ancient
Church. Apostolic succession was broken in the
majority of the churches which proceed from the
Reformation. In the discussions which ensued
later the results are that "on the one side, they
led to strengthening the conviction that only the
Eucharist is valid which is executed by a priest.
To a growing degree the apostolic succession
became a formal criteria torn apart from the
fulness of the life of the church. On the other
side, the tendency arose to concede no more than
an ordering function of the office. The statement
was made with increasing emphasis that the altar
is not the altar of the church, but the 'table of
the Lord'."[17]

---

17. op. cit., FO/64:25, p.14.

3.3 CONSULTATION AT GRANDCHAMP 1965.
NOTES ON THE LORD'S SUPPER
(Prof, J.J. von Allmen[*]).

In accordance with the directives issued by
the Faith and Order Commission after its meeting
at Aarhus in 1964, a consultation was held at
Grandchamp near Neuchatel, Switzerland, from 19-
25 July 1965. This consultation fulfills that
part of the directives which says that a study
guide should be prepared by one or more writers
who should be responsible to the Commission.
Participants came from the Anglican, Lutheran,
Methodist, Orthodox, Reformed and United churches; three Roman Catholic consultants were also
present. A paper titled "Notes on the Lord's
Supper" was presented by Prof. J.J. Allmen of the
University of Neuchatel.

Having highlighted the problems forseen in the
study project and saying that "the Lord's Supper
is the one element of the Church's life which the
world cannot reduce to that which is characteristic of itself", the Professor went on to treat
the subject under six paired headings.

3.3.1 ANAMNESIS AND EPICLESIS.

The church, said the author, did not invent
the Supper, but in celebrating the Supper she
obeys the command of Christ: "Do this in remembrance of me." This anamnesis, remembrance or

---

[*] Prof. J.J. von Allmen is a minister of the
Reformed Church and professor at the University
of Neuchatel.

memorial he defines as: "the ritual evolution of
an event in order to give it its original force,
and the insertion of those who make this anamnesis into that very event which the celebration
commemorates. Consequently it means something
quite different from a mere exercise of memory -
it concerns the re-enactment of what is being
celebrated."[18] What the church remembers or celebrates is a unique event that cannot be isolated,
the whole history of salvation looking up to the
parousia. Explaining this further he said: "By
being the anamnesis of Jesus, of his body and the
blood he shed, the Eucharist connects salvation
with history, while at the same time shedding
over this history the light which makes it com-
prehensible."[19] Because Jesus at the institution
of the Eucharist spoke some words and displayed
some actions, the author submitted that in celebrating the Supper, words and actions should
mutually help to the understanding of each other.
That means that the Supper is necessary for the
understanding of the words and vice versa. Those
who make or celebrate this anamnesis, profit by
what Jesus Christ accomplished once for all, so
that the history of salvation may become the
history of their salvation. The anamnesis of
Christ's passion is therefore a formal participation in the decisive and unfailing event of the
history of salvation.

Alluding to the words Jesus used to close his
eucharistic discourse in the sixth chapter of
John's gospel: "It is the Spirit that gives life,

18. FO/65:33, Geneva, WCC, 1965, p.6.
19. op. cit., p.7.

the flesh has nothing to offer",[20] the author
concluded that since the new covenant is that of
the Spirit, it is therefore through spiritual
food and drink that the church is nourished for
eternal life.

He then defined epiclesis thus: "epiclesis is
the prayer which asks that God, through his Holy
Spirit, will make the Supper truly what Jesus
wanted it to be when he instituted or explained
it."[21] This is understandable from the great
liturgical traditions which shows that the Spirit
is invoked upon the worshippers and the gifts so
that the meal may truly become communion in the
body and blood of Jesus Christ, and make not only
the species, but also the congregation into the
body of Christ. While the East holds that
epiclesis is the means by which the eucharistic
miracle is brought about, the West attributes it
to the words if institution spoken by the
minister. This difference of conceptions regarding
epiclesis depicts further differences between East
and West in their eucharistic theology. The one is
pneumatological while the other is christological.
He submitted that the Reformation protested
against the Roman Mass because of what he called
"that which atrophy and ignorance of the epiclesis
had allowed to spread consciously or unconsciously
throughout the western Church."[22] But he added
that the Reformation did not imagine that the
eucharistic life could be healed and reformed by a
rediscovery of the epiclesis.

I wish to recall immediately that the Roman

---

20. cf. Jn.6:63.
21. op. cit., FO/65:33, p.9.
22. op. cit., p.10.

Catholic Church in her liturgy-reforms according
to the spirit of Vatican II, has given epiclesis
a befitting position in the structure of the new
eucharistic prayers. Epiclesis stand between the
Sanctus and the words of institution and again
after the anamnesis.

3.3.2 NUPITAL COMMUNION AND FRATERNAL COMMUNION.

Here the author treats the eucharist as communion which unites Christ and the Church and
secondly as that which unites the baptized with
one another. The communion between Christ and the
Church is best described by the New Testament as
marriage.[23] Because this communion is neither
vain nor empty, it presupposes the real presence
both of Christ as well as the Church. This communion is doublefold, one is a nuptial fellowship
at the table of the church with her Bridegroom;
the other depicts a mystery of union between
them. To substantiate the mysterious aspect of
this nuptial meal the author quotes Cyril of
Jerusalem who said: "Christ has given to all the
sons of the marriage chamber the enjoyment of his
body and blood", and Theodoret of Cyr: "In eating
the limbs of the bridegroom and in drinking his
blood, we fulfil a nuptial fellowship"[24] In the
same sense, the words of St. Paul should be understood which says: "But anyone who is joined to
the Lord is one Spirit with him."[25] Then he

---

23. cf. Mk. 2:20; Rev.19:7ff; 21:2; 22:17, 20;
    Jn3:29; 2Cor11:2; Mt.22:2ff; 25:1ff.
24. op. cit., FO/65:33, p.13.
25. cf. 1 Cor 6:17.

brings in St. Augustine saying: "The Supper becomes the moment and the place where this 'whole
Christ head and body' is established."[26]
The author sees in this nuptial communion which
the eucharist represents as the only communion
between Christ and the believer to the extent
that it is first of all communion between Christ
and the Church. The nuptial understanding of the
Supper gives a valuable insight into the roll of
the minister who presides at the Eucharist, in
the person of Christ. This nuptial character of
the communion has not only to do with the present
but also with the future, hence: "The future
reminds us that what the present gives of this
communion is no more than a temporal intermit-
tent, clumsy foretaste of an eternal joy, lasting
and complete."[27]

The nuptial communion between Christ and the
Church, which entails fraternal communion of the
members of Christ's body among themselves, is an
eschatological event, which, though genuine and
effective, is at present no more than the promise
of the messianic marriage. This eschatological
event is "the carrying up of believers beyond all
the foreshadowing of the final bringing together
of God's people in the Kingdom to come."[28] This
brotherly communion he maintains is not only
given by Christ as a foretaste of the world to
come, it is also what must be received and even
regained by the believers. This is the essence of
the kiss of peace as shown in the early liturgies. Among the problems that arise from the

26. op. cit., FO/65:33, p.13.
27. op. cit., p.14.
28. ibid.

fraternal communion, two are considered, agape
and inter-communion.

The information about agape is fragmentary, he
said. Agape concerned communal meals probably
ordered according to a liturgical scheme of
Jewish origin. In the early days, it appeared
that the Eucharist was celebrated as the crowing
point of such meals and the typical example would
be that Jesus instituted the Eucharist at the end
of a meal probably, a Passover meal. In the
course of the Church's life these agapes threa-
tened to degenerate either into carousals which
made the eschatological exuberance of christian
gatherings artficial, or into exclusive tables
which finally became sectarian, the author noted.
What resulted was that Paul referred the agapes
back to private houses in order to retain the
Supper alone during the Church's worship. This
prevailed in the church and gradually the agapes
withered away. And long before this, the early
Church genuinely and strongly understood the Eucharist as a profound source of fellowship.

The next problem handled by our author is
inter-communion, which he says becomes a problem
when the Church is divided. As it is certain that
each church during the eucharistic celebration
knows nuptial communion with the Lord, the question then arises on what is to be done when
because of the division fraternal communion stops
at the frontiers of each church. The author
accepts that the problem is difficult enough and
attributed the causes to reciprocal disputes
about the interpretation of the eucharistic event
or about the authority to preside at the eucharist in the Lord's name. The problem is rather

difficult to comprehend when one confronts the
issue that the sixteenth century protest against
the Roman See brought about three churches which
are scarcely in communion with one another.
Further, among the communicants of the divided
churches there is a recognition of oneness at the
level of baptism but among their clergy there is
no such recognition in the area of ordination. He
laments the division of the churches into different confessions and attributes such division to
non-theological factors which do not prevail over
the grace of salvation, and which in any case are
mostly in process of losing the justification for
their existence.

For the author, the solution of the problem of
intercommunion lies in "communion i.e. in the
Eucharist celebrated after the reconciling exchange of the kiss of peace, in unity found once
more". To achieve this he suggests three ways
out: first that those who demand intercommunion
should insist on communion in their own church;
secondly that communicants should be allowed a
more generous use of 'limited open communion' or
communion by economy of dispensation'; and
thirdly that consideration be given to experi-
ments in full communion over a limited period
under close control.

3.3.3 THE SUPPER AS THE REVELATION OF THE LIMITS AND THE FULNESS OF THE CHURCH

Taking as his departure Paul's saying in the first letter to the Corinthians, "The fact that there is only one loaf means that though there are many of us, we form a single body, because we all have a share in this one loaf,"[29] the author said that the Supper consitutes and reveals the Church. Thus in constituting the Church, the Supper reveals her limits. In this way therefore, the baptismal, apostolic and local character of the church are affirmed. While the baptismal character points towards death to oneself as what constitutes the Church, the apostolic imposes on her the duty of mission and the local character confirms that there is the Church of God where the Supper is celebrated. The author used the eucharistic species to show the revelation of the Church's limits. He argues that if the church were to prepare the table of the Lord, then she could use other national food or drinks to celebrate the eucharist, but since it is Christ himself who prepares the table as host, the Mediterranean diet of bread and wine which he used must be retained.

The supper does not only reveal the limits of the Church but its fulness also. For the fact that God made the fulness of his divinity to dwell in Jesus, the latter is found in the former. The fulness of the Church must be sought for and be found in the local church. This is also to affirm that the Supper reveals the structure and

---

29. cf. 1 Cor 10:17.

the mystery of the Church.

At the moment of the Supper the structure of
the Church appears; the different liturgical
functions allow this basic structure to become
clear. In the words of the author himself "This
means, in a negative sense, that any elements of
ecclesiastical structure and organization which
have no connection with the nature of the Church
are therefore inessential or even dangerous."[30]
Thus the Supper provides the key which prevents
the confusion of essential institutions in the
church with its judicial organization. Although
the latter is necessary because of the former,
the two do not coincide even when the judicial
organisation strives to express and protect the
church's essential structure in the best way
possible.

As the Supper is the moment which reveals the
mystery of the church, the author explained it to
mean that the church is both the sign of the
presence of God's Kingdom and the sign of the
presence of the world. Applying this in concrete
terms, he says that each local church where the
Eucharist is celebrated is the catholic church,
and there the whole Christ head and body is present. This fulness of the church manifested in
the local churches should bring about the mutual
recognition of the churches because each sees in
the other the mystery which is its own characteristic. The consequence will therefore be the
mutual recognition of shepherd and flock that
they are in communion with one another respectively; and this eucharistic identity should

_____

30. op. cit., FO/65:33. pp.21-22.

express mutual recognition in love and demon-
strate the unity of the church.

Just as the mystery of the church is in each
local congregation a sign of the presence of the
kingdom of God, so also does it belong to her
mysterious character to be in each local congregation, a sign of the presence of the world. In
effect: "This means that each eucharistic congregation is a visible sign of the real presence of
the world which God has created, loved and saved
in Jesus Christ."[31] For this reason therefore,
the celebration of the Supper concerns the world,
even if the world ignores or ridicules it. During
the eucharistic celebration, creation as it were
asks for and obtains access to the true worship,
and this restores to creation its original purpose, which is doxological. The church is the
world's protector and when she celebrates the
eucharist, which is the memorial of Christ's
death which saves the world, the world's continued existence is guaranteed. Therefore the
author concludes saying that the Supper does not
loosen the ties between the Church and the world,
but on the contrary it reveals more profound
links between them.

3.3.4 LIVING BREAD AND SACRIFICE.

In the first part of this sub-heading the
author considers the Supper as the gift of the
living bread under four points. First he handles
the New Testament terminologies for the Supper.

---

31. ibid.

The New Testament is quite straight forward in
describing the bread and wine used at the Supper.
At the institution of the Eucharist Jesus himself
said of the bread and wine "This is my body..;
this is my blood." St. Paul speaks of 'communion
in the body and blood of Christ'. In the sixth
chapter of the gospel of John, words which could
not fail to scandalize the Jews were used to
allude to the eucharist: "Anyone who does eat my
flesh and drink my blood has eternal life and I
shall raise him up on the last day.."[32] The Eucharist is also called 'the breaking of bread'.
The church further understands the eucharist as
daily bread, manna, and spiritual food. One thing
clear about these terms as they were presented by
the author is that "they presuppose as a matter
of course that the living Christ is truly present
during the Supper, and that in giving himself to
God he causes the communicants to enjoy eternal
life."[33]

The fact of the Supper is that the living Lord
feeds his followers for eternal life through the
eucharistic meal. He gives himself as food for
eternity by means of bread and wine. To establish
a link between this fact and its meaning three
rules are given. First, eucharistic theology
should give an intelligible account of the fact
of which the significance must be given thereby
protecting the eucharist from the two interpretations which threaten it viz: the magical and the
symbolic. The second is to avoid a close correspondence between the fact of the eucharist and

---

32. cf. Jn6: 54-58.
33. op. cit., FO/65:33, p.29.

its meaning. By so doing it will be possible to
distinguish between them and avoid giving a
single interpretation to the meaning lest it be
caught up in the fate of the fact itself.
Thirdly, the liturgical attitude which governs
the theology of the eucharist imposed by the
reality of the fact of the eucharist should not
be made to disappear or called into question.

The next question is, how does the Supper
become this meal of eternal life? The answer is
twofold according to the eastern and western
traditions. The eastern tradition holds that the
miracle of the eucharist is the work of the Holy
Spirit, invoked upon the bread and wine and upon
the church to make them the body of Christ. The
characteristics of this answer is the attention
paid not only to the species but also to the
people and the fact that it is not only bread and
wine that are transformed into Christ's body and
blood but also the congregation. The western
tradition holds the miracle of the Eucharist to
be the work of the Word of God active and power-
ful. Here attention is centered upon the species,
which alone are transformed and the church
communicates in the body and blood of Christ.
What comes to mind immediately from the second
answer is the role of the minister who is to
pronounce those words of institution. One can
also stop short here and ask who calls the
minister and who appoints him to preside over the
Eucharist?

What are the effects of the Supper and how are
these linked with eternal salvation of the communicants? The Supper is an eschatological meal and
therefore it is like an anticipation of the Last

Judgement in the christian community. In the
words of St. Paul, one has to recollect himself
before partaking of the Bread and the Cup lest he
be condemned.[34] The effects of the Supper are
however positive. The church has always taught
that the Supper sets man free from sin and gives
the pardon it promises. The author went further
to enumerate the effects and said: "The Supper
forms the churchly community in one single body.
The Supper feeds and strengthens the new man
implanted by the Holy Spirit in the believers, in
order to help him overcome the old man, who has
now been left behind by baptismal resurrection
with Christ...; finally, the Supper gradually
acclimatizes believers to the life of the kingdom
to come."[35] Other effects of the eucharist are
contained in the words of the Lord himself: "Anyone who does eat my flesh and drink my blood has
eternal life, and I shall raise him up the last
day..."[36] The author perharps having the so
called private Masses in mind, asks why the Roman
tradition attimes celebrates Eucharist without
distributing the communion to the people, so that
they may live in the new life and grow in it,
since the eucharist is the meal that gives eternal life. And to the Protestant tradition he
asks: "Who on earth gave Church leaders the right
to have Sundays without a celebration of the
Eucharist, and to deprive christian people so
often of the meal through which the glorified
Christ desires to live in each of his members?"[37]

---

34. cf. 1 Cor 11:30-32.
35. op. cit., FO/65:33, pp.35-36.
36. cf. Jn 6:54, 56-57.
37. op. cit., FO/65:33, p.36.

The issue of the sacrificial character of the
Eucharist observed the author, has torn the West
apart that it is delicate to approach. He decided
to approach it by seeking first of all, the reasons for which Christ instituted the Eucharist.
He declared that the sacrifice on Calvary is
unique and beyond dispute. Jesus died once for
all, and through his death has offered the only
sacrifice which can save the world. He contended
why Christ was not content to commission his
disciples to tell the world that it could be
saved through Him in order to maintain the uniqueness of the cross, but rather he instituted
the Eucharist, which the author calls the "sacrament of his sacrifice".

His first answer was that "Jesus instituted
the Supper in order that rememberance (anamnesis)
in the biblical sense of the word - might be made
of his sacrifice; i.e. that those who make rememberance of the salvation obtained through the
sacrifice of the cross might be truly and genuinely enabled to benefit from it."[38]
As he mentioned before that Jesus instituted the
Supper so that believers might receive the bread
of life and thus have their share in salvation;
he followed it up with the remark that this bread
which is distributed is sacrificed, separated
like sacrificial victims into body and blood; the
body being broken and the blood drawn into the
cup. He recalls that Paul has no slightest hesi-
tation in comparing the christian Supper[*] with
the pagan sacrifices and that St. John "refrains

38. op. cit., p.38.
*   cf. 1 Cor 10:14-22.

from giving an account of the Last Supper and
assigns the death of Jesus to the Passover Day,
so that the institution of the Supper should be
the actual sacrifice of the cross and not its
anticipation in the context of Christ's last meal
with his disciples."[39]

The second answer, maintains the author, becomes indeed more meaningful as it is preceeded
by the first and that is, that Christ instituted
the Supper to give his followers an example and a
command. That example is the cross itself for it
is first of all sacrifice and reconciliation, the
work of salvation. At the institution of the
Supper, Jesus gave his followers the example of
what they have to carry out. This is clearly
shown in the washing of the feet of his disciples
as recorded by John the Evangelist. He further
submits that "in instituting the Supper, the
sacrament of his sacrifice, Jesus is thus asking
his followers to let the same mind be among themselves which they 'have in Christ Jesus', to take
part through their sacrifice, in his" Further
that "the Supper itself is not the moment when
the christian bears his cross, sacrifices himself, etc. But when it is not simply the most
profound moment of the sacrifice of praise which
the church offers to God through Christ (cf. Heb
13:15), the Supper becomes the key to the sacrifice of christians, the sacrament of Christ's
sacrifice."[40]

Thirdly, he said, the Supper was instituted in
order that the eschatological meal, the meal with
Jesus, should remain present in the church. This

---

39. ibid, p.39
40. op. cit., FO/65:33, p.40.

meal acquired its messianic significance for the
disciples after they had recognized Jesus as the
Messiah. St. Paul also said that through the
Supper Christ's death is proclaimed until he
comes. This means that the Supper will not only
endure the parousia, but rather the parousia will
include the element of proclaiming Christ's
death, which is the sacrificial element.

Summarizing, he said that the Supper un-
doubtedly contains sacrificial references and
wondered why it was over the sacrificial element
of the Supper that the Reformation break occured.
He noted that in the apostolic writings that
sacrificial terminology marks three particular
moments in the celebration of the eucharist viz:
"the eucharistic prayers, the presentation of the
bread and wine for the institution and the likeness of Christ's death, i.e. the breaking of the
bread and the thanksgiving over the Cup."[41] Because of the importance of the problem at stake
the author recommended a further study into the
history of the Supper especially in the West
where the sacrificial element of the eucharist
constitutes a problem. He calls for a further
study also in the theology of the Holy Spirit
because the serious divisions which have not yet
been overcome are pneumatological in origin. He
finally recommends that there be no Sunday without the celebration of the Eucharist and no Eucharist without communion.

---

41. ibid, p.42.

153

3.3.5 PRAYER AND ITS FULFILMENT.

The proposition here is that the Supper sums
up the prayers which the church directs to God in
the name of Jesus Christ. The author goes on to
say that judging from the history of christian
prayer, the Supper is not the centre but the
standard and school of prayer. He argues that if
the Supper were to be removed from the life of
the church, the church would have found herself
condemned and would no longer know how to pray. He
describes the Supper as the true school of prayer
and christian life, adding: "Here, above all, the
faithful learn and relearn how to appear before
God and how to meet the world. The Supper invites
them to find once more the pardon and joy which
was theirs at baptism, to give thanks, to make
intercession, to proclaim the mighty works of
God, to be fully aware of their place within the
Church's catholicity, and to offer themselves to
God as living and holy sacrifice."[42]

But it must be also that the Supper is the
fulfilment of christian prayer or at least that
the Supper is that part of prayer which can already be answered, that is to say, it is the gift
by anticipation of the final accomplishment. "The
Supper is this because it gives Christ, in whom
lies the pledge of all fulfilment - and even
more, who is already the fulfilment in secret of
all genuine prayer"; the Supper is fulfilment
because "there the unique and incomparable nature
of the name of God is given its due; there the
kingdom of God comes to the surface; in it God's

---

42. op. cit., p.45.

will is already accomplished on earth and the
Church gives herself over to this will and offers
herself to God.. But above all, it is at the
Supper that men who have been adopted in Christ
because their baptism has made them share in his
death and resurrection, already dare to say 'Our
Father'to God."[43] Thus this prophetic fulfilment,
which is the meaning of the Supper, gives the
Church an eschatological greatness, and makes her
into a messianic people.

3.3.6 MASS AND EUCHARIST.

The author first of all traced the origin of
the word, mass. It comes from a Latin word -
missa = missio or dimissio - meaning dismissal in
order to fulfil an order, to obey an order to go
out. The term implies a movement of deparutre.
The word Eucharist, means, tanksgiving; it "implies a movement of gathering in, of assembling
together, in order to be able to become an offering of praise." Describing further this movement
of departure the author says: "The holy table
which makes the Church an earthly sacrament of
the heavenly Jerusalem is the place of movement
back and forth. From this table from this commemoration of the history of the whole of salvation, from communion with the living Lord and
with men who have become brothers, from this
awareness of the Church, from this life-giving
meal, from this secret fulfilment of all prayer -
the Church goes into the world in order to be

43. op. cit., p.47

salt and light there, in order to sanctify it and
protect it, to be there a witness to God's forgiveness and love, through knowing herself how to
forgive and to love,"[44] By sending out the Church
into the world, the eucharist thus becomes missionary.

The author maintains that if the holy table is
the place from which the church sets out on mission, it is also the place to which she returns
from mission, loaded with her work in the world,
like the seventy disciples returning, not to
complain, but to rejoice with their Lord over the
dethrowning of Satan and his demons. This coming
back is what he called "The Eucharist-weekly
pilgrimmage of offering, in which the Church,
like the servants in the parable, enters into the
joy of her Master who has returned, in order to
offer him in offering herself, all that she has
gained for him with what he entrusted to her."[45]
Thus the Eucharist in its catholicity receives
back the church which the Mass established in its
apostolicity. Therefore it is impossible for the
eucharist not to be a festival. Concluding he
said: "The supper understood both as Mass and as
Eucharist is one of the essential factors in the
theology of Sunday; not only because in the early
Church it was reserved for Sundays, but also
because it describes Sunday both as the first and
as the eigth day of the week."[46]

In his overall conclusion the author said that
it is necessary to allow the Supper itself to
find once more the fulness and balance of its

---

44. op. cit., FO/65:33, p. 49
45. ibid.
46. ibid.

156

unity, adding: "Only to the extent that the
Supper reconstitutes itself in this unity can it
also contribute to the reconstitution of the
Church in the fulness and balance of unity; for
only thus will the eucharistic struggles which
have torn the Church and wounded her to the heart
be overcome."[47]

3.3.7 REPORT OF THE CONSULTATION AT GRANDCHAMP.[48]

After Prof. J.J. von Allmen had presented his
paper, the group at Grandchamp settled down to a
discussion based mostly on that paper. The report
is seen as a consensus of the opinion of the
group, since it applied the method at Lund Conference, which is a return without prejudice to the
common sources.

I. On the Eucharist and the Church, the report
said that the Eucharist cannot be dealt with in
isolation and affirms that there is a close connection between their understanding of the Eucharist and the doctrine of the Church. But it remarked that where a common understanding of the
sacrament should exist among them, there is bound
to be differences in their understanding of the
nature of the Church and its structure as an
eucharistic community.

The report called for the recognition of the
process of eucharistic tradition arguing that the
eucharistic life could not be derived from the
bibilcal evidence alone; it maintained that the

---

47. op. cit., p.50.
48. My source is FO/65:85.

biblical evidence can help safeguard the Eucharist against corruptions.

The origin of the Eucharist is found in its institution by Christ. Like the church herself, the eucharist is historical in nature. The report submitted that though a general structure was given to the eucharist at its institution, no eucharistic rite is fixed in all its details and therefore there is room for variety and adaptation to different traditions and situations.

As the group discussed the distinction between the eucharistic reality and the eucharistic theology, it maintained that the eucharistic reality, which is the reality that Christ is present among his people, should never be identified with the theology of the eucharist, which is the attempt to understand the mystery therein. Consequently in further ecumenical discussions it may be said that: "The sacrament can never be exhausted by our understanding; that the sacrament can be the same in different expressions, and that unity can be discovered through the living experience of what happens when the Eucharist is celebrated."[49]

II. On Baptism and Eucharist, the report said that the Eucharist is a sacrament of faith and it is celebrated by the people of God and it nourishes in them the gift given in baptism. It directs that christians should prepare for the eucharist through confession of their sins, renewal of obedience in order to celebrate beneficially. The call to witness to Christ addressed to all the baptized is renewed in the Eucharist. The report was worried about the use of ecclesia-

---

49. FO/65:85, p.3.

stical discipline in connection with the eucharist and asked: 'what discipline should properly
be accepted by all those who have been baptized?'

III. Sorting out how the ministry and the
congregation are related to each other, the report submits that the eucharist is the act of the
whole church and that it involves the participation of all the people present in the liturgy. To
fulfil its ministry in the world the congregation
needs the nourishment of a regular eucharistic
life; and to provide the congregation regularly
with the means of grace in the celebration of the
sacrament is one of the purposes of the ordained
ministry. The group was not one in its understanding and interpretation of the ordained ministry, hence its recommendation that apostolic
succession should be further studied as the source
of the divisions.

IV. In this paragraph the group discussed the
structure of the eucharistic celebration. It said
that thanksgiving and anamnesis are closely linked
together and that there should be places for them
in every eucharistic liturgy. The western traditions are asked to make their prayer of thanksgiving more adequate, that is, to reflect the
whole work of the Triune God.

On the invocation of the Holy Spirit (epiclesis), the report said that the whole celebration of the Eucharist depends upon the action of
the Holy Spirit. It maintained that the epiclesis
should be clearly expressed in the liturgy of the
eucharist, but attached no importance to its
particular place in the structure of the eucharistic celebration. This is so because the group is
convinced that the Holy Spirit is at once the

source of renewed life on the Church and also the
guarantor of her continuity.

For the better understanding of consecration,
they recommended that attention should be paid to
its meaning in the early liturgies of the church.
In that period the whole prayer action was
thought of as bringing about the reality promised
by Christ. They hoped that when it is so understood, it might help to overcome the differences
concerning a special moment of consecration. The
report called on all the churches to return,
where applicalbe, to the administration of communion in both species as was instituted by
Christ. It also held that there should be no
celebration of the eucharist without the ministry
of the Word.

V. In the Eucharist our reconciliation with
God is made manifest, for it is above all, communion with God in Jesus Christ. The Eucharist
therefore brings different kinds of people together. The report recognized that in so doing,
the eucharist must be a sign of crossing human
barriers in terms of race, class, nationality,
generation etc. It recommends immediately intercommunion across such barriers within the Church.

They deplored the fact that the historical
relationship between the Eucharist and Agape was
not entirely clear. It went on to say that the
loss of Agape has left a certain vaccum in the
eucharistic life of the church and the danger
therin is that the eucharist can easily lose its
meal character, and be turned into a mere cultic
act. To counteract this, it called on the churches to show their solidarity to the suffering in
the world.

VI. The group here understands the eucharist
both as the act of the local church and as the
act of the Catholic Church. The report declares
that it is in the local church that the church's
eucharistic fellowship is manifestly expressed.
The local church always celebrates the eucharist
in the communion of the whole church both in
heaven and on earth. It also said that "the maintenance of essential elements does not imply
uniformity", and submitted that "catholicity
finds its fulfilment in wide variety."[50]

VII. The group at Grandchamp has this to say
about sacrifice and the Eucharist: "All of us
hold that Christ's sacrifice is unique and cannot
be repeated. All, too, would agree that in the
Eucharist the Church offers herself as a sacrifice of praise to God and service to men. But a
description of the eucharistic act in sacrificial
terms may still conceal divergencies of interpretation."[51] They registered their difference of
opinion when they said: "Some traditions think it
proper to say that there the church 'offers
Christ' to the Father; others object to the phra-
seology and insist that the sacrifice is only
that of ourselves, in praise and thanksgiving."[52]
The group nevertheless expressed satisfaction with
the portion of the report which expressed agreement.

VIII. That the Eucharist is an eschatological
event is also upheld by the report when it said:
"The Eucharist is both anticipation of the communion enjoyed in the kingdom of God and expecta-

---

50. op. cit., FO/65:85, p.6.
51. ibid.
52. ibid.

tion of its fulfilment."[53] As the people celebrate the eucharist, they experience in faith
that the kingdom has come, yet they pray at the
same time for its coming.

Finally the group submitted that the Eucharist
is the centre of all christian worship and the
prayer of the Church par excellence. All other
forms of christian worship should have some clear
relationship with the eucharistic liturgy. It
should also govern the spiritual life of christians, feed their devotion and understanding of
the sacrament.

---

53. ibid.

3.4   BRISTOL 1967: THE HOLY EUCHARIST.

In August 1967, the Faith and Order Commission of the World Council of Churches held its plenary assembly in Bristol, Great Britain. The assembly received reports from different study groups and one of them was on the Eucharist. The study division of the Commission on Faith and Order, after the consultation at Grandchamp in 1965, sent their report to different regional study groups, and asked them to consider the whole problem in general and to examine in detail one or more of the questions raised. The theological commission met at Crêt-Bérard, Switzerland, in April 1967. In the light of the comments which the commission received, it concluded that an ecumenical discussion could be carried on at the following three points: Anamnesis and Epiclesis; Catholicity of the Eucharist; and Eucharist and Agape. The report was therefore presented to the assembly in Bristol, debated and amended and finally edited by the Commission for publication.

3.4.1   THE ANAMNETIC AND EPIKLETIC CHARACTER OF THE EUCHARIST.

Recalling to mind the consensus on the Eucharist reached at Montreal,[54] the report said that attention is being given to anamnetic and epikletic character of the Eucharist in the way it has not done before. It then said: "Christ

---

54. cf. Rodger P.C. and Visher L. (ed.), The Fourth World Conference on Faith and Order, London, S.C.M., 1964, p.73ff.

instituted the Eucharist, sacrament of his body
and blood with its focus upon the cross and resurrection, as the anamnesis of the whole of
God's reconciling action in him."[55] This anamnesis includes not only all that Christ has
accomplished for man and for all creation in his
incarnation, servanthood, ministry, teaching,
suffering, sacrifice, resurrection, ascension and
Pentecost, but also the foretaste of his Parousia
and the fulfilment of the kingdom. In other words
anamnesis includes representation and anticipation in the joyful celebration of the Church. The
report emphasized the fact that this anamnesis is
not only a calling to mind of what is past or of
its significance, it is also the Church's effective proclamation of God's mighty acts. Thus the
anamnetic representation and anticipation are
realized in thanksgiving and intercession. In
thanksgiving the Church proclaims before God his
mighty acts of redemption and requests him to
give the benefits of these acts to every one. So
in thanksgiving and intercession the Church is
united with the Son, the High Priest and intercessor. Thus the anamnesis is the basis and
source of all christian prayer.

The report established a relationship between
anamnesis and epiclesis by saying that "The anamnesis leads to epiclesis, for Christ in his
heavenly intercession prays the Father to send
the Spirit upon his children. For this reason,
the Church being under the New Covenant, confidently prays for the Spirit, in order that it

---

55. New Directions in Faith and Order Bristol
    1967, Geneva, W.C.C. 1968, p.61. Further
    citations as FO. No. 50.

may be sanctified and renewed, led into all truth
and empowered to fulfil its mission in the
world."[56] The report identifies anamnesis and
epiclesis as unitive acts, which cannot be conceived apart from communion. It maintains that
"it is the Spirit who, in our Eucharist makes
Christ really present and given to us in the
bread and wine, according to the words of institution."[57]

They submitted also that the liturgy should
express adequately both the anamnetic and the
epikletic character of the Eucharist because,
anamnesis is the very essence of the preached
Word as it is of the Eucharist; epiclesis is the
invocation of the Spirit upon the people of God
and upon the whole eucharistic action including
the elements. It attaches no importance to the
location of epiclesis in relation to the words of
institution, when the Eucharist is celebrated.

3.4.2 THE CATHOLIC CHARACTER OF THE EUCHARIST.

The report briefly reviewed the Old Testament
usage of the word ecclesia. It did so because of
its conviction that the christian understanding
of the catholicity of the Church and of its local
manifestations are rooted in Judaism. The word
qahal, ecclesia (LXX), referrs originally to the
whole people of God, and in post-exilic times,
the word ecclesia, like synagogue, however came to
apply to the local congregation of believers. The

---

56. FO. No. 60, p.61.
57. ibid.

New Testament, says the report, shows in its
usage of this word, this double signification.
The word Church (ecclesia) and other New Testament descriptions of the church always witness to
the totality of the people of God. Having said
that, the report goes on to draw conclusions.

First, the action of the local congregation of
christians when it celebrates the Eucharist is
seen as having the fulness of catholicity.
Through their sharing of the one loaf, their
unity with the church catholic is demonstrated;
the mystery of redemption is set forth and the
whole body grows in grace. Whenever the Eucharist
is celebrated its catholic character is made
manifest, both as an assurance of redemption and
as a sign of hope to the whole cosmos. This is so
because "the world God is reconciling to himself
is present at every Eucharist: in the bread and
wine, in the persons of the faithful, and in the
prayers they offer for themselves and for all
men."[58] Thus the Eucharist unites the faithful
with the Person of our Lord, and they are transfigured and accepted. In this way the Eucharist
reveals to the world what it must become.

When the local churches celebrate the Eucharist, they experience the wholeness of the Church
and reveal it in its fulness. This catholicity of
the eucharist is therefore made obscure when
there is no communion between one congregation
and the other. The report deplores this lack of
communion and said: "because of its catholicity
the Eucharist is a radical challenge to the 'de-
monic' tendencies in church life toward estrange-

---

58. op. cit., FO. No. 50, p.63.

ment, separation and fragmentation. Lack of local
unity in the church or society constitutes a
challenge to the christians in that place. A
mockery is made of the Eucharist when the walls
of separation destroyed by Christ on his cross
are allowed to persist: those between races,
nationalities, tongues, classes, congregations
and confessions."[59] The report further said that
because the church is found in variety of cultures, the catholicity of the Eucharist therefore
requires that the church be both indigeneous and
contemporary. This then should justify the differences between the church of one generation and
another, and between the church in one nation and
another. To find the mean the report adds: "Catholicity welcomes that 'partiality' which re-
nounces self-realization at the expense of others
and which has allowed itself to be converted by
the Gospel, so that it dies to self and lives to
Christ."[60] The report finally supports a church
maintaining its paricular rite when it finds
herself in another nation or culture. This is
seen as "an expression of that Church's bona fide
intention to serve and honour the Catholic
Church."[61]

3.4.3 EUCHARIST AND AGAPE.

Agape is descriped in the early christian
usage as a communal meal explicitly observed in
the name and presence of Christ. Agape is further
seen as reflecting the self revealed love of God

59. op. cit., p.63.
60. ibid.
61. ibid.

in Christ and the Church; love between christians
and the love which God gives the world through his
believing people. The report discloses that the
precise relation between Agape and the Eucharist
is not clear-cut in the earliest christian practice, and submitted that all communal meals mentioned in the New Testament, when not necessarily
eucharistic were surely intended to be agapeic.

The Eucharist right from its institution includes the element of communal eating and drinking as does the Agape. Further expression of
such agapeic relationship was found in all the
affairs of God's people in the Hebraic and early
christian life. In the eucharistic liturgy these
agapeic implications are expressed: "in the mutual forgiveness of sins; the kiss of peace; the
bringing of gifts for the communal meal and for
distribution to the poor brethren; the specific
prayer for the needy and suffering; the taking of
the Eucharist to the sick and those in prison."[62]
Such ministry between the table of the Lord and
the needy is seen to testify properly to the
redeeming presence of Christ in the world.

The reasons for the separate observances of
the Eucharist and Agape are not fully known. What
was clear is that Agape followed its own ceremo-
nial with emphasis on fraternal responsibility in
human affairs. Later Agape lost its intergity and
came under serious attack.[63] This loss of intergrity no doubt led to the eventual disappearance
of Agape as a regular communal meal in the
church. The report hinted that there is a growing

---

62. op. cit., p.64.
63. cf. 1 Cor 11:21-22; Jude 12, 2 Pet 2:13

interest in the present time for Agape-like
meals, and pleaded that it be given a trial und
surveillance. It recommended that care should be
taken to acknowledge and realize the agapeic
character of the eucharistic meal, in such a
manner that the Lord's Supper may be reognized as
the most desirable Agape. The report advocates
for what it called congregational Agapes, whose
aim should be to stimulate fuller participation
in the whole life of the church and active concern for the world. It called also for inter-
confessional Agapes which may foster christian
fellowship and witness.

3.4.4   REPORT OF SECTION II.

Among members of Section II, that reported on
the Eucharist at the plenary assembly in Bristol,
were three people who belonged to the group that
drew up the original draft. The section benefited
from the presence of these three as they clarified the original intent of the paper when some
editorial changes were made. The section acknowledged the strength of the paper which it says
lies in its conciseness. About the paper the
report said inter alia: "It must be remembered
that this paper does not claim to be a general
theology of the Eucharist, but that it limits
itself to a few significant matters and assumes
previous ecumenical work on this topic and draws
on recent biblical and theological research
field. We believe the paper should have as wide a
circulation as possible among those in the Churches especially entrusted with theology and prac-

tice. The paper has stimulated a most rewarding discussion for us, and we believe it can do so for others. We strongly recommend that the secretariat be authorized to share this document with the member churches and urge its proper printing and distribution."[64]

On the issue of the Eucharist and Agape, Section II, reaffirmed that care must be taken to ensure that agape meals do not become substitute Eucharists; and recommended further study of the matter. Apart from the editorial changes, which were effected before publication, the section made the following recommendations:

It gave the mandate that the paper entitled "The Holy Eucharist" be published as edited. Further that careful study should be made of the Words of Institution of the Lord's Supper, having as its departure, the exegetical, historical and theological details. It calls for a broadened study of the Eucharist with particular attention to the eucharistic faith and doctrine. Because of what the report calls "the growing incidence of intercommunion", it directed that attention should be given to the problem of the ministry in relation to the celebration of the Eucharist. It recognized the usefulness of the regional study groups and called for the formation of same where it does not yet exist. Finally it recommended that a resumé of the emerging ecumenical consensus on the Eucharist be drawn up starting from Lund to Bristol. The fruit of this recommendation is the paper entitled "The Eucharist in Ecumenical Thought" presented at Louvain in 1971, at the general assembly of the Faith and Order Commission.

---

64. op. cit., FO. No. 50, p.141.

3.5 LOUVAIN 1971.

In Bristol, 1967, the Faith and Order Commission accepted the recommendation made by section II, which reported on "The Holy Eucharist". That part of the recommendation reads: "That there be drawn up a résumé of the emerging ecumenical consensus on the Eucharist, drawing on the work of Lund, Montreal, Aarhus and Bristol, and on the work of regional groups and of individual scholars related to the ecumenical discussion of the Eucharist. On the basis of this résumé the draft of a popular booklet, perhaps with illustrations, should be prepared under the direction of the secretariat. Booklets could then be printed separately in the language and idiom of the various countries, in consultation with representatives of National Councils of Churches and with experts in communication. In this way a wider public could be informed about ecumenical liturgical developments."[65]

Complying with this recommendation the Commission's division of studies made the résumé and presented it at Louvain in 1971, at the Commission's general assembly under the title "The Eucharist in Ecumenical Thought". This résumé was drawn up from the World Conferences of Faith and Order at Lund, 1952, Montreal 1963; from the consultation at Grandchamp 1965 organized by the Commission and finally from the Commission's meeting at Bristol 1967. These reports have already been handled partly in the previous chapter and partly in this chapter. A repetition of these

---

65. op. cit., FO. No. 50, p.143.

is not currently envisaged, rather I shall go on
to consider the report: Beyond Intercommunion
presented also at Louvain.

3.5.1 BEYOND INTERCOMMUNION.

The problem of common eucharistic worship has
been the concern of the ecumenical movement right
from the beginning. The results of the attempt to
bring a solution were given in chapter two above,
and indeed as it was treated in Edinburgh, Lund
and Montreal. As a result of the agreement reached
since the Eucharist was taken up as a study project, it became clearer that previous analysis of
the problem of intercommunion are no longer
entirely adequate. Hence the Uppsala assembly of
the World Council of Churches in 1968, asked the
Faith and Order Commission to take up the issue
once more. After its consultation in Geneva, 1969,
the Commission came up with a report which it presented in Louvain, 1971, under the title: Beyond
Intercommunion.

The report started with the appraisal of the
situation. It tells us why the problem should
arise, which is because the eucharist has to do
with the very centre of our christian faith, and
of the life of the church. The Eucharist inesca-
pably is at the heart of the ecumenical movement.
Because of this fact all forms of ecumenical
activities throw up the questions about this
sacrament, its practice and discipline. In discussing the issue of intercommunion two contra-
sting positions emerge. The first group include
those because of the way they understand the

nature of the church and the sacraments, concern
themselves with the maintenance of the manifestation of its true unity, and hold that the
eucharist is the sign and reality of the church's
unity. According to this group "the eucharistic
observance will gather together those who have
found their common life in the Una Sancta as both
the reality of their oneness in Christ and a
witness to it."[66] The other group include those
who hold that the eucharist is not only the sign
of unity but a God given means of grace which
imparts unity and teach that "for those who are
committed to the quest of unity in one body,
common participation in the eucharist is the
proper and grateful use of the means which God
has provided."[67] The paradoxical nature of these
positions were taken note of by the report, and
the study group pledges itself to discover how
best this can be understood and practised.

The membership of the Roman Catholic Church
into the Faith and Order Commission is seen as
affecting the Commission not merely quantita-
tively. The report acknowledges that with this
entry, the whole spectrum of christian churches
is represented in the discussion and the consequence is that the problem of intercommunion or
the question of finding a way to communion in the
eucharist can at last be tackled in its fulness.
The different theological discussions between the
churches are seen to be leading to new possibilities of discussing topics long taken to be
'immovable stumbling block'. The most positive

---

66. Faith and Order Louvain, FO. No. 59, Geneva,
    W.C.C. 1971, p.55.
67. ibid.

thing that emerges is the awareness of the corporate nature of christian existence, a sense
that the eucharistic communion involves a relationship not only with God but also with fellow
christians. The report pointed out that notable
advances were registered in the Second Vatican
Council, the Lambeth Conference of 1968 and the
recent recommendations for implementing in Germany the Arnoldshain Theses of 1957. Ecumenical
activity is seen to be on the increase at the
local level and no longer remains the monopoly of
academicians in the sense that the problem of
worship at ecumenical gatherings "is being raised
more at the local level where many christians
have found that their most significant experiences of fellowship cut across the lines of ecclesiastical separations and are pressing towards
the one eucharist as the adequate expression."[68]
This eagerness of christians towards one another
led to what the report called "acts of common
eucharistic celebrations not in accordance with
the eucharistic discipline of the churches."[69]
The celebration of the Week of Prayer for Christian Unity was given as an example from where
these eagerness arose. The call made by Vatican
Council II, and in turn by the World Council of
Churches' Assembly in Uppsala 1968, to call christians to express their commitment against
hunger, ignorance and oppression and to support
justice, development and peace in the world is
accepted as intrinsic to christian obedience.
Such concerns give new meaning to intentions long

---

68. op. cit., F.O. No. 59, p.56.
69. ibid.

expressed in celebrations of the eucharist and
are full of eucharistic symbolism and significance, the report maintains. The report drew
attention to another important factor that must
not be overlooked. It disclosed that many christians who are wrestling with the issues of their
contemporary world are no longer content with
standard confessional teachings about the meaning
and integrity of worship and about the community
in which worship takes place. They are also said
to be looking for prophetic words and acts in
Christ's work of reconciliation and not only
conciliatory gestures. The report is of the opinion that such a situation may overshadow the
central reconciling thrust of the eucharist and
precipitate division rather than peace and unity
which are the goal. The fundamental question
about the eucharist therefore, is about the true
nature of the human community it both expresses
and makes possible.

The second part of this report is taken to be
a contribution towards the goal of ecumenical
movement, which is unity. Here attempt is made to
state in terms of the intrinsic character of the
eucharist, the goal which the churches are
committed to attain; and part of it concerns the
several perspectives of the eucharist which offer
hope for advance.

The first intrinsic character of the eucharist
to be handled is communion. The report atates
that man is created in and for communion with
God. When man lost this communion the consequence
was that his relationship with his creator,
fellow men and with his environment was distur-
bed. In Jesus Christ, God renews the communion in

all the dimensions. Pointing out clearly the way
this renewal in Christ is accomplished through
the eucharist, the report said: "The Eucharist is
the sacramental event in which this renewed
communion is both celebrated and enacted by the
power of the Holy Spirit. Our sharing at the
Lord's table thus inseparably involves communion
both with God and with our fellow men, in Jesus
Christ. It is the eschatological sign of universal salvation."[70] In the present situation of
divisions in the church, our eucharistic services
should make us question whether we are faithful
to God's will. This should be so because the
celebration of the Lord's Supper will take on its
full meaning and truth if the church itself is a
single body. In the past disunity in the eucharistic communion led to the church's decision to
excommunicate but the present situation of inability to communicate should be seen as a breach
of trust in the gift of communion. The fact that
the churches can now pray together especially
saying the Lord's prayer together and exchaning
the kiss of peace are tokens of reconciliation
that are implicitly eucharistic. This action
points to our common origin and unity and shows
also that "the Church and the Eucharist are signs
and tokens of the same mystery of communion. Both
comprise in one organic whole, the same essential
elements."[71] This communion is also described as
being eschatological, inspiring conversion and
conspiring reconciliation; it is also kerygmatic,
through which communion of faith is also realized.

---

70. op. cit., F.O. No. 59, p.58
71. ibid.

Communion is also sacramental, as a gift of
Christ to his Church. Communion is ministerial
because "the eucharist implies the sacrament of
the royal priesthood as well as that of the apostolic ministry since it is the sacrament both of
the whole Christ offered up and of Christ's handing on (traditio) communion to his Church."[72]
Communion is also missionary because through it
the gift of the ministry is exercised in bringing
the gospel to the people. Finally communion is
said to be cosmic because Christ in the body of
his Church, acts as priest for all creation offering up the entire creation as Eucharist.

The report then rejoices on the agreement
reached so far on the three long-standing controversies, on epiclesis, the real presence and on
the sacrifical character of the eucharist regarding this as a promising sign of progress. It
went further to raise some theological issues
about the eucharist for further study and explo-
ration.

The first issue considers the new awareness in
many traditions about the eschatological nature
of the eucharist, which suggests a new openness
to each other and a new ordering of priorities.
The Church, in the eucharist does not only remember Christ's death under Pontius Pilate but
also looks forward to the final fulfilment of the
kingdom, knowing each time as before, a foretaste
of that reality. This foretaste of the kingdom
calls mankind to reconciliation and to new life.
This foretaste recalls that the ultimate judgement is in God's hand and that judgement will

---

72. ibid.

call into question the lesser acts of judgement
and division. The report notes that it is because
of the joy of the eucharistic anticipation both
in the past century as well as in the present
that proped people to embrace martyrdom, a costly
witness to Christ, and in such period the barriers of division fall away. The question that
comes up to mind is what this should mean for the
balance of our loyalties between that which comes
to us from the past and that which we are called
to envisage in the future.

The next theological issue is about the renewed dynamism of the eucharist considered as the
sacrament which constitutes the fellowship that
is called the church. This fellowship is constituted where the christians listen together to the
proclaimed word and share the broken bread, the
sign of their oneness in the body of Christ. In
this fellowship two distinctions are made between
the churches which understand the Eucharist as
the sign of the unity once given and those who
see it as a means of restoring that unity. The
report submits that the Eucharist is increasingly
known to be both and maintained that as long as
the churches seek regularly, faithfully and rea-
listically to obey Christ's command in the eucharistic celebration, the inherent dynamism of the
sacrament will be made manifest across the present divisions. To realize this would imply confession of sins including the sin of acquiescence
in disunity.

The Eucharist understood as prayer has both
universal and local character. Here the report
re-echoes what has been established earlier in
this study project, as it said: "But there is

hope in recent stress on the biblical teaching
that one, universal eucharist is precisely that
which is incarnate in a huge diversity of local
celebrations and that each of these is not just a
partial and transitory reality but indeed the one
and whole Christ praying in his members."[73] It is
then expected that the Churches which stress
visible unity and continuity in time and space
should show a new awareness of the proper place
of local diversity, while those churches that
stress truth and autonomy of each local community
should also find a need for the structures that
assure wider co-operation and unity. The dangers
that beset stricking a balance are, that the
emphasis on the local level on account of bewil-
dering opinions and situations can appear danger-
ously anarchic and liable to lead to new schisms;
and secondly that a universal discipline of eucharistic practice is neither necessary nor desirable for expressing the unity of the Church.

On the ministry in the church, the report said
that divisions in communion was often centred
around it. It restated what all the traditions
hold about it: "In all christian traditions the
ordained ministry is understood as a service
within the body of the faithful. It is a ministry
given by God but not over or apart from the
people. In the eucharist the whole people together celebrates and offers, in union with the
ministry which presides in the action. The thanksgiving is that of a priestly people who participate in the sacrificial offering of Christ."[74]

---

73. op. cit., F.O. No. 59, p.60.
74. op. cit., p.61.

It is in this context that the ministry should be
understood as a sign of the action of Christ, the
High Priest. Differences centred always on the
Apostolic Succession in the ministry. This the
report said should be better understood as
existing in and for the life of the whole body of
the faithful; and that ordination should be conceived as an act of the Holy Spirit in response
to the prayer of the whole church. In all the
confessions there is a place for the laying on of
hands, and the report explains that the handing
on (traditio), of office must never be understood
in a mechanical or purely historical sense. Still
on the differences that exist, the report says:
"But these differences exist within an area of
agreement which should allow churches which maintain and value historic continuity to recognize in
other bodies at least a tradition of ministering
and a continuity of invocation, and should allow
those who lay less stress on the historic
succession to recognize in bodies which preserve
it an intention to act as the servants of the Word
and the Spirit and thus to reconsider giving
expression to the continuity of ministry in their
own midst."[75]

The report submits that the eucharist is a
celebration of God's reconciling work in the life
of the world. This reconciliation is made manifest in the sharing of Bread. "The sharing of
this bread is the symbol of the sharing of all
bread, the unconditional character of this community the pledge of all society restored in
Christ."[76] This reconciliation which should lead

---

75. op. cit., p.62.
76. ibid.

to unity is contradicted by the growing disunity
among Christ's people bolstered by racial segre-
gation even at the Lord's table. This gives rise
to the question: "In what ways does our eucharistic worship commit us to certain social (political, economic), actions, policies and attitudes
comparable to the recognition that racial segre-
gation at the Lord's table is a denial of Christ?
Conversely, in what ways does the eucharist in-
trinsically free men from enslaving habits and
ideologies."[77] Again, how is this reconciliation
achieved by Christ and celebrated at the eucharist be carried out in missionary work among the
baptized without widening the borderlines?

PRACTICE ON THE WAY.

Having done with the explication of some theological issues on the eucharist, the report goes
on to define the terminologies involved in the
practice. It made it clear that the word intercommunion is one of such terms and that it does
not explain the whole subject matter as it was
thought before. These terminologies are not altogether new, they have appeared earlier under
intercommunion.

The report starts with the terminology that is
the goal we are seeking for in ecumenical
movement.
COMMUNION: This indicates the goal to be achieved
by the ecumenical movement. It depicts the
fellowship willed by Christ. What other terms
that follow, the report says refer to the anomalous situations precipitated by separation.

---

77. ibid.

ADMISSION: This refers to those cases where a
church in celebrating the eucharist admits members of other churches. Such admission are threefold, namely: limited, general or reciprocal.
LIMITED ADMISSION: This term has two meanings. It
is admission based on exceptional pastoral reasons. This is practised by the Orthodox and Roman
Catholic Churches. In the wider sense it is
"based on the awareness that every baptized christian belongs fundamentally to the one communion
of the Church and is directed towards his sanctification in the body of Christ."[78]
GENERAL ADMISSION: This is said to be the regular
practice of a great number of Protestant Churches. This practice also varies. One form of it
is that a number of these churches may invite
baptized and communicant members of other churches to Holy Communion; others extend their invitation to "all who love the Lord Jesus". At times
taking cognisance of the discipline of the other
churches, the minister of the host church may
limit their general invitation.
RECIPROCAL ADMISSION: This term is applicable in
two situations: Firstly, the establishment of
intercommunion by agreement between two churches,
usually in geographically different regions, and
without any question of organic union beign raised; secondly, when two churches are committed to
work for organic union, sometimes within a specified period and enter into this relationship on
the ground that the causes of division between
them have been in principle removed.
COMMON CELEBRATION: This term is used to designate a form of concelebration comprising ministers

78. op. cit., F.O. No. 59., p.63.

from different confessions during a gathering
involving their members. Each participant brings
with him to the celebration what he has received
from faith and ministry. He brings also with him
repentance for disunity, his commitment to overcoming it and his hope in the unity and fulness
that is Christ's will. The conditions for such
celebration have been worked out by one group of
Roman Catholics and Protestant theologians, the
report revealed. These are the conditions verbatim:

(a) it should involve only groups which are already in existence and which have sought the
prior agreement of the churches.

(b) all the participants, clergy and laity,
should have had some considerable ecumenical
experience and thus be theologically and spiritually prepared.

(c) the celebration should not be seen as in any
way habitual but take place in the context of a
conference or meeting with a precise aim, in
study or in action, and including serious doctrinal teaching.

(d) there should be no confusion or doubt left
about the parts played by the celebrating clergy.
Each should perform the actions required for the
authenticity of the sacrament in his church.
There should be no hiding or calling in question
the differences in understanding of the ministry
that still exist.

(e) care should be taken to see that the liturgy
used respects the various rules of the churches,
so that all participants may be able to live the
sacramental action in full communion with their
own churches and so that they all can receive
everything that they receive in their separate
communions.

(f) the celebration should vividly clear the
penitential character of the action (i.e. its
deep relationship with the repentance for which
communion in the blood shed for the remission of
sins cannot but call) and performed in close
connection with prayer for unity, that prayer not
yet fully realized but whose answer is expected
with suffering and hope from the grace of the
Lord.[79]

INTERCELEBRATION: This term applies to those
cases where two or more separated Churches are
prepared reciprocally to allow their ministers to
preside at the eucharistic celebration.

The theological commission which produced this
report did not hide its feelings of dissatisfac-
tion when it said that the restoration of
communion in a single ecclesial fellowship is what
is expected. It has earlier described these other
terms as anomalous.

---

79. op. cit., F.O. No. 59, pp.66-67.

3.6 ACCRA 1974: THE EUCHARIST.

All along Faith and Order Commission has been
discussing Baptism, Eucharist and Ministry but
has never put the results together until after
its general assembly at Accra, Ghana. After the
general assembly at Accra, the Commsission published the convergence on the three subjects
under the title: One Baptism, one Eucharist and a
mutually recognized ministry. We concern ourself
here with the Eucharist.

3.6.1 PREAMBLE.

Right from the beginning one notices that the
document reflects the previous agreements from
the past general meetings of the Faith and Order
Commission. The preamble takes off from baptism
and says that it is the sacrament which incorporates one into the people of God and thus the
worshipping life of the royal priesthood. In the
Eucharist we proclaim and celebrate a memorial of
the saving acts of God. These saving acts of God
made manifest in the incarnation, life, death,
resurrection and ascension of Christ are unique
and therefore cannot be repeated. In the Eucharist we find the centre and climax of the
church's whole sacramental life because Christ
himself is present in the eucharist, 'with all he
has accomplished for us and for all creation'.
The Commission takes note of the limitedness of
the document in the sense that it does not say
everything about eucharistic theology but maintains that the document reflects wide growing
agreement on many aspects of the Eucharist. The
whole report is presented under five sub-headings.

3.6.2 THE INSTITUTION OF THE EUCHARIST.

The Eucharist, according to the document, was
instituted in the contex of the Jewish Passover:
"The Eucharist is the sacramental meal, sequel to
the Passover of Israel, the new paschal of the
people of God, which Christ having loved his
disciples until the end, gave to them before his
death, shared with them after his resurrection
and commanded them to hold until his return."[80]
This meal of bread and wine is not only the sacrament, but also the effective sign and assurance of the presence of Christ who sacrificed
his life for all men and gave himself to men as
the bread of life. Putting all these together the
document declared that: "The eucharistic meal is
the sacrament of the body and blood of Christ,
the sacrament of his real presence." In the Eucharist the promise of the presence of the crucified and risen Christ is fulfilled in a unique
way for the faithful; the faithful are sanctified
and are unified in the eucharist. They are reconciled in love as servants and become agents of
reconciliation in the world. In Christ the faithful are offered up as a living sacrifice, thus in
the eucharist is the full manifestation of the
community of God's people.

---

80. One Baptism, one Eucharist And a mutualy
    recognized Ministry, Geneva, W.C.C., 1975,
    pp.18-20.
    Further quatations as F.O. No. 73.

3.6.3 THE MEANING OF THE EUCHARIST.

Here the eucharist is understood as Thanks-

giving to the Father; as Anamnesis or Memorial of
Christ; as invocation and gift of the Spirit and
finally as Communion within the Body of Christ.

3.6.3.1 THANKSGIVING TO THE FATHER.

The eucharist is considered as a great thanksgiving to the Father for everything he had accomplished, for example, in creation, redemption and
sanctification; for everything which he presently
accomplishes in the church and in the world inspite of the sins of men; and for everything he
will accomplish to bring the kingdom to fulfilment. "Thus the eucharist is the benediction
(berakah) by which the church expresses its
thankfulness to God for all his benefits."[81] That
the eucharist is a sacrifice is expressed by the
document in its understanding as thanksgiving to
the Father. The document has it that "The Eucharist is the great sacrifice of praise by which
the church speaks on behalf of the whole creation. For the world which God has reconciled to
himself is present at every eucharist: in the
bread and wine, in the persons of the faithful,
and in the prayers they offer for themselves and
for all men."[82] In their prayers the faithful are
united to the Person of our Lord and to his intercession, and thus they are transfigured and
accepted. In this way therefore the eucharist
reveals to the world what it must become.

_____

81. op. cit., F.O. No. 73, p.20.
82. ibid.

3.6.3.2 ANAMNESIS OR MEMORIAL OF CHRIST.

The document submits that at the institution
of the Eucharist, Christ's focus was upon the
cross and the resurrection, as the anamnesis of
the whole of God's reconciling action in him.
Anamnesis therefore includes all that Christ
himself accomplished for us and for all creation
in his incarnation, servanthood, ministry, teaching, suffering, resurrection, ascension and
Pentecost, as well as the fortaste of his Parousia and the fulfilment of the kingdom. In other
words Anamnesis includes this representation and
anticipation.
Explaining the fact further the document maintains that anamnesis is not only a calling to
mind of what happened in the past or its significance, it is also the church's effective proclamation of God's mighty acts. In communion with
Christ, the Church therefore participates in this
reality.
The document further explains that this anamnetic representation and anticipation are realized in thanksgiving and intercession. That
means that the church united with Christ, its
great High Priest and intercessor, proclaims
before God the mighty acts of redemption in
thanksgiving, and implores him to make every man
benefit from these acts. Anamnesis of Christ is
further understood by the document as the source
of all christian prayer. The prayer of the christians relies and is united with the continual
intercession of the risen Lord. In the eucharist
therefore "Christ empowers us to live with him
and to pray through him as justified sinners

joyfully and freely fulfilling his will."[83] The
document once again in the context of Anamnesis
of Christ points out acts of sacrifice therein, it
says: "With contrite hearts we offer up ourselves, in union with our Saviour as a living and
holy sacrifice, a sacrifice which must be expressed in the whole of our daily lives. Thus
united to our Lord and to all the faithful before
us and in fellowship with the whole Church on
earth, we are renewed in the covenant sealed by
the blood of Christ."[84] The document relates the
preached word with the eucharist, since the essence of both is the anamnesis of Christ, it
submits that the eucharist should always be celebrated with the ministry of the word.

3.6.3.3 INVOCATION AND GIFT OF THE SPIRIT.

The document draws a clear relationship between anamnesis and epiclesis by saying that "The
anamnesis leads to epiclesis - the Church being
under the New Covenant, confidently prays for the
Spirit, in order that it may be sanctified and
renewed, led into all truth and empowered to
fulfil its mission in the world."[85] Apart from
communion, says the document, anamnesis and epiclesis cannot be conceived. It then went further
to explain Christ's real presence in the Eucharist saying: "It is the Spirit who, in the Eucharist makes Christ really present, and is given to
us in the bread and wine, according to the words

---

83. op. cit., p.21.
84. ibid.
85. ibid.

of institution."[86] The gift of the Holy Spirit in
the eucharist is a foretaste of the kingdom of
God, for through the Spirit, the Church receives
the life of the new creation and the assurance of
the Lord's return. The document ever stresses
that the whole action of the eucharist depends on
the work of the Holy Spirit and recommends that
this epikletic character should find adequate
expression in the words of the liturgy. It
appears that there was no perfect agreement on
the manner and purpose of the invocation of the
Holy Spirit; for according to the document "Some
Churches desire an invocation of the Holy Spirit
upon the people of God and upon the elements;
others hold that the reference to the Spirit may
be made in other ways."[87]

In the opinion of many churches consecration
cannot be limited to a particular moment in the
liturgy, and the document explains that in
various liturgical traditions the epiclesis is
located differently in relation to the words of
institution. To combat further the problem of the
special moment of consecration, the document
refers to the early liturgies where the whole
'prayer action' was thought of as bringing about
the reality promised by Christ.

---

86. ibid.
87. op. cit., F.O. No. 73, p.22.

3.6.3.4 COMMUNION WITHIN THE BODY OF CHRIST.

The document first established that Christ is
present in the eucharistic communion, and that it
is he who nourishes the life of the Church
through it, for this communion takes place within
the body of Christ which is the Church. It went
on to show how all who participate in this communion are united. "The sharing of the common loaf
and the common cup in a given place demonstrates
the oneness of the sharers with the whole Christ
and with their fellow sharers in all times and
places. By sharing the common loaf they show
their unity with the church Catholic, the mystery
of redemption is set forth and the whole body
grows in grace."[88] Having said this the document
points out how the eucharist radically challenges
any form of division and disunity: "Because of
its catholicity, the eucharist is a radical
challenge to our tendencies toward estrangement,
separation, and fragmentation. Lack of local
unity in the Church or society constitutes a
challenge to the christians in that place."[89] It
is then a mockery of the eucharist, maintains the
document, if the separation destroyed by Christ
on the cross should be allowed to resurface in
the life of the Church in any form, either between races, nationalities, tongues or classes.

Then the document went on to talk about solidarity which should derive from the eucharistic
communion of the body of Christ and of responsible concern of christians for one another and

---

88. ibid.
89. op. cit., p.22.

the world. It urged for specific prayer for the
needy and the suffering, the sorrowful and the
perplexed in the celebration of the eucharist,
and further for the care of prisoners especially
in taking the eucharist to them. The reason for
this is that "all these manifestations of love in
the eucharist are directly related to Christ's
own testimony as a servant, in whose servanthood
christians themselves participate by virtue of
their union with him."[90] At this juncture the
document recalls the ministry of deacons and
deaconesses in the early church as having a
role to play in the present time. Lastly it states
that in the eucharistic communion each faithful
member of the body of Christ receives remission
of sins and everlasting life, and is nourished
also in faith, hope and love.

3.6.4   IMPLICATIONS OF THE EUCHARIST.

   The document considers that the first implication that the eucharist has for the Church is her
mission to the world. The Church carries out
her mission to the world by the thanksgiving she
makes to the Father; in the memorial of Christ,
where she is united with its high Priest and
Intercessor and prays for the world, and asks for
the gift of the Holy Spirit, the sanctifier of
creation. Being reconciled in the eucharist, the
members of the body of Christ, become agents of
reconciliation amongst men and bear witness to
the joy of resurrection. They also show their

---

90. op. cit., p.23.

solidarity with the poor and the suffering in the
world.

The second implication that the eucharist has
for the Church is that of putting an end to all
divisions. Here the document emphasizes the importance of local churches which are meant, no
matter how humble, to reveal the wholeness of the
church in its fulness, when they share in the
eucharist. The eucharist points to the unity of
the church. The document points out that it is
through baptism that believers are incorporated
into the body of Christ and are endowed by the
Holy Spirit. Hence it regrets the situation where
the right of the baptized believers and their
ministers to participate in and preside over the
eucharist is called into question. This it maintains, obscures the catholicity of the eucharist,
and submits that "in so far as a church claims to
be a manifestation of the whole Church, it should
recognize that the whole church is involved in
its pastoral and administrative regulations."[91]

3.6.5 THE ELEMENTS OF THE EUCHARIST.

Here the document outlines the elements involved in the celebration of the Eucharist, understood essentially as a simple whole. It is
thus structured:

- proclamation of the word of God;
- intercession for the whole church and the
  world,

---

91. op. cit. F.O. No. 73, p.26.

- thanksgiving for the marvels of creation,
  redemption and sanctification,
- the words of institution,
- the anamnesis,
- the epiclesis,
- prayer for the Lord's coming and of the manifestation of his kingdom,
- the Amen of the whole congregation,
- communion,
- a final act of praise.

To this the document added apologetically that
"This list of liturgical items is not meant to
exclude reference to others, such as the expression of contrition, the declaration of forgiveness of sins, the affirmation of faith in credal
form, the celebration of the communion of saints,
hymns of thanksgiving and praise, and the self
dedication of the faithfull to God."[92]

3.6.6 RECOMMENDATIONS.

The document winds up by making some recommendations. It recommends renewal in the teaching
and liturgy of the Eucharist as a means toward
unity in the eucharistic celebration and communion. It asserts that affirmation of a common
eucharistic faith does not mean uniformity in
either liturgy or practice. It does not object to
the frequent celebration of the eucharist, which
it says deepens eucharistic faith. The document
recommends that the eucharist be celebrated not

---

92. op. cit., p.27.

less frequently as every Sunday or once a week at which every christian should receive communion.

Our document drew special attention at the elements of bread and wine in the eucharist and how they are to be treated. It said inter alia: "The act of Christ, being the gift of his body and his blood (that is himself), the given reality symbolized in the bread and wine, is his body and blood. It is in virtue of the creative word of Christ and by the power of the Holy Spirit that the bread and wine are made sacraments and thus, 'participation in the body and blood of Christ' (1 Cor 10:16). Henceforth, in the deepest sense, by an external sign, they are given reality and remain so in view of their consumption. That which is given as the body and blood of Christ remains given as his body and blood; it must be treated as such."[93]

With this statement in mind, the document said that it should be made known that the primary intention of reserving the elements is their distribution to the sick and those absent from the celebration and that the best way of showing respect to the elements served in the eucharistic celebration is by their later consumption.

Finally the document believes firmly that the problem of intercommunion will be solved "as the churches in their eucharistic experience move toward the fulness which is in Christ."[94]

---

93. op. cit., pp.27-28.
94. ibid.

3.6.7 EVALUATION.

The Accra Text was built up from the materials taken from the previous World Conferences of Faith and Order and from the plenary meetings of Faith and Order Commission of the World Council of Churches. In these meetings there was a gradual growth in agreements in the age-long toothing eucharistic controversies. The text did not solve definitively those controversies and in certain cases conscious of the past problems made statements open to various interpretations. Let us now look into such notions as eucharistic sacrifice and anamnesis; epiclesis and real presence in the way the text presented them.

EUCHARIST: ANAMNESIS AND SACRIFICE.

The Accra Text speaks of the eucharist as sacrifice first in the context of thanksgiving to the Father and secondly in the context of anamnesis. As thanksgiving to the Father the document says: "The Eucharist is the great sacrifice of praise by which the church speaks on behalf of the whole creation."[95] This statement in itself is an ecumenical breakthrough, although it did not say all about the eucharist as sacrifice; but calling to mind the controversies of the past four centuries, since the Reformation, one can commend such convergence of opinion in an ecumenical gathering. Again the document said in paragraph eleven, that "with contrite hearts we offer up

---

95. op. cit., No. 73, p.20.

ourselves, in union with our Saviour as a living
and holy sacrifice, a sacrifice which must be
expressed in the whole of our daily lives."[96]
Considering the above citations in the Roman
Catholic view, one can say that rightly is underlined that the Eucharist is a 'a sacrifice of
praise', it less evidently said it is the real
sacrifice of worship, expiation and reconciliation of Christ. "We offer up ourselves", is also
true, but there should be more, namely the offering in the anamnesis of the death of Jesus. It
should also have been said in this document that
the eucharist is Christ's sacrifice for the whole
creation, and that the church shares in both
offering and being offered along with Christ. Had
these points been clearly stated in our document,
then it could have approximated the Catholics'
understanding of the eucharistic sacrifice.

EUCHARIST: EPICLESIS AND REAL PRESENCE.

The Accra Text presented its teaching on the
real presence of Christ in the Eucharist in three
stages, namely in the paragraph dealing on the
institution, then on the epiclesis and finally on
the recommendation section. In paragraph four of
the document it says: "This meal of bread and
wine is the sacrament, the effective sign and
assurance of the presence of Christ himself, who
sacrificed his life for all men and who gave
himself to them as the bread of life; because of
this, the eucharistic meal is the sacrament of

---

96. op. cit., p.21.

the body and blood of Christ, the sacrament of his real presence."[97] The document put it correctly that Christ is present in the sacrament of the eucharist. It did not go further to handle the manner of this presence. Perharps it wanted to avoid the age long controversy by the Reformation churches on the Catholic doctrine of Transubstantiation. In such ecumenical discussion however, it is priseworthy that the presence of Christ in the Eucharist is unequivocally asserted.

The document went further to say that it is the Spirit who in the eucharist makes Christ really present, and is given to us in the bread and wine, according to the words of institution. This statement tends to bring together the two different traditions of East and West. While one lays emphasis on epiclesis as bringing about the eucharistic miracle, the other holds that it is through the Words of institution spoken by the minister. Traditionally in the Roman Catholic Church, it is well understood that once the words of institution are spoken by the priest (in the person of Christ), the bread and wine become the Body and Blood of Christ. In the structure of the eucharistic celebration the epiclesis and the words of institution are placed in relation to the other. While in the epiclesis the power of God is invoked to intervene and consecrate the gifts proffered by mankind, so that they may become the body and blood of Christ, which is the source of salvation to those who share in communion, the narration of the words of institution

---

97. op. cit., p.20.

accomplish the very sacrifice of Christ which he himself instituted at the Last Supper.[98] The moment of consecration is clear from what is said above. To point out that epiclesis is located differently in different traditions, as the document did in paragraph eighteen, is to play down the importance of epiclesis in determining the precise point during the eucharistic celebration when Christ becomes really present.

The Second Vatican Council in its Constitution on Sacred Liturgy outlined the various ways in which Christ is present among his people. Christ is always in his Church, especially in her liturgical celebrations, in the sacraments, in the holy Scriptures, when the Church prays and sings but "He is present in the sacrifice of the Mass, not only in the person of his minister, "the same one now offering, through the ministry of priest, who formerly offered himself on the cross", but especially under the Eucharistic species."[99] This statement ferries us across to consider what was stated in paragraph thity-four of the document about the special attention that should be given to the eucharistic elements of bread and wine. "That which is given as the body and blood of Christ remains given as his body and blood; it must be treated as such."[100] Behind this statement is the fact of Christ's real presence in the eucharistic elements. The above citation co-incides radically with the reason for the traditional

---

98. cf. Howell Clifford, (translated), General Instruction on the Roman Missal, London, C.T.S., 1973, pp.28-29.
99. cf. S.C. No. 7.
100. op. cit., F.O. No. 73, p.28.

adoration of the reserved sacrament by the Roman
Catholics. But paragraph thirty-five seems to
depreciate this assertion when it maintains that
the purpose of reserving the elements is their
later distribution among the sick and those who
were absent but excluding the idea of adoration.
As a secondary intention, the Catholic tradition
of eucharistic adoration should not be excluded
as much as it must not be imposed an other traditions. The reserved elements are given to the
sick and those absent as the body and blood of
Christ, the sacrament of his real presence. When
the document recommends that the eucharistic
elements should be treated with special attention, why exclude adoration as one of the ways of
giving that 'special attention'?

In paragraph twenty-eight, the document listed
what it called "the elements of the Eucharist".
The document may be misunderstood as if the elements given prominence in the document are only
the essential ones, while the others packed at
the end of the paragraph are not. One would like
to see such elements as the expression of contrition, declaration of forgiveness of sins, profession of faith given their proper position at the
top of the list. In the list the kiss of peace
was conspicuosly missing. It is a sign of reconciliation and love and deserves its rightful
place in this document.

Finally on intercommunion the document says:
"As the Churches in their eucharistic experience
move toward the fulness which is in Christ, the
problem of intercommunion will move toward its

solution."[101] This is another way of saying that
when the Churches are in communion with one
another, the problem of intercommunion will
disappear, because the goal of ecumenical
movement would have been attained.

---

101. op. cit., p.28.

CHAPTER FOUR.

ECUMENICAL EUCHARISTIC STATEMENTS.

4.0 INTRODUCTION.

One of the aims of Faith and Order is to help the Churches to attain visible unity. One of the ways it does this is by organising multilateral dialogues on subjects where there is no conformity either in dogma or practice. In such dialogues convergence agreement is achieved but it is left for the Churches themselves to respond to such agreements or to apply them in their church order; the Faith and Order is always prepared to offer its help. The director of the Faith and Order Commission recently recalled this role of the commission, he said: "We should remember that Faith and Order, before as well as after the founding of the W.C.C., there was and still is a policy that Faith and Order seeks to prepare the way to visible unity, but negotations and con- crete steps leading to the establishment of visible unity have to be undertaken by the chur- ches themselves."[1]

The Faith and Order Commission helps in church union negotiations when its help is elicited and in the bilateral dialogues which have ensued, it sends observers. The bilateral dialogues contri- bute a lot to the ecumenical movement viewed as a unit, and the Roman Catholic Church is at the

---

1. Gassmann G., The Relation between bilateral and multilateral dialogues in: Journal of Ecumenical Studies vol. 23:3, summer 1986, p.370.

forefront. This is confirmed by Dr. Günther
Gassmann himself who said: "I believe rather
that by means of the bilaterals the ecumenical
movement as such has experienced an extension of
its breadth and scope. Through the bilateral
dialogues, but not limited to them, the Roman
Catholic Church has joined the ecumenical movement. This in itself constitutes an unparalleled
quantitative and qualitative extension of the
movement."[2]

We can then say that in the bilateral dialogues the role of Faith and Order towards church
unity is projected. This chapter is therefore
designed to show some churches in dialogue and to
expose their efforts towards understanding the
eucharist together as a means of clearing the
obstacles on the way towards their unity. Three
dialogues between the Catholic Church and other
Churches have been selected; one other selection
is between a group of Protestants and Catholics
and the next one is a dialogue among the Evangelical Churches in Germany in their effort to
attain church communion.

It is interesting to note that each group in
dialogue takes something from the convergence
agreement on the eucharist reached already by
Faith and Order, in its multilaterals. Since
complimentarity exists between the bilateral and
the multilateral dialogues, their inclusion here
is viewed to be profitable to our work. At a
glance one gathers all the reach results attained
in the difficult discussions on the eucharist by
different traditions in dialogue.

Let us now go into the dialogues one after the
other in their chronology.

---

2. op. cit., p.371.

4.1 THE ARNOLDSHAIN THESES 1957.

In the year 1947, the Evangelical Church of
Germany (E.K.D), comprising the Lutherans, the
Reformed and United Churches, in their meeting at
Treysa, passed a motion that led to the formation
of a theological commission to discuss the Eucharist, the main subject at the centre of their
division. The decision that brought about the ten
year long discussion on the eucharist reads: "Die
Kirchenversammlung bittet den Rat der EKD, sich
darum zu bemühen, daß ein verbindliches theologisches Gespräch über die Lehre vom Heiligen
Abendmahl im Hinblick auf die kirchliche Gemeinschaft zustande kommt."[3] The last meeting of the
theological commission took place at Arnoldshain
near Taunus in the Federal Republic of Germany,
and thereafter the result of the ten year discussion was published in eight theses and named
after the venue of the last meeting as Arnoldshain Theses.

The Theses[4] were eight in number. In the
preamble the authors indicated that they considered the essential things about the eucharist as
it is in the bible and as members of the one
Apostolic Church.

THESIS I.

1. The first thesis states that the origin of

---

3. Niemeier G., (Hrsg), Lehrgespräch über das
   Heilige Abendmahl, München, Kaiser Verlag,
   1961, p.34.
4. Source of the theses in German: Abendmahls-
   Gespräch der EKD, 1947-1957, Verlag des
   Amtsblattes der EKd, 1958. My English source:
   Scottish Journal of Theology, vol. 15, March,
   1962, pp.1-3.

the eucharist is based on its institution by
Jesus Christ, and we celebrate it in accordance
with his command.

2. The exalted Lord invites his followers to
the eucharist, and through their participation
they enjoy a foretaste of the future fellowship
in God's kingdom.

THESIS II.

1. In the eucharist, Jesus Christ is present
in the Holy Spirit and acts through his word in
what the Church does.

2. The eucharist is one of the ways in which
Christ bestows upon us the gifts of salvation.

THESIS III.

1. The eucharist is an act of worship in the
name of Jesus.

2. The celebration of the eucharist is bound
up with the preaching of the word.

3. Accompanied by prayer, thanksgiving and
praise, the words of institution are spoken over
the bread and wine, and the bread and wine are
distributed to the congregation

4. In the eucharist, we commemorate the death
of Christ we confess the presence of the risen
Lord in our midst and await his return.

THESIS IV.

For a good fellow-up to the fifth thesis may I
quote the fourth thesis in full: "The words
spoken by Our Lord Jesus Christ when the bread
and wine are offered tell us what He Himself
gives in this Supper to all who participate in
it. He, the crucified and risen Lord, permits us

to participate, through the Holy Spirit to share
in the victory of His Lordship, so that through
Faith in His promise we may receive forgiveness
of sins, life and bliss".[5]

THESIS V.

The authors devoted this thesis to express
what they called 'inappropriate' interpretation
of what happens in the eucharist, having stated
in thesis four, what the eucharist is all about.
The five statements made in this thesis bear
traces of Reformation polemics. They went on to
say that it is inappropriate:

a. to teach that through the words of institution bread and wine are transformed into a supernatural substance and cease to be bread and wine.

b. to teach that act of salvation is repeated
in the eucharist;

c. to teach that the elements of the eucharist
is either purely natural or purely supernatural;

d. to teach about two forms of eating, one
physical and the other spiritual.

e. to teach that physical participation in the
eucharist ensures salvation, or that participation in the body and blood of Christ is a purely
spiritual procedure.

THESIS VI.

1. The thesis states that Jesus our Saviour is
both the beginning and the Lord of a new
creation.

---

5. op. cit., Scottish Journal of Theology, p.2.

2. That through Christ those who receive his
body and blood are united in his body, the
Church, and participate as well in the new
covenant of Christ's blood.

3. That the eucharist is a fellowship of
brethren, which proves that all divisions and
enslavement in this world have been broken down
in Christ; and that amid the redeemed sinners,
the Lord has inaugurated a new humanity.

THESIS VII.

Here the thesis says that the eucharist places
us on the way of the cross. It recalls the weakness of the believers but the victory of Christ
remains concealed through temptation and suffering and that is why "the Lord feeds us through
His Supper, in order to strengthen us for the
struggle into which he sends His people, and to
arm us against sentimentalism and indolence, so
as to prevent us from indulging in false dreams
about the future or from throwing up the gauntlet
in despair."[6]

2. The fellowship bestowed by Christ to us in
the eucharist makes us brothers, which is lived
out in love for one another. Just as Christ the
righteous, who is also free and exalted, has
received us who are bound and debased, so also
must we share all that we are and have with those
who need us.

THESIS VIII.

1. The thesis states that, it is through faith
and not through merit that what is promised is

---

6. op. cit., Scottish Journal of Theology, p.3.

received.

    2. That we should not sin against the great-
ness of the gift of the eucharist and bring
judgement upon us.

    3. That all the members of the church are
called by the Lord to the Last Supper and that
forgiveness of sins is promised to all who long
for his righteousness.

4.1.1 ASSESSMENT.

    The Arnoldshain Theses provoked a lot of
comments among member Churches and individuals in
the EKD, the Evangelical Church of Germany. The
Synod of EKD held in February 1960, received the
Theses with Joy and thanked all those who took
part in the theological discussions and charged
the Councils and Administrators of the member
Churches to ensure the continuation of the promising work already started.

    The response from different member churches of
EKD and from some groups and individuals demands
explanation on, or reject entirely some parts of
the theses. The whole exercise reflects the difference between the eucharistic teaching of
Luther and Calvin. Let us now consider briefly
the affected parts of the theses.
Thesis 2:2

    The committee set up by VELKD, on the
Arnoldshain Theses, evaluated this part positively but added that the eucharist is not just
only one of the ways Christ bestows upon us the
gift of salvation, he does so in a special way in
the eucharist in that he gives us his body and

blood.[7]

Thesis 3.

This thesis concerns the liturgical celebration of the eucharist. Dr. Sasse considers thesis 3:1, a rule in the celebration of the eucharist which excludes the question of private Masses; at the same time he identifies its insufficiency for no provision was made for private communion in the case of the communion of the sick.[8]

Theses 4 and 5.

The Lutherische Theologische Hochschule, Oberursel, considers thesis 4 as denying the Lutheran confession of the eucharist, in the sense that it did not bear witness to the real presence of the truly and substantial body and blood of Christ; neither did it witness to the eating and drinking of the body and blood of Christ with the mouth, nor did it condemn receiving the body and blood of the Lord unworthily.[9] Dr. Sasse questioned the whole formulation of the fourth thesis, and was of the opinion that it would have been better to say: He gives us his real body and his real blood under bread and wine, instead of saying: Christ permits us to participate through the bread and wine in his body and blood given for all.[10]

---

7. cf. Die VELKD zu Arnoldshain in: sartory T., Die Eucharistie im Verständnis der Konfessionen, Reclinghausen, Paulus Verlag, 1961, p.247.
8. cf. Sasse H., Zum Ergebnis des "Abendmahlgesprächs der Evangelischen Kirche in Deutschland 1947-1957", in Niemeier G., op. cit., p.301.
9. cf. Theologische Feststellung zu den Arnoldshainer Abendmahlthesen, Lutherische Theologische Hochschule Oberursel, in: Niemeier G., op. cit., p.39.
10. Sasse H., op. cit., p.302.

Another group understands the formulation of the
thesis as emphasizing only the personal presence
of Christ instead of his real presence.

The Lutherische Bruderkreise in Germany, in
their response said that thesis 5b, has to be
completely rejected if it fails to admit any
teaching of the re-presentation of Christ's sacrifice in the celebration of the eucharist.[11]

Ineffect, thesis 5a and 5b are directed
against the Roman Catholic dogma of transubstantiation and her teaching on the eucharistic sacrifice. But one of the EKD theologians bore
witness to the fact that the Catholic Church has
never taught that the sacrifice of Calvary is
repeated as the thesis presents it rather that it
is re-presented.[12]

In trying to avoid any mention of the sacrificial aspect of the eucharist, the thesis abandoned an important character of the eucharist,
which points to the atonement of our sins by
Christ. In this line of thought, T.F. Torrance
said: "As we have already noted, no interpretation of the Supper is biblically sound which does
not rest upon a doctrine of atonement involving
the aspect of sacrifice, and correspondinly no
doctrine of Eucharistic memorial is adequate
unless it corresponds to that fulness in the
atonement"[13]

---

11. cf. Lutherische Bruderkreise Deutschlands:
    Einspruch gegen die Lehrerklärung der EKD vom
    Heiligen Abendmahl, in: Niemeier G., op.
    cit., p.45.
12. cf., Sasse H., op.cit., p.303.
13. Torrance T.F., The Arnoldshain Theses on Holy
    Communion, in: Scottish Journal of Theology,
    vol 15, March 1962, p.15.

The rest of the fifth thesis reflects the controversy in the eucharistic doctrine of Luther and Calvin, with some exaggerations as Sasse points out regarding 5e: "Wer hat je gelehrt, das leibliche Essen als solches mache heilig."[14]

The purpose of choosing to present the Arnold-shain theses is to give an insight into the internal dialogue among the member churches of EKD, and how they pursued to understand the eucharist together in their quest for intercommunion and church communion.

---

14. Sasse H., op. cit., p.303.
   "Who has ever taught that corporeal eating as such makes one holy". (Translation is mine).

4.2 ANGLICAN / ROMAN CATHOLIC: THE WINDSOR STATEMENT 1971.

4.2.1 HISTORICAL BACKGROUND.

The participation of the Roman Catholic Church in the modern ecumenical movement traces its origin to the Second Vatican Council. The Decree on Ecumenism spelt out the pathways and methods for the Catholics to take part in ecumenical movement.

The first meeting of an Archbishop of Canterbury and the Pope since the Reformation was a courtesy visit on 2 December 1960, of Archbishop Geoffrey Fisher to Pope John XXIII in Rome. This was before the Second Vatican Council, and after the Council, the Archbishop of Canterbury, Michel Ramsey, visited Pope Paul VI in Rome, March 22-24 1966. One of the fruits of this historic visit is the resolution of these two leaders to initiate dialogue between the two Churches, on theological matters and on other areas such as Scripture, Tradition and Liturgy. This was made clear in their common declaration which said inter alia: "...they intend to inaugurate between the Roman Catholic Church and the Anglican Communion a serious dialogue which, founded on the Gospels and on the ancient common traditions, may lead to that unity in truth, for which Christ prayed."[15] A joint preparatory Commission was constituted, which met three times in 1967 and produced the Malta Report 1968. In this report the commission

---

15. Stranky T.F.; Sheerin J.B., (ed.), Doing The Truth in Charity, New York/Ramsey, Paulist Press, 1982, pp.285-286.

recommended among other things that a permanent
Joint Commission be constituted to continue the
work already started. The report also recommended: "the constitution of two joint commissions,
to undertake two urgent and important tasks: One
to examine the question of intercommunion, and
the related matters of church and ministry; The
Other to examine the question of authority, its
nature, exercise and implications."[16]

The recommendations were accepted, but the
commission was rather named Anglican Roman Catholic International Commission. This commission set
fort to work and in 1971 produced an agreement on
the eucharistic doctrine published as Windsor
Statement 1971.

4.2.2 WINDSOR STATEMENT 1971.

The Windsor agreement on the eucharistic doctrine, treats the subject under three sub-
headings, namely: the mystery of the Eucharist,
the Eucharist and the sacrifice of Christ and
finally the presence of Christ.

The first two paragraphs serve as an introduction. There it is made clear that in the course
of history the eucharist has been described under
various names, viz: The Lord's Supper, Liturgy,
holy mysteries, synaxis, Mass, holy communion,
but the document says that 'Eucharist' has become
the most universally accepted term. To bring
about a substantial consensus on the purpose

---

16. Meyer H., Visher L. (ed.), Growth in
    Agreement, New York/Ramsey, Geneva, Paulist
    Press, 1984, p.124.

and meaning of the eucharist, which is an important stage to organic unity, the commission declares its aim by saying: "Our intention has been
to seek a deeper understanding of the reality of
the eucharist which is consonant with biblical
teaching and with the tradition of our common
inheritance, and to express in this document the
consensus we have reached."[17] The document resta-
tes that the relationship with God and with one
another inaugurated by being baptized in Christ,
is deepened through the eucharist and expressed
in a confession of one faith and a common life of
loving service.

4.2.2.1   THE MYSTERY OF THE EUCHARIST.

In handling this sub-heading the document did
not begin with the mystery and God's unknow-
ability in the eucharist, rather it explains what
Christ does, when his people celebrates the eucharistic mystery: "Christ makes effective among
us the eternal benefits of his victory and
elicits and renews our response of faith, thanksgiving and self-surrender. Christ through the
Holy Spirit in the eucharist builds up the life
of the church, strengthens its fellowship and
furthers its mission."[18] In the eucharist also
the identity of the church as the body of Christ
is expressed and effectively proclaimed in partaking of the body and blood of Christ. The

---

17. Modern Eucharistic Agreements, London,
    S.P.C.K., 1973, p.26. Further quoatations as
    Windsor 1971.
18. op. cit., Windsor 1971, p.26.

document clearly brings out another fact in the
mystery of the eucharist when it says that in the
whole action of the eucharist, Christ is sacramentally present through bread and wine, as the
crucified and risen Lord, and offers himself to
his people according to his promise.

Having said what Christ does in the eucharist
the document expresses what the congregation
does, their benefits and anticipation, stressing
also the union and commitment of those who partake of the one loaf, "In the eucharist we proclaim the Lord's death until he comes. Receiving
a foretaste of the kingdom to come, we look back
with thanksgiving to what Christ has done for us,
we greet him present among us, we look forward to
his final appearing in the fulness of his kingdom... When we gather around the same table in
this communal meal at the invitation of the same
Lord and when we 'partake of the one loaf', we
are one in commitment not only to Christ and to
one another, but also to the mission of the
church in the world."[19]

4.2.2.2 THE EUCHARIST AND THE SACRIFICE OF CHRIST.

The document first states what Christ's sacri-
fice was and later links it with the eucharist.
It begins by saying that the redemptive action of
Christ through his death and resurrection took
place once and for all in history. This act of
Christ is presented in sacrificial language:
"Christ's death on the cross, the culmination

---

19. op. cit., p.27.

of his whole life of obedience, was the one,
perfect and sufficient sacrifice for the sins of
the world."[20]
This sacrifice cannot be repeated nor can there
be anything added to what Christ has once and for
all accomplished. The document submits that this
fundamental fact of the christian faith must not
be obscured when an attempt is made to express a
nexus between the sacrifice of Christ and the
eucharist. In a footnote the document referred to
this nexus as it was understood in the early
church and cited the Hebrew tradition as well.
The footnote reads: "The early Church in expressing the meaning of Christ's death and resurrection often used the language of sacrifice. For
the Hebrew, sacrifice was a traditional means of
communication with God. The passover, for example
was a communal meal; the day of Atonement was
essentially expiatory; and the covenant established communion between God and man."[21]

Having said that, the document immidiately
relates the notion to the eucharist by saying:
"Yet God has given the eucharist to his Church as
a means through which the atoning work of Christ
on the cross is proclaimed and made effective in
the life of the Church."[22] Our document went
further to explain how the notion of memorial was
understood in the passover celebration at the
time of Christ which is "the making effective in
the present of an event in the past." This notion, it declared has opened the way to a
clearer understanding of the relationship between

---

20. ibid.
21. op. cit., Windsor 1971, p.31.
22. op. cit., p.27.

Christ's sacrifice and the eucharist. This eucharistic memorial therefore "is no mere calling to
mind of a past event or of its significance, but
the Church's effectual proclamation of God's
mighty acts."[23] The document adds immediately
that "Christ instituted the eucharist as a memorial (anamnesis), of the totality of God's reconciling action in him."[24] The document thereafter
outlines what the church does in the eucharist,
how her members are united with Christ and with
one another in thanking God for his mercies,
praying for the whole church through which they
participate in Christ's self-offering. "In the
eucharistc prayer the Church continues to make a
perpetual memorial of Christ's death, and his
members, united with God and one another give
thanks for all his mercies, entreat the benefits
and enter into the movement of his self-
offering."[25]

4.2.2.3 THE PRESENCE OF CHRIST.

The document on the eucharistic doctrine
asserts the real presence of Christ in the eucharist with clarity. It says: "Communion with
Christ in the eucharist presupposes his true
presence, effectually signified by the bread and
wine which in this mystery become his body and
blood."[26] Our document submits that the real
presence of Christ is better understood in

---

23. ibid.
24. ibid.
25. op. cit., Windsor 1971, pp. 27-28.
26. ibid.

Christ's redemptive acts, whereby "he gives himself, and in himself reconciliation, peace and
life, to his own." It further made two points
clear; that the eucharistic gifts spring out of
the paschal mystery of Christ's death and resurrection, in which God's saving purpose has been
definitely realized; and secondly that the purpose of this eucharistic gift is to transmit the
life of the crucified and risen Christ to his
body the church,so that its members may be more
fully united with Christ and with one another.

It outlined the threefold ways in which Christ
is present: in the proclaimed word, in the person
of his minister, who presides and sacramentally
in his body and blood. That Christ is present in
the eucharist in his glorified nature, the document says: "It is the Lord present at the right
hand of the Father, and therefore transcending
the sacramental order, who thus offers to his
Church, in the eucharistic signs, the special
gift of himself."[27]

The document goes on to deal with the faith of
the believer. "The sacramental body and blood of
the saviour are present as an offering to the
believer awaiting his welcome. When this offering
is met by faith, a life-giving encounter results."[28] It states clearly that Christ's presence in the eucharist is not dependent on the
faith of the individual, for it is no longer a
presence for the believer rather a presence with
him. This wonderful awareness is thus brought to
expression: "Thus, in considering the mystery of

---

27. ibid.
28. ibid.

the eucharistic presence, we must recognize both
the sacramental sign of Christ's presence and the
personal relationship between Christ and the
faithful which arises from that presence."[29]

Stressing the fact that the elements are not
mere signs and that Christ's body and blood become really present and are given, the document
says: "The Lord's words at the last Supper, 'Take
and eat; this is my body', do not allow us to
dissociate the gift of the presence and the sacramental eating."[30] The purpose remains that
when the believers receive what is given they may
be united in communion with the Lord.

In the next paragraph the document concerns
itself briefly with the celebration of the eucharist. It states that the consecratory prayer
leads to the communion of the faithful and the
role of the Holy Spirit is asserted. "Through
this prayer of thanksgiving, a word of faith
addressed to the Father, the bread and wine become the body and blood of Christ by the action
of the Holy Spirit, so that in communion we eat
the flesh of Christ and drink his blood."[31]

What was treated next was the eschatological
dimension of the eucharist. Our document says
that this Christ, who comes to his people in the
power of the Holy Spirit is the Lord of glory. In
the liturgy of the eucharist, the joy of the age
to come is anticipated. This action of the Holy
Spirit the document thus depicts: "By the transforming action of the Spirit of God, earthly
bread and wine become the heavenly manna and the

---

29. ibid.
30. ibid.
31. op. cit., p.29.

new wine, the eschatological banquet for the new
man: elements of the first creation become
pledges and first fruits of the new heaven and
the new earth."[32]

4.2.3 THE ELUCIDATION 1979.

In 1979 the Anglican Roman Catholic International Commission (ARCIC), issued an elucidation
statement on its statement on the eucharistic
doctrine of 1971. It is an attempt to give answer
to the criticisms levelled on the document, and to
offer explanations where there was ambiguity.

On anamnesis, the elucidation text keeps to
the Commission's stand in Windsor Statement, and
says further: "We accept this use of the word,
(anamnesis), which seems to do full justice to
the semitic background. Furthermore it enables us
to affirm a strong conviction of sacramental
realism and to reject mere symbolism."[33]

Again on the issue of sacrifice, the commission identifies two ways in which the word has
been used in the exposition of the christian
doctrine of redemption. First in the New Testament "sacrificial language refers primarily to
the historical events of Christ's saving work for
us", and secondly in the Church's liturgies, the
word is used "to designate in the eucharistic
celebration the anamnesis of this historical
event"; then it concludes: "Therefore it is
possible to say at the same time that there is

---

32. ibid.
33. op. cit., Meyer H., Vischer L., (ed.), p.74.

only one unrepeatable sacrifice in the historical
sense, but that the eucharist is a sacrifice in
the sacramental sense, provided that it is clear
that this is not a repetition of the historical
sacrifice."[34] What the church does in celebrating
the eucharist is that she "gives thanks for the
gift of Christ's sacrifice and identifies itself
with the will of Christ who has offered himself
to the Father on behalf of all mankind."[35]

On the presence of Christ in the eucharist,
the text affirms his sacramental presence in
which God uses the realities of this world to
convey the realities of the new creation, that is
to say "bread for this life becomes the bread of
eternal life." The text goes on to say that "In
the sacramental order the realities of faith
become present in visible and tangible signs,
enabling christians to avail themselves of the
fruits of the once-for-all redemption. In the
eucharist the human person encounters in faith
the person of Christ in his sacramental body and
blood. This is the sense in which the community,
the Body of Christ, by partaking of the sacramental body of the risen Lord, grows into the unity
God intends for his Church."[36] The text submits
that the change intended by God in the eucharist
is the transformation of human beigns into the
likeness of Christ.

The Windsor Statement was silent on the issue
of reserving the eucharist. In this elucidation
text, the Commission traces the origin of the
sacrament back to the early Church, quoting

---

34. ibid.
35. ibid.
36. op. cit., p.75.

Justin the Martyr.[37] The purpose of the reservation is for reception especially by those who are
sick and could not come to the celebration. It
noted also that with time, there developed the
practice of veneration of the sacrament, which in
some places tended to obscure the original purpose. The text at least supported the veneration
of Christ's presence in the consecrated elements
when it said: "If veneration is wholly dissocia-
ted from the eucharistic celebration of the community it contradicts the true doctrine of the
eucharist."[38] The text goes on to explain this
practice of Adoration. "Adoration in the celebration of the eucharist is first and foremost
offered to the Father. It is to lead us to the
Father that Christ unites us to himself through
our receiving of his body and blood. The Christ
whom we adore in the eucharist is Christ glori-
fying his Father. The movement of all our adoration is to the Father, through, with and in
Christ in the power of the Spirit."[39] The text
identifies two groups in this issue. One group
represents those who will practice reservation of
the sacrament in order to administer it later to
those who were unable to attend the eucharistic
celebration. This practice is rightly understood
as an extension of that celebration. The next
group includes those who not only reserve the
sacrament for its later consumption but also for
eucharistic devotion. To this group the text
explains: "Adoration of Christ in the reserved
sacrament should be regarded as an extension of

37. cf. First Apolpgy 65, p.67.
38. op. cit., Meyer H., Vischer L., (ed.), p.76.
39. ibid.

eucharistic worship, even though it does not
include immediate sacramental reception, which
remains the primary purpose of reservation."[40]
The Commission is aware of the third group which
does not accept any kind of adoration of Christ
in the reserved sacrament despite its explanation. It nevertheless concludes: "That there can
be a divergence in matters of practice and in
theological judgements relating to them, without
destroying a common eucharistic faith, illustra-
tes what we mean by substantial agreement. Differences of theology and practice may well co-
exist with a real consensus on the essentials of
eucharistic faith - as in fact they do within
each of our communions."[41]

4.2.4 ASSESSMENT.

The Windsor Statement on the eucharistic doctrine was issued for the declared purpose of promoting organic union between the Anglican and the
Roman Catholic Churches. In the introduction to
the statement signed by the co-chairmen, they
declared that the commission was not all out for
a comprehensive treatment of the subject but
claimed that "nothing essential has been
omitted". Their overriding intention was "to
reach a consensus at the level of faith, so that
all of us might be able to say, within the limits
of the statement: this is the christian faith of
the eucharist."[42]

---

40. ibid.
41. ibid., p.77.
42. op. cit., Windsor 1971, p.25.

While the Second World Conference on Faith and
Order at Edinburgh in 1937, cleared the ground
for an elaborate idea of Christ's sacrifice,[43]
the Montreal Faith and Order Conference came out
clearly to say that the Lord's Supper "is a sacrament of the presence of the crucified and
glorified Christ until he come, and a means
whereby the sacrifice of the cross, which we
proclaim, is operative within the Church."[44]
Despite the fact of this ecumenical background,
the Windsor Statement on the eucharistic doctrine
declines to call the eucharist a sacrifice, and
when it did, as in the elucidation text, it did
so showing signs of constraint. The commission
should have called the eucharist a sacrifice and
then use the theory of the memorial (anamnesis),
as it did to drive home the doctrine that "Yet
God has given the eucharist to his church as a
means through which the atoning work of Christ on
the cross is proclaimed and made effective in the
life of the Chruch."[45] To call the eucharist a
sacrifice would not be a problem for the Roman
Catholic members of the commission, the difficulty perhaps lies on the Anglican side. For as
one of them wrote, having said that the one subject that epitomised the tearing apart of Catholic and Protestant in the sixteenth century was
the sacrifice of the mass: he cited Cranmers
assertion and the Council of Trent's anathema and
concluded: "To what extent there may have been
mutual misunderstanding is debatable, but that

---

43. cf. footnote No. 25 of chapter Two above.
44. Rodger P.C., Vischer L. (ed.), The Report
    from Montreal London, SCM, 1964, p.74.
45. op. cit., Windsor 1971, p.27.

the rift was great is undeniable, and it was a
rift in which the Church of England was clearly
set on the Protestant side over against the
Church of Rome. With these harshly defined positions behind us, what hope had our commission of
reaching a consensus on this thorny matter."[46]

The commission asserts the presence of Christ
in the eucharist. It did not attempt to explain
the how of the presence, rather the word transubstantiation, an issue of past controversy was
treated as a footnote. The terminology is to be
understood as affirming the fact of Christ's
presence and of the mysterious and radical change
which takes place, and does not intend to explain
the manner of the change.

The commission never mentioned the issue of
reservation, which is a custom known from the
patristic times, nor the question of eucharistic
adoration in the 1971 Statement. It handled the
matter in its elucidation text of 1979. From that
explanation, it remains a fact that there are
some who would not accept the practice of eucharistic worship, and the concluding point calls
for tolerance. In the Catholic Church, eucharistic worship and adoration is a custom which
developed gradually. The Windsor Statement did
not specify the role of the ministerial priest,
who presides at the eucharistic celebration, nor
did it say something about who is the qualified
minister of the eucharist. It left open therefore
whether ordination is necessary for the one who
presides over the eucharist.

---

46. Charley Julian W. (ed.), The Anglican Roman
    Catholic Agreement on the Eucharist,
    Bramcote, Notts, Grove Books, 1972, p.16.

One notices that in the two main issues which
the commission handles, sacrifice and the real
presence, that the members are not perfectly
agreed on the notion of sacrifice or its
application to the eucharist, nor on the extent
to which Christ's presence in the eucharist
implies a transmutation of the elements.

4.3   GROUP OF LES DOMBES.

The inter-confessional Group of Les Dombes was founded in 1937 by Abbé Paul Coutier of Lyons. He was the promoter of the Week of Prayer for Christian Unity. After he had secured the support for his proposal for universal prayer in 1936, he sought to form a doctrinal working group of Catholic priests and Protestant pastors at the Trappist Monastery of Les Dombes. The Abbot of the monastery offered him the hospitable refuge which he sought. Thus, the seed of a modest institution was planted which grew and flourished until today.

The ideas of the group have converged at certain outstanding points viz: The Church as the Body of Christ, 1958; The Authority and Presidential Role of the Ministry, 1959; The Apostolic succession, 1960.[47] In 1964, the group took up the study of the Holy Spirit and the Eucharist. Their aim in studying the eucharist was to remove from it all the cotroversy that had built around it since the Reformation. Two texts were produced on the eucharist, one doctrinal, and the other pastoral. It is interesting to note that the group knows the work of Faith and Order on the Eucharist.

---

47. cf. Modern Eucharistic Agreement, London; SPCK, 1973, p.35.

4.3.1 DOCTRINAL AGREEMENT ON THE EUCHARIST.

The agreement is presented under ten sub-
headings with recommendations made at the end.
The first three paragraphs serve as the introduction. The group observed that there is an
increase of fellowship in the feelings of christians who celebrate the eucharist and proclaim
the gospel. These christians want to fulfill a
mission and to bear witness together to the same
Christ by word and deed and through their eucharistic celebration. This led the group to carefully study the call and significance for mutual
eucharistic hospitality among christians and then
came to the decision that the condition for
mutually sharing at the Lord's Table depends on
reaching a substantial agreement on what the
eucharist is.

4.3.1.1 THE EUCHARIST: THE LORD'S SUPPER.

The group says that the eucharist is the sacramental meal, the new paschal meal of the
people of God. Christ gave the eucharist to his
disciples to celebrate in the light of his resurrection until his next coming. Explaining further
the document says: "This meal is the effective
sign of the gift that Christ made of himself as
the bread of life, through the sacrifice of his
life and his death and by his resurrection."[48]

---

48. Gaughen Pamela (translated), Group of Les
    Dombes, Toward a Common Eucharistic Faith,
    Agreement between Roman Catholics and
    Protestants, in: Modern Eucharistic
    Agreement, London, SPCK, 1973, p.57. Further
    quotations as: Group of Les Dombes.

It is in the eucharist that Christ fulfills in a
surpassing manner his promise to be among those
who gather in his name.

4.3.1.2 THE EUCHARIST: ACT OF THANKSGIVING TO THE FATHER

As expressed in an earlier agreement by Faith
and Order Commission, the Group of Les Dombes
joins them to say that the eucharist is the great
act of thanksgiving to the Father for all the
works of creation and redemption of the world,
and for what he does presently for the coming of
his kingdom. In the eucharist, therefore the
church gives thanks to God for all his benefits.
The document employs the sacrificial language and
says: "The Eucharist is the great sacrifice of
praise in which the Church speaks in the name of
all creation. For the world which God reconciled
with himself in Christ is present at each eucharist."[49] The eucharist also opens up to the world
the way to its transfiguration.

4.3.1.3 THE EUCHARIST: MEMORIAL OF CHRIST.

The document submits that Christ instituted
the eucharist as a memorial (anamnesis) of his
whole life and above all of the cross and resurrection. Christ is present in this memorial, with
everything he has accomplished for all creation;
and this memorial is a foretaste of his kingdom.

---

49. op. cit., p.58.

When the church celebrates this memorial, Christ
acts through her and this implies re-presentation
and anticipation. The memorial is not a mere
recalling to mind of past event or its significance, rather it is "the effective proclamation
by the Church of the great work of God." The
church participates in this reality from which it
draws its life by its communion with Christ.

The church lives out this memorial in thanksgiving and intercession. The document explains
how in this memorial the church presents to the
Father a perfect sacrifice: "Making the memorial
of the passion, resurrection, and ascension of
Christ, our High Priest and Mediator, the Church
presents to the Father the one perfect sacrifice
of his Son and asks him to accord every man the
benefit of the great work of redemption it proclaims."[50]

The members of Christ benefit from his perfect
sacrifice and in commemorating it they also offer
themselves with Christ. "Thus united to our Lord,
who offers himself to his Father, and in communion with the universal Church in heaven and on
earth, we are renewed in the covenant sealed with
the blood of Christ and we offer ourselves as a
living and holy sacrifice which must be expressed
in the whole of our daily life."[51] The document
also submits that the proclaimed word of God and
the eucharist are the essential content of the
memorial of Christ.
Both go hand in hand for the ministry of the word
is directed towards the eucharist and the eucharist

---

50. op. cit., p.58.
51. ibid.

in turn implies and fulfils the word.

4.3.1.4 THE EUCHARIST: GIFT OF THE SPIRIT.

Our document maintains that the memorial
(anamnesis) implies the invocation of the Spirit
(epiclesis). It is Christ in his heavenly intercession who asks the Father to send his Spirit to
his children. The church in turn prays with confidence for the Spirit, who will renew her in
truth and strengthen her to fulfil her mission in
the world.
The role of the Spirit is further explained.
"It is the Spirit which, invoked over the congre-
tation, over the bread and wine, makes Christ
really present to us, gives him to us and enables
us to perceive him."[52] The product of anamnesis
and epiclesis is communion, because being directed towards our union with Christ, it cannot be
accomplished independently of the communion.
Hence the gift of the Holy Spirit is regarded as
a foretaste of the kingdom of God; thus the
church receives the life of the new creation and
the assurance of the Lord's return. In order to
clear the issue of the moment of consecration,
the document says that it recognizes the eucharistic prayer as a whole to posses the character
of an epiclesis.

---

52. Group of Les Dombes, p.59.

4.3.1.5 THE SACRAMENTAL PRESENCE OF CHRIST.

The document recognizes the eucharist as the
gift of Christ's person. Having quoted the words
of the institution of the eucharist the group
affirms: "We accordingly confess unanimously the
real, living, and effective presence of Christ in
this sacrament."[53] Christ's presence in the eucharist does not depend on the faith of the individual but at the same time faith is required to
discern his presence. It is Christ himself who
freely binds himself in his words and in the
Spirit to the sacramental act, the sign of his
given presence.

The elements of bread and wine are the signs
of Christ's gift of his body and blood. The bread
and wine are made the sacrament of the body and
blood of Christ by virtue of Christ's creative
word and by the power of the Holy Spirit; and
"They are henceforth, in their ultimate truth,
beneath the outward sign, the given reality, and
so they remain, since their purpose is to be
consumed."[54] With the statement, "what is given
as the body and blood of Christ remains given as
his body and blood and requires to be treated as
such", the group begins to handle the issue of
reservation of the sacrament. To the Roman Catholic side, it requests that they point out through
preaching and cathechesis, that the primary purpose of reserving the elements used in the eucharistic celebration is for its distribution to the
sick and those absent. And to the Protestant side,

_____

53. ibid.
54. ibid.

it reminds also that the best means be adopted of
showing respect due to the elements that have
served for the celebration of the eucharist,
which is to consume them subsequently, without
precluding their use for the communion of the
sick.

4.3.1.6 THE EUCHARIST: COMMUNION IN THE BODY OF CHRIST.

The attempt here is to stress the union of all
in Christ, who share in his body and blood. The
sharing of the one bread and the one cup in a
given place, makes the communicants one with
Christ, and one with another, at all times and in
all places. The membership of the communicants to
the universal church is manifested through the
sharing of the one bread; to their eyes the
mystery of redemption is revealed and the whole
body grows in grace. In a nutshell, therefore,
"The communion is thus the source and strength of
all community life among christians."

The contradiction in the life of the communicants is here deplored. First of all, Christ by
his cross, has broken down all the barriers that
separate men. This means that we cannot communicate with Christ in truth if the barriers he has
broken persist in the church especially that
which separates races, nationalities, languages,
classes and denominations.

The document outlines also what the believer
receives in the eucharist according to Christ's
promise as: "the remission of his sins and everlasting life and is fed with the food of faith,

hope, and love". The fellowship in the eucharistic communion in the body of Christ, in the opinion of the group, should be expressed in the liturgy: "by the mutual forgiveness of sins, the kiss of peace, the offering of gifts to be used for community meals or for distribution to brothers in need, the brotherly welcome extended to all regardless of political, social or cultural differences."[55]

4.3.1.7 THE EUCHARIST: A MISSION IN THE WORLD

For the church to be itself, its mission is part of its life and this mission traces its origin back to the eucharist, and in the eucharist also is the church fully itself and is united with Christ in his mission. The Church carries out her mission when in the eucharistic thanksgiving she prays for the world and in the eucharistic memorial, where she is united with Christ the Redeemer and Mediator, the church prays for the world, in the invocation of the Holy Spirit to sanctify and renew creation.

The church carries out her mission in the world through her members, who are first of all reconciled in the eucharist, and thereafter become servants of reconciliation among men and bear witness to the joy of the resurrection. They identify themselves with those suffering by giving them hope and witness the love of Christ in service and combat. The implications of their communion with Christ and with one another in-

---

55. op. cit., Group of Les Dombes, p.59.

cites them to the course of those who are deprived of food, justice and peace. The document
then called the eucharist "the feast of the perpetual apostolic harvest, in which the Church
rejoices for the gifts received in the world."[56]

4.3.1.8 THE EUCHARIST: BANQUET OF THE KINGDOM.

The eschatological dimension of the eucharist
is considered under this sub-heading. The document submits that "Our Lord instituted the eucharist for the time from his ascension until his
coming again." In this period of hope, the eucharist not only directs our thoughts to the Lord's
coming, it brings it near to us. For "it is a
joyful anticipation of the heavenly banquet, when
redemption shall be fully accomplished and all
creation shall be delivered from bondage."[57] The
eucharist therefore enables the church to take
new heart and to perservere in the midst of
suffering and strife. The document sees the final
gathering as an ecumenical meeting place. "This
Church that Christ feeds throughout its pilgrimage perceives, above and beyond the divisions
that still persist, that the eschatological
meeting-place is an ecumenical meeting-place,
where Israel and all the nations will be gathered
into one people."[58]

---

56. op. cit., Group of Les Dombes, p.62.
57. ibid.
58. ibid.

4.3.1.9 THE PRESIDENCY OF THE EUCHARIST.

The document first talks about Christ, how he
gathers together and feeds his church at the meal
over which he presides. This sign of Christ's
presidency is given in the presiding minister who
represents him. Christ calls him and sends him.
The mission of the minister has its root on that
of the apostles and it is transmitted to the
church by the imposition of hands and the invocation of the Holy Spirit. This transmission implies the continuity of the ministry, fidelity to
apostolic teaching, and a life lived according to
the gospel.

The role or sign of the minister consists in
the fact that to the congregation he is a pointer
or sign that Christ is the master of the eucharist. The minister is also the person sent to
signify God's action in the worshipping congregation; the link between the local community and
other communities in the minister and the worshipping community vis-à-vis Christ the Lord, is
thus synthesized: "In their mutual relations, the
eucharistic gathering and its president live
their dependence on the one Lord and great High
Priest. In its relation to the minister, the congregation is exercising its royal priesthood
conferred on it by Christ, the priest. In his
relation to the congregation, the minister is
living his presidency as the servant of Christ,
the pastor."[59]

---

59. ibid, p.63.

In conclusion the group expressed their awareness for further clarifications as regards the
permanence of the sacramental presence of Christ
in the eucharist, and the precise place of apostolic succession in the ministry. The group did
not claim to have exhausted the mystery of the
eucharist which it says is beyond all understanding. It calls for the abandonment of everything that is marked by controversy within the
various denominations to allow for joint participation in the eucharist.

The group finally recommended that eucharistic
communion should no longer be with-held from
christians whose faith corresponds to that professed in this agreement on the eucharist.

4.3.2 PASTORAL AGREEMENT.
THE MEANING OF THE EUCHARIST.

The group of Les Dombes indicated in the general introduction to both texts, that the work and
agreement on the Pastoral Agreement on the eucharist was embarked upon on the request of chap-
lains and youth movements, Catholics and Protestants alike. The text, they directed should be
read as a prolongation of the doctrinal agreement
on the eucharist.

I. The text takes off once again from the
institution of the eucharist; the biblical texts
are quoted and thereafter it concludes: "With
these words he invited his disciples to repeat
his action and christians to respond to that

invitation by coming together to celebrate the eucharist."[60]

II. In the eucharist we gather around Christ to meet him. During this gathering the decisive events whereby we are reconciled to God and to one another are made present and real, but they are not repeated. Christ, who embraces the congregation in his offering commits them to love and to serve their brothers.

III. The text affirms the real presence of Christ in the eucharist, and goes on to show that in consuming the bread and wine of the eucharist, it is the whole person of Christ that is consumed. The eucharist nourishes the life received at baptism, and prepares for its fulfilment in our resurrection.

IV. The text submits that the eucharist is celebrated in the Holy Spirit, and depicts the action of the church in the invocation. "In the eucharistic prayer the Church asks for the promised coming of the Holy Spirit in order to receive and discern the presence of our Lord and to draw life from his death and resurrection."[61]

V. In the fifth paragraph the text treats the minister of the eucharist. Just as Christ chose his apostles, maintains the text, so also today does he choose the ministers to gather the church together in prayer and guide her in its mission. In the eucharistic celebration, the presence of the minister serves as the sign of Christ himself presiding at the meal whereby he gives his body

---

60. op. cit., p.65.
61. op. cit., p.66.

to be eaten. The minister is that sign of communion between the local church and the universal
church.

VI. The eucharist is described as a force for
the liberation of mankind. Christ freed and reconciled man through his works of redemption. He
carries on this work through the action of the
Holy Spirit and the ministry of the church. On
accepting his invitation to the eucharistic meal,
we are also accepting the responsibility to carry
out his mission and to follow in his footsteps.
That implies that the christians will have to
fight against the forces of oppression, destruc-
tion and death in order to reconcile all things
and everything to God.

VII. Finally the eucharist is described as the
source of unity. This is so because the eucharist
is given to us to be eaten and by this action the
participants are united with Christ and with one
another. "When Christ gives himself to us in the
eucharist, he is leading us towards union in his
body, with all communicants at all times and in
all places. Thereby he receives our hope of reaching it and strengthens our will to strive for
it."[62] Inspite of the gift of the eucharist, the
source of unity the christians live in the state
of separation and disunity. The text calls this a
scandal and deplores the inability of the christians to overcome their confessional differences. The text emphasizes the more, the gift of
unity in the eucharist saying: "As Christ inten-

---

62. op. cit., p.67.

ded it, the gift of the eucharist overrides our
divisions, not by denying or concealing them, but
by giving us today the pledge and effective sign
of the unity he is always asking his Father: 'May
they all be one...so that the world may believe.' "[63]

4.3.3 ASSESSMENT.

The Group of Les Dombes has the intention of
producing a common eucharistic creed, which will
eventually allow communion of the separated churches in the eucharist. Their intention also includes ridding this mystery of the controversy
that was built around it since the Reformation.
The group claimed to have reached agreement as to
what is essential in the doctrine of the
eucharist.

How did the group treat the eucharist as a
sacrifice? Like the Windsor Statement, the Group
of Les Dombes did not call the eucharist a sacrifice. It only said that 'the eucharist is the
great sacrifice of praise in which the church
speaks in the name of all creation'. It is in the
issue of memorial (anamnesis) that the document
came out boldly and described the celebration of
the eucharist in terms of sacrife presented to
the Father by the church. Memorial itself is not
merely calling to mind of a past event rather it
is "the effective proclamation by the church of
the great work of God." In celebrating the me-

---

63. ibid.

morial of Christ, "the Church presents to the
Father the one perfect sacrifice of his Son and
asks him to accord every man the benefit of the
great work of redemption it proclaims." The one
perfect sacrifice of Christ is also the sacrifice
of atonement for the sins of man, through which
Christ brought about reconciliation between God
and man. As the document talked about memorial as
re-presentation, the notion of atonement can be
said to be inclusive. This does not mean that
Christ suffers anew in each eucharistic memorial,
but rather through the celebration of the
memorial, we are purified and our sins are forgiven.

The group did not border itself with the moment of consecration, rather it recognizes the
eucharistic prayer as a whole, as having the
character of epiclesis.

The document asserts Christ's real presence in
the eucharist. The duration of Christ's presence
in the reserved element was not handled satis-
factorily. For the group, the eucharistic elements are destined to be consumed and there was
no mention of eucharistic adoration or worship of
the reserved sacrament, although this is a living
custom in the Roman Catholic Church.

The document took a step forward in considering the minister of the eucharist. It
recognized the person of the minister as a
sign of unity that links the local church with
the universal church. It failed to point out what
meaning that is to be given to the apostolic
succession, in determining the proper minister of
the eucharist. It shows some ambiguity when it
said that the apostolic succession is given to

the church through the imposition of hands and
the invocation of the Holy Spirit without relating it at once to the minister through whom it
is transmitted.

4.4   LUTHERAN / ROMAN CATHOLIC.

4.4.1 HISTORICAL BACKGROUND.

During the Second Vatican Council contact was established between the Roman Catholic Church and the Lutheran World Federation. This contact led to the formation of a Lutheran/Roman Catholic Working Group, which met at Strasbourg, France, in August 1965 and in April 1966. Later in 1967, the authorities of the two Churches appointed a study commission of international composition and assigned to it the topic "The Gospel and the Church". The commission did its work and the result known as the "Malta Report", was published in 1972.

In 1973 a mixed commission of six members from each side was created. The new commission had two principal assignments: (a) the discussion of the Malta Report at the local church level, in ecumenical institutes, etc and (b) a deepened study of doctrinal points arising from the Malta Report. At the commission's meeting in January 1974, agreement was reached that these points centre on themes of the eucharist and ministry with special concern for the episcopacy. Thereafter two sub-commissions were created, the one was assigned the eucharist, the other the ministry.

The task for the sub-commission handling the eucharist "was not to produce an original study in the strict sense but rather to produce a synthesis of the various documents that have been published as the results of various colloquia while of course adapting them to the current

problems in the Lutheran/Catholic situation."[64]
The document on the eucharist was worked over in
two sessions of the full commission meeting at
Strasbourg, France, in March 1966, and in
Paderborn, Federal Republic of Germany in March
1977. Thereafter it was published in 1978 after
slight revision.

Our document, the Eucharist, has two major
parts. The first part is tagged 'Joint Witness',
and it expresses what the Lutherans and the
Catholics are able to confess jointly; the second
part named `Joint Tasks', identifies and
discusses points of disagreement. The first has
seven sub-headings while the second has three.

JOINT WITNESS.
4.4.2 THE LEGACY OF CHRIST ACCORDING TO THE
SCRIPTURE.

The document takes off with the narration of
the institution of the eucharist, quoting the
scriptural sources: Mt26:26-29; Mk 14:22-25;
Lk22:16-20; 1Cor11:23-26; and thereafter says:
"In this new passover meal the Lord gave himself
as nourishment to his disciples and thus, in
anticipation of his glory, made them partkers in
his work, life and suffering."[65]

---

64. S.P.C.U. IS (1977) No. 33, p.21.
65. Lutheran/Roman Catholic Joint Commission, The
    Eucharist, Geneva, The Lutheran World
    Federation, 1980, p.4. cf. S.P.C.U. IS (1979)
    No. 39 pp. 22-35.
    Further quotations as: The Eucharist.

4.4.2.1 MYSTERY OF FAITH.

Our document submits that the eucharist is a
mystery of faith in the fullest sense of the
word. The only possibility open to human beings
to recognize the mystery, is through God's self
communication and even at that, it enters the
range of our vision only to the extent that the
Lord wills and effects. Therefore the only way in
which the eucharist is accessible to us is
through the divine gift of faith.

It is this divine gift of faith that is responsible for the attitudes and actions of those
who participate in the eucharistic celebration.
The eucharistic community of life grows out of the
community of faith through the Holy Spirit. The
christian faith is that which is essentially
shared with all fellow believers. In this sense
therefore: "The Eucharist is primarily an affair
of the community and through this individuals.
Like the 'new covenant', 'the blood of the
covenant' given in the eucharist...is granted to
the new people of God and thus to its members."[66]

The document goes on to say that all grace and
truth are now in our midst, in our Lord present
in the eucharist, which is also a mystery of
faith. The mystery of faith as it is celebrated
in the eucharist reflects different phases of
salvation, namely: God's good creation for which
we give thanks and praise; bread and wine,
earthly things taken into the process of salvation and healing, is followed by basic feature of
human life, eating and drinking and communal

66. op. cit., The Eucharist, p.5.

celebration and action; thus "the union of christians with their Lord and with each other is
both the proclamation and the beginning of God's
kingdom in our midst and a promise of the coming
fulfilment."[67]

The mystery of the eucharist unites us to the
ultimate mystery of the triune God. Thus our
heavenly Father is the source and final goal of
the eucharistic event; the incarnate Son of God
is the living centre of the eucharistic event,
and the Holy Spirit is the immesurable power of
love which gives the eucharist life and lasting
effect. This profound mystery of the eucharist is
clearly expressed in the doxology that comes at
the end of many eucharistc prayers.

"Though him, with him, in him
in the unity of the Holy Spirit
all honour and glory is yours, almighty Father
now and forever. Amen."[68]

The next three sub-headings is so structured
to correspond to the role of the Tinity, in the
order in which they are mentioned in the
doxology.

4.4.2.2 THROUGH, WITH AND IN CHRIST.

It is only through Jesus Christ that the eucharist exists. He celebrated it first in the
circle of his disciples and commissioned them to
celebrate it in his remembrance until he comes
again. It is Christ who prepares the Supper and

---

67. ibid.
68. op. cit., p.5.

extends the invitation. The conscious and active
participation of the believers in the eucharistic
event is made possible and actual through Christ.
It is through Christ that the ministers who
preside at the eucharistic celebration are called
and commissioned, and their service thus shows
that the congregation is not the master of the
eucharist, but Christ living in his Church.

Speaking about the presence of Christ in the
eucharist the document says first and foremost
that "through him we can celebrate the Eucharist
with him", and that the wonder of his presence
occurs in the power of his grace alone. It went
further to enumerate the different modes of
Christ's presence. It quoted from the agreement
reached in the United States of America between
Lutherans and Catholics on this issue. This includes that Christ is present in his body, the
people of God; in baptism for it is he who bapti-
zes; in the scriptures and in the proclamation of
the gospel; and in the poor and the distressed.
Quoting also from Windsor Statement, it underlines Christ's mode of presence in the eucharist
and then sums up by saying: "In the sacrament of
the Lord's Supper Jesus Christ, true God and true
man, is present wholly and entirely, in his body
and blood, under the signs of bread and wine."[69]

The presence of Christ in the eucharist is
real, true and substantial. The manner of the
real presence can scarcely be expressed in words,
rather trusting on the promise of Christ at the
institution of the eucharist, the two traditions
speak of his presence as sacramental, supernatural

---

69. op. cit., The Eucharist, p.7.

and spiritual. These terms have different connotations in the two churches, but both join hands
in rejecting a spatial or natural manner of presence as well as an understanding of the sacrament as only commemorative or figurative.

On anamnesis, the document made the corresponding paragraph from the Accra Text, its own by
quoting it verbatim.[70] That is to say, that
Christ instituted the eucharist, sacrament of his
body and blood with its focus upon the cross and
resurrection, as anamnesis of the whole of God's
reconciling action in him. Christ is present in
the anamnesis and anamnesis is understood as the
foretaste of his Parousia and the fulfilment of
the kingdom.

Having asserted that Christ is present in the
eucharist and explained what anamnesis implies,
the document goes on to show what the christians
together with Christ do in the eucharist. "With
him and through his grace we have passed from
death to life. Participating in the eucharistic
sacrament, we are on pilgrimage with him from
this world to the world to come. Endowed and
quickened by his Spirit we may hand on his love
and so glorify the Father. The more powerless we
are to offer to God a worthy sacrifice so much
more shall we be taken up by the power of Christ
into his offering."[71] Then summarising this
thought it joins its voice with the Group of Les
Dombes in saying: "Thus united to our Lord, who
offers himself to his Father, and in communion
with the universal Church in heaven and on earth,

---

70. cf. The Eucharist, Accra Text, No. 8.
71. op. cit., The Eucharist, p.7.

we are renewed in the covenant sealed with the
blood of Christ and we offer ourselves as a
living and holy sacrifice which must be expressed
in the whole of our daily life."[72]

The document links beign-with-Christ to the
climax of beign-in-Christ. In his offering of
himself as nourishment under the signs of bread
and wine, the Lord shows himself to be the
"living bread which came down from heaven."[73]
Receiving this food in faith the believer is
taken into communion with Christ, which is
likened to the communion of the Son with the
Father.[74] The climax of this beign-in-Christ is
demonstrated from John's gospel: "He who eats my
flesh and drinks my blood abides in me, and I in
him".[75] And furthermore: "He who eats this bread
will live for ever." The document shows also that
this union with Christ is not just with an individual, rather "In giving himself Christ unites
all who partake at his table: the many become
"one body" (1Cor10:17). In the power of the Holy
Spirit, they are built up as the one people of
God. The eucharistic meal is thus the source of
the daily new life of the people of God who
through it are gathered together and kept in one
faith."[76]

---

72. op. cit., p.8. cf. Dombes I, No. 11.
73. cf. Jn 6:51.
74. cf. Jn 6:57.
75. cf. Jn 6:56, 58.
76. op. cit., The Eucharist, p.8.

4.4.2.3 IN THE UNITY OF THE HOLY SPIRIT.

Before the document goes on to speak about the
Holy Spirit and the eucharist it mentioned the
following facts: that Jesus Christ, during his
earthly life, did all things in the Holy
Spirit;[77] That he offered himself as a sacrifice
in the power of the Spirit;[78] and it is through
the Holy Spirit that he conquered sin and death
and rose from the dead and lives in his Pentecost
community. It is also through the Spirit that
Christ is at work in the eucharist. The christians, therefore are to remain bound to Christ
and continue his work through the Spirit. For the
christians to make their own, all that the Lord
gives, is possible only through the Holy Spirit,
and this shines out clearly in the liturgy during
the invocation of the Holy Spirit.

What then happens in the eucharist through the
Holy Spirit is put in this way: "In remembrance
of the intercession of Christ, its high priest,
the Church asks with confidence for his spirit,
in order to be renewed and sanctified through the
eucharistic gifts and so strengthened to accomplish its mission in the world. In the power of
the Holy Spirit the bread and wine become the
body and blood of Christ through the creative
word. The spirit of love causes the sacrament of
love to become real in that the divine love seeks
us in our earthly reality in order to bring us
home again."[79]

The congregation which celebrates the eucharist

---

77. cf. Lk4:1, 14, 17-21.
78. cf. Heb9:14.
79. op. cit., The Eucharist, p.9.

cannot simply celebrate except that it received
the faith through the Holy Spirit. So, then, when
the invocation of the Spirit is made, it is the
prayer for a living faith which prepares the
congregation to celebrate the anamnesis of
Christ. The document underlines the importance of
the presence of the Holy Spirit within the believers to appropriate the eucharist, which is a
means of salvation for the world.

At this juncture the document speaks briefly
about the eschatological aspect of the eucharist
and the role of the Holy Spirit. The sub-heading
seven is devoted to this aspect later. The document then says: "In the fruits of the Holy Spirit
- the love, joy and peace which believers receive
in the Eucharist in a special way - the ultimate
fulfilment of all things is anticipated. The
Eucharist is the meal celebrated in expectation
of his coming in glory for the strenghtening of
the faithful. The invocation of the Holy Spirit
is (accordingly) a plea for the future world to
break into our present one."[80]

Our document now speaks about the relationship
between the church and the eucharist. It starts
with baptism through which one becomes incorporated into the body of Christ, the Church. All
are baptized by the one Spirit into the one body;
are nourished by the body of Christ; and through
the Holy Spirit become ever one body.[81] Hence it
concludes: "The Eucharist and the Church are
thus, in manifold ways, linked together in a
living bond."[82] The document further submits that

---

80. ibid.
81. cf. 1Cor12:13; 10:17.
82. op. cit., The Eucharist, p.9.

the christians by partaking of the body and blood
of Christ, become what they receive. That is to
say that through the eucharist, the life of
Christ becomes the life of his people and his
Spirit. The eucharist then is the source and
climax of the Church's life, and one can also
say: "without the eucharistic community there is
no full ecclesial community, and without the
ecclesial community there is no real eucharistic
community."[83]

This statement is true not only of the congregation gathered locally to celebrate the eucharist but also of the universal church; so that
the sharing of the one loaf and the common cup in
a place may signify the oneness of the sharers in
all times and places. This trancends the limits
of earthly reality for the Holy Spirit unites us
with those who have gone before in faith, and have
been called to eternal communion with God. The
unity bestowed by Christ lives on inspite of the
fact of sin against this unity in various ways
and a call is made for a united action against
the forces that tend to perpetuate this disunity.

4.4.2.4 GLORIFICATION OF THE FATHER.

In line with its doxological presentation of
the eucharist, the document begins this sub-heading by saying that "The union with Christ into
which we are drawn in the Eucharist through the
power of the Holy Spirit ultimately leads to the
eternal Father. This occurs at different levels

---

83. op. cit., p.10.

and in varying, yet internally related ways."[84]

The first of these internally related ways considered is the eucharist as proclamation. The eucharist as a whole is understood as proclaiming the greatness and mercy of God. Each of the eucharistic elements receives a particular significance appropriate to its nature. Among these are: the confession of sins; the reading and exposition of the scriptures; the recitation of the early christian creeds. Others are bread and wine, which "are first and foremost gifts of the Father that epitomize his creation", and finally the eucharistic meal; thus "each eucharistic meal testifies to that love for the whole world made manifest on the cross by God who gave his son for the world. 'For as often as you eat this bread and drink this cup, you proclaim the Lord's death until he comes.'"[85]

The next way is thanksgiving which is linked with proclamation. The eucharist is explained in terms of thanksgiving to the Father. We thank the Father in the eucharist for all that he has accomplished in creation, redemption and sanctification of man and the world. We thank the Father also for what he accomplishes now in the Church and in the world, and for everything that he does in bringing his kingdom to fulfilment. In a nutshell: "The eucharist is the benediction (berakah) by which the Church expresses its thankfulness to God for all his benefits."[86]

The congregation expresses this thanksgiving to God verbally as well as materially. The self-

---

84. ibid.
85. ibid. p.11.
86. ibid.

giving of Christ and the promise of the kingdom
makes us concious of the fact that God is the
giver and we ourselves as the servant of these
gifts. Hence "in the offering of bread and wine
we praise God who through our work provides us
with the earthly gifts necessary for our life. We
offer ourselves and share one with the other what
has been given us."[87]

The congregation at the eucharistic celebration intercedes for all men, for the needs of the
world, for the concerns of the faithful and of
those who have special responsibilities in the
church and society. In this way the church is
united with the intercession its Lord is making
before the Father in heaven, and pleads through
the world, the foretaste of which she has received in the eucharist in faith and hope through
the Holy Spirit.

The next inter-related way of speaking about
the eucharist is praise. The document submits
that the eucharist is the great sacrifice of
praise by which the church speaks on behalf of
the whole creation. This praise was once silenced
through the fall of man and brought to life again
through Christ. The eucharistic assembly sings
its praise to worship the Father in spirit and in
truth, especially in the Preface and Sanctus.

Next the document speaks about self-giving, in
other words about sacrifice. It states that the
Lord is present in giving his body for his own,
and in pouring out his blood for them. He is
present among us as the one given by the Father
in the Holy Spirit, and also as the one giving

---

87. ibid.

himself to the Father and for mankind in the Holy
Spirit. In this way, he gives himself and wills
to continue to be effective. The Church, the
celebrating community is drawn into this act of
self-offering and the more it is drawn to it, the
more it lives to the greater glory of God. The
Church which proclaims Christ's death, that is,
his sacrifice, is summoned to be taken up in this
sacrifice, so that in dying with its Lord, the
Church will be prepared to rise with him.

The union of himself which Christ offers,
affects the desires and acts of his people, so
much so that when the Church carries out the
Lord's command: "Do this in rememberance of me",
'it comes in contact with the sacrifice of Christ
anew: it receives new life from him and the power
to die with him."[88]

Applying the notion of memorial as it is
understood in the passover celebration at the
time of Christ, the document established a relationship between Christ's sacrifice and the eucharist.[89] It went on to say: "In the memorial
celebration of the people of God more happens
than that past events are brought to mind by this
power of recall and imagination. The decisive
point is not that what is past is called to mind,
but that the Lord calls his people into his presence and confronts them with his salvation. In
this creative act of God, the salvation event
from the past becomes the offer of salvation for
the future."[90]

The benefits that come to those who celebrate

---

88. op. cit., The Eucharist, p.12.
89. cf. Windsor Statement, No. 5.
90. op. cit., The Eucharist, p. 13.

the eucharist are then outlined. They are incorporated in Christ's life, passion, death and
resurrection; they receive the fruit of Christ's
offering of his life, and of the entire reconciling saving act of God; they are set free and
united with God and with one another. They give
thanks "for all his mercies, entreat the benefits
of his passion on behalf of the whole church,
participate in these benefits and enter into the
movement of self-offering."[91] Moreover in faith,
they are taken as the body of Christ into the
reconciling sacrifice which equips them for self-
giving and enables them through Christ to offer
spiritual sacrifices in service to the world. In
the Lord's Supper then is rehearsed what is practised in the whole christian life and as our
document put it: "with contrite hearts we offer
ourselves as a living and holy sacrifice, as a
sacrifice which must be expressed in the whole of
our daily lives."[92]

To round this section, the document brings out
what the two churches could say together in their
understanding of the eucharist as sacrifice. "Our
two traditions agree in understanding the Eucharist as a sacrifice of praise. This is neither
simple verbal praise of God, nor is it a supple-
ment or a complement which people from their own
power add to the offering or praise and thanksgiving which Christ has made to the Father. The
eucharistic sacrifice of praise has only become
possible through the sacrifice of Christ on the
cross: therefore this remains the main content of

---

91. ibid.
92. ibid.

the Church's sacrifice of praise. Only 'by him,
with him, and in him who is our great High Priest
and Intercessor we offer to the Father, in the
power of the Holy Spirit, our praise, thanksgiving and intercession.'"[93]

4.4.2.5 FOR THE LIFE OF THE WORLD.

The document takes off here by stating that
Jesus Christ, his life and movement towards the
Father is meant for the life of the world. The
eucharist is related to the world, in that "the
world which God in Christ reconciled with Himself
is present at each eucharist: in the bread and
the wine, in the persons of the faithful and in
the prayers they offer for all humankind. Thus
the eucharist opens up to the world the way to its
transfiguration."[94] The eucharist also reveals to
the world what it is and what it is to become,
and concentrates in itself all dimensions of
historical growth, for it is "rooted in the past,
translated into reality in the present, and
directed to the future". In the eucharistic unity
the new unity of mankind begins to emerge. This
unity in the eucharist shows itself, when at the
invitation of the same Lord, the believers partake of the same loaf, and through it they become
one in commitment to Christ, to one another and
to the mission of the Church in the world.

As the eucharist is directed towards the
salvation of the world, so also are the christians

93. ibid.
94. op. cit., The Eucharist, p.14. cf. Dombes I,
    no.8.

who celebrate it called to service to the world.
These christians are capable to carry this
responsibility to the world because in the
eucharist, they are reconciled with God in Christ
and they in turn become servants of reconciliation among men and witnesses of the joy of resurrection. They manifest their solidarity with
the suffering and fight against injustice in the
world. Their action is particularly necessary to
ward off social, national or racial divisions in
the Church, for such divisions may not only precipitate schism in faith, but also contradict the
nature of the Church and render its witness ineffective and its sacramental celebration unw-
orthy.

4.4.2.6 WITH A VIEW TO THE FUTURE GLORY.

The eschatological dimension of the eucharist
is considered here. It opens well with the remark
that "in the Eucharist we proclaim 'the Lord's
death until he comes.'" In the eucharist the
future glory is promised, as well as revealed and
mediated. The form and the effect of the eucharist, says, our document, are a promise of the
eternal glory to which we are destined, and a
sign pointing to the new heaven and to the new
earth towards which we are moving. Then quoting
from the Group of Les Dombes, it says: "That is
why the eucharist directs our thoughts to the
Lord's coming and brings it near to us. It is a
joyful anticipation of the heavenly banquet, when
redemption shall be fully accomplished and all

creation shall be delivered from bondage."[95]

The eucharist enables us to understand the future glory as the boundless and eternal wedding feast to which we are invited by the Lord. It turns our gaze to the promised eternal kingdom of unlimited freedom and righteousness. Hence "Those who celebrate together are called to join personal commitment and communal service, and thereby to point to that fulfilment of personal and social life which belongs to the glory of God, the glory in which by his grace we may share."[96]

The eucharist is spoken of in terms of mediation to attain the promise which lies in the future. As John the Evangelist put it, "He who receives the bread of life has eternal life."[97]

The future then is opened to him in a mysterious way so that one can say that the everlasting life does not begin in the future, but is already present in anyone who is united with the Lord. In other words the future world breaks into our present through the eucharist even now.

In conclusion, the document says: ""Thus, by giving the eucharist to his Church, which in its weakness, will live to the last in the midst of suffering and strife, our Lord enables it to take new heart and to persevere"; he gives it the power to work untiringly for the renewal of the life and structures of the world. The life of the world to come promised, disclosed and mediated to believers, shall and must become effective already in this world."[98]

---

95. op. cit., p.15. cf. Dombes I, no. 29.
96. ibid.
97. Jn6:54.
98. op. cit., The Eucharist, p.16.

4.4.3 COMMON TASKS.

The second part of our document identifies and discusses points of disagreement. The overall intention is that "controverted positions which hinder complete fellowship of faith and Eucharist must be recognized, described and faced with the purpose of recognizing and overcoming what is divisive."[99]

4.4.3.1 EUCHARISTIC PRESENCE.

The first among the controverted issues to be discussed was the presence of Christ in the eucharist, focusing attention on the Catholic doctrine of Transubstantiation. The Council of Trent teaches that "by the consecration of the bread and wine a change is brought about of the whole substance of the bread into the substance of the body of Christ our Lord, and of the whole substance of the wine into the substance of his blood. This change the holy Catholic Church properly and appropriately calls transubstantiation."[100] The Lutherans contend that this terminology is a rational attempt to explain the mystery of Christ's presence in the eucharist, and

---

99. op. cit., p.17.
100. DS 1641, quoted according to: Rahner K. (ed.), The Teaching of the Catholic Church, New York, Alba House 1967, p.288.

therefore do not accept it. As we already saw in
the Windsor Statement and mentioned in this document, transubstantiation is intended as a confession and preservation of the mystery character of
the eucharistic presence; it is not intended as
an explanation of how this change occurs.[101] With
this explanation and the fact that Catholics and
Lutherans confess the real, true and substantial
presence of Christ in the eucharist,[102] the disagreement on this issue is thus minimised, but
disagreement continues on the question of the
duration of the eucharistic presence.

The Catholics have the custom of reserving the
sacrament first and foremost for its use for the
communion of the sick and secondly for eucharistic worship and adoration. The Lutherans argue
that the eucharistic adoration deviates from the
meal character of the eucharist. For the
Lutherans the best way of showing respect to the
elements is their eventual consumption. It is
necessary to recall what the two churches hold
together to see to what extent that will help us
to appreciate or solve the problem. In this document it is said: "Catholic and Lutheran christians together confess that the eucharistic
presence of the Lord Jesus Christ is directed
toward believing reception, that it nevertheless
is not confined only to the moment of reception,
and that it does not depend on the faith of the
receiver however closely related to this it might
be."[103]

In order to find a solution to the problem, it

---

101. cf. Windsor Statement, no. 6, note 2.
102. cf. op. cit., The Eucharist, p.7. no. 16.
103. op. cit., p.18.

is interesting to point out what two scholars, a
Lutheran and a Catholic, both members of the
commission said in an essay jointly written on:
"The Presence of Christ in the Eucharist." They
wrote: "Although the Reformers called for an
attitude of respect towards the residual consecrated elements, they condemned the Catholic
custom that required "the bread (to be) locked up
in the tabernacle or (to be) carried about as a
spectacle and for adoration", because the Lord's
Supper and the presence of Christ are wholly
orientated towards reception."[104] The two
scholars explained the Catholic side further
saying: "It is true that even the Catholic side
says the use of the consecrated host for the
communion of the sick, and not its adoration, is
the 'first and original purpose' of its reservation. At the same time, however, one has to note
that adoration of the reserved sacrament has been
very much a part of Catholic life and a meaningful form for many centuries."[105] Then they
pleaded together saying: "However, the remaining
difference between Catholic and Lutheran practice
need not call into question retrospectively the
common profession of Christ's real presence. This
divergence is closely connected with the
different understandings of the modus praesentiae
and -like this latter- need not touch the
"essence" of the real presence."[106]

The remedy suggested by our document is "It

---

104. Meyer H., Pfnür V., The Presence of Christ
     in the Eucharist, in: op. cit., The
     Eucharist, p.65.
105. ibid.
106. ibid.

would be good 'for Catholics to remember, particularly in catechism and preaching, that the
original intention in preserving the eucharistic
gifts was to distribute them to the sick and
those not present', and for Lutherans 'the best
means should be adopted of showing respect due to
the elements that have served for the celebration
of the eucharist, which is to consume them subsequently, without precluding their use for communion of the sick."[107]

4.4.3.2 EUCHARISTIC SACRIFICE.

The next point of dispute is about the eucharistic sacrifice. The document first of all
stated what the Catholics and the Lutherans can
say together on this issue, in these words: "Catholic and Lutheran christians together recognize
that in the Lord's Supper Jesus Christ 'is present as the crucified who died for our sins and
rose again for our justification, as the once-
for-all sacrifice for the sins of the world.'
This sacrifice can be neither continued, nor
repeated, nor replaced, nor complemented; but
rather it can and should become effective ever
anew in the midst of the congregation. There are
different interpretation among us regarding the
nature and extent of this effectiveness."[108]
Once again it is what the Council of Trent
teaches on this matter that is the bone of contention. The council teaches that in each eucha-

---

107. op. cit., The Eucharist, p.19.
108. op. cit., p.20.

rist "a true and proper sacrifice is offered".[109]
That the eucharistic sacrifice is truly propitiatory; and has the effect that we obtain mercy and
find grace in seasonable aid; that it is rightly
offered not only for the sins, punishments,
satisfactions and other necessities of the faithful who are living, but also for those departed
in Christ but not yet fully purified;[110] that the
victim is one and the same, the same now offering
by the ministry of priests who then offered himself on the cross, the manner of offering alone
being different.

The fears of the Lutherans vis-á-vis the Catholic position is then expressed by the document: "The Lutherans have feared that the understanding of the Eucharist as propitiatory sacrifice is contrary to the uniqueness and complete
sufficiency of the sacrifice of the cross and
calls in question Christ's exclusive mediation of
salvation."[111]

The Catholic position regarding the eucharist
as propitiatory sacrifice is explained by one of
her scholars in a write up. He explained: "Now
the German sühnen like the Latin expiare was at
one time understood in two different senses: the
generic sense of purify, remove a stain or an
obstacle which prevents our being united to God or
his being pleased with us; or with a more juridi-
cal emphasis - to cancel guilt or sin by under-
going punishment for it. From the Catholic point
of view it is obvious that the mass is a pro-

---

109. cf. DS 1751.
110. cf. DS 1743.
111. op. cit., The Eucharist. p.21.

pitiatory sacrifice in the generic sense that it
makes God pleased with us...Catholics cannot call
the mass expiatory or Sühnopfer in the sense that
Christ could still suffer, or suffer afresh,
punishment for the sins of the world or gain
merit afresh as he did on the cross."[112]

The position of the two churches is further
explained by the document. On the Catholic side,
it is held that the believers are included in
Christ's offering, not externally rather each
derives from him and points to him. The gift
which they bring to the heavenly Father, is
wholly and completely a free, unmerited gift of
the love of God which is in no way merited by
man. This act allows no sort of self-complacency
and self-righteousness to arise. What the people
offer can also be understood in these terms:
"Christ has become completely ours, he is our
head. Of ourselves we have nothing and are unable
to do anything. Therefore we do not point to
ourselves but to him. Of ourselves we cannot
offer God praise, glory and honour, but we offer
Christ; he is praise, glory and honour."[113] The
document quoted from the previous agreement in
U.S.A. between Catholics and Lutherans to support
this position: "The members of the body of Christ
are united through Christ with God and with one
another in such a way that they become participants in his worship, his self-offering, his
sacrifice to the Father. Through this union bet-

112. Vagaggin C. Observations on the Catholic-
     Lutheran Joint Commission's Document on the
     Eucharist, in: S.P.C.U. IS (1979) No. 39,
     p.37.
113. op. cit., The Eucharist, p.20.

ween Christ and christians, the eucharistic
assembly "offers Christ" by consenting in the
power of the Holy Spirit to be offered by him to
the Father. Apart from Christ, we have no gifts,
no worship, no sacrifice of our own to offer to
God. All we can plead is Christ, the sacrificial
lamb and victim whom the Father himself has given
us."[114]

On the Lutheran side the document says: "The
Lutheran Reformation affirmed the understanding
of the Lord's Supper as a sacrifice of thanksgiving in return for the sacrifice of the cross
present in the sacrament. This sacrifice is an
expression of faith and happens in such a way
"that we offer with Christ, that is, that we cast
ourselves upon Christ with unwavering faith in
his testament and we do not appear otherwise
before God with our prayer, praise and sacrifice
than through Him and His means (of salvation) and
that we do not doubt that He is our Pastor and
Priest before God's face in heaven. The 'eucharistic sacrifice', thus understood is performed
by those reconciled in faith, and expressed in
thanks and praise, in invoking and confessing
God, in suffering and in all the good works of
believers.""[115]

Before summarising this section the document
expressed thanks to ecumenical dialogue which has
helped the two sides to understand each others
interpretations, and these interpretations help
mutually in improving, deepening and enlivening
each others position. The document recorded four

---

114. ibid. cf. U.S.A. III, 1.2b.
115. ibid.

areas of convergence, namely:

(a) that the sacrifice of the Mass according to the Catholic doctrine is the making present of the sacrifice of the cross, and not its repetition, nor does it add anything to its significance.

(b) that according to Catholic doctrine the ex opere operato should witness in the context of the sacramentalogy, to the priority of God's action. The Lutherans stress this priority as well.

(c) that the understanding of opus operatum does not exclude the believing participation of the whole worshipping community. The document notes that God's action calls for their participation and makes it possible.

(d) That the conviction that the eucharistic fruits extend beyond the circle of those present at a celebration does not diminish the importance of active believing participation. But how this extends to those who are not present at the celebration is entirely dependent on the sovereign love of the Lord; and finally that God's freedom is not limited by intercession and intentions at Mass for specific persons, the living as well as the dead.

4.4.3.3 EUCHARISTIC COMMUNION.

The central problem here is the so called private Masses and its corresponding question mark on the communal-meal-character of the eucharist and secondly the question of communion under both species.

The document affirms that for the Lutherans
and the Catholics, the communal-meal-character is
an essential aspect of the eucharist. It recognizes as well that on the Catholic side, according
to Vatican II, the superiority of the communal
celebration, especially at mass, involving the
presence and active participation of the faithful
is underlined, "even though every Mass has of
itself a public and social nature."[116] The document submits that Catholics as well as Lutherans
are convinced that communion under both species
belong to the complete form of the eucharist. The
document brings out the fact that in the Catholic
celebration of the eucharist, the faithful are
for the most part given only the species of
bread. It recognizes that communion under one
specie was introduced for practical reasons,
which are also known to the Lutherans, and also
for the conviction that Christ is fully present
under both species and that the reception in one
kind constitutes no dimunitive effect. The document also recalls that the liturgical reform of
Vatican II has extended the possibilities of
receiving the eucharist in both kinds, and then
concludes saying: "if differences in doctrine and
practice continue to persist in this area, they
no longer have a church-dividing character."[117]

---

116. cf. SC. 27; DS 1747.
117. op. cit., The Eucharist, p.23.

4.4.3.4 EUCHARISTIC MINISTRY.

The crucial point here is that of the minister of the eucharist. Although the document says that Catholics and Lutherans are convinced of the leadership role of the minister in the celebration of the eucharist, there are still obvious differences. It recalled the teaching of Vatican II, which says: "The ecclesial communities separated from us lack that fullness of unity with us which should flow from baptism, and we believe that especially because of the lack of the sacrament of Orders they have not preserved the genuine and total reality of the Eucharistic mystery."[118]

The problem here touches on the following areas: apostolic succession, episcopate, presbyterate and the eucharist. For the Lutherans, 'the ecclesial office is a divine institution', they do not clasify ordination as a sacrament. The document did not attempt to give a solution as it did in the previous cases. It only recalled that the Malta Report had proposed mutual recognition of Lutheran and Catholic ministries as "something to be examined seriously."[119] At the beginning the commission said that questions which concern the eucharist will be answered in its discussion on the ministry; now it did only pose questions rather than give solutions or point towards convergence. It then says: "...it must be asked, among other things how the Lutheran Churches

---

118. UR. 22.
119. cf. Meyer H. Vischer L. (ed.). op. cit.,
     p.183.

regard a Eucharist celebrated without an ordained
minister. It must also be asked, in view of the
Lutheran interpretation and practice of ordination, how the Roman Catholic Church evaluates the
Eucharist celebrated in the Lutheran Church."[120]
What needs to be clarified, according to the
document, is the importance and ecclesiological
ordering of the ministry, and what consequencies
it has for the structure of the church.

4.4.3.5 EUCHARISTIC FELLOWSHIP.

Here is also envisaged the issue of intercommunion. Our document states that the christians of
both churches confess together that Jesus Christ
joins together all those who are joined to him.
For the Catholics, eucharistic communion with
Christ includes those who departed in the Lord.
Here the church remembers the saints who have
gone into the heavenly joy, thanks God for the
grace granted them in this life and commends
itself to their intercession.
The Lutherans, though they give expression in
thanksgiving and in intercession to the communion
of the heavenly and earthly congregation, do
not deny their heavenly intercession. They do
not intercede for the dead in their eucharistic
celebration.
In the Catholic doctrine, it is understood
that the eucharistic fellowship calls for and
fosters actual community of faith within the
church. In other words the eucharist really con-

---

120. op. cit., The Eucharist, p.24.

tains what is the very foundation of the being
and unity of the church. The document outlines
these as: the ministerial power which Christ gave
to his apostles and to their successors, the
bishops along with priests; the unity of the
ministry, exercised in the name of Christ; and
the faith of the Church, which is expressed in
the eucharistic action itself. Under this background the Vatican II, teaches that common worship (communicatio in sacris), may not be regarded as a means to be used indiscriminately for
the restoration of christan unity.[121] Admission
to the Catholic celebration of the eucharist is
possible, given sufficient reasons.

In this issue, the Lutheran attitude is more
permisive than that of the Catholic. The
Lutherans use their own yard stick, perhaps the
concept of the church as essentially invisible,
and of its consequent unity. They therefore emphasize that the communion practice of the separated churches must receive their orientation
from that which is demanded of the church by the
ministry of reconciliation among men. And they
decry that "a celebration of the Lord's Supper in
which baptized believers may not participate
suffers from an inner contradiction and from the
start, therefore does not fulfil the purpose for
which the Lord established it."[122]

---

121. U.R. 8
122. op. cit., The Eucharist, p.26.

4.4.3.6   LITURGICAL FORM.

On the onset, the document submits that the
truth affirmed in faith about the eucharist must
shape the content and form of the liturgy. Both
sides are asked to go on improving the form of
eucharistic celebration in accordance with the
Lord's will, with the needs of every period and
of the liturgy itself as an indispensable means
of ecumenical dialogue on this subject. The general principle is stated: "The best way toward
unity in eucharistic celebration and communion is
the renewal of the eucharist itself in the different churches in regard to teaching and
liturgy."[123] In making this recommendation, the
document does not lose sight of unity in diversity. However the document pointed out the basic
elements in the celebration of the eucharist
which call for greater agreement. Among these
are: "proclamation of the word of God, thanksgiving for the acts of God in creation and
redemption together with the remembering of the
death and resurrection of Christ, the words of
institution in accordance with the witness of the
New Testament, the invocation of the Holy Spirit
on bread and wine and on the congregation, intercession for the church and the world, the Lord's
prayer and eating and drinking in communion with
Christ and every member of the Church."[124]
The document did not wind up without each side
making a demand from the other. The Lutherans
would like the Catholics to seek:

---

123. ibid.
124. ibid, p.27.

(a) the avoidance of the so called private masses.

(b) better use of the possibilities for proclamation within each celebration of the eucharist.

(c) the administration of holy communion under both species.

The Catholics in turn would like the Lutherans to seek:

(a) more frequent celebrations of holy communion.

(b) a greater participation by the congregation as a whole.

(c) a closer link between liturgy of the word and of the sacrament.

These requests reflect the differences in practice of which the document says that they must join together in clarifying and overcoming them. The faithful of the two churches are called upon to show interest for the reception of the agreement.

4.5 ORTHODOX / ROMAN CATHOLIC.

HISTORICAL BACKGROUND:

Communion between the Orthodox Church and the
Roman Catholic Church broke down in the year
1054. Attempts were made to restore communion at
the Council of Florence 1438-45. The result was
short lived.

The Secretariat for the Promotion of Christian
Unity, initiated visits to the heads of the
Eastern Patriarchates during the preparation for
the Second Vatican Council. The result was that
some churches of The Eastern Orthodox sent official observers to the conciliar sessions. As
one author rightly described it: "Thus began an
increasing 'dialogue of charity by the exchange
of visits, letters and theological conversations
between the leaders of the Holy See and these
Eastern Churches."[125] One of the greatest
achievements of the renewed contacts is the common
declaration of Pope Paul VI and Patriarch Athenogoras I, on 7 December 1965, in which the mutual
excommunication of 1054, which led to the schism
of East and West, was lifted. The declaration
stated inter alia: "They also regret and wish to
erase from the memory and midst of the Church the
sentences of excommunication which followed them,
and whose memory has acted as obstacle to a
rapprochement in charity down to our own days,
and consign them to oblivion."[126] Being aware
that the cancellation of the sentences of ex-

---

125. Stranky F.T., Sheerin, J.B. (ed.), Doing the
     Truth in Charity, New York/Ramsey, Paulist
     Press, 1982, p.177.
126. op. cit. p.179

communication alone cannot put an end to the
differences, ancient and modern, between the two
churches, the declaration spoke of initiating a
dialogue "which will lead them, with the help of
God, to live once again for the greater good of
souls and the coming of the kingdom of God, in
the full communion of faith, of brotherly concord
and of sacramental life which existed between
them throughout the first millenium of the life
of the Church."[127]

The contact re-established by Pope Paul VI,
and Patriarch Athenogoras I, survived them and
indeed to their glory. Hence Pope John Paul II,
and the Ecumenical Patriarch Dimitrios I, paid a
glowing tribute to their predecessors in their
common declaration on the Feast of St. Andrew 30
November 1979 saying: "We are grateful to our
predecessors, Pope Paul VI and Patriarch
Athenogoras I, for everything they did to reconcile our Churches and cause them to progress in
unity."[128] In the same common declaration, the
Pope and the Patriarch announced the commencemnt
of the theological dialogue and made known the
list of the members of the mixed Catholic-Ortho-
dox Commission. The common declaration disclosed
the aim of the dialogue in these words: "This
theological dialogue aims not only at progressing
towards the re-establishment of full communion
between the Catholic and Orthodox sister-Churches, but also at contributing to the multiple
dialogues that are developing in the christian
world in search of its unity."[129]

---

127. ibid.
128. op. cit., p.212.
129. ibid, p.213.

In 1978, the mixed technical preparatory commission of theologians worked out the plan of the dialogue, which was later approved by the Roman Catholic Church and all the Orthodox Churches.

In 1980, from May 29 - June 4, the Joint Commission for the Theological dialogue between the Orthodox and Roman Catholic Churches met for the first time at the Greek islands of Patmos and Rhodes. The Joint Commission adopted in common and unaimously as the agenda of the first phase of the dialogue, the approved plan of the mixed technical preparatory commission of theologians. The precise themes for the initial theological studies were chosen and three sub-commissions were set up. A mixed co-ordinating committee was established whose duty it is to assure the progress of the dialogue.[130] The meeting accepted as the general method of the commission, to start with what both churches have in common and by developing this, to touch upon from inside and progressively the points upon which agreement does not exist. The first topic chosen was "The Mystery of the Church and the Eucharist in the light of the mystery of the Holy Trinity."

The three sub-commissions set forth to work separately and the first group met at Cheretogne (Belgium), in October 5-9, 1980; the second at Rome, December 27-30, 1980; and the third at Belgrade in 1981. The co-ordinating committee met at Venice from 25-30 May, 1981. The task of the co-ordinating committee was to examine the results of what had been accomplished by the three

---

130. cf. S.P.C.U. IS (1980) No. 44, p.102.

sub-commissions on the theme they were assigned at Rhodes. The committee drafted a synthesis of the work of the sub-commissions, sent it to all the members of the commission along with the reports of the three sub-commissions. These documents served as the working paper at the next plenary session, which was held at Munich, in 1982.[131]

The discussions in Munich centred around questions of the nature of the eucharist, its expression of the activity of the Holy Trinity in the economy of salvation; the relationship of the eucharist to the church and the centrality of the eucharist for an understanding of communion within the local churches in the universal church. The commission later issued a document which was sent to the two churches; and to that document we turn our attention.

4.5.1 THE MYSTERY OF THE CHURCH AND OF THE EUCHARIST IN THE LIGHT OF THE MYSTERY OF THE HOLY TRINITY.

The document is presented as one, but in three sub sections without sub-titles. At the introductory note the commission claimed that in carrying out its function, they intend to express together a faith which is the continuation of that of the apostles. The topic is of great importance in the sacramental perspective of the two Churches.

---

131. cf. S.P.C.U. IS (1981) No. 45 p.27; No. 46, p.58.

4.5.1.1 PART I.

The first part is dedicated to answering the question: "What is the relation between the Eucharist celebrated around the Bishop by the local Church and the mystery of the one God in the commission of the three Persons?"[132] The report began by stating some basic facts about the mystery of Christ. He is the incarnate Son of God, dead and risen from death; it is he alone who has conquered sin and death. When therefore the sacramental nature of the mystery of Christ is spoken about it serves at the same time as a means of calling to mind the possibility given to man through Christ, to experience the kingdom of God here and now, through the material and created realities. In this mode, the unique person and event of Christ exist and operate in history starting from Pentecost and reaching to the Parousia. The eternal life given to the world by God through the event of Christ, is contained in earthen vessels and remains given as a foretaste.

At the Last Supper, Christ instituted the eucharist, gave his body to his disciples for the life of many. The report explained that this gift is made by God to the world, but in sacramental form, and the eucharist exists from then on as the sacrament of Christ himself, the foretaste of eternal life. Therefore "The sacrament of the Christ event thus becomes identical with the sacrament which incorporates us fully into Christ."[133]

---

132. S.P.C.U. IS (1981) No. 46, p.58.
133. S.P.C.U. IS (1982) No. 59, p.107. (It is my source of the report, pp.107-112).

Christ's incarnation, death and resurrection
are from the beginning realized according to the
Father's will, in the Holy Spirit. The Spirit,
which proceeds eternally from the Father, manifests himself through Christ, prepared the Christ
event. The report submits that Christ is the
sacrament par excellence; the Father gave him for
the world and Christ continues to give himself for
the many in the Spirit, who alone gives life.
This sacrament is a reality which can only exist
in the Spirit.

The document has the following to say about
the Church and the eucharist: It recalls that the
evangelists were silent about the action of the
Spirit in their account of the Last Supper, but
the document maintains that the Spirit was ever
closely united to the incarnate Son for the exe-
cution of the Father's work. It is after Christ's
glorification that the Spirit pours out himself
and thereby manifest himself. Through the outpouring of the Spirit, the Lord Jesus Christ
enters into his sacramental mode in this world.
Thus the Pentecost simultaneously completes the
paschal mystery and inaugurates the last times.
Hence "The Eucharist and the Church, body of the
crucified and risen Christ, become the place of
the energies of the Holy Spirit."[134]

Through baptism in the name of the Trinity,
believers form one body, and when the church
celebrates the eucharist it realizes what it is,
the body of Christ. By baptism and confirmation,
the members of Christ are anointed by the Spirit
and grafted into Christ and by communion in the

134. ibid.

body and blood of Christ, they grow in that
mystical divinization which makes them dwell in
the Son and the Father through the Spirit.
Putting this in another form the document says:
"Thus, on the one hand, the Church celebrates the
eucharist as expression here and now of the
heavenly liturgy; but on the other hand, the
eucharist builds up the church in the sense that
through it the Spirit of the risen Christ
fashions the Church into the body of Christ."[135]
The eucharist is then described at once as the
true sacrament of the Church, the sacrament of
the total gift of the Lord, in which the Lord
manifests himself before his own, for the growth
of his body, the Church. In its anticipation for
the judgement of the world and its final transfiguration, the pilgrim church celebrates the
eucharist until her Lord comes.

Next the document concentrates on the role of
the Spirit in the mission of Christ, and in the
celebration of the eucharist.

It is the Spirit who prepares the coming of
Christ through the prophets; he directs the
history of the chosen people towards Christ; of
the Holy Spirit was Christ conceived by the
Virgin Mary and the Spirit opens the hearts of
men to receive his word. The Spirit manifests
Christ in his work as saviour, the gospel which
is himself and of which the eucharistic celebration is the anamnesis. In this memorial, the
ephapax is truly but sacramentally present. The
eucharist is therefore the proper time (kairos)
of the mystery of Jesus Christ.

---

135. ibid, p.108.

It is the Spirit also who transforms the
sacred gifts into the body and blood of Christ in
order to bring about the growth of the body, the
Church. In this sense the report maintains that
the entire celebration is an epiclesis, which
becomes more explicit at certain moments. Again
it is the Spirit that unites into communion with
the body of Christ, those who share the same
bread and the same cup. From there on, the Church
manifests itself as the sacrament of the Trinitarian koinonia, the dwelling place of God with
men. Finally "The Spirit, by making present what
Christ did once for all - the event of the
mystery - accomplishes it in all of us. The relation to the mystery, more evident in the eucharist, is found in the other sacraments, all acts
of the Spirit. That is why the eucharist is the
centre of sacramental life."[136]

The report goes on to explain the eucharistic
celebration as the making present of the trinitarian mystery of the church, when taken as a
whole. The sequence runs like this: from the hearing of the word of God, one passes on to the
thanksgiving offered to the Father, and then to
the memorial of the sacrifice and communion made
possible, thanks to the prayer of epiclesis said
in faith. The epiclesis is understood not only as
an invocation for the sacramental transforming of
the bread and wine, but also as a prayer for the
full effect of the communion of all in the
mystery revealed by the Son. The presence of the
Spirit is thus extended to all the church by the
sharing of the sacrament of the body and blood of

---

136. ibid.

Christ. It also means that the Spirit, which
proceeds from the Father is communicated to us
particularly in the eucharist by the Son, upon
whom he reposes in time and in eternity. This
eucharistic mystery is accomplished in the prayer
in which the words of institution and the invocation of the Spirit, epiclesis, are spoken in
faith. This prayer entreats the Father, through
the Son, to send the Spirit, so that in the unique offering of the incarnate Son, everything may
be consumated in unity.

The believers unite themselves to Christ
through the eucharist. In this union Christ
offers himself with them to the Father and they
are opportuned to offer themselves to each other,
as Christ offers himself to the Father for the
many, and by so doing, he gives himself to men.
The first part is concluded by pointing to the
fullness of the church reflected in the light of
the Trinitarian koinonia. "This consumation in
unity brought about by the one inseparable operation of the Son and the Spirit, acting in reference to the Father in his design, is the Church
in its fulness."[137]

4.5.1.2 PART II.

The second part is answering the question
"What is the relation between the Eucharist celebrated around the Bishop by the local Church and
the mystery of the one God in the commission of

---

137. ibid.

the three Persons?"[138] The report draws from the
New Testament witness to say that the Church
exists in history as a local church, though as
the Church of God, but in a given place. This
church manifests itself when it is assembled. The
determining factor for this assembly is the eucharist. "This assembly itself, whose elements
and requirements are indicated in the new Testament is fully such when it is eucharistic synaxis. When the local church celebrates the eucharist, the event which took place 'once and for
all' is made present and manifested."[139] A notable sign of the local church is its unity, for
there is neither male nor female, slave nor free,
Jew nor Greek. A new unity is rather communicated, which overcomes divisions and restores communion in the one body of Christ. This unity
transcends racial, socio-political, psychological
or cultural unity, for "It is the 'communion of
the Holy Spirit' gathering together the scattered
children of God." In this sense, the newness of
baptism and confirmation bears its fruit, in that
through the power of the body and blood of Christ
filled with the Holy Spirit, there are healed all
sins whose forms contradict God's design.

The unity of the local church spoken about
recognizes the plurality of Christ's members. In
itself it is a mystery of many persons in the
likeness of Trinitarian koinonia communicated to
men in the church through the eucharist. "This is
why the Church finds its model, its origin and
its purpose in the mystery of God, one in three

138. S.P.C.U. IS (1981) No. 46, p.58.
139. op. cit., S.P.C.U. IS (1982) No. 49, p.109.

persons. Further still, the eucharist thus understood in the light of the Trinitarian mystery is
the criterion for functioning of the life of the
Church as a whole."[140]

Next the report speaks about the elements that
stand out when the local church gathers around
its bishop or the priest in communion with him,
celebrates the eucharist. The eucharistic celebration shows how the koinonia takes shape in the
celebrating church.

The koinonia is eschatological. It is the
newness which comes in the last times. It presupposes conversion and reconciliation. The eucharist forgives and also heals sins, since it is
the sacrament of the divinizing love of the
Trinity.

The next element is that the koinonia is
kerygmatic. What is particularly evident here is
that the event of the mystery is not only announced in the celebration, but is actualy realized
in the Spirit. The word of God is proclaimed to
the assembly and the response of faith is given by
all. The unity of faith brought about in the
kerygma is inherent in the eucharistic koinonia,
and the bishop witnesses to the orthodoxy of the
symbol of faith by virtue of his apostolic
succession. "Thus the eucharist is inseparably
sacrament and word since in it the incarnate word
sanctifies in the Spirit."

The koinonia is at once ministerial and pneumatological, and the eucharist is its manifestation par excellence. This is so because the entire
assembly, each one according to his rank, is

---

140. ibid.

minister of the koinonia. Koinonia is a gift of
the Trinitarian God and also a response of men.
This response in faith is put into practice while
carrying out the mission received in baptism
according to one's rank in the body of Christ.

In the next paragraph, the document discusses
the ministry of the bishop. The bishop's ministry
is neither tactical nor pragmatic but an organic
function. In his episcopal consecration, the
bishop receives sacramentally, not juridically,
the Spirit of the Lord, which confers on him the
authority of servant which Christ received from
the Father, and which he received in a human way
by his acceptance in his passion.

The bishop's function is closely bound to the
eucharistic assembly over which he presides. In
the exercise of his function, it becomes clear
that the bishop and his church are bound together, and cannot be separated from each other.
For the eucharistic unity of the local church
implies communion between the president and the
people; the word which the minister transmits is
that which he receives from his church that is
faithful to tradition; and the intercession which
the bishop sends to the Father is that of his
entire church praying with him.

The bishop's function at the local church also
include: discerning the charisms and taking care
that they are exercised for the good of all, in
faithfulness to the apostolic tradition; as a
servant of Christ the Lord, he is also the
minister of unity, imitating the Lord to gather
into unity the children of God. It is he who
presides over the eucharist of the local church.
As the president at the offering of the entire

community, the bishop appears as minister of Christ fashioning the unity of his body and thereby creating communion through his body. This union of the community with him is of the order of mysterion and "it is that union expressed and in the eucharist which is prolonged and given practical expression in the 'pastoral' relations of teaching, government and life." Hence the ecclesial community is called to be the outline of a human community renewed.

The report goes on to the next paragraph to show how a profound communion exists between the bishop and the community, thus showing that the apostolic succession is embodied in the local church. In the ancient church, it recalled that the people elected their bishop, for they guaranteed his apostolic faith. But once the bishop is ordained in the prayer of the assembly and by the laying on of hands by the neighbouring bishops, through which he receives the ministerial grace of Christ, he becomes in his church the guarantor of apostolicity and the one who represents it within the communion of churches. Apostolic succession is understood as something more than a mere transmission of powers, rather "it is a succession in a Church which witnesses to the apostolic faith, communion with the other apostolic faith."[141] Because the bishop is the guarantor of the apostolic faith in his church and represents it within the community of churches, explains why in his church every eucharist can only be celebrated in truth if presided over by him or by a presbyter in communion with him.

---

141. ibid, p.110.

The ministry of presbyters exists in relationship to that of the bishop. "Through the ministry
of presbyters, charged with presiding over the
life and the eucharistic celebration of the communities entrusted to them, those communities grow
in communion with all the communities for which
the bishop has primary responsibility."[142] In
this context the diocese can be explained in
terms of a "communion of eucharistic communities", and it is the function of the presbyters
to link these to the eucharist of the bishop and
to nourish them with the apostolic faith of which
the bishop is the witness and guarantor. In their
functions, the presbyters should ensure that the
christians become the authentic witnesses of
fraternal love in response to the sacrifice of
Christ in which they are nourished.

4.5.1.3 PART III.

The third and last part concentrates on the
relationship between the universal church and the
local church. In other words it answers the question "What is the relation between these Eucharistic celebrations of the local church and the
communion of all the local churches in the one,
holy church of the one God in three Persons."[143]
The report re-iterates the fact that the body of
Christ is unique; and secondly that there is only
one church of God. The eucharistic assemblies
have the same identity, because, they celebrate

142. ibid.
143. S.P.C.U. IS (1981) No. 46, p.58.

with the same faith, the same memorial, and participate in the eating of the same body and drinking of the same blood of Christ into which they have been incorporated by the same baptism. Therefore "if there are many celebrations, there is nevertheless only one mystery celebrated in which all participate. Moreover, when the believer communicates in the Lord's body and blood, he does not receive a part of Christ but the whole Christ."[144]

The report then submits that the local church which celebrates the eucharist gathered around its bishop is not a section of the body of Christ, but is "truly the holy Church of God, the body of Christ, in communion with the first community of the disciples and with all who throughout the world celebrate and have celebrated the memorial of the Lord."[145] This depicts also that the multiplicity of local eucharistic assemblies (synaxes) do not divide the church, but rather shows its sacramental unity.

The document emphasizes that the koinonia presupposes unity in diversity, and then applies it to show the universality of the local churches. The text reads: "Since Christ is one for the many, as in the church which is his body, the one and the many, the universal and local are necessarily simultaneous. Still more radically, because the one and only God is the communion of three persons, the one and only church is a communion of many communities and the local church a communion of persons. The one and unique church

---

144. op. cit., S.P.C.U. IS (1982) No. 49, p.111.
145. ibid.

finds her identity in the koinonia of the
churches."[146]

Two conditions are named which the local
church that celebrates the eucharist must fulfil
in order to be truly within the ecclesial communion. The first is called: Catholicity in time;
that means, that the mystery of the church lived
by the local church must have the same identity
with the mystery lived by the primitive church.
The second is called: mutual recognition among
local churches, and what is here presupposed is
communion in the same faith.

The bonds of communion which are found among
these churches as indicated in the New Testament
are: communion in the sacraments; communion in
the diversity of charism; communion in reconciliation and communion in the ministry. The report
says that the agent of this communion is no other
than the Spirit of the risen Lord. "Through him,
the Church universal, catholic, integrates diversity or plurality, making it one of its own
essential elements."[147]

Through their attachment to the apostolic
communion, the bishops are bound together; thus
the episkope of the local churches is linked to
the college of the apostles. By forming a college
rooted in the Spirit by the unique witness to the
faith of the apostolic group, the bishops should
be united among themselves not only in faith,
charity, mission and reconciliation, but also
should have in common the same responsibility and
the same service to the church. In other words

---

146. ibid.
147. ibid., p.112.

each bishop exercises the episkope of his local
church and that of the universal church as well.
It is in the people of God that he exercises it
in communion with the living tradition which the
bishops of the past handed on. The communion of
bishops with one another is demonstrated vividly
at an episcopal ordination through the presence
of the neighbouring bishops, and as the report
put it, this "produces a thorough fusion between
his solicitude for the local community and his
care for the Church spread throughout the
world."[148] Finally on the universal episkope and
how it is exercised the document says: "The episkope for the universal Church is seen to be entrusted by the Spirit to the totality of local
bishops in communion with one another. This communion is expressed traditionally through conciliar practice."[149]

4.5.1.4 EVALUATION.

As is evident from the document, it is given
in three sections without subtitles. In effect
each section was answering the corresponding
question that was posed by the Joint Commission
at Rhodes, and later assigned to the three sub-
commissions.

In answering the first question the document
presents the eucharist as the sacrament of Christ
himself, and the relationship between the eucharist and the church in a perspective which is

---

148. ibid.
149. ibid.

known as eucharistic ecclesiology. This is one of the perspectives in which the mystery of the church can be treated as the document itself points out.

The second part of the document concentrates on the theology of the local church. The local church is seen as an assembly of believers with their bishop in the eucharistic celebration. This eucharistic assembly constitutes the church. The attempt is made here to discover the ecclesiological implication of the community gathered with its bishop to celebrate the eucharist.

Finally the third part treats the relationship between the universal church and the local church in the light of the eucharist and its celebration. The universal church is here understood as the communion of several local churches. Each local church must recognize in the other the identity of the mysteries of the one and only church. Among these churches are found bonds of communion in areas of faith, hope, and love, in sacraments and also in the ministry. This communion takes place at different levels; at the local church under the presiding bishop, at the regional level and at the universal level, bishops being in communion with one another, as a sign of the communion of local churches making up the universal church. The universal episkope is exercised by the bishops in a conciliar practice.

EUCHARISTIC ECCLESIOLOGY.

Our document can be seen as a solid result in
the ecumenical discussion on the area of sacramental and eucharistic understanding of the
church. In other words the relationship between
ecclesiology and the eucharist, is clearly ex-
plored.

In modern times the father of the eucharistic
ecclesiology is said to be the Russian emigrant
theologian, Nikolay Afanasév (1893-1966). He
presented his basic thoughts on the subject
matter in the article he wrote in 1934 titled
"Zwei Vorstellungen von der katholike ekklesia."
In his book, Peter Plank re-presented the
thoughts of his mentor.[150] The fundamental idea
here is the identification of the church with the
eucharistic assembly. The church is defined
thereafter as an assembly gathered to celebrate
the eucharist. The eucharistic ecclesiology is
the theology of the local church as the body of
Christ. This stands in contrast to the theology
of the People of God.

According to Afanasév the passage, Mt
18:20,[151] found its best explication in Ignatius
of Antioch, in his letter to the Smyreans. There
the bishop wrote: "Wherever the bishop appears,
let the people be there; just as wherever Jesus
Christ is, there is the Catholic Church."[152]

---

150. cf. Put'45 (1934) 16-29; and, Plank P., Die
     Eucharistieversammlung als Kirche, Würzburg,
     Augustinus Verlag, 1980, p.49ff.
151. Mt18:20: For where two or three meet in my
     name, I shall be there with them. (Jerusalem
     Bible).
152. Sm, 8,2; quoted acc. to: Jurgens A.W., The
     Faith of the Early Fathers vol. one,
     Collegeville, Minnesota, The Liturgical
     Press, 1970, p.25.

The autor then argued: "Eine solche Versammlung
im Namen des Herrn im Sinne Mt18:20, ist aber als
eine eucharistische zu verstehen, denn "Als Zentrum einer solchen Gemeinde erscheint nicht mehr
der Tempel von Jerusalem, sondern die eucharistische Gabe."[153] The author explains further:
"In der eucharistischen Gabe is Christus voll und
ganz gegenwärtig. So macht der eucharistische
Leib Christi diejenigen, welche an ihm teil-
nehmen, die eucharistische Versammlung, ebenfalls
zum wahren Leib Christi. Dieser ist die Fülle der
katholike ekklesia."[154] Another passage of Ignatius writings which was of interest to Afanas'ev,
to show that the bishop and the community celebrate the one eucharist in unity, is taken from
his letter to the Philadelphians. Ignatius wrote:
"Take care, then to use one Eucharist, so that
whatever you do, you do according to God: for
there is one Flesh of our Lord Jesus Christ, and
one cup in union of His Blood; one altar, as
there is one bishop with the presbytery and my
fellow servants, the deacons."[155] Correspondingly
the author wrote: "Damit ist die notwendige ge-
genseitige Verwiesenheit von Bischof und Gemeinde
ausgesagt. Kirche kann nur dort sein, wo der

---

153. op. cit., Plank P., pp.50-51.
     "Such an assembly in the name of the Lord in
     the context of Mt.18,20 is to be understood
     as a eucharistic community, because "the
     Temple of Jerusalem does not appear to
     constitute such a community, but the
     eucharistic gift."" (Translation is mine).
154. ibid.
     "In the eucharistic gift, Christ is really
     and truly present. Therefore the eucharistic
     body of Christ, incorporates all those who
     participate in Him, the eucharistic
     assembly, into the real body of Christ. This
     is the fulness of the katholike ekklesia."
     (Translation is mine).
155. Phil.4,1, cf. Jurgens W.A., op. cit., p.22.

Bischof ist, weil ohne den Bischof die Eucharistie nicht vollzogen werden kann. Aber auch der
Bischof ist nur da Bischof, wo die Gemeinde ist,
denn ohne Versammlung der Gläubigen kann ebenfalls Eucharistie nicht begangen werden."[156]

According to Afanas^ ev, Ignatius of Antioch
represents what he calls the qualitative concept
of the Church universal. This idea implies that
every local church is the church in its fulness.
Christ is the same in every local church; no
local church should dominate the other, for
Christ is not divisible. The local church is an
object of love for the other, and what happens in
one is accepted by the other through the process
of reception. The author denies the necessity of
a visible head in the church as a sign of the
bond of love between the churches. He wrote:
"Weder einem Kirchenfürsten, einer Vorrangstel-
lung des Apostels Petrus, noch einem einzigen
Bischof ist die sichtbare Gewalt über die katholike ekklesia anvertraut, sondern jedem einzelnen
Bischof in seiner Kirche - in Übereinstimmung mit
seiner Gemeinde."[157]

---

156. op. cit., Plank P., p.52.
     "The essential and mutual reference between
     the bishop and the community is thus
     explained: The church is there, where the
     bishop is, because there can be no eucharist
     without the bishop. Also the bishop is there
     a bishop, where there is a community,
     because without the assembly of believers,
     the eucharist cannot be celebrated."
     (Translation is mine).
157. op. cit., Plank Peter, p.54.
     "Neither a church prince with the special
     position of the apostel Peter nor any other
     bishop is entrusted with the visible power
     of the katholike ekklesia, but every bishop
     in his church corresponding to his
     community." (Translation is mine).

Afanas'ev holds Cyprian of Carthage as the
model of quantitative ecclesiology. He demonstrates this by presenting St. Paul's eucharistic
ecclesiology and how Cyprian interpreted Paul.
The citations are from Paul's letter to the
Corinthians, namely: "Just as a human body,
though it is made up of many parts, is a single
unit because all these parts, though many, make
one body, so it is with Christ. In the one Spirit
we were all baptised, Jews as well as Greeks,
slaves as well as citizens, and one Spirit was
given to us all to drink." "The fact that there
is only one loaf means that, though there are
many of us, we form a single body because we all
have a share in this one loaf." Thirdly: "Now you
together are Christ's body; but each of you is
different part of it."[158]

These three citations represent the Pauline
example of the eucharistic orientated community
and the meaning of the ecclesiology of an individual community. But Cyprian understood it differently, for he wrote: "The church is one, however
widely she has spread among the multitude through
her faithful increase."[159] The author is not
completely satisfied with the position of
Cyprian, for he thus reacts: "Dem liegt die Vor-
stellung zugrunde, daß die Kirche über die ganze
Welt hin - auch empirisch gesehen - eine einzige
ist, welche in einzelne kirchliche Gemeinden
untergliedert ist."[160] He says that Cyprian's

---

158. 1 Cor 12:12-13; 1 Cor 10:17; 1 Cor 12:27.
159. De Unitate Ecclesia, quoted according to:
     op. cit., Jurgens W.A., p.221.
160. op. cit., Plank P., p.54.
     "It underlies that the church all over the
     world, even empirical, is one which is sub-
     divided into single ecclesial community."
     (Translation is mine).

conception is the same with Pauline ecclesiology
only that the former misunderstood the latter.
For Paul the participants at the eucharistic .
celebration become one as a whole, that is in the
living body of Christ. This unity is mystical as
well as empirical. While Paul considers the individual christian, Cyprian looks at the individual community. And from there he speaks about
the universality of the church. In Cyprian's
thought, the unity of these churches is found in
the unity of the episcopate. The author continues
his commentary on Cyprian saying:
"Das Wesen der Einheit des Episkopates tritt nach
Cyprian sogar leuchtender hervor als die Einheit
der Kirche; die Einheit des Episkopates ist näm-
lich eine concors numerositas, d.h. eine Vielzahl
von Einzelbischöfen, geeint in herzlicher Bruder-
liebe (concors), die im Übereinklang besteht,
welcher, wie einzelne Töne, eine Harmonie formt.
Jeder Bischof hat gleiche Rechte, weil er, als
Glied der übereinstimmenden Vielheit, direkt vom
Apostel Petrus die volle hierarchische Vollmacht
empfängt. In seiner Gemeinde steht er anstelle
Christi, vice Christi, weshalb er auch über ihm
keine Gewalt gibt, von welcher er abhinge."[161]

---

161. op. cit., p. 56 "The essence of the unity of
     the episcopate according to Cyprian stands
     out more prominently than the unity of the
     church itself; the unity of the episcopate
     is namely a concors numerositas, i.e., a
     multitude of bishops, united in brotherhood,
     which exists in harmony like single tones,
     which form a sound. Every bishop has equal
     rights, because as a member of a correspon-
     ding multitude, he receives the full
     hierarchical power given directly by Apostle
     Peter. In his community, the bishop repre-
     sents Christ, vicar of Christ, that is why
     there is no power over him upon which he is
     dependent." (Translation is mine).

It is a fact that Cyprian maintains the equality of the bishops, but in practice he writes to
the bishop of Rome explaining to him how the
church in his region flourishes and about its
problems too.

The ecclesial character of the eucharist is
found in the teaching of the Second Vatical Council. The Constitution on the Church shows clearly
the rediscovery of the eucharistic ecclesiology.
In article 26, of the Constitution we read:
"A bishop, marked with the fulness of the sacrament of orders, is 'the steward of the grace of
the supreme priesthood," especially in the Eucharist, which he offers or causes to be offered and
by which the church constantly grows." The local
church is understood to be the church of Christ,
"This Church of Christ is truly present in all
legitimate local congregations of the faithful
which, united with their pastors, are themselves
called churches in the New Testament. For in
their own locality these are the New People
called by Christ, in the Holy Spirit and in much
fulness." In these local churches the bishop is
the symbol of unity and he regulates every legitimate eucharist. "In any community existing
around an altar, under the sacred ministry of the
bishop, there is manifested a symbol of that
charity and "unity of the Mystical Body," without
which there can be no salvation. In these communities, though frequently small and poor, or
living far from any other, Christ is present."
Finally we read from the same article that:
"Every legitimate celebration of the Eucharist is
regulated by the bishop, to whom is committed the
office of offering the worship of christian

religion to the divine majesty and of administering it in accordance with the Lord's command-
ments and with the Church's laws, as further
defined by his particular judgment for his
diocese."[162]

That the local church is constituted where the
bishop is and the eucharist celebrated is emphasized also in the Council's decree on the
Bishop's Pastoral Office in the Church. The
Catholic Church is present in the local church.
"A diocese is that portion of God's people which
is entrusted to a bishop to be shepherded by him
with the co-operation of the presbytery. Adhering
thus to its pastor and gathered together by him
in the Holy Spirit through the gospel and the
Eucharist, this portion constitutes a particular
church in which the one, holy, catholic Church of
Christ is truly present and operative."[163]

In various parts of the Council's documents
the importance of the local church is stressed
and shown to be the church of Christ in its fulness.

In the document that is being assessed, there
is a lot of emphasis on the local church, which
manifests itself when it celebrates the eucharist. This notion goes back to the New Testament
and was expressed sharply by Ignatius of Antioch.
The bisop is the bond of koinonia in his church,
and every eucharist is either celebrated by him
or at his mandate. The document is aware of the
plurality of persons in the koinonia and likened

---

162. L.G. 26.
163. C.D. 11.

it to the mystery of God, one in three divine
persons. The document also identified the universal Church, the one Church of God, with the
koinonia of the local churches. Each bishop at
his consecration is endowed with the spirit of
episkope both for his church and for the universal church. The bishops form a college in the
manner of the apostolic group and exercise the
universal episkope through conciliar practice.
The document therefore failed to recognize in the
person of the bishop of Rome the sign of the bond
of unity of the bishops, and consequently the
right to universal episkope. The issue concerns
also the problem of authority in the church.

It is difficult to reconcile the stand of the
mixed commission and the teaching of the Roman
Catholic Church on the issue of the bishop of
Rome serving as the bond of the episcopal unity
and the universal episkope entrusted to him. The
fathers of the Second Vatican Council pointed out
clearly that the bishop of Rome, the Roman
Pontiff, is the bond of the collegial union of
bishops and the individual bishop is also the
principle of unity in his particular church. The
fathers stressed this point in the context of the
relationship between the local churches and the
universal church. The fathers said: "This collegial union is apparent also in the mutual relations of the individual bishops with particular
Churches and with the universal Church. The Roman
Pontiff as the successor of Peter, is the perpetual and visible source and foundation of the
unity of the bishops and the multitude of the
faithful. The individual bishop, however, is the
visible principle and foundation of unity in his

particular Church."[164] The relationship of the
bishops to the Roman Pontiff does not jeopardise
their complete pastoral care of their local churches. The council fathers have this to say on the
issue: "Nor are they to be regarded as vicars of
the Roman Pontiff, for they exercise an authority
which is proper to them and are quite correctly
called 'prelates', heads of the people whom they
govern. Their power, therefore, is not destroyed
by the supreme and universal power. On the contrary
it is affirmed, strengthened, and vindicated
thereby."[165]

The primacy of the Roman Pontiff among his
brother bishops found its clear expression in
Cyprian of Carthage, in his book, De Unitate
Ecclesiae. He wrote: "...Indeed, the others were
that also which Peter was; but a primacy is given
to Peter, whereby it is made clear that there is
but one Church and one chair. So too, all are
shepherds, and the flock is shown to be one, fed
by all the Apostles in single-minded accord. If
someone does not hold fast to this unity of
Peter, can he imagine that he still holds the
faith?"[166]

As it is pointed out earlier, the issue concerns authority in the church. The mixed commission of Orthodox and Roman Catholic Churches,
should have borrowed a leaf from the Anglican/
Roman Catholic International commission, which has
issued a statement on authority and brought to
the lime light the universal episkope which is

164. L.G. 23.
165. L.G. 27.
166. De Unitate Ecclesiae, 4,2. Quoted acccording
    to: op. cit., Jurgens W, A., p.220.

due to the bishop of Rome among the communion of
Churches. The commission said: "The importance of
the bishop of Rome among his brother bishops, as
explained by analogy with the position of Peter
among the apostles, was interpreted as Christ's
will for his Church. On the basis of this analogy
the First Vatican Council affirmed that this
service was necessary to the unity of the whole
Church. Far from overriding the authority of the
bishops in their own dioceses, this service was
explicitly intended to support them in their
ministry of oversight. The Second Vatican Council
placed this service in the wider context of the
shared responsibility of all the bishops. The
teaching of these councils shows that communion
with the bishop of Rome does not imply submission
to an authority which would stifle the distinctive features of the local churches. The purpose
of the episcopal function of the bishop of Rome
is to promote christian fellowship in faithfulness to the teaching of the apostles."[167]

Our document submits that the universal episkope of the church is carried out by the bishops
in communion with one another, through conciliar
practice. Although the document said that the
commission has not said the final word about it,
it did not indicate the importance of the bishop
of Rome in order to realize the conciliar practice. It is necessary then to point out what
others have said on the matter in ecumenical
dialogue. Once again the Anglican/Roman Catholic
International Commission comes to mind: "Among

---

167. Meyer, H., Vischer L. (ed.), Growth in
     agreement, New York/Geneva, 1984, p.93.

the complex historical factors which contributed
to the recognition of conciliar decisions considerable weight is attached to their confirmation
by the principal sees, and in particular by the
see of Rome. At an early period other local churches actively sought the support and approbation
of the church in Rome; and in course of time the
agreement of the Roman see was regarded as necessary to the general acceptance of synodal
decisions in major matters of more than regional
concern, and also, eventually, to their canonical
validity. By their agreement or disagreement the
local church of Rome and its bishops fulfilled
their responsibility towards other local churches
and their bishops for maintaining the whole
church in the truth. In addition the bishop of
Rome was also led to intervene in controversies
relating to matters of faith - in most cases in
response to appeals made to him, but sometimes on
his own initiative."[168]

Our document lays importance and correctly
too, on the mutual recognition of the identity of
the mystery of the church between local churches.
Communion in the same partriarchate or region
implies unity of faith and calls for the exercise
of fraternal correction in humility. This regional communion it maintains, should extend further
to the communion between sister churches. It is
necessary to see this communion realized beyond
sister churches, to the universal church, where
this fraternal correction in humility will be
practised. But now is this going to be practicable without some one serving as that bond of

---

168. op. cit., p.95.

unity in the koinonia of churches, and therefore
exercising universal episkope? A solution to this
question can be found once again in the statement
on authority issued by the Anglican/Roman Catholic International Commission. Writing on the
conciliar and primatial authority in the church
the statement says: "If God's will for the unity
in love and truth of the whole christian community is to be fulfilled, this general pattern
of the complimentary primatial and conciliar
aspects of episkope serving the koinonia of the
churches needs to be realized at the universal
level. The only See which makes any claim to
universal primacy and which has exercised and
still exercises such episkope is the see of Rome,
the city where Peter and Paul died. It seems
appropriate that in any further union a universal
primacy such as has been described be held by
that see."[169]

The problems that face the mixed commission of
Orthodox and Roman Catholic Churches must not be
underestimated. The position of the Orthodox
Church on the issue of the primacy of Rome was
made clear in the speech of welcome made by
Patriarch Dimitrios I, in 1973, to the President
of the Secretariat for the Promotion of Christian
Unity, Cardinal Willebrands. The Patriarch said:
"Um deutlich aufrichtig und ehrlich uns selbst
und gegeneinander, aber auch der ganzen Welt
gegenüber zu sein, müssen wir wiederholen und
betonen, daß kein einziger Bischof in der
Christenheit ein Privileg, göttliches oder
menschliches, über die ganze eine, heilige,

169. op. cit., p.97.

katholische und apostolische Kirche Christi be-
sitzt. Wir alle - sei es in Rom, sei es in dieser
Stadt... - sind einzig und allein Mitbischöfe
unter dem einzigen obersten Hohenpriester, dem
Haupt der Kirche, immer unserem Herrn Jesus
Christus, nach der von jeher kirchlich anerkann-
ten hierarchischen Ordnung."[170]

This statement should be weighed vis-á-vis the
position of the Roman Catholic Church on the
issue of primacy and authority of the bishop of
Rome in the universal Church as it is taught by
the Second Vatican Council. The council fathers
taught: "But the college or body of bishops has
no authority unless it is simultaneously conceived of in terms of its head, the Roman Pontiff, Peter's successor, and without any lesse-
ning of his power of primacy over all, pastors as
well as the general faithful. For in virtue of
his office, that is, as Vicar of Christ and
pastor of the whole Church, the Roman Pontiff has
full, supreme, and universal power over the
Church. And he can always exercise this power
freely."[171] About the primacy of the Roman

---

170. cf. Episkepsis 4 (1973) No. 90, 18. quoted
     here according to: Rauch Albert, Imhof Paul
     (Hrsg.), Die Eucharistie der Einen Kirche,
     München, Kaffke, 1983, p.116.
     "In order to be distinct, sincere and honest
     to ourself, to one another and to the whole
     world, we must repeat and emphasize, that no
     individual bishop in christianity, possesses
     divine or human priviledge over the one,
     holy, catholic and apostolic church of
     Christ. We all, be it in Rome, or in this
     city...are nothing but fellow bishops, under
     the same High Priest, the head of the
     church, always our Lord Jesus Christ,
     according to the traditional ecclesiastical
     recognized hierarchichal order."(Transla-
     tion is mine.)
171. L.G. 22.

Pontiff in ecumenical council, the Council also
said: "The supreme authority with which this
college is empowered over the whole Church is
exercised in a solemn way through an ecumenical
council. A council is never ecumenical unless it
is confirmed or at least accepted as such by the
successor of Peter."[172]

The root cause of the difference between the
two sister-churches is well observed by Kallis
Anastasios in one of his writings. He wrote:
"Hier begegnen sich zwei Kirchen, die trotz ihrer
weitgehenden Glaubensübereinstimmung unterschied-
liche Kirchenstrukturen und divergierende ekkle-
siologische Kriterien aufweisen. Für die Katholische Kirche gelten, wie auch die jüngste Erfah-
rung zeigt, die Unfehlbarkeit des Papstes und
seine universale Jurisdiktion nach wie vor als
die letzten ekklesiologischen Kriterien. Dagegen
ist das orthodoxe Denken von einer eucharistischen Ekklesiologie, von der Theologie der
Lokalkirche bestimmt, die zudem einen pneumatolo-
gischen Charakter trägt."[173]

---

172. L.G. 22.
173. Kallis Anastasios, Eucharistische
Ekklesiologie-Theologie der Lokalkirche. Die
eucharistische Struktur der Kirche, in: op.
cit., Rauch A., Imhof Paul (Hrsg.), pp.116-
117.
"Here are two churches, who inspite of their
almost common faith, have different
ecclesial structures and divergent
ecclesiological criteria. For the Catholic
Church still maintains, as recent experience
shows, the infalibility of the Pope and his
universal jurisdiction as the final
ecclesiological criteria. In contrast the
Orthodox thinking is fixed on a eucharistic
ecclesiology, the theology of the local
church, which contains a pneumatological
character. (Translation is mine).

Cardinal Ratzinger in his evaluation of the
common eucharistic text produced by the mixed
commission of Orthodox and Roman Catholic Churches reveals that among the Orthodox Churches the
eucharistic ecclesiology is also found to be
narrow. It is so because there exists differences
among the Orthodox Churches themselves as one
would not believe and among them there is no
general agreement on the so called eucharistic
ecclesiology. In the words of the Cardinal himself: "Nun in diesem Gespräch hat sich gezeigt,
daß der Gegensatz in der Form, wie ihn etwa die
Ekklesiologie von Afanasieff vermuten ließe,
nicht da ist. Auch für die orthodoxen Kirchen ist
diese rein ortskirchliche Ekklesiologie zu eng.
Auch sie meint, die fast ausschließliche Betrach-
tung der Kirche von der Eucharistie her lasse
wichtige Gesichtspunkte aus... Zunächst einmal
hat sich gezeigt, daß auch die Orthodoxe viel
unterschiedlicher ist, als man möchte. Es besteht
keineswegs eine allgemeine Zustimmung zu der
vorhin genannten eucharistischen Ekklesiologie."[174] He substantiates this statement by
citing an example of some orthodox Russian theologians in exile who develop another ecclesiology

---

174. cf. KNA-Öki Information No. 30, 21. July 1982,
     pp.11-12.
     "As the discussion now reveals, the contrast
     in the form is not there as supposed in the
     ecclesiology of Afanasieff. For the Orthodox
     Church as well, this pure ecclesiology of
     the local church is too tight. It holds also
     that the almost exclusive view of the church
     based on the eucharist excludes important
     points of view... wherefore as it is shown
     that the Orthodox is much more varied as one
     wishes. There is no common agreement on the
     above named eucharistic ecclesiology."
     (Translation is mine.)

using the Trinity, one God in three Persons, as a
model. They maintain that: "So wie es in der
Trinität, nicht gleichsam einen Obersten und
Untergeordneten gibt, sondern nur die völlige
Einheit Gottes aus der völligen Kommunion der
drei Personen besteht, so gibt es auch in der
Kirche nicht gleichsam einen Vorrang und daneben
Zu- und Untergeordnete, sondern die Einheit der
Kirche ist nach dem trinitarischen Modell der
vollen Gleichheit aufzufassen."[175]

Another theologian sees our text as being
valid for a strong eucharistic ecclesiology for
the two Churches. He wrote: "Das Dokument darf
als Ausdruck der beiden Kirchen inzwischen er-
starkten eucharistischen Ekklesiologie gelten,
welche die in Eucharistie und Sakramenten vorge-
gebene Gemeinsamkeit als ein so fundamentales
Einheitspotential kennzeichnet, daß demgegenüber
die herkömmlichen Differenzen kirchenrechtlicher
und systemtheologischer Art ihre kirchenspaltende
Kraft zu verlieren scheinen."[176]

---

175. op. cit., p.12.
     "As in the Trinity, there is no superior and
     subordinate as it were, but only full unity
     of God by full communion of the three
     Persons, that is why also there is no
     preference and besides no superior and
     subordinate in the church, but the unity of
     the church is to be understood according to
     the Trinitarian model of equality "by full
     equality."" (Translation is mine).
176. Schulz, H.J., Die Beziehungen zu den ortho-
     doxen Kirchen, in: Löser W., (Hrsg.), Die
     Römisch-Katholische Kirche, Frankfurt, Evan-
     gelisches Verlagswerk, 1986, p.367. "The
     document can be counted as the expression of
     the two Churches for the growing eucharistic
     ecclesiology, which is indicating such a
     fundamental potential unity in the eucharist
     and the sacraments as alleged togetherness,
     but on the other side the traditional dif-
     ferences in canon law and systematic theo-
     logy appear to lose the ecclesial splitting
     power." (Translation is mine.

The document shows that the Eucharist is the
central point in the Church and that it is the
eucharist that builds up the church. With the
eucharist at the centre the equality of the churches is presupposed. The document also shows
agreement as regards the office of the bishop,
ordained by the imposition of hand, and under
whose presidency the eucharist is validly celebrated.

The document did not make any mention of
intercommunion between the two sister churches.
The Orthodox stand in this issue is clear and one
of them restated it recently. He said: Die Intercommunion kann also nicht der Weg, sondern nur
die Krönung der Wiederherstellung der Einheit im
Glauben, in der Liturgie und in der kirchlichen
Ordnung und im kirchlichen Leben zwischen den
beiden Kirchen sein."[177] On the other hand, a
Catholic theologian asks: "...ist dann nicht
vielmehr in der liturgischen und bekenntnis-
mäßigen Überlieferung eine an sich auch Komm-
uniongemeinschaft schon tragende wirkliche Glau-
benseinheit gegeben, der gegenüber theologische
Differenzen vor allem als Ausdruck unterschiedlicher lokaler Tradition erscheinen, wie solche
auch in der Alten Kirche etwa zwischen der anti-
ochenischen und alexandrinischen Vätertheologie

---

177. Zaphiris C., Der Theologische Dialog
     zwischen der Orthodoxen und der Römisch-
     Katholischen Kirche, in: Ökumenischen
     Rundschau 32 (1983), p.61.
     "Intercommunion cannot be the way, but only
     the crowing of the restoration of unity in
     faith, in the liturgy and in ecclesiastical
     order and in the ecclesiastical life between
     the two Churches." (Translation is mine).

bestanden."[178]

The last word is not yet said by the two
sister-churches and there is still a burning hope
that the two churches will one day be in communion with each other and celebrate the eucharist
together. The aim of this dialogue is said to be
double. Firstly, it is aimed at re-establishment
of full communion between the two Churches, and
secondly to contribute to the multiple dialogues
going on in the christian world in search of its
unity. It will be regrettable if the efforts put
in, result only in attaining the secondary aim
while the first and the most important is unat-
tained due to inherent differences in the structure of the church. The christian world is wat-
ching with interest the two sister-churches to
take the lead towards christian unity.

---

178. Schulz, H.J., op. cit., pp.367-368.
    "... is the true unity of faith not already
    given in the liturgical and confessional
    tradition as well as in the communion
    fellowship? Theological differences presume
    simply to be the expressions of different
    local traditions as one can already find in
    the early church, e.g. the differences bet-
    ween the Antiochian and the Alexandrian
    Fathers of the church. (Translation is
    mine).

CHAPTER FIVE.

ROMAN CATHOLIC VIEW-POINTS.

That the Roman Catholic Church joined the modern ecumenical movement is the hand work of the Second Vatican Council. A Council which emphazises the spirit of aggiornamento, brought about the liturgical reform and stated its principles on ecumenism in her Decree on Ecumenism promulgated in 1964.

The ecumenical movement has since then witnessed Churches in dialogue with one another and the Roman Catholic Church is at the fore front. The Catholic Church is also in dialogue with the World Council of Churches, and has formed with that Council since 1965, a body known as Joint Working Group. Since 1968, the Catholic Church is a member of the Commission on Faith and Order of the World Council of Churches, and her representatives took part in the discussions that produced the Lima convergence text on Baptism, Eucharist and Ministry. Here is the witness of two great ecumenists on the Catholic Church's entry into the ecumenical movements: "The intensification of bilateral interconfessional dialogues at world level coincided with the end of the Second Vatican Council. This was no accident. For when the Roman Catholic Church decided to participate actively in the ecumenical movement, this brought into the dialogue a Church which sees itself as a spiritually structurally united, worldwide communion with a strong conviction of its special identity as the Church of Christ."[1]

The Eucharist has always been a topic at the centre of the conversations in the various dialogues between the Catholic Church and other Churches. The discussions featured the presence of Christ in the Eucharist as well as the eucharist as a sacrifice and intercommunion. Other areas include eucharistic worship and the reservation of the sacrament.

This chapter is designed to briefly give an insight into the Roman Catholic teaching and practice on the Eucharist. This attempt will help to evaluate the efforts being made by the representatives of the Catholic Church during the bilateral dialogues and the multilateral dialogues to understand the mystery of the eucharist together with their dialogue partners. It will help to understand the stand of the Catholic Church vis-a-vis the convergence text on the eucharist. In doing this, we have chosen to present the Catholic teaching on the eucharist as it is presented in the Encyclical of Pope Paul VI, Mysterium Fidei. Greater attention will be paid on those controversial areas that engaged Faith and Order Commission with much difficulty at its discussion of the eucharist, such as the real presence, eucharist as a sacrifice and the eucharistic worship.

---

1. Meyer H. and Vischer L., (eds.), Growth in Agreement, New York, Ramsey, Genevy, Paulist Press, 1984, p.3.

5.1 POPE PAUL VI.: MYSTERIUM FIDEI.

A SHORT HISTORICAL BACKGROUND.

The attempt by some theologians to understand and explain anew the Real Presence of Christ in the Eucharist, the dogma of Transubstantiation, is the proximate cause of writing the encyclical, Mysterium Fidei. The lokale of this new attempt is predominantly in Holland.

In his article, E. Schoenmaeckers[2] delved into the religious and societal awakening in the Netherlands after the Second World War. He described the Netherlands as a nation that was locked up to itself before the war and after the war it confronted itself with her isolationism. By fighting against the strong patriachal system in the family it stumbled into the crisis of authority in the Church which resulted into a crisis of faith. He described the christian life in the Netherlands in these words: "Das kirchliche Leben in den Niederlanden macht gegenwärtig den Eindruck der Modernen Kunst: formlos und chaotisch. Gutes ist mit sehr Ungutem gemischt, Heiliges mit Unheiligem, Aberglaube und Unaberglaube sind bis zur Unkenntnis im religiösen Aufwand getarnt."[3]

It is in such atmosphere that the dogma of Transubstantiation came under discussion in Holland. Prof. Schillebeeckx traced the historical development of the crisis in Holland under three

---

2. Schoenmaeckers E., Die Katholische Kirche der Niederlande in der Krise der Gegenwart, in: Orientierung 28 (1964) pp. 19-22.
3. op. cit., p.21.

stages, in one of his articles[4] in 1966. He remarked that after the war, the renewal of Catholic theology of sign had a clear effect on the
eucharistic theology, in the sense that the
Scholastic saying: "Sacramentum est in genere
signi" applies also to the eucharist. That is to
say: "...one should seek to appraise the proper
mode of the real presence without departing from
sacramentality or from the "sacramentum-signum";
the sign itself, this particular eucharistic
sign, should be able to account for the proper
mode in such a way that there would no longer be
an opposition between the "sacramentum-signum"
and transubstantiation, yet so that this sacrament would infinitely transcend the more peripheral sacramentality of the six other sacraments. Transubstantiation is profoundly real,
but it is so within the framework of the category
of sacramentum-signi."[5] He classified the second
factor to be in the philosophical order. This
concerns the renewed debate on the notion of
substance among the neo-scholastics. The tendency
for neo-scholasticism was to restrict the concept
of substance to spiritual beings, and to deny the
same to artificial beings like bread and wine.
The result was that the distinction between substance and accidents in the Aristotelian sense
was vigorously attacked, and this prompted several theologians to undertake a historical analysis of the Council of Trent to determine
whether or not the Council in defining the dogma

---

4. Schillebeeckx E., Transubstantiation,
   Transfinalization, Transfiguration, in:
   Worship 40:6 (1966) 324-338.
5. op. cit., p.326.

of Transubstantiation, had avoided Aristotelian
doctrine.[6] The third factor, he attributed to the
Second Vatican Council's liturgical reform and
the appreciation for the several "real presences"
of Christ as defined by the Council.[7]

The new thought form, existential phenomeno-
logy, developed in the Netherlands exerted influence in the discussion. This new thought form
lays emphasis on the personal conception of man
and the manner in which human beings relate to
God, to their fellow human beings and to the
world in which they live in. In this new spiritual climate, the Eucharist is considered as a
community meal, in which the Lord himself is the
host, and the congregation the guest. Bread and
wine are sacramental gifts of the Lord, and the
means through which the Lord expresses his love
and grace and are therefore realized. Through the
means of this modern thought, some theologians
attempted to explain anew the real presence of
Christ and to replace transubstantiation with new
terminologies: transignification and transfina-
liztion.[8] Public opinion among Catholics was
aroused in Holland by the expression of Father
Smits in which he said: "after the consecration
the bread remained bread and the wine remained
wine."[9]

The bishops of the Netherlands reacted through
their Pastoral Letter of 9 May 1965 and restated

---

6. ibid. p.327.
7. cf. S.C. 7.
8. cf. Fragen der Theologie und des religiösen
   Lebens, Herder Korrespondenz 19 (1964-65),
   p.517.
9. cf. Schillebeeckx E., op. cit., p.330.

the authentic teaching of the Church on the Eucharist as defined by the Council of Trent. The bishops described the Eucharist in these words: "God meets his people in the celebration of the Eucharist, the covenant sacrifice of his Son, our Lord and brother. In order that we may fully and completely take part in this sacrifice and covenant, the Lord invites us to eat his flesh and to drink his blood. To be at the table of the Lord is more than coming together with the Lord and with one another for a festivity. Through the holy Communion we participate in the sacrificial death of the Lord, and we are in the deepest sense of the word, accepted in the new covenant of everlasting life which is promised."[10] The bishops enumerated the different ways in which Christ is present in his Church and added that his presence in the eucharist is not independent of his other mode of presence in the Church. Then they restated the Church's teaching on the real presence of Christ in the eucharist, and said that it does not come into any theological discussion. The bishops also said: "The believe on the real presence of Christ in the eucharist belongs to our christian heritage, which can never be abandoned. If presently in the Church the presence of the Lord under the eucharistic forms is being discussed, this discussion does not touch the question whether he is really present. What can only be discussed in the Church is the manner and art of approaching and describing this mystery of faith...we mean that we can leave

---

10. Quotation according to: Heder Korrespondenz, op. cit., p.159. (Translation is mine).

to the free discussion of theologians, the manner
of this presence as long as the change of bread
and wine into the body and blood of the Lord and
the reality of his presence in the eucharistic
forms are recognized."[11]

On the eve of the last session of the Second
Vatican Council, Pope Paul VI, published the
encyclical, "Mysterium Fidei".[12] The Pope stated
clearly what occasioned his encyclical in these
words: "We have become aware that there are a
number of speakers and writers on this sacred
mystery who are propagating opinions that are
likely to disturb the minds of the faithful and
to cause them considerable mental confusion on
matters of faith. Such opinions relate to Masses
celebrated privately, to the dogma of transubstantiation and to eucharistic worship. They seem
to think that, although a doctrine has been defined once by the Church, it is open to anyone to
ignore it or to give it an interpretation that
whittles away the natural meaning of the words or
the accepted sense of the concepts."[13] Having
mentioned the three areas in which disquieting
views on the eucharist are being expressed, the
Pope went down immediately to correct such views
and said: "It is not right to exalt the "community" Mass, so-called, to the detriment of
Masses which are celebrated privately. Nor is it
right to be so pre-occupied with considering the
nature of the sacramental sign that the impres-

---

11. ibid. (Translation is mine)
12. AAS. 57 (1965) 753-774. Quotations here
    according to C.T.S., London, 1965: Mysterium
    Fidei.
13. Paul VI. Mysterium Fidei, C.T.S. English
    Translation, London, 1965, p.7.

sion is created that symbolism - and no one denies its existence in the most holy Eucharist -
expresses and exhausts the whole meaning of
Christ's presence in this sacrament. Nor is it
right to treat of the mystery of transubstantiation without mentioning the marvellous change of
the whole of the bread's substance into Christ's
body and the whole of the wine's substance into
his blood, of which the council of Trent speaks,
and thereby make these changes consist of nothing
but a 'trans-signification' or a 'transfinalisation', to use these terms. Nor finally, is it
right to put forward and to give expression in
practice to the view which maintains that Christ
the Lord is no longer present in the consecrated
hosts which are left when the sacrifice of the
Mass is over."[14]

We shall now go on to present the Pope's teaching on the eucharistic presence, the eucharist
as a sacrifice and the eucharistic worship.
Thereafter the opinions of some theologians will
be presented.

5.1.2 THE MYSTERY OF FAITH.

The Holy Father, before presenting the teaching of the Church on the blessed Eucharist
chose first and foremost to remind us that the
subject he was about to handle is the Mystery of
Faith. The purpose for this is to alert the christians to reject any poisonous rationalism on
this mystery for which many martyrs bore witness

---

14. ibid.

with their blood, and in which many Fathers of
the Church professed their faith. In approaching
this mystery, he recommends steadfast adherence
to divine revelation in preference to following
human arguments. To support this view he quoted
some Fathers and also St. Thomas, the Angelic
Doctor who said: "The existence in this sacrament
of Christ's real body and real blood 'cannot be
grasped by sense-experience but only by the faith
which has divine authority as its support'".[15]
From the scripture, the Pope took another
example, where many of Christ's disciples drew
back because Christ talked about eating his flesh
and drinking his blood. But the apostles stayed
put, after Peter had professed his faith and that
of others in the promise of Christ: "Lord, to
whom shall we go? You have the words of eternal
life."[16] The Pope then insists that in the
investigation of this mystery the magisterium of
the Church has to be followed as a guide because:
"The Redeemer has entrusted the word of God, in
writing and tradition, to the Church's magisterium to keep and to explain;" he quoted St.
Augustine to augument his position: "What has
since ancient times been preached and believed
with true Catholic faith throughout the Church is
still true if it is not susceptible of rational
investigation or verbal explanation."[17]

The Pope is not against further investigation
into the mystery of Faith. He insists that

---

15. op. cit., p.10; cf. also Summ Theol. IIIa,
    q 75a 1c.
16. ibid. cf. also Jn6:61-69.
17. ibid. cf. also St. Augustine, Cont-Julian VI,
    5,11; PL 44, 829

the traditional formulas used in expressing the
faith must be adhered to and that no one may
presume to alter it at will in the pretex of new
knowledge. In the contex of the dogma of transubstantiation he said: "It is equally intolerable that anyone on his own initiative should
want to modify the formulas with which the Council of Trent has proposed the eucharistic mystery
for belief."[18] The formulas which the Church
employs in proposing dogmas of faith express
concepts which are not tied to any specified
cultural system, nor are they restricted to any
one theological school. The theologians are reminded that in the exposition of their findings,
the meaning must always be retained which the
Church has once declared, because "this enables
the unalterable truth of faith to survive as
progress is made in the understanding of faith."

5.1.3   THE EUCHARISTIC REAL PRESENCE.

Following the footsteps of the Constitution on
the Sacred Liturgy of the Second Vatican Council,
Pope Paul VI, enumerates seven different ways of
Christ's presence in the Church.[19] In his
enumeration, the Pope goes beyond the Council, in
so far as he included that Christ is present in
the social life of the Church. In effect therefore Christ is present in his Church when she
prays, in her social life and actions, in her
faith and works of charity, in the proclamation

---

18. ibid.
19. cf. S.C. 7.

of the word of God, in the ministry of her presbyters, in the administration of the sacraments
in general; but his mode of presence is more
sublime in the sacrament of the Eucharist. He
lays emphasis on the reality of Christ's presence
in these different ways and of the eucharistic
real presence he adds: "It is called the 'real'
presence, not in an exclusive sense as though the
other forms of presence were not 'real', but by
reason of its excellence. It is the substantial
presence by which Christ is made present without
doubt, whole and entire, God and man."[20]

The Pope rejects two explanations of this form
of presence as erroneous first, if one should
conceive it to be an omnipresence of the pneumatic nature of Christ's body in glory; and secondly if one considers it symbollically on the
assumption that the eucharist consists of nothing
but an efficacious sign of Christ's spiritual
presence and of his close union with his faithful
members in the Mystical Body.

On the issue of eucharistic symbolism, the
Pope says that it is particularly related to the
unity of the church. After a survey of the doctrines of the Fathers and the Doctors of the
schools, the Council of Trent taught that our
Lord left the Eucharist in his Church "as a
symbol...of the unity and the charity with which
he wanted all christians bound and joined together, and thus the symbol of the single body of
which he himself was the head."[21] The Pope

---

20. Paul VI, Mysterium Fidei, op. cit., p.18.
21. op. cit., p.19; cf. DS 1638; and Council of
    Trent, Decr. de SS. Eucharistia,
    introuchtion.

further cited Didache and St. Cyprian to buttress
his explanation and said that St. Paul preceded
them in his letter to the Corinthians, where it
is said: "Because there is one bread, we who are
many are one body, for we all partake of the one
bread."[22] From the teaching of the Council of
Trent and from the words of Christ at the institution of the Eucharist, the Pope says that all
insist that we profess: "The Eucharist is the
flesh of our Saviour Jesus Christ; the flesh
which suffered for our sins and which the
Father, of his kindness, brought to life." To
this he adds what Theodore of Mopsuetia taught to
the people concerning this subject: "The Lord did
not say: "This is the symbol of my body and this
is the symbol of my blood." He said: "This is my
body and my blood." He is teaching us not to pay
attention to the nature of the object presented
to the senses, it has been changed into flesh and
blood by thanksgiving and the words pronounced
over it."[23]

The Holy Father then restated the dogma of
transubstantiation as was defined by the Council of
Trent."...the Council of Trent openly and simply
professes that in the bountiful sacrament of the
holy Eucharist, after the consecration of the
bread and wine, our Lord and Saviour Jesus
Christ, true God and man, is contained truly,
really and substantially under the appearance of
the objects that the senses can perceive."[24]

The Pope goes on to explain this dogma. He

22. cf. Didache, 9.1; Cyprian Epist. ad Magnum,
    6; 1Cor 10:17.
23. Paul VI, Mysterium Fidei, op. cit., p.20.
24. ibid. cf. also DS 1636.

most importantly remarks that the real presence
of Christ in the Eucharist through transubstantiation in itself oversteps the laws of nature,
and in order to avoid any misunderstanding of
this mode of presence, he calls everyone to be
docile to the voice of the Church through her
teaching and prayer. The Church teaches that
Christ becomes present in the sacrament of the
eucharist precisely by a change of the bread's
whole substance into his body and the wine's
whole substance into his blood; and this substantial change she gives the suitable and accu-
rate name of transubstantiation. The Pope then
admits that after the consecration bread and wine
are transignified and transfinalised only in the
ontological sense. Because of the importance of
the statement, I beg to quote him in detail. The
Pope said: "When transubstantiation has taken
place, there is no doubt that the appearance of
the bread and appearance of the wine take on a
new expressiveness and a new purpose since they
are no longer common bread and common drink, but
rather the sign of something sacred and the sign
of spiritual food. But they take on a new expressiveness and a new purpose for the very reason
that they contain a new 'reality' which we are
right to call ontological. For beneath these
appearances there is no longer what was there
before but something quite different. This is so
in very fact and not only because of the valua-
tion put on them by the Church's belief, since on
the conversion of the bread and wine's substance,
or nature, into the body and blood of Christ,
nothing is left of the bread and the wine but the
appearances alone. Beneath these appearances

Christ is present whole and entire, bodily present too, in his physical 'reality', although not in the manner in which bodies are present in place."[25] The pope then warned against the sensual physical conception of the eucharistic change and called everyone to assent to the words of Christ which have the power to change, transform, and transelement the bread and wine into his body and blood. The power that performs this action is the same power of the almighty God that created the universe out of nothing. The case of Berengarius was mentioned as one who through human reason's difficulty refused the eucharistic change, which led to the drawing up of a statement of oath which he took.

5.1.4 OPINIONS.

I would like here to present the opinions of two Dutch theologians whose writings generated some heat on the issue of transubstantiation and the third as the mediator. Thereafter the explanation of Cardinal J. Ratzinger and the intervention of the German Bishop's Conference on the issue of the real presence of Christ and the dogma of transubstantiation.

---

25. Paul VI, Mysterium Fidei, op. cit., p.21.

Prof. Schoonenberg.

In his articles[26] which appeared in 1964 and
1965, he started by analyzing the concept
'presence', and landed at discussing the risen
Lord in the Eucharist, as his central point. He
differentiates two forms of 'presence': the spatial presence and the personal. The spatial presence is described as the conglomoration of
things or togetherness of people, whose relationship is impersonal and therefore only local.
Personal presence always means communication, and
it is very intensive when it is interpersonal.
This presence effects a unity, without the loss
of personal identity. Every person can in thought
and in willing be personally present in another
without the two being spatially together. The
characteristics of personal presence are, the
free decision to offer oneself, the spiritual
openness in which both become one, without loss
of selves. A human being is most fructfully present in another when his presence is both bodily
and personal.

God is only freely and personally present but
never locally. In the historical Jesus, God was
both spatially and bodily present in the world.
After Christ's resurrection, he is only spiritually and personally present where he is believed in. He is as the transfigured Christ in

---

26. Schoonenberg P., Tegenwoordigheid, in: Verbum
    31 (1964) Eucharistische Tegenwoordigheid; De
    Herant 95 (1964). also in: De Jijd Dec. 21,
    1964.
    My German sources are: Herder Korrespondenz
    19 (1964-1965) 517-518
    Schillebeeckx E., Die Eucharistische
    Gegenwart zur Diskussion über die
    Realpräsenz, Düsseldorf, Patmos, 1967.

his entirety with us, although our human eyes
cannot see him. By implication of what the Constitution on the Sacred Liturgy said about the
various ways in which Christ is present in his
Church, our author lays emphasis on Christ's
presence in the congregation that has gathered to
celebrate the Eucharist. That is to say , that
Christ is already present before the bread and
wine are consecrated. Through the Eucharist,
however, his personal presence is brought near to
us.

The presence of Christ under the sign of bread
and wine is characterized as real, because
through them his presence is realized in us. The
Lord offers his body and blood under the sign of
bread and wine as food and as a sign of the covenant. Bread and wine are offered as food so that
through it the reality of the Lord becomes effective in us. In the eucharist we do not receive
under the form of bread and wine Christ locally
present, rather it is the invisible, risen Lord,
who offers his body as food through the sign of
bread. The eucharistic bread can be compared with
a gift which the Lord offers. Our author says
that the dogma of transubstantiation does not
mean that the Lord bodily descends down from
heaven and that we must not speak of physical or
chemical change of bread and wine. After consecration, the bread receives a new meaning. For
him therefore, transubstantiation is transfinalisation or transignification. The bread means
the real self-offering of the Lord. Because this
gift takes place under the sign of bread, which
must be eaten, the physical reality of bread must
also remain after the consecration so that its

function as a sign can be fulfilled, he concluded.

After the publication of the encyclical, Mysterium Fidei, Prof. Schoonenberg expressed his
opinion once again on the dogma of transubstantiation.[27] His point of departure here is that
the mystery of the real pressence of Christ in the
eucharist in the dogma of transubstantiation by
the Council of Trent, can be expressed in a new
terminology, like transfinalisation and transignification, without violating the fact of the
real presence. He contended that the terminology
transubstantiation current in the time of the
Council of Trent cannot be valid in all other
times. "Dies galt für die Zeit des Konzils, es
galt offensichtlich nicht für jene Zeit, da dieser Ausdruck noch nicht vorhanden war, und
braucht nicht für immer gelten."[28] He argued that
as the Council Fathers of Trent did not depart
from the teaching of the Council of Constance,
that the Fathers of Trent employed Aristotelian
categories in their doctrine of transubstantiation. He then asked whether our confession of
faith in the eucharistic mystery is tied down to
the model, substance/accident or whether there is
another possibility of explaining this mystery?
For our author, the answer to this question is

---

27. Schoonenberg P., Inwieweit ist die Lehre von
    der Transsubstatiation historisch bestimmt?
    in: Concilium 3 (1967) 305-311.
28. op. cit., p.305.
    "This is valid at the time of the Council,
    without doubt it does not need to be valid
    always, because this expression does not yet
    count and does not need to be valid for every
    time." (Translation is mine.)

obviously positive for he wrote: "Daraus sieht
man, daß die Glaubensformulierung eines Konzils,
wie die jedermanns, niemals adäquat von einer
zeitgebundenen theologischen Interpretation zu
trennen ist. Sicherlich nicht für jene selbst,
die sie aussprechen. Für uns aber, die später
kommen, ist dies, wenigstens teilweise, wohl
möglich."[29] Backed by this conviction, and taking
into account the explanation of the eucharistic
symbolism of Mysterium Fidei (44), as relating to
the unity of the Church, and the use in number
(46) of the words transignification and transfinalisation, (but only in the ontological
sense), hence transubstantiation, our author
concludes that the encyclical leaves room for the
teaching on transubstantiation to be expressed
with other words: "Somit läßt auch diese Enzyklika Raum für eine Transsubstantiationslehre in
weiterem Sinne, die nach verschiedenen Seiten
entfaltet werden kann."[30]

L. Smits.
   His articles appeared in Dutch in 1964 and
1965 on the real presence of Christ in the

---

29. ibid. p.307.
    "That is why the formulation of creed of a
    council as of any other, can never be
    separated from the interpretation current at
    the time. There is no doubt for those
    who proclaim it. But for us, coming later,
    this is a least partly possible."
    (Translation is mine.)
30. ibid, p.311.
    "That is why the encyclical gives a place for
    the teaching of transubstantiation in all its
    meaning which can be developed in different
    ways." (Translation is mine.)

Eucharist.[31] After his detailed study on transubstantiation, he came to the conclusion that since
this doctrine was born in an era of polemics,
that the danger exists of seeing the presence of
the Lord in the form of bread and wine to be
static. The personal presence of the Lord in the
form of bread and wine remains central to his
writings. He said that food and drink in everyday
life count as a sign of friendship and love when
they are offered as gifts. The donor identifies
himself with the gifts which at the same time
become part of his personality. Food becomes in
this way a sign of personal solidarity; sign of
the incarnation of what it signified.

In the eucharist, the Lord incarnates his love
in bread and wine. The offering of bread and wine
means the self-oblation of the Lord. For him the
dogma of transubstantiation can be understood
from the doctrine of the hypostatic union. Just
as in Christ, the humanity becomes God and the
humanity is no longer independent, but is taken
up in a higher mode of existence, so also bread
and wine in the eucharist are taken up into the
mode of existence of the risen Lord, and thereby
receive a higher mode of existence. Bread and
wine take hold of the Lord and become so to say
part of his heavenly existence. The consecrated

---

31. Smits L., Nieuw Zicht op de werkelijike
    tegenwoordigheid van Christus in die
    Eucharistie, De Bazuin 48:9 (1964). Van onde
    naa Nieuwe transsubstantiatieleer, De Herant
    95 (1964); cf. De Bazuin 48:23 (1965).
    My German sources of these articles are:
    Herder Korrespondenz 19 (1965-1965) 518;
    Beinert, W., Die Enzyklika "Mysterium Fidei"
    und die neuere Auffassungen über die
    Eucharistie, ThQT 147:2 (1967) 159-176.

bread is not in itself the body of the Lord, it
is rather taking hold of the Lord. Because bread
takes hold of the Lord, it becomes the body of
Christ. Christ is really present.

Prof. Schillebeeckx.

His contribution to the discussion on the
eucharistic presence in Holland is contained in
the book he published in 1965[32] and in an article
in 1966[33]. He acknowledged the attempts made by
some theologians to formulate anew the eucharistic teaching; he no doubt took note of the
onesidedness of this new attempt, for he wrote:
"Was mir bei vielen neueren Versuchen, das Dogma
modern, eben als kathlolisches Dogma, zu deuten,
ein methodischer Grundfehler zu sein scheint, ist
die Tatsache, daß man das Dogma von einer modernen Phänomenologie aus neu interpretiert, ohne
klarzumachen, was z.B. das Dogma von Trient von
mir als gläubigen Katholiken fordert."[34] To balance this onesidedness he undertook to inquire

---

32. Schillebeeckx E., Die eucharistische Gegen-
    wart zur Diskussion über die Realpräsenz,
    Düsseldorf, Patmos, 1967.
33. Schillebeeckx E., Transubstantiation, Trans-
    finalization, Transfiguration, in Worship:
    vol. 40, 6 (1966).
34. Schillebeeckx E., op. cit., Die euchari-
    stische Gegenwart zur Diskussion über die
    Realpräsenz, p.12.
    "What appears to me personally by the diffe-
    rent attempts to interprete the dogma mo-
    dernly, just as Catholic dogma, is the me-
    thodical error, the fact that the dogma is
    interpreted by modern phenomenology, without
    making it clear, for example, what the dogma
    of Trent is demanding from me personally as a
    Believer." (Translation is mine.)

into the definitions of real presence and transubstantiation as the Council of Trent handled
them. He explained that the Fathers of the Council in handling the issue of the eucharistic
change used the word transubstantiation to express their conviction that the bread and wine
are really changed into the body and blood of
Christ. He argued that "the conciliar fathers at
Trent, while thinking in the Aristotelian categories which were theirs, intended to define
dogmatically the reality proper to the eucharistic presence, that is, our Catholic eucharistic faith, and not the categories which they
used in discussing and formulating this properly
eucharistic presence."[35] This point counteracts
the opinion of Schonnenberg as we saw above.

From the historical analysis of the Council of
Trent, our author distinguishes three points in
the dogma of transubstantiation namely: that of
faith, which is the biblical affirmation of the
real presence proper to the eucharist, which is
clearly distinguished from a purely symbolical
presence and from real presence proper to the
other sacraments. The second is the ontological:
i.e. the affirmation of the substantial change of
bread and wine as demanded by the eucharistic
presence; this is also the affirmation of the
realistic character or of the ontological dimension of the presence of Christ in the sign of
bread and wine; it is the 'conversio totius
entis' as St. Thomas called it. Thirdly is the
issue of the word transubstantiation, in the

---

35. Schillebeeckx E., op. cit., Worship, pp.327-
    328.

manner it is presented on the level of philosophy
of nature. Thereafter he concludes: "From this
analysis, compared with the interpretation of the
Greek fathers, who spoke of "transelementatio" or
of a "conversio substantialis" in an ontological
sense that was, however, completely foreign to
the Aristotelian philosophy of nature, it appears
that, even though the conciliar fathers of Trent
were all thinking in Aristotelian categories
(each in his own manner), the dogma itself is
foreign to the Aristotelian categories of "substance" and "accidents" "[36] The professor maintains that, that word transubstantiation should
be retained so long as it expresses an ontological change, but when it does not agree with modern philosophy of nature it can be reinter-
preted. He also says that the way the dogma of
transubstatiation is explained leaves the door
open to a conceptual presentation of the dogma
different from the medieval and Thomistic conception. "The dogma obliges the Catholic to admit
the profound realism, or the ontological dimension, of the eucharistic presence in such a way
that after the consecration the reality present
is no longer ordinary or natural bread and wine,
but our Lord himself in the presence of bread and
wine which has become sacramental. This leaves
the door open to a conceptual presentation of the
dogma different from the medieval and Thomistic
conception."[37] He sees the attempt to explain the
real presence anew as a return to the patristic
position of emphasizing the res sacramenti of the

---

36. op. cit., pp.331-332.
37. ibid.

eucharist. In his words: "Because the 'new'
emphasis is concerned with the intimate presence
of Christ in the hearts both of the individual
believer and of the community of Christians, the
eucharist must remain on the level of interpersonal relationship: of the presence of one person
to another person. For man each interpersonal
presence is communicated by means of a spatial,
visible, tangible, and even tasted presence. But
in this case the spatial presence, that is, the
body and the corporeal elements receive a new
dimension: they become signs of a person who is
present, signs which effect this presence, and
signs which are real because they 'realize' this
presence."[38] Consequently our author sanctions
the new terminology: transignification and transfinalisation so long as their meaning is ontological "...whereas in the eucharist we ought to be
concerned with an interpersonal relationship in
which Christ gives himself to man by means of
bread and wine which, by this very gift, have
undergone a transfinalization and an ontological
and therefore radical transignification."[39]

Referring to the encyclical, Mysterium Fidei,
he remarks that it admits the new terminology but
on condition that it has a profound ontological
content: "The encyclical admits transfinalization
and transignification on condition that they are
not considered as an extrinsic designation or as
a peripheral change, but rather as having a profound and ontological content."[40]

---

38. ibid. pp.335-336
39. ibid.
40. ibid.

Cardinal Ratzinger J.

In his article[41], the Cardinal did not only
hold firm to the ontological quality of substantial change on the dogma of transubstantiation,
he also attempted a critical assessment of the
eucharistic theology of Calvin and Luther as an
ecumenical slant. He distinguished between the
metaphysician and the physisist and adds that
when we talk about substantial change, in the
understanding of the metaphysician, it does not
touch the area of the physisist. Applying this
concretely to our subject matter he wrote: "Die
eucharistische Wesensverwandlung ist kein physi-
kalisches Geschehen, weil das "Wesen", die "Substanz", von der hier gesprochen wird, außerhalb
des Bereiches der Physik und des physikalisch
Erscheinenden liegt."[42] The physisist is concerned about the impression the thing makes but
the metaphysician is more interested on the nature of the thing. However, he says, "Die eucharistische Verwandlung aber bezieht sich per der-
finitionem nicht auf das, was erscheint, sondern
auf das, was nie erscheinen kann. Sie vollzieht
sich außerhalb des physikalischen Bereichs. Das
heißt aber ganz deutlich gesagt: Physikalisch
chemisch gesehen vollzieht sich an den Glauben

---

41. Ratzinger J., Das Problem der
    Transsubstantiation und die Frage nach dem
    Sinn der Eucharistie, in: ThQT 147,2 (1967)
    129-158.
42. op. cit., p.150.
    "Transubstantiation is not a physical event,
    because the "matter", the "substance", which
    we are talking about is outside the area of
    physics and physical appearances.
    (Translation is mine.)

Schlechterdings nichts."[43] In this context he
goes on to say that there is no contrast between
the teaching on transubstantiation and the consubstantiation of Luther; but he rejected consubstantiation as the co-existence of two substances. He wrote: "Es wird sichtbar, daß "Transsubstantiation" gar keinen Gegensatz zu "Konsubstantiation" bedeutet, wenn letztere einfach
sagen soll, daß Brot und Wein als physikalisch-
chemische Größen unverändert weiter bestehen.
Freilich wird man gerade, wenn man das für
selbstverständlich ansieht, sagen müssen, daß das
Modell der Konsubstantiation, d.h., eines Neben-
einander zweier Substanzen, die man beide im
gleichen Sinn "Substanz" nennen könnte und müßte,
philosophisch und theologisch zu vordergründig
und oberflächlich bleibt."[44]

The Cardinal did not go out of his way to re-
interpret the dogma of transubstantiation in the
sense of seeking new terminology like the Dutch,
rather he stuck to the Thomistic terminology and

---

43. ibid. p.153.
   "Transubstantiation is dealing by definition,
   with what never appears. It takes place
   outside physical action. Clearly that means:
   looking at it from the point of view of
   physics and chemistry nothing really
   happens." (Translation is mine.)
44. ibid, p.153.
   "It is obvious that there is no contrast
   between transubstantiation and consubstantiation, because consubstantiation simply means
   that bread and wine continue to exist without
   change in their physical and chemical constitution. But it must be said that in the case
   of accepting the model of "consubstantiation"
   as two substances co-existing side by side
   both as substances seems to be too superfi-
   cial considered by philosophical and theological view." (Translation is mine.)

inquired about reality. He furthermore explained:
"Transsubstantiation aber besagt, daß sie auf-
hören, in der dem Geschöpf zukommenden Weise
einfach in sich selbst zu stehen und daß sie
statt dessen zu reinem Zeichen Seiner Anwesenheit
unter uns werden... Sie sind nun so in ihrem
Wesen, in ihrem Sein, Zeichen, wie sie vorher in
ihrem Wesen Dinge waren."[45]

About the manner of Christ's presence in the
eucharist, he maintains with St. Thomas that
Christ is present 'secundum substantiam', that is
to say that "Christus is anwesend seinem wesent-
lichem Selbstsein nach, in das Er die Kreatur
einbezieht, dadurch, daß Er sie zu Zeichen Seiner
Anwesenheit macht. Anwesend is Seine durch das
Kreuz hindurchgegangene Liebe, in der er sich
selbst (die "Substanz" Seiner selbst): Sein von
Tod und Auferstehung geprägtes Du als heilsschaf-
fende Wirklichkeit uns gewährt."[46] He rejects
using the doctrine of ubiquity to explain the
real presence as well as Calvin's local presence
of Christ at the right hand of God. He concluded
his reflection in an ecumenical tone:

---

45. op. cit., p.152.
   "But transubstantiation means that they stop
   to exist for themselves but to become a pure
   sign of His presence among us. They are now
   in their nature, in their being, signs as
   they have been ordinarily in their
   existence." (Translation is mine.)
46. op. cit., p.154.
   "Christ is present in his essential way of
   existence, in what he is, including all the
   creatures by making them into the sign of His
   presence. He is present in his love for what
   he suffered on the cross, in which he grants
   us through His death and resurrection the
   salvation reality stamped by He himself."
   (Translation is mine.)

"..."Transsubstantiation" gerade vom ursprüng-
lichen Sinn des Begriffs her in einer Weise zu
verstehen ist, die weder denkerisch unvertretbar
noch kirchentrennend ist."[47]

THE GERMAN BISHOP'S CONFERENCE.

The German Bishop's Conference in its Pastoral
Letter[48] of 22 September 1967, devoted some paragraphs to the mystery of the Eucharist. It was
their intention through their teaching to safeguard the dogma of transubstantiation from any
misunderstanding; for they noted also that the
concept "substance", as it underlies the concept
"Transubstantiation" is no longer current in its
right understanding, especially in modern
times. The Bishops explained the word, transubstantiation, (Wesensverwandlung), to mean that,
according to the words of institution by Christ,
the eucharistic food is no longer bread, but
really the body of the Lord. Taking the word
transubstantiation as it stands, the bishops say
that it admits other terms to bring out its full
meaning for the reason that these sacramental
signs still point towards something that is not
yet fulfilled. In their own words: "Die Er-

---

47. op. cit., p.158.
    "Transubstantiation from the original sense
    is to be understood as neither rationally
    indefensible nor as what divides the church."
    (Translation is mine.)
48. Sekretariat der Deutschen Bischofskonferenz,
    Hrsg., Schreiben der deutschen Bischöfe an
    alle, die von der Kirche mit der
    Glaubensverkündigung beauftragt sind, Trier
    Paulinus-Druckerei, 1967.

gänzungsfähigkeit des Begriffes "Transsubstantiation" macht es dabei möglich, zur Beschreibung
dieses Heilgeheimnisses auch andere Aspekte her-
anzuziehen. Die Zeichen dieses Sakramentes weisen
darauf hin, daß es nicht schon mit seinem Dasein
seinen ganzen Sinn erfüllt; durch das Zeichen von
Speise und Trank für die verborgene Realität
dieses Sakramentes wird vielmehr deutlich, daß es
"als geistliche Speise der Gläubingen gegeben
ist." "[49]

The bishops in line with the encyclical,
Mysterium Fidei, teach that after consecration,
the bread and wine take on a new expressiveness
and a new purpose, that is to say, they become
transignified and transfinalized. These words,
transignification and transfinalization are new,
but what they express is not new. "Durch die neue
Zeichenhaftigkeit (Transsignification) wird aus
dem natürlichen Brot die geistliche Speise, durch
die neue Bestimmung ("Transfinalisation") wird
die neue Speise zur Speise für das ewige Leben.
Die Worte "Transsignification" und "Transfinalisation" sind neu, das mit ihnen Gemeinte jedoch
nicht. Die Grundlage für die Bestimmung, welche
der Herr aussprach mit den Worten: "Nehmet hin
und esset, dies ist mein leib (Mt.26,26), ist die
Wirklichkeit, daß Brot und Wein in Leib und Blut

---

49. op. vit., No. 45, p.25.
   "The ability of complementing the term transubstantiation enables us to draw other
   aspects of describing this salvation mystery.
   The signs of this sacrament show that it is
   not yet fulfilled by its existence; but
   through the sign of food and drink for the
   hidden reality of this sacrament, it becomes
   clear that it is given as spiritual food to
   the believer." (Translation is mine.)

Christi verwandelt sind. Darum kann Transsubstantiation durch Transfinalisation verdeutlicht,
aber nicht ersetzt werden."[50] The bishops laid
emphasis on the real presence and warned against
any attempt to endanger the faith in the name of
better knowledge. They maintained that Transubstantiation as a definitive element of the Catholic teaching on the eucharist should not be taken
as an intellectual solution to the salvation
mystery of God's descent, rather: "es wird im
Gegenteil gerade dadurch die Konkrete, alles
Begreifen übersteigende Leibhaftigkeit festge-
halten, die dem im Abendmahlshandeln vergegen-
wärtigten Kreuzestod Christi und der Inkarnation
überhaupt entspricht."[51] The bishops carefully
explained that in transubstantiation the change
that takes place is ontological, although the
form of bread and wine remain after the consecration. "Die Lehre von der Transsubstantiation

---

50. ibid.
    "Through the new expressiveness (transignifi-
    cation) bread becomes divine food; through
    the new transfinalization, the new food be-
    comes food for eternal life. The words "tran-
    signification" and "transfinalization" are
    new, but what they are expressing is not new.
    The basis for the definition given by the
    words of the Lord: Take and eat, this is my
    body (Mt.26,26), is the reality that bread
    and wine are changed into the body and blood
    of Christ. That is why transubstantiation is
    confirmed by transfinalization, but does not
    replace it." (Translation is mine.)
51. ibid. No. 46.
    "Just on the contrary is confirmed the
    concrete, all understanding, transcending
    corporeity which corresponds to the
    eucharistic celebration, the representation
    of the death and incarnation of Christ."
    (Translation is mine.)

setzt ihrerseits allerdings voraus, daß eine
Wirklichkeit mehr enthält, als was die Alltagser-
fahrung oder die Naturwissenschaft erreichen
können, und daß sich somit in jenen Dimensionen
wirklich etwas ändern kann, die für diese Empire
nicht erreichbar sind."[52]

5.1.5   EUCHARIST AS SACRIFICE.

The issue of the sacrificial character of the
eucharist was not among the areas in which the
Holy Father mentioned that opinions exist which
cause considerable mental confusion; but at the
bilateral and multilateral discussion in ecumenical circles, it has remained a burning issue.
Here then is what the Pope said about the matter
in Mysterium Fidei.
   The Pope went straight to the matter and gave
the summary and the summit of the Church's doctrine which is: "By means of the eucharistic
mystery, the sacrifice of the cross, achieved
once on Calvary, is marvellously symbolised,
continually recalled to the memory, and its saving virtue is applied to the remission of the
sins which are daily committed by us."[53] Re-
casting the event at the Last Supper, the Holy

---

52. ibid. No. 47.
   "The dogma of transubstantiation presupposes
   that the reality must include more than the
   common experience or what physical science can
   offer and therefore can really change something in these dimensions which cannot be
   reached by these empiricals.
53. A.A.S. 57 (1965), quoted according to
   English translation C.T.S. publishers, op.
   cit., p.13.

Father said that Christ the Lord, as the Mediator
of the New Covenant ratified that covenant with
his blood as Moses ratified the Old Covenant with
the blood of oxen. He saw in Christ's command:
"Do this in remembrance of me", as his wish that
his sacrifice should be capable of constant renewal in the eucharistic offering. He pointed out
that the early Church was loyal to this command
as was clearly indicated in the Acts of the
Apostles.[54] St. Paul in his letter to the Corinthians forbade the Christians to participate in
the pagan sacrifices for the fact that they have
become partakers at the Lord's table.[55] This new
oblation of the new covenant was foretold by
Malachy.[56] Bringing all this together the Holy
Father said that the Church in keeping with the
Lord's instruction and that of the apostles "has
always offered it not only for the sins, punishments, satisfactions and needs of the faithful
still alive but also for those who have died in
Christ but are not yet fully cleansed."[57]

By recalling the teaching of St. Cyril of
Jerusalem the Pope brought out the Church's teaching on the propitiatory character of the eucharistic sacrifice: "When the spiritual sacrifice -
worship without bloodshed - is completed, we
entreat God over that victim of propitiation for
the common peace of the Church...For we believe
that the souls for whom prayer is offered while

54. cf. Acts 2:42, "These remained faithful to the
    teaching of the apostles, to the brotherhood,
    to the breaking of bread and to the prayer."
55. cf. 1 Cor10:14-16.
56. cf. Mat. 1:11.
57. Paul VI, Mysterium Fidei, op. cit., no.30,
    p.14.

the sacred and awe-inspiring victim lies present,
will obtain the greatest help from this...we too
offer prayers to God for the dead, even if they
are sinners. Not that we weave a garland; but we
do offer Christ sacrificed for our sins, in the
effort to earn merit and favour from God's cle-
mency both for them and for ourselves."[58] On
speaking about the public nature of the Mass the
Pope brought out clearly what belongs to this
sacrifice, an action of Christ and the Church:
"The Church indeed, in the sacrifice which she
offers, is learning to offer herself as a universal sacrifice; she is also applying to the whole
world for its salvation, the redemptive virtue of
the sacrifice of the cross, which is unique and
infinite."[59]

The Second Vatican Council in its Constitution
on Sacred Liturgy stressed the importance of the
liturgy especially as it is through the liturgical celebration that the divine eucharistic sacrifice, the work of our redemption is exercised.
The conciliar Fathers placed the eucharist at the
centre of the life of the local Church. In the
context of the eucharistic sacrifice, the council
Fathers said: "At the Last Supper, on the night
when he was betrayed, our Saviour instituted the
Eucharistic Sacrifice of His Body and Blood. He
did this in order to perpetuate the sacrifice of
the cross throughout the centuries until he
should come again, and so to entrust to his beloved spouse, the Church, a memorial of his death
and resurrection: a sacrament of love, a sign of

---

58. ibid.
59. ibid, No. 32, p.15.

unity, a bond of charity, a paschal banquet in
which Christ is consumed, the mind is filled with
grace, and a pledge of future glory is given to
us."[60]

The German Bishop's Conference in their Pastoral Letter of 1967, which we have mentioned
above, bore an eloquent witness to the eucharist
as a sacrifice. The bishops explained that in the
liturgical action of the holy Mass, the precious
legacy of the Lord to his Church, the institution
of the Holy Eucharist by Christ together with his
obedience unto death is re-presented in which
Christ the high Priest ratified the new and everlasting covenant and made his death on the cross
into a sacrifice. In the celebration of the Mass
therefore, the sacrifice of the cross and the
glorification of the Lord are re-presented and
become present. This means that the institution
of the eucharist by Christ cannot be separated
from his death On the cross. Hence they maintained: "Darum hat die heilige Messe auch Opfer-
character in dem vollen Sinn des Kreuzesopfers,
welches sakramental, im Zeichen und geheimnis-
voll, dargestellt und gegenwärtig wird."[61] The
re-presentation of the sacrifice of Christ on the
cross is the focal point in the bishops' teaching
and they made no mention of the propitiatory
character of the sacrifice of the Mass, rather
they emphasized that: "Der neue Bund verlangt die
Bundestreue des neuen Gottesvolkes und darum bei
der Teilnahme an der heiligen Messe die vorbe-
haltslose Hingabe der Gläubigen als christliche

---

60. S.C. 47; cf. also Nos. 2,41
61. Sekretariat der Deutschen Bischofskonferenz,
    Hrsg., op. cit., pp.22-24 "Therefore the holy
    Mass has a sacrificial character in the full
    sense of the sacrifice of the cross, which is
    sacramentally represented and made present in
    signs and mystery" (Translation is mine).

Grundhaltung überhaupt."[62]

I would like to mention one theologian's contribution to this issue. In his article[63], Cardinal
Ratzinger made a contribution towards the understanding of the sacrificial character of the
eucharist celebrated in the Mass, having recourse
to the biblical sources. Taking note that
Luther's rejection of the sacrifice of the Mass
as a relapse from faith into the law, the Cardinal says that the christian art of sacrifice
lies in receiving with thanksgiving, the presence
of the sacrifice of Christ and our fulfilment
from him. In his judicious consultation of the
biblical texts on the institution of the Eucharist, he grouped them into two: Matthew/Mark and
Luke/Paul. He discovers that each is marked by
the Old Testament theology and embodies as well
its concept of sacrifice. About the first group
he says: "Das eigentliche Zentrum der Thora, der
Bundesgedanke und seine kultische Realisierung
reicht so in diese Abendmahlsworte hinein und
erhält von da aus einen neuen Sinn. Das Abendmahl
erscheint in Parallel zum Bundesgeschehen am
Sinai und zu Seiner die Geschichte Israel fortan
durchziehenden kultischen Besiegelung, freilich
so, daß der neue Moses-Jesus - zugleich selbst
das Bundesblut dieser Bundesliturgie dahin-
gibt."[64] He maintains that unquestionably it is
through the concept of the "bundesblutes", blood
of the covenant, that the idea of sacrifice en-

---

62. ibid.
63. Ratzinger J., Ist die Eucharistie ein Opfer?,
    in: Concilium 3 (1967) 259-304.
64. op.cit., p.301.

ters into the event of the Eucharist. "Die Liturgie des Lebens und des Sterbens Jesu Christi wird als Bundesopfer angelegt, das den mosaischen Ansatz auf höherer Ebene aufgreift und zu seinem eigentlichen Sinn fügt."[65]

Again our author says that the Pauline type refers to the covenant theology of the prophets with its sharp criticism on the cult, which puts a question mark on the self-sufficent mark of the cultic affair; in this context therefore: "Das Abendmahl des Herrn steht nun da als die Erfüllung dieser geistigen Linie, wo wie es vorhin als die Erfüllung des Gesetzes aufgefaßt war."[66]

Applying the image of the servant of God's Songs of Deutro Isaiah, he spots out the medium between the cultic aspect of Matthew/Mark and the prophetic aspect of Luke/Paul. "Die Gottesknechtidee ist die einigende Mitte, die beide verbindet und so Gesetz und Propheten eins werden läßt. Damit haben wir den eigentlichen Kern des in den Abendmahlswörter liegenden neutestamentalichen Opferbegriffs gefunden. In diesem Gedenken sind das Gesetz und die Propheten, der Kult und die Kultkritik, gleichermaßen an ihrem Ziel angelangt."[67] In Jesus Christ therefore, the cult has found its meaning and is fulfilled, hence "Er selbst ist der Kult und in diesem Verständnis das Abendmahl ein Opfer, das wir danksagend empfangen, das in unserem Gedenken wahrhaft in unsere Mitte tritt."[68]

Thereafter he explains the meaning of memorial

---

65. ibid.
66. ibid.
67. op. vit., p.302.
68. ibid.

in the Old Testament, as being central to the
nature of sacrifice, a means of re-presentation,
"Indem Israel der Heilsgeschcihte gedenkt, empfängt es sie als Gegenwart, tritt es in diese
Geschichte ein und wird ihrer Wirklichkeit teil-
haft."[69] He concludes saying that thanksgiving
and sacrifice are not opposed to each other,
rather they define each other mutually.

5.1.6 EUCHARISTIC WORSHIP

In the dialogues in which the Catholic Church
is engaged with Protestant Churches and in the
Faith and Order discussions on the eucharist, the
reservation and worship of the eucharist outside
of Mass have been seriously discussed. The Holy
Father mentioned the eucharistic worship as one
of the areas in which disquieting opinions have
been expressed.

In the encyclical, Mysterium Fidei, the Pope
cited examples from the practice of the early
Church, which show that Christ is venerated in
the sacrament and that reservation of the eucharist orginated from the early Church. He recalled
how the Christians in times of persecution, in
the absence of a priest or deacon, would refresh
themselves daily with the Eucharist. He further
explains: "This cult of worship which ought to be
bestowed on the sacrament of the Eucharist has
been offered by the Church outside as well as
within the rites of the Mass, she still does so,
by using the greatest care in preserving conse-

---

69. ibid. "Through it Israel reflects on the
    salvation history, receives it as in the
    present, enters into this history and
    participates in its reality" (Translation
    is mine.)

crated Hosts, presenting them to the people for
their solemn veneration, carrying them in procession to the joy of the people in their
crowds."[70] It is the Church's faith in the real
presence of Christ which links the old practice
and the present one. Out of this same faith, the
feast of Corpus Christi sprung up and "many
customs of eucharistic piety have derived from
this faith and under the inspriation of divine
grace, they have increased from day to day. With
their help the Catholic Church strives, in an
almost competitive spirit, to render honour to
Christ, to thank him for his great gift, to im-
plore his mercy."[71]

In his exhortation to promote the eucharistic
cult, the Pope designates this cult as the
meeting-point and goal of other forms of piety.
The christians are exhorted to take part daily in
the eucharistic sacrifice, to receive holy communion and give thanks to the Lord for this great
gift. By their participation "they should be
united to God by the sacrament and draw strength
from it to restrain lust, to wash away the slight
faults of daily occurrence and to take precau-
tions against the more serious sins to which
human frailty is liable."[72]

The Pope devoted some time to explain the need
to pay visit to the reserved Eucharist and the
fruits derived therefrom. "Such a visit is a
proof of gratitude, a pledge of love, an observance of the adoration due to Christ the Lord
present in the Blessed Sacrament." On the fruits

---

70. Paul VI., Mysterium Fidei, op. cit., p.25.
71. op. cit., p.26.
72. op. cit., p.27

derived therefrom he said "Anyone therefore, who
bestows a singular devotion on the worshipful
Eucharist and makes the effort to return a prompt
and generous love to Christ, who has an infinite
love for us, gains delight of heart and enjoyment
to no small degree; he learns by experience and
fully comprehends the great value of the life
hidden with Christ in God and the efficacy of
engaging in conversation with Christ. Nothing on
this earth holds more delight, nothing is more
effective for covering the road to sanctity."[73]
The Holy Father further described the eucharist
beautifully to encourage the faithful to have
interest in the eucharistic cult. The eucharist is
the sign and cause of the unity of the Mystical
Body of Christ. In the eucharistic cult the faithful are sustained in their entreaty for the
Church's unity and peace.

The Instruction on Worship of the Eucharistic
Mystery of May 25 1967, published by the Sacred
Congregation of Rites stated clearly the purpose
for the reservation of the Eucharist. The Congregation wrote in line with the Council of Trent
and said: "It would be well to recall that the
primary and original purpose of the reserving of
the sacred species in Church outside Mass is the
administration of the Viaticum. Secondary ends
are the distribution of communion outside Mass
and the adoration of Our Lord Jesus Christ concealed beneath these same species."[74] The text

---

73. op. cit., p.28
74. Instructio de cultu mysterii eucharistici,
    AAS, 59 (1967) 539-573, Sacred Congregation
    of Rites, 25 May 1967; quoted according
    English translation, St. Paul Editions,
    Boston, U.S.A., pp.31-32, No.49.

made it clear that the presence of Christ in the
reserved species demands adoration. "The reservation of the sacred species for the sick... led to
the praiseworthy custom of adoring the heavenly
food which is preserved in Churches. This practice of adoration has a valid and firm foundation, especially since belief in the real presence of the Lord has as its natural consequence
the external and public manifestation of the
belief."[75] The Instruction reminds the faithful
of something they should bear in mind when they
adore Christ present in the sacrament and that
is: that this presence of Christ in the sacrament
derives from the sacrifice of the Mass and is
directed toward both sacramental and spiritual
communion.

The German Bishop's Conference in their afore
mentioned Pastoral Letter justified the eucharistic worship outside Mass, because of the lasting
presence of Christ in the sacrament of the altar.
They pointed out that this type of cult is fully
approved and promoted by the Church for centuries
and that it has brought to the spiritual life
enermous fruits; and at the end they warned: "Es
wäre daher sicher unberechtigt und unkirchlich,
die Anbetung Christi in diesem Sakrament außerhalb der Messe in Mißkredit zu bringen."[76]

---

75. idem.
76. ibid.
     "It would be unjust and unecclesiastical to
     discredit the worship of Christ in this
     sacrament outside the Mass." (Translation is
     mine.)

5.1.7 SUMMARY.

As we said at the beginning of this chapter,
our purpose is to expose the Catholic teaching on
the eucharist, as it is expressed in the encyclical, Mysterium Fidei. The encyclical itself is an
internal matter for the Catholics. The encyclical
as an official teaching organ of the Magisterium,
serves also as a means of restating the dogma of
the Church when the Pope notices that false
opinions are being propagated by any individual
or group against any doctrine of the Church.

The encyclical does not rule out that progress
can be made in the understanding of the faith, as
is evident in the case we have examined, it only
appeals that while explaining the doctrine of the
Church the original meaning declared by the
Church must be retained. This makes it possible
for the theologians representing the Catholic
Church in the various ecumenical dialogues to
work with their counterparts together towards a
convergence agreement on matters of faith and
doctrine.

It is my intention to leave the expositions as
they are for the time being, as they will later
come to be applied in the next chapter.

5.2 THE NEW ORDER OF MASS.

The Faith and Order Commission in its general
assembly at Bristol in 1967, which we have presented in chapter three above, adopted a report
on the Holy Eucharist. In the report, the general
assembly held that the liturgy should express
adequately both the anamnetic and the epikletic
character of the eucharist because, anamnesis is
the very essence of the preached Word as it is of
the Eucharist. At the same time epiclesis was
defined as the invocation of the Spirit upon the
people of God and upon the whole eucharistic
action including the elements. Earlier on at the
consultation at Grandchamp in 1965, which marked
the beginning of eucharist as a study project by
Faith and Order Commission, the Roman Catholic
Church was accused of neglecting the role of
epiclesis in the structure of the eucharistic
celebration. It also recalled that in the past
the East has emphasized the role of epiclesis as
bringing about the eucharistic miracle, while the
West emphasized the Words of institution as
accomplishing the same eucharistic miracle. The
Faith and Order Commission at Bristol maintains
that "it is the Spirit who, in our Eucharist
makes Christ really present and given to us in the
bread and wine, according to the words of institution."[77]
The presentation of the New Order of Mass is
designed to show how the eucharistic liturgy is
celebrated by the Roman Catholic Church after the
implimentation of the reforms ordered by the

---

77. cf. note 57 of chapter three of this work.

Second Vatican Council; it will show the importance attached to the restored epiclesis and its
relation to anamnesis in the structure of the
eucharistic prayers. Let us now turn over to the
text itself, starting with a short history about·
the New Order of the Mass.

5.2.1 PRELIMINARY HISTORY.

The Second Vatican Council in its Constitution
on the Sacred Liturgy, (Sacrosanctum concilium),
laid the foundation for the revision of the Roman
Missal, which implies as well the reform of the
structure of the Mass. In undertaking the reform
of the Sacred liturgy, the Council had the good
of the Christians in mind and their active participation in the sacred rites, for the Constitution itself says: "In order that the Christian
people may more securely derive an abundance of
graces from the sacred liturgy, holy Mother
Church desires to undertake with great care a
general restoration of the liturgy itself. For the
liturgy is made up of unchangeable elements
divinely instituted, and elements subject to
change... In this restoration, both texts and
rites should be drawn up so that they express
more clearly the holy things which they
signify."[78] For the full understanding of the
rites which are to be revised, the Council directed that a careful investigation be carried out
which should be theological, liturgical and pastoral.[79]

---

78. S.C. 21.
79. S.C. 23.

In the paragraphs devoted to the Eucharist,
the Council gave the following instructions about
the revision of the rite of the Mass: "The rite
of the Mass is to be revised in such a way that
the intrinsic nature and purpose of its serveral
parts, as also the connection between them, can
be more clearly manifested, and that devout and
active participation by the faithful can be more
easily accomplished. For this purpose the rites
are to be simplified, while due care is taken to
preserve their substance. Elements which with the
passage of time, came to be duplicated, or were
added with but little advantage are now to be
discarded. Where opportunity allows or necessity
demands, other elements which have suffered in-
jury through accidents of history are now to be
restored to the earlier norm of the holy
Fathers."[80]

The Constitution on the Sacred Liturgy was
promulgated on 4 December 1963, and a few weeks
later, Pope Paul VI, set up the machinery for the
implimentation of the Council's liturgy reforms.
On 25. January 1964, he formed a Liturgical Council consisting 10 Cardinals, 32 Bishops and about
200 experts as consultors, coming from 26 countries.[81] On 29 February 1964, the Liturgical
Council began to work. The Council organized
itself under twelve study groups[82], each group
undertaking a specific assignment. There was a
study group for the structure of the Mass and

---

80. S.C. 50
81. Lengeling E.J., Die neue Ordnung der
    Eucharistiefeier, Münster, Verlag Regenberg,
    1970, p.25.
82. op. cit., p.28

another for the eucharistic prayers, just to
mention but a few.

The work of the Liturgical Council on the
revision of the Roman Missal was presented to the
Synod of Bishops of 1967 and votes were conducted
and taken. After necessary corrections and amend-
ments were made the New Order of Mass was ready
for promulgation.

In his Apostolic Constitution, Missale
Romanum, of 3. April 1969, Pope Paul VI, promulgated and restored the Roman Missal. Three days
later, by his command the Sacred Congregation of
Rites published the New Order of Mass together
with the General Instruction on the Roman Missal.

In the Apostolic Constitution, the Pope revealed that three new Eucharistic Prayers were
introduced; and for pastoral reasons and to facilitate concelebration, he ordered that the
Words of Institution by our Lord should be the
same in all forms of the Eucharistic Prayer. As
for the Order of the Mass, the Holy Father said
that 'the rites have been simplified, due care
having been taken to preserve their substance'.
The Pope mentioned other areas affected by the
revision other than the Order of Mass, Eucharistic Prayer and scripture readings: "Besides
these, other elements of it have been thoroughly
investigated and considerably modified. These are
the Proper of the Season, the Proper of the
Saints, the Common of the Saints, the Ritual
Masses for particular occasions, and the Votive
Masses. In all of these special attention has
been given to the Collects. Their number has been
increased so that they may better correspond with

the needs of our own times..."[83] In conclusion
the Pope expressed the hope that the New Missal
will be received by the faithful as an aid
"whereby all can witness to each other and
strengthen the one faith common to all, since it
enables one and the same prayer expressed in so
many different languages, to ascend to the heavenly Father through our High Priest Jesus Christ
in the Holy Spirit - a prayer more fragrant than
any incense."[84]

The General Instruction on the Roman Missal
explains in detail how the Eucharist is to be
celebrated. It specifies the structure of the
Mass, the role of the priest and the people during the celebration. Before it went into the
structure of the Mass the General Instruction has
this to say about the Mass: "The celebration of
the Mass, as an action of Christ and the people
of God hierarchically ordered, is the centre of
the whole Christian life for the universal
Church, the local Church and for each and every
one of the faithful. For therein is the culmina-
ting action whereby God sanctifies the world in
Christ and men worship the Father as they adore
him through Christ the Son of God. The mysteries
of man's redemption are in some way made present
throughout the course of the year by the celebration of Mass. All other sacred celebrations and
the activities of the Christian life are related

---

83. Paul VI, Apostolic Constitution, Missale
    Romanum, AAS (quoted according to: Howell C.,
    English translation, London, C.T.S., 1973,
    p.5.
84. op. cit., pp. 5-6

to the Mass; they spring forth from and culminate in it."[85]

5.2.2 THE STRUCTURE OF THE MASS.

The General Instruction on the Roman Missal stated that "The Mass is made up of two parts, the Liturgy of the Word and the Liturgy of the Eucharist. They are so closely connected with each other that together they constitute but one single act of worship. In the Mass both the table of God's word and the table of Christ's Body are prepared, so that from them the faithful may be instructed and nourished. There are also some introductory and concluding rites."[86] On the point that the Liturgy of the Word and the Liturgy of the Eucharist constitute a single act of worship, the Sacred Congregation of Rites in its Instruction on Worship of the Eucharistic Mystery laid emphasis on that, for it says: "Pastors should therefore carefully teach the faithful to participate in the whole Mass showing the close connection between the Liturgy of the Word and the celebration of the Lord's Supper, so that they can see clearly how the two constitute a single act of worship. For the preaching of the Word is necessary for the administration of the sacraments, in as much as they are sacraments of faith, which is born of the Word and fed by it...When therefore the faithful hear the Word of

---

85. G.I. no. 1. quoted according to: Howell C., op. cit., p.14.
86. op. cit., p.16

God, they should realize that the wonders it
proclaims culminate in the Paschal Mystery, of
which the memorial is sacramentally celebrated in
the Mass."[87] Let us now concern ourself with the
individual parts and elements of the Mass in the
whole structure.

5.2.3 THE LITURGY OF THE WORD.

    A. INTRODUCTORY RITES.
    a. Entrance Antiphon.
    b. The Priest venerates the altar, thereafter
       makes the sign of the cross together with
       the people.
    c. The Penitenital Rite.
    d. The Gloria.
    e. The Collect or opening prayer.

The Entrance Antiphon deepens the unity of the
people and introduces us to the mystery of the
season. Within the sanctuary there stands that
which is the very heart of the Church - the
altar. Entering the sanctuary the priest vene-
rates the altar with a kiss. The Penitential act
consists of an acknowledgment by all of their
sins and the priest concludes it by praying for
God's forgiveness. Then an appeal for mercy,
(Kyrie), is made if it is not included within the
penitential act. The Gloria is an ancient and
very venerable hymn by which the Church gathered

---

87. Eucharisticum Mysterium No. 10, quoted
    according to N.C.W.C. Translation, St. Paul
    editions, Boston, p.11.

in the Spirit praises and prays to the Father and
the Lamb. The Introductory Rites conclude with a
prayer which expresses the theme of the celebration and addresses a petition in the people's
name to God the Father through the mediation of
Christ in the Holy Spirit.

B. THE LITURGY OF THE WORD.

a. First Reading.

b. Responsorial Psalm.

c. Second Reading.

d. Allelluia.

e. Gospel.

f. Homily.

g. The profession of Faith.

h. The prayer of the Faithful.

The first reading is usually taken from the
Old Testament (except in the season of Easter), a
recall of the aspirations of the ancient Jews
fulfilled in Christ. Then a Psalm is read or
sung; when it is read, the people respond. The
second reading is taken from the New Testament
Letters of the Apostles, followed by Allelluia
except in the season of Lent. The Liturgy of the
Word reaches its climax in the reading of the
Gospel, which deals directly with God's manifestation in Jesus Christ. As a rule, the Homily
develops some points of the Bible readings of the
day. Thereafter the people make the Profession of
Faith whose purpose "is to express the assent and
response of the people to the scripture readings
and homily they have just heard, and to recall to
them the main truths of the faith, before they

begin to celebrate the Eucharist."[88]

5.2.4 THE LITURGY OF THE EUCHARIST.

   a. Preparation of the Gifts.
   b. The Eucharistic Prayer.
   c. Communion Rite.

At the beginning of the eucharistic liturgy
the bread and wine destined to become the Body
and Blood of Christ are brought to the altar. The
Offertory Antiphon is intended to accompany the
procession in which the gifts are carried to the
sanctuary. The Preparation of the Gifts is concluded by an invitation to the people to pray
with the priest, and by the prayer over the Gifts
which leads into the eucharistic prayer.
   The Eucharistic Prayer will be demonstrated
with the second Eucharistic Prayer, and the elements will be vividly outlined.

EUCHARISTIC PRAYER TWO.

Celebrant: The Lord be with you.
People: And also with you.
Celebrant: Lift up your hearts.
People: We lift them up to the Lord.
Celebrant: Let us give thanks to the Lord our
             God.
People: It is right to give him thanks and
             praise.

_____

88. G.I. no. 43, Howell C., op. cit. p.25

PREFACE:

Father, it is our duty and our salvation,
always and everywhere to give you thanks through
your beloved Son, Jesus Christ.
He is the Word through whom you made the universe,
the Saviour you sent to redeem us.
By the power of the Holy Spirit
he took flesh and was born of the Virgin Mary.
For our sake he opened his arms on the cross;
he put an end to death
and revealed the resurrection.
In this he fulfilled your will
and won for you a holy people.
And so we join the angels and the Saints
in proclaiming your glory
as we sing (say):
SANCTUS:

Holy, holy, holy Lord, God of power and might,
heaven and earth are full of your glory. Hossanna
in the highest. Blessed is he who comes in the
name of the Lord.
Hossanna in the highest.
EPICLESIS:

Lord, you are holy indeed, the fountain of all
holiness. Let your Spirit come upon these gifts
to make them holy, so that they may become for us
the body and blood of our Lord, Jesus Christ.
INSTITUTION NARRATIVE AND CONSECRATION:

Before he was given up to death, a death he
freely accepted, he took bread and gave you
thanks. He took the bread, gave it to his diciples, and said:
Take this, all of you, and eat it:
This is my body which will be given up for you.

When supper was ended, he took the Cup. Again
he gave you thanks and praise, gave the cup to
his diciples, and said: Take this, all of you,
and drink it: This is the cup of my blood, the
blood of the new and everlasting covenant. It
will be shed for you and for all men so that sins
may be forgiven. Do this in memory of me.

ACCLAMATION:

Priest: Let us proclaim the mystery of faith.

People: When we eat this bread and drink this
         cup, we proclaim your death, Lord Jesus,
         until you come in glory.

ANAMNESIS AND OBLATION:

In memory of his death and resurrection, we
offer you, Father, this life-giving bread, this
saving cup. We thank you for counting us worthy
to stand in your presence and serve you.

SECOND EPICLESIS:

May all of us who share in the body and blood
of Christ be brought together in unity by the
Holy Spirit.

INTERCESSIONS: (FOR THE CHURCH).

Lord, remember your Church throughout the
world; make us grow in love, together with N. our
Pope, N. our bishop, and all the clergy.

(FOR THE DEAD).

Remember our brothers and sisters who have
gone to their rest in the hope of rising again;
bring them and all the departed into the light of
your presence.

(IN COMMUNION WITH THE SAINTS).

Have mercy on us all; make us worthy to share
eternal life with Mary, the virgin mother of God,
with the apostles, and with all the saints who
have done your will throughout the ages. May we

praise you in union with them, and give you glory
through your Son Jesus Christ.
DOXOLOGY:
Through him, with him, in him,
in the unity of the Holy Spirit,
all glory and honour is yours,
almighty Father, for ever and ever.
People: Amen.

The Eucharistic Prayer begins with thanksgiving which finds its clearest expression in the
Preface. The priest in the name of all the people
of God offers praise and thanksgiving to God the
Father for the work of redemption or for some
particular aspect of it, according to the day,
feast or season. Then the entire congregation in
union with the heavenly powers sings or says the
Sanctus, which is regarded as an integral part of
the eucharistic prayer itself.

The epiclesis is a special petition by the
Church that the power of God should intervene to
consecrate the gifts proffered by mankind, so
that they may become the body and blood of
Christ. The second epiclesis is a petition for
the sanctification and unity of those who share
in the body and blood of Christ.

In the Anamnesis the Church fulfilling the
command she has received from her Lord through
the apostles, celebrates the memorial of Christ,
calling to mind especially his blessed passion,
his glorious resurrection and his ascent to
heaven. It is through this very memorial that
the Church, assembled here and now, offers the
holy Victim to God the Father in the Holy Spirit.

The intercessions express the truth that the

Eucharist is celebrated in union with the whole
Church in heaven and on earth, and that sacrifice
is offered for her and for all her members living
and dead, since all of them are called to share
in the redemption and salvation acquired through
the body and blood of Christ.

The doxology brings the eucharistic prayer to
a close; it is an expression of the praise of
God, emphasized and concluded by the people's
acclamation.

THE COMMUNION RITE.
   a. The Lord's Prayer.
   b. The Rite of Peace.
   c. The Breaking of Bread.
   d. Agnus Dei.
   e. Invitation.
   f. Communion.
   g. Communion Antiphon.
   h. Pause.
   i. Post-communion.

In the Lord's Prayer, we ask for our daily
bread which, for Christians means also the eucharistic bread; we beg forgiveness of our sins, so
that those to whom the Holy Things are given may
in truth be holy.[89] By word and gesture the
people pray for peace and unity in the Church and
the whole human family, and express their love
for one another before they share the one bread.[90]
In early Christianity the Eucharist was known as

89. G.I. no. 56a, op. cit., p.30.
90. ibid.

"The Breaking of Bread." "The purpose of breaking
the bread is not merely practicable; it is also
intended to convey a meaning. It means that
through communion, we though many in number,
become one body because we eat one Bread of Life
which is Christ."[91] Having broken the bread the
priest drops a part of the host into the chalice.
About this action J. Jungmann wrote: "While in the
oldest documents the commingling of the two species, during which a particle of the host is
dropped into the chalice, was interpreted as the
union of the two species to constitute one single
whole - the body and blood of the one Christ -
the Syrian documents seem to indicate that a
deeper significance was attached to this action.
After Christ's body and blood had been re-presented under the two separate species by the double
consecration, and his Passion and death had
thereby been symbolized, the sacred gifts had to
be re-presented now before communion as the food
of immortality, as the living unity of the risen
Lord's body and blood."[92] Meanwhile the Agnus Dei
is sung or recited by the people. The priest
receives the Body and Blood of Christ and distri-
butes them also to the people. In the course of
this, communion hymn is sung or the communion
antiphon recited. After Communion the priest and
the people settle down for a few moment of silent
prayer; thereafter the priest invites all to
Post-communion prayer. The people associate themselves with this prayer by adding their Amen.

---

91. ibid.
92. Jungmann J., The Mass, Collgegeville,
    Minnesota, The Liturgical Press, 1976, p.208.

THE CONCLUDING RITES.
  a. The priest greets the people and gives them
     his blessing.
  b. Finally comes the formal dismissal of the
     assembly who may now return to their daily
     lives of good works, praising and blessing
     God.

The presentation of the liturgical structure
of celebrating the Eucharist in the Roman Catholic Church here is for its use in evaluating the
Lima Liturgy in the next chapter and secondly to
show how the elements that formed part of the
eucharistic celebration and which are topics for
discussion in the Faith and Order dialogue on the
eucharist, are translated into Catholic liturgy
of the Eucharist.

5.3 EXKURS: ANAMNESIS.

The Eucharist has often been described in the
Faith and Order documents in its study project on
the eucharist in terms of Anamnesis. In the Lima
Convergence Text on the Eucharist the description
reads: "The Eucharist is the memorial of the
crucified and risen Christ, i.e. the living and
effective sign of his sacrifice, accomplished once
and for all on the cross and still operative on
behalf of all humankind. The biblical idea of
memorial as applied to the eucharist refers to
this present efficacy of God's work when it is
celebrated by God's people in liturgy."[93] A brief
biblical survey of the word in its liturgical
context will perhaps throw more light into its
application and understanding of the eucharist.

The word Anamnesis comes from the Greek word
avamvesis, meaning: rememberance, commemoration,
memorial. One author is of the opinion that the
word is untranslatable into English, for memorial, commemoration, remembrance suggest that
the person or deed commemorated is past and absent, whereas anamnesis means exactly the
opposite. He defined anamnesis in these words:
"It is an objective act, in and by which the
person or event commemorated is actually made
present, is brought into the realm of the here
and now. And the eucharist, as the early Church
understood it, is the 're-calling' before God of
the one sacrifice of Christ in all its accomplished fullness so that it is here and now opera-

---

93. World Council of Churches, Baptism, Eucharist
    and Ministry, Geneva, 1982, p.11.

tive by its effects in the souls of the redeemed."[94] The revered Odo Casel categorises the
definition of anamnesis into subjective and objective. In the subjective sense, anamnesis, i.e.
memorial, remembrance "is the capability of our
spirit, to retain images formed from experiences
and things which are far from us either in time
or space."[95] The objective, he calls cultic memorial. It is objective, that is, it exists inspite
of myself. Something happens in the cult which
does not depend on a human person as its subject.
Hence he calls anamnesis also a mysterium.

5.3.1 OLD TESTAMENT.

To come to grips with the word memorial, in
Hebrew (zikkaron), and its meaning in the Old
Testament, we have to begin from the institution
of the Passover Feast in the Book of Exodus. A
detailed survey is not to be undertaken; suffice
it to cite a few examples. Before the tenth pla-
gue in Egypt, Yahweh instituted the Passover
Feast. The Israelites were to celebrate it to
mark their delivery out of Egypt, generation
after generation. After giving the laws that
would guide the celebration Yahweh concluded with
Moses saying: "This day is to be a day of remembrance for you, and you must celebrate it as a
feast in Yahweh's honour. For all generations you

---

94. Davies J.G., (ed.), A Dictionary of Liturgy &
    Worship, London, SCM, 1972, p.25.
95. Warnach V., (Hrsg.), Odo Casel, Das
    christiliche Opfermysterium, Wien, Köln,
    Styria, 1968, p.492. Cf. also Thurian Max,
    Eucharistie, Stuttgart-Mainz, Kreuzverlag,
    1963, p.16.

are to declare it a day of festival, for ever."[96]
The Israelites are to keep to the rules and ordinances governing this feast when they have
taken possession of the promised Land and should
their children ask why they keep the rituals they
should answer: "It is a sacrifice of the Passover
in honour of Yahweh who passed over the houses of
the sons of Israel in Egypt, and struck Egypt but
spared our houses."[97] In the same Deuteronomic
form, the reason for the feast of the Unleavened
Bread could be explained to the children in these
words. "This is because of what Yahweh did for me
when I came out of Egypt. The rite will serve as
a sign on your forehead, and in that way the law
of Yahweh will be ever on your lips, for Yahweh
brought you out of Egypt with a mighty hand."[98]
Earlier on as Moses talked to the people about
the feast of Unleavened Bread, he said: "Keep
this day in remembrance, the day you came out of
Egypt, from the house of slavery, for it was by
sheer power that Yahweh brought you out of it; no
leavened bread must be eaten."[99] In each case
where the word remembrance is used, it refers to
the event of the Israelites delivery` from Egypt
made present. This idea of actualizing the past
in the present during the celebration is vivid in
the Book of Deuteronomy. Thus the legislation on
the celebration of Passover Feast and the feast of
Unleavened Bread was given: "Observe the month of
Abib and celebrate the Passover for Yahweh your
God, because it was in the month of Abib that

---

96. Ex.12:14
97. Ex.2:26.
98. Ex.13,8-9.
99. Ex.13,3-4.

Yahweh your God brought you out of Egypt by
might."[100] The following verses 3 and 6 reinforce
the idea that the participants in the rite of the
Pasch are by that fact themselves participants in
the historical Exodus. The verses read: "You must
not eat leavened bread with this; for seven days
you must eat it with unleavened bread, the bread
of emergency, for it was in great haste that you
came out of the land of Egypt." "But only in the
place where Yahweh your God chooses to give his
name a home, there you must sacrifice the Passover, in the evening at sunset, at the hour at
which you came out of Egypt." On the question of
representing the Exodus event in the Passover
celebration, Thurian wrote: "The Jewish Passover
permits liturgically to re-experience the liberation from the Egyptian servitude, which is a sign
of the great eschatological liberation on the day
on which the Messias will come."[101]

The Paschal Feast in the Old Testament is
understood as a sacrifice with three dimensional
memorials: the past, the present and the future.
On the past as a dimension of the Paschal memorial Daly said: "The past is present in this
feast because, regardless of what the original
significance of the Pasch might have been, it had
been historicised as a memorial of the Exodus
event quite early in Israel's literary history.
The liturgy, however, did not merely recall, it
also actualized or made present i.e. re-presented, the Exodus event, making of it in a real
sense, a present reality for those taking part in

---

100. Dt. 16,1.
101. Thurian Max, Eucharistie, op. cit., p.28.
     (Translation is mine.)

the feast."[102] A further indication of the presence of the past in the Paschal feast is the
increasing tendency of the Jewish tradition to
consider every significant event of the Old
Testament, that is, every event of salvation
history as a Paschal event. Thus, even before
christianity, the Paschal feast had already become a comprehensive compendium of salvation
history.[103]

How then does the present have the memorial
dimension in the Paschal celebration? Daly again
wrote: "The present dimension is not exhausted
merely by the fact that the past Exodus event was
thought to be re-presented by the participants in
the feast; the participants in the Paschal rite
were considered also to be the recipients of
salvific action and here and now. This comes from
the character of the Pasch both as memorial and
as a sacrifice."[104]

The Paschal memorial has a future dimension or
is eschatological. This is embedded in the Jewish custom which considers the original Exodus
Pasch to be the model or archtype of the final
salvation event to take place at the end of history. In this context Schildenberger wrote: "The
old salvation act itself is not simply a past
event as in the case of human activities, so that
the Passover in its festival proclamation or
festival reading would only appear to be a remembrance feast or something of the past; this feast,

---

102. Daly R.J., Christian Sacrifice, Washington,
     D.C., The Catholic University of America
     Press, 1978, p.199.
103. op. cit., p.100
104. op. cit., p.200

started in faith implies and guarantees that the
old saving action of God is still actual and
shall manifest itself in the new saving actions
until it finds its end in the eschatological
saving act of Yahweh and until salvation brings
eternity."[105]

5.3.2 NEW TESTAMENT.

The Synoptic writers place the Last Supper and
death of Christ in a Paschal framework. John sees
Jesus sacrificed as a Paschal Lamb (Jn. 19,36),
and Paul sees the decisive Christian event as the
sacrificing of Christ our Pasch (1Cor 6,7).
Before we go on to examine anamnesis, resul-
ting from Christ's mandate at the Last Supper,
let us briefly survey a few instances in which
the word anamnesis occured in the New Testament.
Heb.10:3, reads: "Instead of that, the sins are
recalled year after year in the sacrifices." This
is the case where the sacrifice of the Old Law
was compared with the sacrifice of Christ. In the
old law the sins are recalled yearly, a sign that
these sacrifices could not remove sins. In contrast, the once and for all sacrifice of Christ
on the cross has taken away the sins of men.
Another example is taken from Acts 10:4, "...your
offering of prayer and alms, the angel answered,
has ascended as a memorial before God." This is

---

105. Schildenberger J., Der Gedächtnischarakter
     des alt- und neutestamentalichen Pascha, in:
     Neunheuser B., (Hrsg.), Opfer Christi und
     Opfer der Kirche, Düsseldorf, Patmos, 1960,
     p.87. (Translation is mine).

the case of Cornelius, a Roman Centurion. Again
Mt.26,13; Mk14,9; "I tell you solemnly, wherever
in all the world this Good News is proclaimed,
what she has done will be told also, in remembrance of her." This is the case of the woman who
anointed the head of Christ at Bethany in Simon
the leper's house. Because some were indignant at
her action, Christ intervened in her favour using
the words cited.

In the first instance the word memorial was
used in view of sins to be forgiven; in the second it is the memorial of prayer and charity and
the third is in remembrance of a saint.

Now let us turn to the mandate Christ gave to
his apostles to celebrate the eucharist until he
comes in glory. "Do this in memory of me." These
words are found once in Lk22,19, and two times in
Paul, 1Cor11,24;25. Paul himself says that when
the christians celebrate the eucharist "they are
proclaiming the Lord's death" (1Cor11,26). The
mandate has to be understood in the context of
what Christ did and said. The words "my body
which will be given up for you...my blood which
is for you (or for many), for the forgiveness of
sins", (Mt 26,26ff), re-present the Lord in the
sacrifical condition of his death. In these words
he anticipated his sacrificial death on the
cross. Hence Schildenberger maintains: "Do this
in memory of me", i.e. the action of the apostles
in which they repeat exactly, what Jesus did
particularly now in his last Paschal meal, shall
be a remembrance of his person. It is also unequivocally a remembrance of his sacrificial

death."[106]

Interpreting Christ's mandate to bring out the
meaning of the memorial Thurian wrote: "This
memorial is not simply a subjective remembering,
but a liturgical action; not only a liturgical
action which makes the Lord present, but also a
liturgical action, which evokes before the Father
in memorial the unique sacrifice of the Son."[107]
A. Gerken explains this mandate in twofold.
Firstly the eucharistic anamnesis in the liturgical setting is the representation of Jesus and
his works especially his saving death and resurrection. He compares the eucharist with the Passover Feast. As the Passover in the Old covenant
re-presents the fundamental saving act of God,
the delivery from Egypt and the assurance to the
Israelites in the sense that God remembers his
own; so also the eucharistic celebration is the
representation of the basic saving act of the new
covenant, the death and resurrection of Christ.
He brings out the eschatological character of the
memorial in his second explanation. St. Paul
expressly said it in his narration of the institution. The eucharist celebration is the prayer
for the coming of Christ in glory. In other words
the eucharist is the liturgical celebration of
the covenant people in via through history,
liberated from the servitude of sin are on the
way to the future glory, the final community with
Christ in the kingdom of the Father.[108]

---

106. op. cit., p.88 (translation is mine).
107. Thurian Max, op. cit., p.159. (Translation
     is mine).
108. Gerken A., Theologie der Eucharistie,
     München, Kösel, 1973, p.39ff.

At this juncture we can join our voices with
Faith and Order Commission to say that: "Christ
himself with all he has accomplished for us and
for all creation (in incarnation, servanthood,
ministry, teaching, suffering, sacrifice, resurrection, ascension and sending of the Spirit) is
present in this anamnesis, granting us communion
with himself. The eucharist is also the foretaste
of his parousia and of the final kingdom."[109]

The eucharist then is the anamnesis of the
sacrifice of Christ on the cross. That is to say
that in celebrating the eucharist the sacrifice
of the cross is sacramentally represented. Applying the biblical explication of anamnesis
therefore, it is possible to call the eucharist a
sacrifice. This is what the Council of Trent did
in its twenty-second session, in defining that
the salvation of mankind is effected by the
sacrifice of the cross; that the Holy Mass is not
a sacrifice independent of that of the cross but
a re-presentation of it; and that at the Last
Supper Christ made an offering and commanded the
apostles to do likewise.[110] The great ecumenist
Max Thurian is of the opinion that in the biblical context of anamnesis, it is possible to
speak about the eucharist in terms of sacrifice.
In the same line of thought, Schmaus wrote that
anamnesis is employed in the theological explanation of the identity between the sacrifice of the
cross and the eucharistic sacrifice.[111]

---

109. BEM, op. cit., no.6., p.11.
110. cf., DS 1738, 1741-1743.
111. Schmaus M., Der Glaube der Kirche, Band 2,
    München, Max Hueber Verlag, 1970.
    cf., Thurian M., op. cit., p.204 ff.

5.4 INTERCOMMUNION (COMMUNICATIO IN SACRIS).

This section is designed to expose the Catholic Church's stand on the issue of intercommunion, known as communicatio in sacris. The subject matter, intercommunion has featured prominently in the discussion of Faith and Order since the World Conference at Edinburgh. In chapters two and three of this work, the issue intercommunion has been presented wherever it has been treated in the different general assemblies of Faith and Order Commission. In the World Conference at Lund, Section V reported on intercommunion. The definitions at Lund was improved upon at Louvain, in the report: Beyond Intercommunion. We presented as well in chapter three, a programme worked out by a group comprising Protestants and Catholics on inter-celebration.

Now let us examine the official stand of the Catholic Church on intercommunion. It belongs to the Secretatiat for the Promotion of Christian Unity (SPCU), to issue directives on the Catholic Church's stand or teaching on intercommunion. But before we go on to present the directives let us briefly ex-ray the origin of SPCU.

5.4.1 A BRIEF HISTORY OF SPCU.

On January 1959, Pope John XXIII announced his intention to convoke an "Ecumenical Council for the Universal Church." In his clarification six months later, he made it clear that only bishops in communion with the See of Rome would assemble at the Council. Later in the year, Archbishop

Jaeger of Paderborn, described as "Germany's foremost leader in ecumenical discussions",[112] contacted a Jesuit priest, later Cardinal A. Bea, then one of the Pope's advisers, with the suggestion of discussing with the Pope to establish 'a commission for the union of Christians'; such a commission when founded would be an explicit instrument in guiding the Council's ecumenical dimensions of Church renewal and in facilitating communications with other christians. This move made by the Archbishop yielded a good result.

In his Mortu Proprio, "Superno Dei nutu", of 5 June 1960, Pope John XXIII, instituted among the twelve preparatory conciliar bodies, the Secretariat for the Promotion of Christian Unity, and appointed Augustine Cardinal Bea its president. The Pope stipulated that the Secretariat would enable: "those who bear the name of Christians but are separated from this Apostolic See...to follow the work of the Council and to find more easily the path by which they may arrive at the unity for which Christ prayed."[113]

From 1960-1965, the SPCU was directly concerned about the Second Vatican Council. In the preparatory years it issued invitation to world confessional bodies like The Lambeth Conference, The Lutheran World Federation and the Oriental Churches to send observers at the Council's sessions. Besides other liason activities of the

---

112. Stransky T.F., and Sheerin J.B. (ed.), Doing the Truth in Charity, New York, Paulist Press, 1982, p.7.
113. Superno Dei nutu: AAS 52 (1960), p.436, quoted here according to: Stransky T.F., Sheerin J.B. (eds.), op. cit., p.7.

Secretariat, the Council owes to SPCU, the draft
of three conciliar documents, namely: Decree on
Ecumenism, Declaration on Religious Freedom and
Declaration on Non-Christians.[114]

A detailed account of the activities of SPCU
is not forseen in this work; suffice it to say
that it has been a useful organ of the Catholic
Church in the field of ecumenism since its inception.

After the Council, Pope Paul VI, confirmed the
SPCU as a permanent organ of the Holy See, alongside the creation of two Secretariats, one for
Non-Christians and the other for Non-Believers.
In his Constitution on the Roman Curia reform,
Regimini Ecclesiae universae, of 15 august 1967,
Pope Paul VI specified the competence of SPCU in
these words: "it shall foster relations with
Christians of other Churches, execute those Vatican decree which bear on ecumenism, see to the
right interpretation and carrying out of ecumenical principles, establish or encourage and coor-
dinate national and international Catholic ecumenical organisations, institute official dialogues with other Churches and Christian communities, and delegate official Catholic observers
to Christian meetings, while also inviting non-
Catholic observers to Catholic meetings."[115]

Little wonder then, that on the issue of
intercommunion, it belongs to the portfolio of
SPCU to issue a directory in the name of the

---

114. cf. Krüger H., Löser W., (Hrsg.), Ökumene
     Lexikon, Frankfurt, Verlag Otto Lembeck
     etc., 1987, p.309
115. Regimini Ecclesiae universae: AAS 59 (1967),
     pp.918-919, quoted according to: Stranky
     T.F., Sheerin T.B. (ed.) op. cit., p.8.

Catholic Church. Before going on to examine the
instruction on intercommunion let us briefly look
into another document: The Ecumenical Directory,
for the former presupposes the latter and refers
to it.

5.4.2 THE ECUMENICAL DIRECTORY, MAY 1967.

As we have seen above, it belongs to the SPCU
to execute those Vatican decrees dealing on ecumenism. The first step taken by the SPCU was to
issue a directory for the application of the
discussions on ecumenical matters rising from the
Second Vatican Council. The Ecumenical Directory
was approved by Pope Paul VI, and was issued on
14 May 1967.

The Directory which took off with the stipula-
tion of setting up ecumenical commissions on the
diocesan and territorial levels, considered also
what it called spiritual ecumenism. To the latter
belongs also, what the Directory called sharing
in liturgical worship. This is further sub-divided into: sharing in liturgical worship with our
'Separated Eastern Brother' and with 'other Separated Brethren'.

By quoting from the Council's decree on Ecumenism, the Directory reiterates the principles
on which common worship is based: on the unity of
the Church which ought to be expressed; and
sharing in means of grace.[116] The Directory
specified in article 40 the ecclesiological and
sacramental basis that can allow some sharing in

---

116. cf., U.R. 8

liturgical worship and even the eucharist with
the separated Eastern brothers. Indeed this is a
recall of what the Council says on the Decree on
Ecumenism, and which applies also to the Decree
on Eastern Catholic Churches. This basis reads:
"Although these Churches are separated from us,
they possess true sacraments, above all - by apostolic succession - the priesthood and the Eucharist, whereby they are still joined to us in a
very close relationship. Therefore, given suitable circumstances and the approval of Church
authority, some worship in common is not merely
possible but is recommended."[117] Such circumstances according to the document are those that
affect individuals in which the unity of the
Church is not at jeopardy or intolerable risks
involved, but in which salvation itself and the
spiritual profit of souls are urgently at
stake."[118] The Episcopal Conference or Synod is
entrusted with the responsibility of verifying
the circumstances before extending permission for
sharing in the reception or administration of the
sacraments of penance, Holy Eucharist or anointing of the sick to the separated Eastern
Brothers, after satisfactory consultations with
the competent authorities of the separated oriental Church.[119]
Besides cases of necessity, admission to these
sacraments of the oriental brother is possible
when circumstances arise that make it materially
or morally impossible over a long period for one

---

117. U.R. 15., cf. also O.E. 26-29.
118. cf., O.E. 26.
119. cf., The Ecumenical Directory (Part One), IS
    2 (1967), p.10.

of the faithful to receive the sacraments in his
own Church.

On the other hand, sharing in liturgical worship with the separated brethren of the West, the
Directory stated what concerns us in this work in
article 55. The Directory submits that it is a
community which celebrates the sacraments, which
signifies their oneness in faith, worship and
life. "Where this unity of sacramental faith is
deficient, the participation of the separated
bretheren with Catholics, especially in the
sacrament of the Eucharist, penance and anointing
of the sick, is forbidden."[120] The Directory
makes concession on the basis that the sacraments
are signs of unity and sources of grace. The
conditions that may warrant admission of the
separated brother from the West to the sacraments
in the Catholic Church are: in danger of death,
or in urgent need for example: during persecution, or in prisons, and if he has no access to a
minister of his own Communion and spontaneously
asks a Catholic priest for the sacraments, "so
long as he declares a faith in these sacraments
in harmony with that of the Church and is rightly
disposed."[121] It is left to the discretion of the
local bishop or Episcopal Conference to judge the
aforementioned conditions and in other cases or
urgent necessity as well. While in the case of
Oriental Church reciprocity is recommended, in
the case of the separated bretheren of the West,
Catholics in similar circumstances are advised to
ask for these sacraments only from a validly
ordained priest.

---

120. op. cit., p.11.
121. ibid.

5.4.3 INSTRUCTION CONCERNING CASES WHEN OTHER CHRISTIANS MAY BE ADMITTED TO EUCHARISTIC COMMUNION IN THE CATHOLIC CHURCH, JUNE 1972.

The Instruction designated as pastoral, is set to give answer to the question: in what circumstances and what conditions can members of other Churches and ecclesial communities be admitted to the eucharistic communion in the Catholic Church? Before giving solutions to the question, the two principles on which the Instruction is based are exposed, namely: The Eucharist and the mystery of the Church and the Eucharist as spiritual food.

5.4.3.1 THE EUCHARIST AND THE MYSTERY OF THE CHURCH.

The first principle is based on the close link between the mystery of the eucharist and the mystery of the Church. The Instruction submits that the eucharist contains really what is the very foundation of the being and unity of the Church; that is the body and blood of Christ offered in sacrifice and given to the faithful as the bread of eternal life. This sacrament of the body and blood of Christ given to the Church which constitutes the Church embodies three elements namely: the ministerial power which Christ gave to his apostles and to their successors, bishops along with the priests, to make effective sacramentally his own priestly act; the unity of the ministry which is to be exercised in the name of Christ in the hierarchical order; the faith of the Church, which is expressed in the eucharistic action itself. The Instruction thus concludes: "The sacrament of the Eucharist, understood in its entirety with these three elements, signifies an existing unity brought about by Him, the unity of the visible Church of Christ which cannot be lost."[122]

The second way in which the mystery of the eucharist is linked to the mystery of the Church reveals itself in the celebration of the Mass. "The celebration of Mass, the action of Christ and of the people of God hierarchically ordered, is the centre of the whole Christian life, for the universal Church as for the local Church and for each Christian. Celebrating the mystery of Christ in the Mass, the Church celebrates her own mystery and manifests concretly her unity."[123] The assembled faithful represent the community of the people of God united in one faith, offer the sacrifice through the hands of the priest, who is acting in the name of Christ. Thus the celebration of the Mass is of itself a profession of faith in which the whole Church recognizes and expresses itself. These acts are detectable when we consider the eucharistic prayers and their meaning, in the various parts of the Mass, and in the liturgy of the Word with emphasis on its catechetical principles.

The relation between the local celebration of the Eucharist and the universal ecclesial communion emphasized by the special mention in the eucharistic prayers, of the Pope, the local

---

122. IS 18 (1972), pp.3-4.
123. ibid.

bishop and the other members of the episcopal
college, is another fact that links the mystery
of the eucharist and the mystery of the Church.
The document rounds off this section by
declaring: "What has been said here of the
Eucharist as centre and summit of the Christian
life holds for the whole Church and for each of
its members, but particularly for those who take
an active part in the celebration of Mass and
above all for those who receive the Body of
Christ."[124]

5.4.3.2 THE EUCHARIST AS SPIRITUAL FOOD.

The second principle is based on the fact that
the Eucharist is the spiritual nourishment of
those who receive it. For according to the faith
of the Church, in the eucharist the body and
blood of Christ is given as food of eternal life.
Hence for the baptized: "The Eucharist is spiritual food, a means by which they are brought to
live the life of Christ himself, are incorporated
more profoundly in Him and share more intensely
in the whole economy of his saving mystery."[125]
Quoting from the scriptures the Instruction pointed out that the Eucharist is both the sacrament
of full union with Christ and of the perfection
of spiritual life, thereby emphasizing its necessity.[126]

The eucharist as a spiritual food effects also

---

124. ibid.
125. ibid.
126. ibid., cf. also Jn6:53-58.

the union of the Christian receiver with Christ.
This union of the faithful with Christ, the head
of the mystical body, effects also the union of
the faithful themselves with each other. In this
sense the eucharist is not simply a means of
satisfying exclusively personal aspirations,
however lofty they may be. The unity of the
faithful symbolized in their sharing of the eucharistic bread is expressed in St. Paul's teaching:
"Because there is one loaf, we who are many, are
one body, for we all partake of the same
loaf."[127] The document encourages frequent communion emphasizing that "spiritual need of the
Eucharist is not therefore merely a matter of
personal spiritual growth: simultaneously, and
inseparably, it concerns our entering more deeply
into Christ's Church, 'which is his body, the
fulness of him who fills all in all.'"[128]

The document then goes on to give the principles that govern intercommunion.

5.4.4 GENERAL PRINCIPLES GOVERNING ADMISSION TO
        COMMUNION.

The document started off by saying that the
Catholics are in communion with one another when
they celebrate the eucharist because they are
united in one faith. This is to be the case when
the Christians are reunited in the one and the
same Church. It is because of the problem which
divided christendom creates that the question of

---

127. 1Cor10,17.
128. JS 18 (1972), p.4., cf. also Eph. 1, 23.

intercommunion arose. It is the extra-ordinary
case that the document considers. For it is
normal for the separated brethren to have recourse to the ministers of their communities for
communion according to their conscience. The
document has in mind those who in certain circumstances cannot have recourse to their own
ministers, but rather turn to the Catholic priest
and request for the eucharistic communion.

The instruction refers to the Ecumenical
Directory which has spelt out what has to be done
so that the intergrity of ecclesial communion and
the good of souls may be simultaneously safeguarded. Two principles are behind the Ecumenical
Directory. The first is that the strict relationship between the mystery of the eucharist and the
mystery of the Church can never be altered,
irrespective of whatever pastoral measures to be
taken in a given case. This is so because: "of
its very nature celebration of the Eucharist
signifies the fullness of profession of faith and
the fullness of ecclesial communion."[129] This
principle, the Instruction emphasizes, must not
be obscured and must remain the guide in this
field.

In the second instance the document gave the
examples of such particular cases when admission
to the eucharistic communion in the Catholic
Church might be possible and maintained that such
admission does not obscure the principle mentioned before. The document named the cases in
these words: "Admission to Catholic eucharistic
communion is confined to particular cases of

---

129. IS 18 (1972), p.5.

those Christians who have a faith in the sacrament in conformity with that of the Church, who experience a serious spiritual need for the eucharistic sustenance, who for a prolonged period are unable to have recourse to a minister of their own community and who ask for the sacrament of their own accord; all this provided that they have proper dispositions and lead lives worthy of a Christian."[130] This spiritual need, maintained the document, must be understood as "a need for an increase in spiritual life and a need for a deeper involvement in the mystery of the Church and of its unity."[131]

In the next paragraph we present the reasons given by the document for giving different directions between the oriental churches and other Christians.

5.4.5 DIFFERENCES, IN VIEW OF THESE PRINCIPLES, BETWEEN MEMBERS OF THE ORIENTAL CHURCHES AND OTHER CHRISTIANS.

As we said already, the Ecumenical Directory gave different directives for the admission to holy Communion of a separated Eastern Christian and of Other Christians. Our document now gives the reason for such apparent discrimination. The Eastern Churches, it said, though separated from the Catholic Church, have true sacraments; they preserved the apostolic succession; have the priesthood and the eucharist; in this way they

---

130. ibid.
131. ibid.

are united to the Catholic Church in close ties,
and this reduces the risk of obscuring the relation between eucharistic communion and ecclesial
communion.

In the case of Other Christians whose eucharistic faith differs from that of the Catholic
Church, and which do not have the sacrament of
Orders, admitting them to the eucharist entails
the risk of obscuring the essential relation
between eucharistic communion and ecclesial communion. This is the reason, the Instruction maintains, why their case is differently treated by
the Ecumenical Directory and envisages admission
only in exceptional cases catergorized as "urgent
necessity". It is in such exceptional cases that
profession of faith in the eucharist in conformity with the Catholic Church is demanded,
but in the case of the Orthodox Christian the
demand is not made for "he belongs to a Church
whose faith in the Eucharist is conformable to
our own."[132] This goes to explain why in the case
of Separated Eastern brethren reciprocity was
envisaged, but in the case of other Christians,
Catholics are forbidden to ask for sacraments
except from validly ordained ministers.

The document concludes with an explanation on
the designated authority referred to in Ecumenical Directory, No.55.

5.4.6 AUTHORITY THAT DECIDES PARTICULAR CASES.

The Ecumenical Directory, article 55, allows a

---

132. ibid.

wider body of authority to judge and verify the
cases of necessity. The Instruction now directs
that if similar cases recur often in a given
region, that the episcopal conference can give
general directions. Besides it falls to the
bishop of the diocese to make a decision for he
alone will know all the circumstances of particular cases.

The Instruction explains that "other cases of
such urgent necessity" mentioned in the Ecumenical Directory, are not confined to situations of
suffering and danger. It cites an example with a
situation in the diaspora. In such a case those non-
Catholic Christians scattered in a Catholic region, often deprived of help of their own communion and unable to get in touch with it, except
at great trouble and expense, can be admitted to
the Catholic eucharistic communion, after the
bishop of the place has verified that they
satisfy the conditions set out in the Ecumenical
Directory.

5.4.7 EVALUATION.

The pastoral Instruction we have just presented laid down the norms for admitting a non-Catholic Christian in the eucharistic communion.
This is in effect the declaration on how common
worship with other Christians could be possible
within the Catholic Church in response to the
conciliar Decree on Ecumenism. This conciliar
document on the issue of 'communicatio in sacris'
reads: "As for common worship, however, it may
not be regarded as a means to be used indiscrimi-

nately for the restoration of unity among Christians. Such worship depends chiefly on two principles: it should provide a sharing in the means of grace. The fact that it should signify unity generally rules out common worship. Yet the gaining of a needed grace sometimes commends it."[133]

The Instruction offers a wider presentation of the two principles. The doctrinal reason for the regulations are based on two principles namely: the relationship between the Eucharist and the Church and secondly the meal character of the eucharist. The Instruction lays great emphasis on the close link between the relationship of the mystery of the eucharist and the mystery of the Church. The Church is presented in its entity as an eucharistic assembly. The eucharistic celebration is central to the self-realization of the Church. These ideas run through the whole Instruction.

The first principle when considered closely, one notices that it is based on the doctrinal factor that the eucharist is a sacrifice. Through the apostolic succession, the bishops and priests along with them, represent the one sacrifice of Christ in the eucharistic celebration. Thereafter the meal character which is the second principle comes into play.

The ecclesiological dimension of the two principles, sacrificial character and meal character of the eucharist, always go hand in hand and are spoken about together in the text. A non-Catholic community stands near or far from the Catholic

---

133. U.R. 8.

Church in so far as its eucharistic doctrine agrees with that of the Catholic Church, with particular reference to the sacrament of Orders, apostolic succession, real presence, transubstantiation. Whoever possesses this eucharistic conception is in union with the Catholic Church, and to him can the communicatio in sacris be granted. This is where the weight of the first principle lies for it demands the profession of faith in the eucharist that corresponds to that of the Catholic Church, from those cases of necessity before admission.

The second principle is based on the eucharist as a meal, as communion which has the effect to nourish spiritually those who receive it as the body and blood of Jesus Christ, as the food of eternal life. The other effect is that through the communion the Christian is united intimately with Christ and also with his fellow Christians. The Instruction specifies that the spiritual need for requesting eucharistic communion must be that of the baptized individual. The baptized individual has the right to eucharistc nourishment.

While the first principle predominantly concerns the doctrinal aspect of the eucharist, the second is primarily pastoral. That means as well that the second principle is subordinate to the first but equally important. The pastoral point of view can be effective only when in the doctrinal area there is no difference. That may explain why at the presentation of the Instruction, the secretary of the SPCU said inter alia: "These two statements are of equal importance and have both to be safeguarded, whatever may be the pastoral decisions which pastors are called upon to make in particular circumstances. As it is, generally speaking, on the second statement that those who ask for 'eucharistic hospitality' in the Church base their request, the Instruction aims to remind those concerned what may not be done at the expense of the first statement in which the indestructible bond between the Eucharist and the Church is underlined."[134]

It is now necessary to point out the basic difference between the Catholic Church's handling of inter-communion and that of the Faith and Order Commission. Faith and Order treats the issue by considering two Churches as it is clear by the definitions; the Instruction by the Catholic Church considers the individual baptized person who has a spiritual need for eucharistic communion. The ecclesiological dimension and the sacramental basis contribute to the Catholic Church's restrictive approach; but these two factors were not underlined in the treatment of the Faith and Order. While in the opinion of the Faith and Order inter-communion is regarded as a means to unity, the Catholic Church insits that communicatio in sacris is a sign of unity not a means to it. Nevertheless, both are in agreement that communion is the goal of ecumenical movement, as Faith and Order defined it at Louvain. Faith and Order also catergorizes the practice of intercommunion in the Catholic church and Orthodox Church under Limited Admission.[135]

A glance at a few examples of the decisions of

134. Harmer J., Doctrinal reasons for the
     Instruction in: IS 18 (1972), p.7.
135. cf. note 78 of chapter three of this work.

either a national Synod or Bishop's Conference,
shows that the reasons for this Limited Admission
allowed in the Catholic Church are that underlined in the documents we have just examined. It
is the fact that eucharistic communion demands
unity of faith; the different conceptions of the
Church in relation to the eucharist; and the
different understanding or lack of ordained
ministry.

The German Bishops' Synod in 1976 in their
decision enumerated the conditions for admitting
any Christian from another confession into the
eucharistic communion as follows: conciousness of
incorporation through baptism in the fellowship
of believers, agreement with the faith of the
church as regards the eucharist, longing for
communion with Christ in the eucharist, personal
connection with the life of the Catholic Church,
conciousness for the unity of the Church and an
exemplary christian life.[136] On whether a Catholic should be allowed to participate in the eucharistic communion of the Evangelical Church,
the bishops said to their faithful: "The Synod
cannot at present approve of a Catholic sharing
in the eucharistic celebration of the Evangelical
Church. It cannot be ruled out that a Catholic -
following his own conscience - may, in his own
particular situation, find reasons which make him
view his sharing in the Lord's Supper as a spiritual necessity. He should reflect that such a
sharing is not in harmony with the bond between
the Eucharist and ecclesial communion, particu-

---

136. cf. Gemeinsame Synode der Bistümer in der
       Bundesrepublik Deutschland, Freiburg, Basel,
       Wien, Herder, 1976, p.215.

larly as regards the understanding of ministry. As
he ponders the decision he feels called upon to
think, he should not put his allegiance to his
own Church at risk, neither should his decision
be equated with a denial of his own belief and of
his own Church, and it should not appear as such
to other people."[137]

In the same context, the French Episcopal
Commission for Unity, gave reasons why eucharistic hospitality should not be habitual in its
decision passed on to their priests in 1983.
Among the reasons they gave are: "The tradition
of the undivided Church also always made communion in the same ecclesial faith the condition
for sharing in the Eucharist. Because eucharistic
communion and ecclesial communion cannot be separated: the Church makes the Eucharist and the
Eucharist makes the Church. Christ's eucharistic
body is ordained for the building up of his
ecclesial body. Communion in the same Eucharist
therefore involves communion in the same Church,
just as it presupposes sharing the same
faith."[138]

Finally the Bishop's Conference of Switzerland
on the question of eucharistic hospitality taught
that there exists a close relationship between
the unity of the Church in faith and the reception of the eucharist. In other words, eucharistic communion presupposes communion in faith.
That is why a Catholic receives the eucharist in
his Church with other Catholics who confess the

---

137. op. cit., p.216; English translation
     according to One in Christ 4 (1983), pp.387-
     388.
138. cf. One in Christ 4 (1983), p.387.

same faith as he does. The bishops underlined the difference in the understanding of minstry as one of the reasons for not allowing intercommunion. They warned that it would be a deceit to allow a Protestant minister to co-oparate in the eucharistic celebration of the Catholic church, for that would mean instituting error rather than promoting christian unity.[139] It would mean allowing a representative of another Church to officially exercise his ministry among those with whom he has no common faith neither in the Eucharist nor in the understanding of the ministry.

---

139. cf. Schweizerischen Kirchenzeitung, 11. September 1986, Eucharistische Gastfreundschaft.

CHAPTER SIX.

BANGALORE TO LIMA.

6.1 RECAPITULATION.

Our task has been to trace and analyse the
discussion on the eucharist by Faith and Order
Commission of the World Council of Churches. In
the first chapter we dealt with the beginnings of
the Faith and Order Movement and its first World
Conference at Lausanne in 1927. There the eucharist was discussed among sacraments in general.

The second chapter which started with the
Second World Conference of Faith and Order at
Edinburgh, saw also the formation of the World
Council of Churches with Faith and Order as its
component part. In this chapter there was an
ecumenical break through on the statement on the
eucharist; intercommunion as a topic featured as
well. We saw also two other World Conferences at
Lund and Montreal, 1952 and 1963 respectively,
but now as Commission on Faith and Order. In the
first case the discussion centred on intercommunion and ways of worship; in the second, the
eucharist was discussed prominently. The chapter
was concluded with the events going on in the
Roman Catholic Church, which is not a member of
the World Council of Churches and which has not
joined the modern ecumenical movement. This
event, the Second Vatican Council, prepared the
ground for the active participation of the Catholic Church in the ecumenical movement.

The third chapter brought us to the scene
where the Eucharist was taken up as a study pro-

ject by Faith and Order Commission following the
recomendation at Aarhus in 1964. The discussion
on the eucharist kicked off with the consultation
at Grandchamp in 1965. The discussion continued
through Bristol to Louvain and culminated at
Accra in 1974. The result of the study was published and sent to the Churches for the first
time asking them to send their response.

In chapter four we saw the Churches in dialogue and the eucharist being at the centre of
their discussion. The Faith and Order Commission
encouraged such bilateral dialogues and gave its
assistance at invitation. The fifth Chapter opened
up the Roman Catholic view on the doctrine of the
eucharist, the eucharistic liturgy and intercommunion.

This present chapter shall take off from where
we stopped on the study project on the eucharist.
The response of the Churches to the Accra Text
resulted in the revision of the text and its
perfection. This took place between the Commission's Plenary meetings at Bangalore 1978, and
Lima 1982. Let us now review the study process.

6.1.2 BANGALORE TO LIMA.

The Commission on Faith and Order on its plenary meeting at Accra in 1974, issued three
agreed statements under the title: "One Baptism,
One Eucharist and a Mutually Recognized Ministry." The Fifth Assembly of the World Council of
Churches at Nairobi, 1975, decided to send the
agreed statements to its member Churches and
requested them to respond by the end of 1976. The

Council asked the Faith and Order commission to
revise the statements in the light of the responses for the Sixth Assembly. A large number of
official replies were received. At a consultation
at Crêt-Bérard, near Lausanne in 1977, the Standing Commission reviewed the replies; the reply
to the response was thereafter published under
the title: "Towards an Ecumenical Consensus:
Baptism, Eucharist, Ministry; Faith and Order
Paper No. 84."

BANGALORE 1978.

At Banalore, the Faith and Order Commission in
its plenary meeting was confronted with the
problem of the best ways of proceeding with the
revision of the three agreed statements on
Baptism, Eucharist and Ministry. In the light of
the replies from the Churches it came to the
following decisions: the statements must be preceded by an adequate introduction; to avoid misunderstanding, the statements have to be spoken
of in terms of a convergence; a commentary has to
be embodied in the text, whose function among
others will be to make clear not only the
positions which were being excluded on hitherto
controversial questions but also the central
areas in which variety of expression might be
acceptable.[1] The timetable for the revision
exercise was mapped out with a view to presenting
it to the plenary Commission meeting in 1981.

---

1. cf. Commission on Faith and Order, Sharing in
   one Hope Bangalore 1978, Lausanne, Imprimerie
   La Concorde, 1978 p.248 ff.

TAIZÉ 1979.

The Standing Commission of the Faith and Order held its annual meeting at Taizé in 1979. The Director of the Commission, Dr. Vischer, reported that after the meeting at Bangalore a steering Group was formed to take charge of the revision exercise. The report mentioned also that four consultations were held on special aspects of the texts. These were at Louisville, Kentucky, with the Baptists; in Chambesy` and two others in Geneva, one for the Forum on Bilateral conversations and the other on study consultation on episcopé and episcopate.[2] The steering Group reported that it has completed the draft on the statement on Baptism and Eucharist, which were discussed by the standing commission in plenary session. At Taizé, the Standing Commission drew up a new timetable which placed the plenary meeting of the Commission on Faith and Order in 1982 instead of 1981. This is to allow time for broad consultations before the final text is composed.

ANNECY 1981.

The next meeting of the Standing commission of Faith and Order took place at Annecy, France in 1981. The steering Group reported of its completion of the drafts on the revised statements on Baptism, Eucharist and Ministry together with a

---

2. cf. Minutes of the Meeting of the Standing Commission 1979, Taizé, FO No. 98, p.21 ff.

preface. It was able to achieve this after meeting three times in the year 1980.[3] At Annecy, the Standing commission announced that the plenary meeting of the Commission on Faith and Order will take place at Lima, Peru in 1982. The Commission also decided that the drafts of the revised statements should be sent to all the members of the commission on Faith and Order, and looked forward to meeting in November 1981, for the final corrections in the light of the comments that would be made by the members. The standing commission expressed deep appreciation and thanks to the steering Group for the work well done and hoped that the 1982 meeting of the Faith and Order Commission will mark a new phase in the ecumenical programme.

LIMA 1982.

The Commission on Faith and Order held its plenary meeting at Lima, Peru, from 2-16 January 1982. Among the five study projects tackled were that on Baptism, Eucharist and Ministry. At the plenary session of 5 January, the BEM project was discussed and areas of special concern were identified for immediate attention and action of the designated editors. On 12 January during the plenary session the BEM project was presented for adoption by the Commission. The motion that was put to the plenary commission reads: "The Commission considers the revised text on Baptism, Eu-

---

3. cf. Minutes of the Meeting of the Standing Commission 1981 Annecy, FO No. 106, p.6.

charist and Ministry to have been brought to such
a stage of maturity that it is now ready for
transmission to the churches in accordance with
the mandate given at the Fifth Assembly of the
World Council of Churches, Nairobi 1975, and reaffirmed by the Central Committee, at Dresden
1981."[4] The motion was seconded by Prof. Geoffrey
Wainwright, (Protestant), Fr. Jean Tillard,
(Roman Catholic), and Prof. Zizioulas (Orthodox).
Following a period of reading, proposed revisions
were discussed paragraph by paragraph. Thereafter
the vice Moderator, John Deschner, repeated the
motion and called for the vote. The motion passed
unanimously without negative votes or absten-
tions.[5]

This unanimous vote marks the end of a study
process on the eucharist going back to the First
World Conference of Faith and Order in Lausanne,
1927. "It also marks the first time in the ecumenical movement that theologians of such varied
backgrounds (Protestants, Orthodox and Roman
Catholics) from around the world have spoken so
harmoniously on fundamental matters of doctrine."[6]

Let us now concern ourself with the convergence text on the Eucharist, which is our subject
matter.

---

4. Kinnamon M., (ed.), Towards Visible Unity,
   Vol. I, Minutes and Adresses, FO. No. 112,
   Geneva, WCC, 1982, p.83.
5. op. cit., p.84.
6. op. cit., p.1.

6.2   THE EUCHARIST: LIMA CONVERGENCE TEXT.

The Lima text on the eucharist is divided into
three parts, namely: the institution, the meaning
and the celebration of the eucharist. The meaning
of the eucharist is sub-divided into: eucharist
as thanksgiving to the Father; eucharist as anamnesis of Christ; eucharist as invocation of the
Spirit; eucharist as communion of the faithful
and eucharist as the meal of the Kingdom.

In this presentation of the eucharistic text,
the divisions are followed as they appear in the
agreed statement. It is to be recalled that the
Lima convergence text is on Baptism, Eucharist
and Ministry, denoted from now as BEM. We are
concerned in this work with the eucharistic text,
denoted from now with an E. The quotations will
be marked with E and the corresponding number of
the paragraph in the text, e.g. E1 or E2 etc. The
convergence text BEM is published by the World
Council of Churches in 1982 as Faith and Order
Paper No. 111.

6.2.1   THE INSTITUTION OF THE EUCHARIST.

The text opend with the statement that the
eucharist is a gift which the Church receives
from the Lord. The institution account by St.
Paul was cited, 1Cor. 11:23-25, and the synoptic
sources were given as well namely: Mt.26:26-29;
Mk.14:22-25; Lk.22:14-20. The document draws a
relationship between the Last Supper and the
different meals of Jesus during his ministry both
before and after the resurrection, saying: "Thus

the eucharist continues these meals of Jesus
during his earthly life and after his resurrection, always as a sign of the kingdom." El.
The Passover memorial of Israel's deliverance
from bondage is a prefiguration of the eucharist.
Thus the eucharist "is the new Paschal meal of
the church, the meal of the New Covenant, which
Christ gave to his disciples as the anamnesis of
his death and resurrection, as the anticipation
of the Supper of the Lamb (Rev.19:9)" El. The
document denotes this meal as sacramental, which
Christ commanded his disciples to remember and
thereby to encounter him as the continuing people
of God until his return.

The eucharist derives its form from the Last
Supper and employs symbolic words and actions.
"Consequently the eucharist is a sacramental meal
which by visible signs communicates to us God's
love in Jesus Christ, the love by which Jesus
loved his own to the End." El. In the course of
history the eucharist has acquired many names,
viz, the Lord's Supper, the breaking of bread,
the holy communion, the divine liturgy and the
Mass. The document submitted that the celebration
of the eucharist is the central act of the
Church's worship.

6.2.2 THE MEANING OF THE EUCHARIST.

The analysis of the meaning of the eucharist
begins with what is ultimately signified by the
liturgical action. "The eucharist is essentially
the sacrament of the gift which God makes to us
in Christ through the power of the Holy Spirit."

E2. In the eating of the bread and drinking of
the wine, the eucharistic meal, Christ grants
communion with himself and God himself gives life
to the body of Christ, renewing each member. Thus
this gift of salvation is received by every christian through communion in the body and blood of
Christ. Furthermore in accordance with Christ's
promise, each baptized member of the body of
Christ receives in the eucharist the assurance of
the forgiveness of sins and the pledge of eternal
life.

The document maintains that the eucharist is
essentially one complete act, and goes on to
analyse the rest of this section along the lines
of the chief themes of the liturgical forms of
the ancient eucharistic liturgies of the East and
West and shows how they relate to the mystery
dimension of the eucharist.

6.2.2.1 THE EUCHARIST AS THANKSGIVING TO THE
         FATHER.

This paragraph begins with the affirmation
that the eucharist is both Word and Sacrament; it
is also the proclamation and celebration of the
work of God. The document then gives the content
of the eucharist as thanksgiving to the Father:
"It is the great thanksgiving to the Father for
everything accomplished in creation, redemption
and sanctification, for everything accomplished
by God now in the Church and in the world in
spite of the sins of human beings, for everything
that God will accomplish in bringing the Kingdom
to fulfillment." E3. In the eucharist therefore,

the Church expresses thanks for God's benefits.

The world and humankind which Christ has reconciled with God are present in the eucharistic
celebration. This is evident in the bread and
wine, in the persons of the faithful and in their
prayers for themselves and for all people. Thus
"the eucharist is the great sacrifice of praise
by which the church speaks on behalf of the whole
creation."

This sacrificial prayer is acceptable to the
Father because Christ the High Priest unites the
faithful of his Church to himself and includes
their prayers and intercession, for "this sacrifice of praise is possible only through Christ,
with him and in him." E4. Therefore in faith and
thanksgiving, the bread and wine, fruits of the
earth and human labour, are presented to the
Father. The eucharist as the meal of the kingdom
anticipates what the world is to become: "an
offering and hymn of praise to the creator, a
universal communion in the body of Christ, a
kingdom of justice, love and peace in the Holy
Spirit." E4.

6.2.2.2 THE EUCHARIST AS ANAMNESIS OR MEMORIAL
         OF CHRIST.

The word Anamnesis (memorial), is a key concept in the Lima convergence text, in the sense
that it opens up the way to solving the disputed
issues between the christian Churches. This concerns the issue of how or whether the memorial is
a sacrifice and secondly the manner of the presence of the Lord Jesus Christ in the memorial

celebration.[7]

The document defines the eucharist in terms of anamnesis in these words: "The eucharist is the memorial of the crucified and risen Christ, i.e. the living and effective sign of his sacrifice, accomplished once and for all on the cross and still operative on behalf of all humankind." E5. It is in the liturgy celebrated by God's people that the efficacy of God's work is made present, hence "Christ himself with all that he has accomplished for us and for all creation (in his incarnation, servanthood, ministry, teaching, suffering, sacrifice, resurrection, ascension and sending of the Spirit) is present in this anamnesis, granting us communion with himself." E6. The eucharistic anamnesis points to the future, "until he comes in glory", hence the document points out that the eucharist is the foretaste of His parousia and of the final kingdom. The anamnesis therefore, "is not only a calling to mind of what is past and its significance. It is the Church's effective proclamation of God's mighty acts and promises." E7.

Since anamnesis has not only to do with the past but also with the present and future, the document says that it is both representation and anticipation which are expressed in thanksgiving and intercession. The document goes in E8 to describe what the church does in celebrating the memorial of Christ in these words: "The Church, gratefully recalling God's mighty acts of redemption, beseeches God to give the benefits of these

---

7. cf. Löser W., Die Konvergenzerklärung von Lima, in: ThPh 60 (1985), p.485.

acts to every human being. In thanksgiving and
intercession, the Church is united with the Son,
its great High Priest and Intercessor." E8. The
document comes out openly in a sacrificial
language and thus describes the eucharist as "the
sacrament of the unique sacrifice of Christ, who
ever lives to make intercession for us. It is the
memorial of all that God has done for the salvation of the world." E8. Following this line of
thought the document declares that what God has
willed and accomplished in the incarnation, life,
death, resurrection and ascension of Christ, he
does not repeat. "These events are unique and can
neither be repeated nor prolonged." However, in
the eucharistic memorial, the Church offers its
intercession in communion with Christ, our great
High Priest.

In the commentary to E8 the document refers to
the Catholic teaching on the propitiatory character of the eucharist and says: "It is in the
light of the significance of the eucharist as
intercession that references to the eucharist in
Catholic theology as "propitiatory sacrifice" may
be understood. The understanding is that there is
only one expiation, that of the unique sacrifice
of the cross, made actual in the eucharist and
presented before the Father in the intercession
of Christ and of the Church for all humanity."
EC8.

Our document further submits that the anamnesis of Christ is the basis and source of all
christian prayer. Hence our prayer relies upon
and is united with the continual intercession of
the risen Lord. All this culminates in the eucharist, where Christ empowers us to live with him,

to suffer with him and to pray through him as
justified sinners, joyfully and freely fulfilling
his will.

With reference to Rom.12,1 and 1Pet.2,5, the
document declares that "in Christ we offer ourselves as a living and holy sacrifice in our
daily lives"; and that this spiritual worship
acceptable to God "is nourished in the eucharist,
in which we are sanctified and reconciled in
love, in order to be servants of reconciliation
in the world." E10. In the eucharistic communion
the christians are not only united with their
Lord, but also with the saints and martyrs, and
thus they are renewed in the covenant sealed by
the blood of Christ.

The preached word and the eucharistic meal
have their common content in the anamnesis of
Christ; they therefore reinforce each other,
hence the document concludes "The celebration of
the eucharist properly includes the proclamation
of the Word." E12.

The next paragraph, E13, deals with the presence of Christ in the eucharist. The real presence of Christ in the eucharist has been a turbulent issue in the discussion on the eucharist.
One notices that the problem is not completely
solved as is evident in the commentary to E13.
The document has paved the way with the earlier
statement on the anamnesis. Now it says that the
words and acts of Christ at the institution of
the eucharist stand at the heart of the celebration, and rounds up saying: "the eucharistic meal
is the sacrament of the body and blood of Christ,
the sacrament of his real presence." E13. The
document acknowledges the various presence of

Christ among his own, but designates his mode of
presence in the eucharist as unique. It is so
because "Jesus said over the bread and wine of
the eucharist: "This is my body...this is my
blood..." Then the document declares: "What
Christ declared is true, and this truth is fulfilled every time the eucharist is celebrated";
and furthermore "The Church confesses Christ's
real, living and active presence in the eucharist." E13. In conclusion, the document makes it
clear that Christ's real presence in the eucharist does not depend on the faith of the individual, but to discern the body and blood of Christ
faith is required.

The commentary to E13 confirms the fact that
perfect agreement on the question of the real
presence of Christ under the eucharistic elements
is not yet there. After saying that many churches
believe that by the words of Jesus and by the
power of the Holy Spirit, the bread and wine of
the eucharist become, in a real though mysterious
manner, the body and blood of the risen Christ
i.e., of the living Christ present in all his
fullness, it goes on to say that some other churches, while affirming a real presence of Christ
at the eucharist, do not link that presence so
definitely with the signs of bread and wine.
EC13. The document throws the decision back to
the churches, whether this difference could be
accomodated in the convergence agreement.

6.2.2.3 THE EUCHARIST AS INVOCATION OF THE SPIRIT.

Our document has already described the eucharist as a thanksgiving to the Father and as a memorial of the crucified and risen Christ. Now it
speaks about the epikletic character of the eucharist. It says: "The Spirit makes the crucified
and risen Christ really present to us in the
eucharistic meal, fulfilling the promise contained in the words of institution." E14. Perhaps
to maintain a balance in the age long debate
between East and West on the issue of what brings
about the eucharistic miracle the power of the
Holy Spirit,or the words of Christ at the institution, the document says: "The presence of
Christ is clearly the centre of the eucharist,
and the promise contained in the words of institution is therefore fundamental to the celebration." E14. However the eucharistic celebration
is presented in the light of the trinatarian
action. "Yet it is the Father who is the primary
origin and final fulfilment of the eucharistic
event. The incarnate Son of God by and in whom it
is accomplished is its living centre. The Holy
Spirit is the immeasurable strength of love which
makes it possible and continues to make it effective." E14. The document singles out the role of
the Spirit from the Triune bond as one who makes
the historical words of Jesus present and alive.
On the assurance that Jesus' promise in the words
of institution will be answered, the church at
the eucharistic liturgy prays to the Father for
the gift of the Holy Spirit in order that the
eucharistic event may be a reality.
    The commentary to E14, points out that as an

activity of the Church, the eucharist is a prayer
addressed to the Father for the fulfilment of the
promise of the Last Supper through the sending of
the Spirit. This corresponds to the understanding
of the early liturgies that the whole 'prayer
action' brings about the reality promised by
Christ and offers as possible solution to the
historical debate about a special moment of consecration.

The document, having emphasized the relationship between the words of institution, Christ's
promise and epiclesis, was confident that "it is
in virtue of the living word of Christ and by the
power of the Holy Spirit that the bread and wine
become the sacramental signs of Christ's body and
blood."E15.

The commentary to E15 lists three approaches
towards understanding the mystery of the real and
unique presence of Christ in the eucharist. The
first approach refers to those who are content
merely to affirm this presence without seeking to
explain it: the second concerns those who consider
it necessary to assert a change wrought by the
Holy Spirit and Christ's words, in consequence,
there is no longer just ordinary bread and wine
but the body and blood of Christ; the third points
to those who have developed an explanation of the
real presence which, though not claiming to
exhaust the significance of the mystery, seek to
protect it from damaging interpretations. The
first two corresponds to the different beliefs of
the churches found in commentary EC13. The third
mentions theological explanations. Thereby it is
implied that the ecumenical problem is reduced to
the different beliefs of the churches mentioned in

commentary E13.

The document, putting together what it has
earlier said, submits that "the whole action of
the eucharist has an 'epikletic' character because it depends upon the work of the Holy
Spirit." E16. The invocation of the Holy Spirit
in the liturgy of the eucharist is expressed in
varied words. On why the church confidently invokes the Spirit, the document says, it is in
order that it may be sanctified and renewed, led
into all justice, truth, and unity, and empowered
to fulfil its mission in the world. It is therefore the Holy Spirit, who through the eucharist
gives a foretaste of the kingdom of God, in which
the Church receives the life of the new creation
and the assurance of the Lord's return.

6.2.2.4   THE EUCHARIST AS COMMUNION OF THE
          FAITHFUL.

In the previous paragraph the eucharistic text
dealt with the trinitarian dimension of the eucharist, now it turns over to the ecclesiological
aspect. It begins with these words: "The eucharistic communion with Christ who nourishes the life
of the church is at the same time communion within the body of Christ which is the Church. The
sharing in one bread and the common cup in a
given place demonstrates and effects the oneness
of the sharers with Christ and with their fellow
sharers in all times and places." E19. It is in
the eucharist that the community of God's people
is fully manifested. In other words, in the eucharist the local church actualizes itself as the

body of Christ and so in communion with Christ,
the participants manifest and deepen their union
with one another. The universal quality of the
local church is made manifest in its eucharistic
celebration because, "eucharistic celebration
always have to do with the whole church, and the
whole church is involved in each local eucharistic celebration." E19. Therefore when a church
claims the manifestation of the whole church, it
has the obligation to order its life properly,
taking into account the interests and concerns of
other churches.

The commentary to E19, affirms the principle
that baptism incorporates the believer into the
body of Christ and so grounds the right to full
participation in the eucharist of the Church.
Having already in E19, established the relation
between the local eucharist and the whole church,
the document laments that the catholicity of the
eucharist is less manifest when the right of the
baptized and their ministers to participate and
preside over eucharistic celebration in one
church is not recognized by the members and offi-
cials of another church. Also the problem of
excluding baptized children from the eucharist, a
practice of some churches, is raised on the
grounds that baptism gives a fundamental right to
the eucharist.

The next paragraphs emphasize the social and
ethical implications of the eucharist. The document puts it this way: "The eucharist embraces
all aspects of life. It is a representative act
of thanksgiving and offering on behalf of the
whole world. The eucharistic celebration demands
reconciliation and sharing among all those re-

garded as brothers and sisters in the one family
of God and is a constant challenge in the search
for appropriate relationships in social, economic
and political life." E20. What then follows is
simply logical: All kinds of injustice, racism,
separation and lack of freedom are radically
challenged when we share in the body and blood of
Christ. The eucharist restores human personality
and dignity, and in it the believer is involved
in the central event of the world's history.
Hence the document calls on all the participants
in the eucharist to join in the restoration of
the world's situation and human condition, and
concludes with a note of challenge which our
inconsistency throws upon us vis-à-vis our communion in the eucharist: "The eucharist shows us
that our behaviour is inconsistent in face of the
reconciling presence of God in human history: we
are placed under continual judgment by the persistence of unjust relationships of all kinds in
our society, the manifold divisions on account of
human pride, material interest and power politics
and, above all, the obstinacy of unjustifiable
confessional oppositions within the body of
Christ." E20.

In this paragraph the document speaks about
the liturgical forms and services in which the
solidarity based on the eucharistic communion is
expressed. "Solidarity in the eucharistic communion of the body of Christ and responsible care
of christians for one another and the world find
specific expression in the liturgies: in mutual
forgiveness of sins; the sign of peace; intercession for all; the eating and drinking together,
the taking of the elements to the sick and those

in prison or the celebration of the eucharist
with them." E21. The document relates these manifestations of love in the eucharist to Christ's
servanthood, in which christians participate, and
makes a comparison between the incarnation and
the liturgy and at the end calls for the restoration of the ministry of deacon and deaconess, to
minister between the table of the Lord and the
needy. "As God in Christ has entered into the
human situation, so eucharistic liturgy is near
to the concrete and particular situation of men
and women." E21.

6.2.2.5 THE EUCHARIST AS MEAL OF THE KINGDOM.

The document now looks beyond the church in
its appreciation of the eucharist, and exposes
the eschatological dimension of the eucharist
which it calls the meal of the kingdom. It is
this in so far as it is the final renewal of
creation and its foretaste; secondly in so far as
signs of this renewal are present in the world
wherever the grace of God is manifest and human
beings work for justice, love and peace. The
document then says: "The eucharist is the feast
at which the church gives thanks to God for these
signs and joyfully celebrates and anticipates the
coming of the Kingdom in Christ." E22.

The indication once again is that the world to
which renewal is promised is present in the eucharistic celebration. The world present in
the thanksgiving to the Father, in the memorial
of Christ, and in the invocation of the Holy
Spirit. Through the eucharist the community is

nourished to serve as agent of reconciliation in
the world and witness to the joy of the resurrection. The celebration of the eucharist itself is
a participation in God's mission of preaching the
gospel of the kingdom, service to neighbour and
witness of fidelity. E25.

The section is rounded off by pointing out
that the weakness of the christians lies in the
fact of their division. The eucharist is there to
heal this division, for it is entirely the gift
of God which transforms christians into the image
of Christ and makes them his effective witnesses.
Through the eucharist, the precious food for
missionary, the christians are equipped to confess Christ and so draw others into the eucharistic assembly. But insofar as Christians cannot
act in full fellowship at the eucharistic table,
their missionary witness is weakened. E26.

6.2.3   THE CELEBRATION OF THE EUCHARIST.

The document presents a list of typical elements found historically in the eucharistic
liturgies, with an observation that the eucharistic liturgy is essentially a single whole. The
elements are found in E27.

The suggestion is made that all churches
should test their liturgies in the light of the
growing eucharistic agreement, as the best way
towards unity in eucharistic celebration. It is
observed as well that liturgical reform movement
has brought the churches closer in the manner of
eucharistic celebration, but this does not imply
uniformity in either liturgy or practice. E28.

The commentary to E28 cites opinion of some
who hold that local food and drink might serve
better than bread and wine 'to anchor the eucharist in everyday life', in places where the traditional elements are not commonly found.

The next paragraph treats the presiding
minister at the eucharistic celebration. Christ
is both victim and the priest. "In the celebration of the eucharist, Christ gathers, teaches
and nourishes the Church. It is Christ who invites to the meal and who presides at it. He is
the shepherd who leads the people of God, the
prophet who announces the Word of God, the
priest who celebrates the mystery of God." E29. This
presidency of Christ is in most churches signified by an ordained minister. The role of this
presiding minister is twofold. He is "the ambassador who represents the divine initiative and
expresses the connection of the local community
with other local communities in the universal
church." E29.

It is recommended that the eucharist be celebrated frequently, at least every Sunday, to
commomerate the resurrection. The frequent celebration of the eucharist is recommended also
because it deepens the faith, and christians are
encouraged to frequent communion as well.

The reservation of the sacrament of the eucharist is one of the practices that has not
found perfect agreement in this ecumenical discussion. Here the document observes that reservation of the sacrament by some churches is linked
to their stress on Christ's continued presence in
the consecrated elements. This is contrasted with
the practice of other churches which place the

main emphasis on the act of celebration itself and
on the consumption of the elements in the act of
communion. The document then directed that the
elements should be treated with special attention, and appealed to the churches to respect the
practices and piety of the others, and closed
with the suggestion: "That, on the one hand, it
be remembered, especially in sermons and instructions, that the primary intention of reserving
the elements is their distribution among the sick
and those who are absent, and on the other hand,
it be recognized that the best way of showing
respect for the elements served in the eucharistic celebration is by their consumption, without
excluding their use for the communion of the
sick." E32.

Finally the text closes with the observation
that: "the increased mutual understanding expressed in the present statement may allow some churches to attain a greater measure of eucharistic
communion among themselves and so bring closer
the day when Christ's divided people will be
visibly reunited around the Lord's Table." E33.

6.2.4 EVALUATION

Having presented the Lima Eucharist text, I
would now like to review it from a Catholic view-
point highlighting the controversial points.

The document described the origin of the eucharist, with Jesus command for its repetition.
Its eschatological character was pointed out;
being the christian Pasch it prefigured the Passover meal, and it is the anamnesis of Christ's

death and resurrection. All this correspond to
the teaching of the Second Vatican Council on the
institution of the eucharist where we read: "At
the Last Supper, on the night when He was betrayed, our Saviour instituted the Eucharistic
Sacrifice of His Body and Blood. He did this in
order to prepetuate the sacrifice of the Cross
throughout the centuries until He should come
again, and so to entrust to His beloved spouse,
the Church, a memorial of His death and resurrection: a sacrament of love, a sign of unity, a
bond of charity, a paschal banquet in which
Christ is consumed, the mind is filled with
grace, and a pledge of future glory is given to
us."[8]

At the very end of E1, the document describes
the eucharist as being central to the worship of
the church. "Its celebration continues as the
central act of the church's worship." E1. This is
also contained in the teaching of Vatican II, on
the portion devoted to the People of God in the
Dogmatic Constitution on the Church. There it is
said: "Taking part in the Eucharistic Sacrifice,
which is the fount and apex of the Whole Christian life, they offer the divine Victim to God,
and offer themselves along with It."[9] This goes
to indicate that the church is the eucharistic
community.

The description of the origin of the eucharist
provides an adequate preliminary statement of the
new Testament witness to the continuity and dis-
continuity between the meals of Jesus' public

8. SC. 47.
9. LG. 11.

life, the Last Supper, the resurrection meals and
the eucharist of the Church. Any further elabora-
tion must include, above all, additional diffe-
rentiation among these meals: the open-ended
meals of Jesus' public life at which none were
excluded, the closed circle of the Last Supper,
the corresponding closed circle of the resurrection meals, and the eucharist of the church.

THE EUCHARIST AS THANKS-GIVING TO THE FATHER.

The convergence eucharistic text makes it
clear that the eucharist is both word and sacrament, E3, i.e. it is a proclamation and celebration of the work of God. Already at the institution narrative, Paul says that the eucharistic
celebration is the proclamation of Christ's death
until he comes in glory. In the past the Catholic
Church was accused of emphasizing sacraments to
the neglect of the proclamation of the Word. The
constitution on the Sacred Liturgy bears witness
that the Catholic Church emphasizes both Word and
sacrament. In this consitution we read: "That the
intimate connection between words and rites may
be apparent in the liturgy: In sacred celebrations there is to be more reading from holy
Scripture, and it is to be more varied and suitable... Its character should be of a proclamation of God's wonderful works in the history of
salvation, that is, the mystery of Christ, which
is ever made present and active within us, especially in the celebration of the liturgy."[10]

---

10. SC. 35.

The document uses the sacrificial language in presenting the eucharist as thanksgiving to the Father, for it says: "The eucharist is the great sacrifice of praise by which the Church speaks on behalf of the whole creation"[11] In a similar tone Schmaus wrote: "The eucharist is adoration, thanksgiving, and praise in that it constitutes the self-offering of the Church to God through Jesus Christ in the Holy Spirit. This action involves the recognition of God as the Lord and as the God of gracious mercy."[12] Describing the ends of the eucharistic sacrifice in his encyclical, Mediator Dei, Pope Pius XII, mentions thanksgiving as one of them, in these words: "The second end is the giving of due thanks to God. Only the divine Redeemer, because He is the most beloved Son of the Eternal Father and fully knows His unbounded love, could offer Him a worthy hymn of thanksgiving. This is what He intended, this is what He willed, when at the Last Supper, He gave thanks. Hanging on the Cross He continued to give thanks; He continues to do so in the august Sacrifice of the altar, which is called by the name of Eucharist, or 'thanksgiving'; for this is 'truly worthy and just, right and salutary'."[13]

---

11. E4.
12. Schmaus M., Dogma 5, The Church as Sacrament, London, Sheed and Ward, 1975, p.129.
13. Mediator Dei, AAS 39 (1949), quotation according to, CTS, translation, No. 76, p.34.

THE EUCHARIST AS MEMORIAL OF CHRIST.

The Lima convergence text on the eucharist
employed the biblical concept of anamnesis and
the invocation of the Spirit, epiclesis, to overcome the controversial issue of the sacrifical
character of the eucharist. At least the document
says: "The eucharist is the memorial of the crucified and risen christ, i.e. the living and
effective sign of his sacrifice accomplished once
and for all on the cross and still operative on
behalf of all humankind."[14]
The Catholic stand on the eucharist as a propitiatory sacrifice is consigned to commentary to
E8. This commentary corresponds to the traditional scholastic eucharistic theology. According
to Catholic theology the sacrifice of the cross
is sacramentally present in the eucharist in
order that its propitiatory effects may be applied
to the participants and those whom intercession is
made. So the eucharist is propitiatory because it
is a rite of application of the once expiation of
the cross. Intercession is a concrete way of
application of the expiation of the cross in the
eucharistic litury. However the council of Trent
teaches that the eucharist is propitiatory sacrifice because it effects propitiation as a "true
and proper sacrifice." In other words, each eucharist is a propitiatory sacrifice not simply
because it is of application of the one expiation
of the cross. Rather because each eucharist is a
rite of offering, it is a rite of application of
the fruits of the cross." And inasmuch as in this

---

14. E5.

divine sacrifice which is celebrated in the Mass there is contained and immolated in an unbloody manner the same Christ who once offered himself in a bloody manner on the altar of the cross, the Holy Council teaches that this is truly propitiatory and has this effect that if, contrite and penitent, with fear and reverence, we draw nigh to God, 'we obtain mercy and find grace in seasonable aid' (Heb. 4, 16)...Wherefore, according to the tradition of the Apostles, it is rightly offered not only for the sins, punishments, satisfactions and other necessities of the faithful who are living, but also for those departed in Christ but not yet fully purified."[15]

But our document speaks of anamnesis of the sacrifice of Christ. This notion is safeguarded by the Council of Trent as well. "...whereby that bloody sacrifice once to be accomplished on the cross might be represented, the memory thereof remain to the end of the world, and its salutary effects applied to the remission of those sins which we daily commit, declaring himself constituted 'a priest forever according to the order of Melchisedech' (Ps. 109:4)"[16] That is further to say that there is also a ritual acceptance of this offering of the sacrifice of Christ to the community through the offical priestly act of ritual-liturgical proclamation. Moreover this ritual acceptance is an offering. In the anamnesis offering prayer the priest offers Christ to the Father in his own name and that of the community. For our document also says: "In

15. DS 1734.
16. DS. 1739

Christ we offer ourselves as a living and holy
sacrifice in our daily lives..."[17]

The offering of Christ's sacrifice by the
Church takes place at the moment of the sacramental representation of the sacrifice of the cross,
that is, at the recitation of the account of
institution when the priest acts in persona
Christi. At this moment the bread and wine are
changed into the body and blood of Christ. "Hence
the transubstantiation of the bread and wine co-
incides temporally with the sacramental representation of the sacrifice of the cross. At this
moment the church appropriately unites itself to
the once-for-all sacrificial act of Christ sacramentally present."[18] The anamnesis offering,
which follows the recitation of the account of
institution, is generally interpreted as a kind
of affirmation of what takes place at the moment
of consecration when the Church unites itself in
faith with the offering of Christ himself made
visible in the act of the priest and so offers
itself in, with and through Christ.

The official Catholic documents clearly distinguish between two activities of the faithful:
they offer Christ and they offer themselves. The
Constitution on the Sacred Liturgy teaches: "the
Church, therefore earnestly desires that Christ's
faithful ...should give thanks to God; by
offering the Immaculate Victim, not only through
the hands of the priest, but with him, they

---

17. E19.
18. Kilmartin E.J., Lima Text on Eucharist, in:
    Fahey M.A., (ed.), Catholic perspectives on
    Baptism, Eucharist, and Ministry, Lanham, New
    York, etc., 1986, UPA Press, p.148.

should learn to offer themselves too."[19] The idea
that the faithful should learn to offer themselves in union with the priest seems to allude
to the anamnesis offering prayer wherein the
priest expresses in his own name and that of the
Church the intention of self-offering. The Decree
on the Ministry and Life of priests gives the
following instructions to priests regarding the
faithful: "So priests must instruct them to offer
to God the Father the divine Victim in the sacrifice of the Mass, and to join to it the offering
of their own lives."[20] Here the close connection
between the offering of Christ and self-offering
is made.

THE EUCHARIST AS INVOCATION OF THE SPIRIT.

The eucharist is according to the Lima eucharistic text, thanksgiving to the Father, memorial
of Christ and invocation of the Spirit. It is a
trinitarian event. The invocation of the Spirit,
epiclesis, is in the past especially in the early
Church and in the Orthodox liturgy strongly emphasized. Today the restoration of epiclesis in
all the churches has a new liturgical meaning.[21]
This return towards the tradition of the early
church has opened up new accesses to both liturgy
and theology. J. Tillard justifies the role of
the Holy Spirit in the liturgy in these words:
"Since the essential purpose of the eucharist is

19. sc. 48. cf. also G.I. Nos. 55-56.
20. P.O. 5. cf. also G.I. Nos. 55-56.
21. cf. Löser W., op. cit., ThPh 60 (1985).
    p.488.

to lead the Church towards this gift, it is only
in the power of the Holy Spirit that the eucharist can be accomplished."[22] In the text we read:
"The Spirit makes the crucified and risen Christ
really present to us in the eucharistic meal,
fulfilling the promise contained in the words of
institution."[23] The emphasis is on the fact that
the presence of Christ in the eucharist is
brought about through the power of the Holy
Spirit and the words of institution. Tillard saw
in the formulation of E15, an apparent settlement
of the debate between the East and West on what
brings about the miracle of the eucharist. "The
Lima document rightly emphasizes this while at
the same time refraining from any precipitate
settlement of the debate between East and West;
in other words, it is careful to connect the role
of the Spirit with that of the words of the Lord
Jesus."[24]

The Lima document clearly states that "It is
in virtue of the living word of Christ and by the
power of the Holy Spirit that the bread and wine
become the sacramental signs of Christ's body and
blood."[25] This corresponds to what in the Catholic theology is designated with transubstantiation.[26] The document avoided this terminology.
But in the commentaries 13, and 15, transubstantiation is implicity referred to. In commentary
15, the corresponding sentence is: "others con-

22. Tillard, J.M.R., The Eucharist, gift of God,
    in: Thurian M. (ed.), Ecumenical Perspectives
    on BEM, Genevy, WCC, 1983, p.106.
23. E15.
24. Tillard J.M.R., opcit., p.106.
25. E15.
26. cf. Löser W., op. cit., p.489.

sider it necessary to assert a change wrought by
the Holy Spirit and Chirst's words, in consequence of which there is no longer just ordinary
bread and wine but the body and blood of Christ."
The first alternative in commentary 13, and the
second alternative in commentary 15, are the same
and correspond to the Catholic theology of the
real presence of Christ, brought about by transubstantiation. The alternatives as a whole show
the extent of different conceptions of the theology of the real presence of Christ among the
christian Churches. The Roman Catholic doctrine
on the real presence of Christ has been treated
in detail in the previous chapter of this work.

The commentary 14, emphasized the intrinsic
relationship between the words of institution,
Christ's promise, and the epiclesis, and concludes that in the early liturgies the whole
'prayer action' was thought of as bringing about
the reality promised by Christ. This statement is
designed by the document to solve the issue of
the moment of consecration. In the structure of
the eucharistic prayer in the tradition of the
Catholic Church, immediately after the epiclesis,
comes the recitation of the words of institution.
After that it is believed that the bread and wine
have become the body and blood of Christ and in
temporary order, the liturgical anamnesis
follows.

The eucharistic prayer both manifests the
unity between the Church and Christ and the
distinction between the Church and Christ. Only
in thanksgiving to the Father for the gift of
Christ does the Church speak the eucharistic
words of Christ through the priest and so receive

the gift of the Father's love. The Church does
not dare to give the impression that it acts
immediately in place of Christ. Through the
thanksgiving prayer it makes its relation of
dependence on the true host of the meal visible
in the rite.[27]

THE EUCHARIST AS COMMUNION OF THE FAITHFUL.

As Tillard rightly observed, one of the major
rediscoveries of contemporary ecclesiology is the
radical connection between the identity of the
Church and the community's participation in the
Lord's Supper.[28] In the eucharist the memory of
Christ's suffering is celebrated in the form of a
meal. To participate in the eucharist means to
have a share in the body and blood of the Lord.
The Lima text clearly identifies the eucharist as
a sign and cause of ecclesial communion. "The
eucharistic communion with Christ who nourishes
the life of the Church is at the same time communion within the body of Christ which is the
Church."[29]

This is also taught by the Second Vatican
Council, for it said: "Truly partaking of the
body of the Lord in the breaking of the Eucharistic bread, we are taken up into communion with
Him and with one another. Because the bread is
one, we though many, are one body, all of us who
partake of the one bread. (1Cor.10:17."[30]

---

27. cf. Kilmartin E.J., op. cit., p.152.
28. Tillard J.M.R., op. cit., p.106.
29. E19.
30. L.G. 7. cf. also L.G. 3, 11.

The unity presumed and effected in and through the celebration extends beyond the local Church in its sociological and geographical identity to eucharistic celebrations of all times and places. The whole church is involved in each local celebration of the eucharist. This same doctrine is expressed vividly in the Vatican II's document on the Church. There it says: "In any community existing around an altar, under the sacred ministry of the bishop, there is manifested a symbol of that charity and unity of the Mystical Body, without which there is no salvation. In these communities, though frequently small and poor, or living far from any other, Christ is present. By virtue of Him the one, holy, catholic and apostolic Church gathers together. For the partaking of the Body and Blood of Christ does nothing other than transform us into that which we consume."[31] In this same view our document holds that: "It is in the eucharist that the community of God's people is fully manifested. Eucharistic celebrations always have to do with the whole Church, and the whole Church is involved in each local eucharistic celebration."[32]

In refernce to commentary 19, it is necessary to point out that in the present experience of the Church baptism alone does not suffice for admission to the eucharistic communion. It has become necessary to emphasize the unity of faith, the same understanding of the ministerial priesthood, ecclesial relation to the mystery of eucharist, as conditions for admission. The Catholic

---

31. L.G. 26.
32. E19.

Church places some age limit, to childrens admission to holy Communion. This is in view of the fact that the eucharist does not consist only in the eating and drinking of the body and blood of Christ; the proclamation of the Word by which we are fed belongs to it. It is more correct to admit children to communion when they are capable of being fed by the word and nourished by the eucharist. This is in line with the teaching that the eucharist is both word and sacrament.

In identifying the relationship between eucharist and the kingdom of God, the Lima text presents the Church as offering the thanksgiving for the renewal already achieved and anticipating the full arrival of the kingdom. The eucharist is not simply a means of nourishment for the daily life of faith. It is the meal of the risen Lord with his Church, the anticipation of the banquet of the kingdom.

The text correctly points out the missionary aspect of the eucharist. Christ assembles his community at a point in order to send it to all people. He gives himself in the eucharist to be given in turn by believers to the world. The preaching of Christ to all the people therefore has a eucharistic background.

THE CELEBRATION OF THE EUCHARIST.

The list of elements for the liturgical celebration of the eucharist are those found in various traditions. The elements correspond to those found in the eucharistic liturgy of the Catholic Church. Although the document employed

the biblical explanation of anamnesis to
explain the sacrificial character of the eucharist, the anamnesis prayer omits any reference to
the offering of the sacrifice of Christ which it
traditionally includes.

The commentary 28, expresses the view that in
certain parts of the world, where bread and wine
are not customary or obtainable, it is sometimes
held that local food and drink serve better to
anchor the eucharist in every day life. It is
here appropriate to remind ourselves that the
church teaches that the liturgy is made up of
unchangeable elements divinely instituted, and
elements subject to change.[33] Bread and wine
belong to the elements divinely instituted. In
carrying out Christ's command "Do this in remembrance of me", it is just appropriate to use the
elements Christ himself used and the words he
used, otherwise it would no longer be the anamnesis of christ that is being celebrated. In-
culturation or incarnation of the gospel could
take place successfully in those parts of the
world alluded to without altering the constitu-
tive elements so central to the eucharistic
mystery.

The role of the presiding minister as representative of Christ is mentioned, as the one
who represents the divine initiative, and
connects the local church to the universal. But
can more be said other than this? Could the
priestly service of the president not find an
adequate place here as it is well described in
the text on the ministry? There we read:

33. S.C. 21.

"...But they may appropriately be called priests
because they fulfil a particular priestly service
by strengthening and building up the royal and
prophetic priesthood of the faithful through word
and sacraments, through their prayers of intercession, and through their pastoral guidance of
the community."[34] In the Catholic Church every
legitimate eucharist is presided over by the
bishop or at his mandate, by a priest in communion with him. The eucharistic sacrifice is
offered by a priest in persona Christi.

The issue of reservation of the sacrament was
already anticipated in E15, by the statement
"They remain so for the purpose of communion" but
was elaborately treated in E32. The teaching of
the Catholic church on this issue was explained in
the previous Chapter. The primary purpose for
reservation of the sacrament is for the communion
of the sick; adoration remains a secondary purpose. The document is correct when it said that
the reservation of the eucharist by some churches
is grounded on the conviction of christ's continued presence in the consecrated elements
after the celebration. Why should one think that
Christ withdraws his presence after the temporal
moment of the liturgical celebration from the
elements which remain? When Christ relates himself to this concrete point of reference in the
celebration in a definitive way, the church has
no option than to believe; the elements remain
sacrament of his self-giving after the celebration. The special attention required in treating
the elements recommended by the document should

---

34. M17.

not exclude adoration if the document accepts
their use for the communion of the sick. Here the
Lima text can borrow a leaf from ARIC statement
on the issue: "...Differences arise between those
who would also regard it as a means of eucharistic devotion. For the latter, adoration of
Christ in the reserved sacrament should be regarded as an extension of eucharistic worship
which remains the primary purpose of reservation.
Any dissociation of such devotion from this primary purpose, which is communion in Christ of all
his members, is a distortion in eucharistic
practice."[35]

The text rounds off with a reference to
possible eucharistic sharing between separated
churches as a means of fostering the unity of the
whole church. As we have shown before in chapter
five, eucharistic hospitality is not encouraged
in the Catholic Church, except in the cases of
necessity. The Catholic Church demands unity in
faith, and fullness of ecclesial communion as
prerequisites for eucharistic communion. The goal
of the ecumenical movement is full communion;
this can be given to us by God himself through
Jesus Christ his only Son in the Holy Spirit.

---

35. ARIC, Elucidation 1979, No. 8.

6.3   THE LIMA EUCHARISTIC LITURGY.

6.3.1 ORIGIN.

In October 1981, Max Thurian was given the
mandate to prepare a eucharistic liturgy for the
plenary meeting of the Faith and Order Commission
in Lima 1982.[36] There are two reference points to
this mandate, namely: to illustrate through the
liturgy the solid theological achievements of the
Faith and Order document, Baptism, Eucharist and
Ministry; to create the possibility for a good
number of christians, as well as the liturgists
of many traditions to participate actively.[37]
Thurian confessed that the experiences he gathered as observer at the meetings of the Liturgical
Commission, that executed the Vatican Council's
liturgy-reform were of great help to him.[38] As
his method, Thurian chose to look into the traditional liturgical documents to find out what are
the substantial liturgical points that correspond
to baptism, eucharist and ministry; at the same
time being mindful of the different christian
traditions in the way they pray.[39]

The Lima eucharistic liturgy was used for the
first time on 15 January 1982 at Lima; for the
second time at the Ecumenical Centre Chapel in
Geneva on 28 July 1982 during the meeting of the
Central Committee of the World Council of Churches; and thirdly at the Sixth Assembly of the
World Council of Churches in Vancouver on 31 July
1983.

---

36. cf. Thurian Max, Die Eucharistische Liturgie
    von Lima, in: Liturgisches Jahrbuch 34
    (1984), p.20
37. op. cit., p.21 and p.23.
38. op. cit. p.22.
39. idem. p.20.

6.3.2   THE STRUCTURE OF THE LIMA EUCHARISTIC LITURGY.

A comparison with the Roman Missal, shows that the structure of the Lima liturgy is similar to the Roman Catholic Order of the Mass, obviously with certain differences, e.g. the opening prayer and the entrance rite which have the flavour of the Reformed Church liturgy. Other exceptions are: the symbolic action of venerating the altar and the washing of the hand are not included in the Lima liturgy. The invitation to offertory prayer and the offertory prayer itself are lacking in the Lima liturgy. Instead of praying for the forgiveness of sins, the Lima liturgy comes up with a prayer of absolution; instead of dismissal, the Lima liturgy speaks about word of mission.

The Churches that have similar liturgical structure with the Lima liturgy are: Reformed Church of France (1955), Church of South India (1963), Lutheran Church of Sweden (1974), Church of England (1980).

According to the Lima eucharistic convergence text the eucharistic celebration includes the proclamation of the Word and the Communion of the members of the Body of Christ in the power of the Holy Spirit. E31. Taking this as a prelude Max Thurian, the author of the Lima liturgy explains that the eucharistic liturgy consists of three parts, which reflect what is said in E29: Christ assembles, teaches and nourishes the Church in the eucharistic celebration. The three parts are: the introductory part, the liturgy of the Word, and the liturgy of the eucharist. The three parts

are elaborated by Thurian in these words: "The
introductory part unites the people of God in
confession, supplication and praise (confession
of sins, litany of the kyrie, and the Gloria).
The second part, the liturgy of the Word, begins
with a prayer of preparation. It includes the
three proclamations: of a prophet (first lesson),
an apostle (second lesson), and Christ (the
Gospel). Then the voice of the Church is heard in
the sermon, making the eternal word contemporary
and living. The sermon is followed by silent
meditation. The faith of the Church is then
summarized in the Creed and all human needs presented to God in the intercession. The third
part, the liturgy of the eucharist, consists of
the great eucharistic prayer, preceded by a short
preparation and followed by the Lord's Prayer,
the sign of peace and communion."[40]

We shall now present the elements in the whole
structure retaining the number given to each in
the original Lima Eucharistic Liturgy, pointing
out resemblances and differences between it and
the liturgy of some churches or confessions.

6.3.3 LITURGY OF ENTRANCE.

1. Entrance Psalm or hymn.
2. Greeting; wording is from 2Cor.13:13. It is
   the same in the Roman Missal. It resembles the
   liturgy of the Reformed Church in France and
   Holland (1955); also of Consultation on Church
   union in U.S.A (1978)

---

40. Thurian M.; Wainwright G., (eds.), Baptism,
    and Eucharist Ecumenical convergence in
    celebration, Geneva, Wm. B. Eerdmans, 1983,
    p.241.

3. Confession
4. Absolution:

As it is indicated by the author, the wordings of the confession said by the people and the absolution spoken by the celebrant are taken from the Lutheran Book of Worship, U.S.A. and Canada, 1978.

5. Kyrie Litany.

This is according to Greek liturgy and is found also in the Roman Missal. Confer also Lutheran Church in U.S.A. and Canada (1978); Taizé 1959. The wordings of this litany is based on BEM.

6. Gloria.

A hymn of praise from the Western liturgy. Here Thurian comments that "from the beginning of the liturgy, therefore, place is provided for the three fundamental attitudes of Christian prayer: penitence, supplication and praise."[41]

6.3.4 LITURGY OF THE WORD.

7. Collect.

This prayer is understood as opening the liturgy of the word and this is according to the tradition of the Reformed Church, which regards it as invocation of the Spirit on the biblical texts and the homily. The content of the prayer here is based on the theme of BEM.

8. First Lesson. (O.T., Acts, or Revelation).

Three readings are known to the Church of

---

41. op. cit., p.243.

South India since 1950; Reformed Church of
Netherlands, 1959; Lutheran Churches in U.S.A.
1958; Taizé 1959; Roman Missal 1969.

9. Psalm or Meditation

10. Epistle.

11. Allelluia.

12. Gospel.

13. Homily.

14. Silence.

15. Credo.

   The creed used at Lima is Nicene-
   Constantinopolitan creed without the
   filioque. Thurian explains that this happened
   "in an ecumencial spirit of fidelity to the
   original text of the Nicene creed."[42]

16. Intercession.

   Thurian says that he adopted the pattern and
   style of the litany of Pope Gelasius (492-
   496). The layout of the first three intentions
   is similar to the instructions in the Vatican
   II's Constitution on the Liturgy (SC 53). The
   last three intentions, in content are
   orientated towards BEM.

6.3.5 LITURGY OF THE EUCHARIST.

17. Preparation.

   Thurian again explains that the eucharist
   begins with a presentation of the bread and
   wine, accompanied by two benedictions from
   the Jewish liturgy. This is found in the
   Roman Missal as well. However in the bene-

---

42. idem. p.244.

dictions are lacking the expression: "we have
this bread to offer", and "we have this wine
to offer", as they are found in the Roman
missal.

The third part of the prayer is worded according to the liturgy of the Reformed Church of
France, 1955; it is taken from Didache 9,4.
For the response of the people, Maranatha!
"come Lord Jesus", confer 1Cor.16,22; Didache
10,6.

18. Dialogue.
19. Preface.

The eucharistic prayer begins with the preface, the great thanksgiving to the Father
for the works of creation and redemption.
This preface also takes its themes from BEM.

20. Sanctus.
21. Epiclesis I.

The positioning of the first epiclesis before
the words of institution correspond to the
tradition found in the eucharistic prayers of
the Roman Missal. In the liturgy of the Orthodox Church, the epiclesis, words of institution are placed together and not divided
into consecratory epiclesis, words of institution and second epiclesis.

The wordings of the post-sanctus is the
same used in the liturgy of the Reformed
Church of France, 1977. And Thurian states
that the reminder of the work of the
Holy Spirit in the history of our salvation
is inspired by the liturgy of St. James in
the fourth century.[43] For Thurian as well, the

---

43. op. cit., p.244.

epiclesis does not only consecrate the bread
and wine, but also the ordained ministry, and
the fellowship of believers. In the epiclesis
therefore, the ordination of the celebrant is
renewed as well as the baptism and confirmation of the whole community.[44]

22. Institution.

The narration here ended with "Great is the
mystery of faith". This was integrated in the
Old Roman Sacramentary. In the current Roman
Missal, after the elevation of the Cup, the
priest invites the congregation saying: let
us proclaim the mystery of faith, and it
responds with an acclamation. Here the acclamation of the congregation is taken from
1Cor.11,26.

23. Anamnesis.

Thurian explains that: "The anamnesis is the
celebration of the "memorial of our redemption". The sacrifice of the cross and the
resurrection, made present and active for us
today in the eucharist, is central in the
anamnesis."[45] In the Lima liturgy certain
events are emphasized because they correspond
to the themes of BEM.

24. Epiclesis II.

A second epiclesis then invokes the Holy
Spirit upon the congregation, a fresh outpouring consequent on communion in the Body
and Blood of Christ.

The wordings here according to Thurian are

---

44. Thurian M., Die Eucharistische Liturgie von
    Lima, in: Liturgisches Jahrbuch, 34 (1934),
    p.28.
45. Thurian M., Wainwright G., op. cit., p.245.

influenced by the third and fourth echaristic prayer of the Roman Missal.

25. Commemorations.

In the Western tradition, our author explains, this is where we mention all those for whom we wish especially to pray, remember those who precede us in the faith, and all the cloud of witness by whom we are compassed about.[46] The commemoration is similar to the Roman Canon, the tradition of the Eastern Church, and the liturgy of the Church of England 1548.

The Lima liturgy prays first for the Church mentioning its four characteristics; then for the threefold ministry of bishop, presbyter and deacon; the prayer for the dead is the same as in eucharistic prayer IV of the Roman Missal; the mentioning of the patriarchs and prophets, corresponds to the Eastern liturgy, apostles and martyrs as in eucharistic prayers I and III of the Roman Missal. Thurian submits that the wordings of the commemoration are inspired by the Consultation of Church Union in U.S.A.

26. Conclusion.

The eucharistic prayer concludes with the trinitarian doxology traditional to Western liturgies.

27. The Lord's Prayer.

The introduction to the Lord's Prayer recalls the unity of all christians in baptism, which incorporates them into the Body of Christ, and gives them life by one Spirit.

---

46. ibid.

28. The Peace.

   The prayer introducing the giving of peace
   and sign of reconciliation is similar to that
   found in the Roman Missal with a slight
   difference at the close.

29. The Breaking Of The Bread.

   The tradition of the Reformed Church is
   followed here with the wordings from
   1Cor.10,16. In the Roman Missal, the bread is
   broken in silence, and a particle put into
   the chalice.

30. Lamb of God.

31. Communion.

32. Thansgiving Prayer.

   The theme of the thanksgiving prayer is based
   once again on the document of BEM.

33. Final Hymn.

34. Word of Mission.

   After the final hymn, before the blessing,
   the presiding minister may give a brief
   message of dispatch on mission.

35. Blessing.

6.3.6 EVALUATION.

   The Lima liturgy is in the first instance an
illustration of the theological convergence on
Baptism, Eucharist and Ministry. That this illustration could be embodied in the eucharistic
celebration goes to support the statement on the
eucharistic text that "Its celebration continues
as the central act of the Church's worship." El.
One of the aims of the Lima liturgy was to give
christians of different confessions the opport-

unity to take part in the common eucharistic
celebration. It is an ecumenical break-through
that at Lima in 1982, christians of different
confessions celebrated the eucharist together,
eventhough all could not go to communion
especially the Orthodox and the Roman Catholic
representatives. It is necessary to recall that up
to the event in Lima in 1982, the Faith and Order
Commission has not held such celebration during
its plenary meetings. In the past communion
services could be organized with the possibility
of an invitation to open communion.[47]

The event at Vancouver, where the Lima liturgy
was used for the third time, during big gatherings, prompted this enthusiastic statement: "Der
große, vom Erzbischof von Cantebury geleitete,
ökumenische Gottesdienst im Zelt von Vancouver
war der bisher geschlossenste Beweis, daß es
möglich ist, miteinander Gottesdienst zu feiern,
ohne den Eindruck einer losen Zusammenfügung
heterogener liturgischer Elemente zu erwecken."[48]
The report has it that at Geneva, where the Lima
liturgy was used for the second time, the gospel
was read by an Orthodox Metropolitan, and at

---

47. cf. Communion services at ecumenical
    gatherings, in: Rodger P.C., and Vischer L.,
    eds., The Fourth Conference on Faith and
    Order, The Report from Montreal, London, SCM,
    1963, p.76 ff.
48. ÖR 33 (1984), p.197.
    The great ecumenical service in the Tent at
    Vancouver, presided over by the Archbishop of
    Canterbury, was until now the most uniting
    prove that it is possible to celebrate divine
    service together without creating the
    impression of a loose connecting
    heteregeneous liturgical elements."
    (Translation is mine.)

Vancouver the gospel was taken by the Catholic bishop of Würzburg.[49] This co-operation in the entrance rite and Liturgy of the Word is seen by Thurian as underlining our deep fellowship in the one baptism and in the same holy bible, especially now that we cannot yet concelebrate and partake at the same table of the Lord.[50] Thurian was also of the opinion that communion and concelebration cannot take place without being planned, rather we should be thankful for our common faith in view of the eucharistic mystery, which can only be authentic in obedience to the intention of Christ and in agreement with the tradition of the Apostles.[51]

The Lima liturgy in itself is not an official rite. Unlike the Lima convergence text on BEM, it was not voted for nor adopted in the plenary session of Faith and Order Commission at Lima.[52] About its authority Max Thurian said: "The Lima liturgy is not the only possibility: the convergences registered in BEM could be expressed in other liturgical forms, according to other traditions, spiritualities or cultures. No "authority" attaches to this particular liturgy, save that accruing to it from the fact of its having been used on certain significant ecumenical occasions."[53]

The Lima liturgy included all the elements

---

49. Thurian M.m op. cit., Liturgisches Jahrbuch, p.23.
50. idem. p.23.
51. Thurian M., op. cit., p.23.
52. Kasper W., Auf dem Weg zur Einheit, in: Gottesdienst, 19. 12 (1985), p.89.
53. Thurian M., Wainright G., eds., op. cit., p.241.

tabulated in the eucharistic convergence text E27. Let us review its use of sacrificial language in the liturgical expression as well as epiclesis, anamnesis and real presence.

Already in the eucharistic text, we read that the whole of the eucharist has an epikletic character, E16. This is brought out prominently in the liturgical celebration. The two epiclese, encompassing the words of institution and anamnesis, characterize the eucharist as the work of the life-giving Spirit of God. God is implored to send his Spirit upon the Eucharist: "Upon your eucharist send the life-giving Spirit..." In accordance with E16, the liturgical text says: "May the outpouring of this Spirit of Fire transfigure this thanksgiving meal that this bread and wine may become for us the body and blood of Christ." (No.21). The communion epiclesis, after pleading for the acceptance of the offering, through which we are reinstated in the covenant prayed that "as we partake of Christ's body and blood, fill us with the Holy Spirit that we may be one single body and one single Spirit in Christ, a living sacrifice to the praise of your glory." (No.24).

The eucharistic convergence text tells us that it is by the words of institution and the power of the Holy Spirit that the bread and wine become the body and blood of Christ. E15. In the liturgical setting, just before the words of institution we read: "May this creator Spirit accomplish the words of your beloved Son, who, in the night in which he was betrayed..." The illustration is very correct.

In the anamnesis, the re-presentation of the sacrifice of Christ, which include not only his

death, resurrection and ascension but also his
incarnation, found expression in the liturgical
text. Perhaps conscious of the commentary to E8,
the liturgical text goes on: "we proclaim
Christ's resurrection and ascension in glory,
where as our Great High Priest he ever intercedes
for all people; and we look for his coming at
last, then "united in Christ's priesthood, we
present to you this memorial. Remember the sacrifice of your Son and grant to people everywhere
the benefits of Christ's redemptive work."
No.28). There was no mention of we offer you this
sacrifice... In the Catholic eucharistic prayer,
for example, it would read: "Father, calling to
mind the death your Son endured for our salvation, his glorious resurrection and ascension
into heaven, and ready to greet him when he comes
again, we offer you in thanksgiving this holy and
living sacrifice..."[54] This avoidance of, 'we
offer' indicates the difference in the theological understanding regarding the eucharist as a
sacrifice among the churches, despite the meaning
of anamnesis, applied in the text.

Taking the Lima liturgy as it is, one can say
that it remained faithful to the theological text
which it illustrated. The structure corresponds
to the Roman Missal with some exceptions, the
liturgical wordings are not similar. In its
essence it is commendable.

---

54. cf. Eucharistic Prayer III, of Roman Missal.

6.4 THE RESPONSE OF THE CHURCHES.

The convergence text of Baptism, Eucharist and
Ministry (BEM), was unanimously approved by the
plenary meeting of the Faith and Order Commission
in a motion proposed by the Vice Moderator, John
Deschner in Lima on 12 January 1982. This means
that the document has reached a stage of maturity
to be transmitted to the Churches, for their
official reaction and response.

The document BEM was designated as a convergence
text not as a consensus text. This was clearly
explained in the preface to BEM in these words:
"As demonstrated in the Lima text, we have already achieved a remarkable degree of agreement.
Certainly we have not yet fully reached "consensus" (consentire), understood here as that
experience of life and articulation of faith
necessary to realize and maintain the Church's
visible unity. Such consensus is rooted in the
communion built on Jesus Christ and the witness
of the apostles. As a gift of the Spirit it is
realized as a communal experience before it can
be articulated by common efforts into words. Full
consensus can only be proclaimed after the Churches reach the point of living and acting together."[55]

On the strength of this explanation the Churches were asked to prepare an official response to
the text at the highest appropriate level of
authority, to reach the Faith and Order Secretariat by 31 December 1984. The Sixth Assembly of

---

55. Baptism, Eucharist and Minstry, FO No. 111,
    Geneva, WCC, 1982, preface, p. ix.

the World Council of Churches in Vancouver 1983,
strengthened the request for the response from the
Churches and extended the date to 31 December
1985. The Assembly also confirms that the BEM
document is rather a convergence statement not a
consensus text. "In speaking of "Baptism,
Eucharist and Ministry" as a "convergent statement", we do not imply that full agreement has
already been reached. Rather, we speak of a statement which arises out of diverse ways of expressing the same faith, but which points to a common
life and understanding not yet fully attained or
expressed. Nevertheless, this unity remains the
goal of the ecumenical task. These expressions
"bend towards each other." These convergences give
assurance that despite a diversity of traditions
the churches have much in common in their understanding of the faith. The "Baptism, Eucharist and
Ministry" text, however, is not yet a "consensus
statement", meaning by that term "that experience
of life and articulation of faith necessary to
realize and maintain the Church's visible
unity"."[56]

The Assembly explained the difference between
response and reception of the BEM text, in the
light of the term "reception" as applied to the
decisions of the ancient ecumenical Councils or
Synods. It goes on to say: "It is important to
distinguish the "process of reception" and the
"official response". The "official response",
which is requested at a relatively early date, is
intended to initiate a process of study and comm-

---

56. Gill D., (ed.) Gathered for Life, official
    Report, Geneva, Wm. B. Eerdmans, 1983, p.46.

unication in which each church will attempt to
provide an answer to the four preface questions,
answers which are not simply the response of
individuals or groups within the church but
which, in some sense, understood by the church
itself, are given on behalf of the church. This
"official response" is explicitly not understood
to be the church's ultimate decisions about "Baptism, Eucharist and Ministry", but rather the
initial step in a longer process of reception.
This "process of reception" is something which
each Church will have to understand in terms of
its own tradition..."[57]

The Faith and Order Commission invites the
churches to prepare an official response to the
text in the light of the following four statements regarded as questions:

"- the extent to which your church can
recognize in this text the faith of the Church
through the ages;

- the consequences your church can draw from
this text for its relations and dialogues with
other churches, particularly with those churches
which also recognize the text as an expression of
the apostolic faith;

- the guidance your church can take from this
text for its worship, educational, ethical, and
spiritual life and witness;

- the suggestions your church can make for the
ongoing work of Faith and Order as it relates the
material of this text on Baptism, Eucharist and
Ministry to its long-range research project "Towards the Common Expression of the Apostolic
Faith Today."[58] The Faith and Order Commission

---

57. ibid.
58. Baptism, Eucharist and Ministry, op. cit.
     p.x.

in turn promised to compare all the official
replies received, to publish the results, and to
analyze the ecumenical implications for the churches at a future World Conference on Faith and
Order.

Over 170 Churches have sent in their official
reports, and these have been published in four
Bands, and the next two Bands are expected to be
published in March 1988.[59] To delve into the
responses alone can afford material for a dissertation in itself. Here we have chosen to present
the responses of some major churches or confessions as samples. In this selection the Orthodox
and the Roman Catholic Churches are represented;
the rest are Reformation Churches except the
Baptists. The responses are presented in this
order: Romanian Orthodox Church, Church of England, Evangelical Lutheran Church in Bavaria
(FRG); Netherlands Reformed Church and Reformed
Churches in the Netherlands; American Baptist
Churches in the USA; Evangelical Church of Westphalia, and The Roman Catholic Church. We are
concerned here with the response to the
eucharistic text.

6.4.1 ROMANIAN ORTHODOX CHURCH.

The Orthodox Church of Romania has a total of
17,000,000 members in 15 dioceses. Altogether
there are 8,165 parishes grouped in 5 metropoli-
tanates. The Church has 8,545 priests and 2,702
monks and nuns. In 1885, the Romanian Orthodox

---

59. cf. Faith and Order, Information No. 4 Feb.
    1988, p.4.

Church was granted autocephalous status through a Tomos issued by the Ecumenical Patriarch Joachim IV. Today the Metropolitan of Bucharest is its Patriarch.[60]

RESPONSE.

In the introduction to the response, the Romanian Orthodox Church, expresses its appreciation on the efforts being made through BEM to achieve Christian unity. It described the document as a theological convergence, and remarked that it contained certain statements which the Church could not accept because they do not meet the Orthodox teaching. However it values the document as an important step towards convergence on three out of the seven sacraments of the Church.

The response is presented in the following order: elements of convergence; critical remarks; and suggestions concerning the eucharist.

ELEMENTS OF CONVERGENCE.

In the underlisted points, the Romanian Orthodox Church recognizes the apostolic faith on the eucharist in its general aspects:

- sacrament instituted by Jesus Christ at the Last Supper.

---

60. Source of this information: cf. van der Bent A.J., (ed.), Handbook member Churches, Geneva, WCC, 1985, pp.172-173.

- thanksgiving to the Father for everything he
  accomplished for us: creation, redemption and
  sanctification.
- anamnesis of the crucified and risen Christ.
- The Church recognizes as well from the Lima
  eucharist text, the statements -, the eucharist
  as:
- sacrament of Christ's real, unique and
  objective presence;
- sacrament of Christ's body and blood by the
  invocation and work of the Holy Spirit;
- sacrament of the community with Christ and his
  ecclesial body; and as
- sacrament of the communion of the church.

Other areas of convergence recognized by this
church include the ackowledgment by the eucharistic text of the eschatological dimension of the
eucharist as anticipation and as foretaste of the
coming of the kingdom in Christ; and the recommendation for frequent celebration of the eucharist, and the emphasis on the communitary and
social implications of the eucharist.

CRITICAL REMARKS.

The church does not agree with the use of the
word 'sign' to clarify the eucharist vis-à-vis
the acceptance of the sacramental character of
the eucharist, for example, "The eucharist is the
living and effective sign of his sacrifice" E5.
The response contended that "the 'sign' only
indicates without expressing the reality of the
sacrament by which the body and the blood of

Christ, which carry the grace of the Holy Spirit, are given."[61] Hence it rejects the other names in which the eucharist is described, namely: sacramental meal, the Lord's supper, divine liturgy and Mass, for not bringing out the sacramental character of the Last Supper.

The response affirms the relation between the eucharist and the other meals of Christ as part of the economy of incarnation and understands them as the prefiguration of the eucharist.

The response remarks that the statement: "The anamnesis of Christ is the very content of the eucharistic meal", E12. denotes a shift of importance from the real presence of Christ onto anamnesis or memorial presence of Christ, without emphasizing the fundamental unity of the Son and the Holy Spirit in the eucharist.

The next remark speaks for itself: "The statement according to which in the eucharist the faithful is empowered to live as a "justified sinner" E9, is alien to the apostolic tradition, since the apostle Paul teaches that the faithful becomes a new being in Christ (Gal.3:27; 6:15)."

Finally, the response remarks that the statement on the invisible celebrant of the eucharist is correct, but categorizes as ambiguous and equivocal, where the text regarded the priest as a sign of Christ, E29. Its contention is: "whereas, the holy scripture clearly shows that the celebration of the eucharist depends upon the charismatic and sacramental state of the cele-

---

61. The response of the Romanian Orthodox Church to BEM is found in: Thurian M., (ed.), Churches respond to BEM Vol III, Geneva, WCC, 1987, pp.4-14.

brant (Lk.22:29; Rev.20:19)."

The Romanian Orthodox Church values the theological convergence on the eucharist as an important basis for further general and bilateral
theological discussions for unity, but it is of
the opinion that they do not justify the eucharistic intercommunion suggested in the document in
E33.

On the eucharist and the pastoral mission of
the church, the official response says that in
the Orthodox Church, it is understood that eucharistic communion supports and deepens the ecclesial communion and plays an important role in the
renewal of the christian spiritual life, and
concluded that the eucharist should be received
in purity, by the help of the sacrament of confession which forgives sins citing: (Acts.19:16;
1Cor.11:27-30).

SUGGESTIONS CONCERNING THE EUCHARIST.

In order to achieve a full consensus on the
eucharist the Romanian Orthodox Church suggests
that the underlisted aspects should be thoroughly
re-analyzed and clarified:

a. The reflection on the work of the Holy Trinity
   in the eucharist: in anamnesis and epiclesis;
b. the sacrifice-sacrament relation in the eucharist; an argumentation of the real presence of
   Christ in the eucharist, as a result of the
   change of the gifts, bread and wine, into the
   body and blood of Christ brought about through
   the work of the Holy Spirit;
c. the understanding of the eucharist as a per-

manent updating of the entire economy of salvation in the church, through Christ, in the Holy Spirit. This suggestion is occasioned by the statement from E8, which says: "What it was God's will to accomplish in the incarnation, life, death, resurrection and ascension of Christ, God does not repeat. These events are unique and can neither be repeated nor prolonged." This statement is classified as separating the eucharist from the economy of salvation;

d. a thorough analysis and more variety in presenting the relation between the physical body of Christ taken from Mary, the eucharistic body and the ecclesial body of the Church of Christ, with a view to a better understanding of the nature and significance of the eucharist as the Church's permanent partaking of the life of Christ and as our participation in the death and resurrection of Christ;

e. a thorough analysis of the relation between the participation in the eucharist and the confession of the whole faith of the church.

f. clarification that the eucharist is the final act of the full incorporation into the body of Christ in christian initiation, making it clear that the eucharist is the essential sacrament for the growth in Christ, when it is received after the pardoning of sins through confession.

g. clear affirmation of the administering of the eucharist to adults and infants.

6.4.2 CHURCH OF ENGLAND.

The origin of the Church of England goes back
to the year 1534, when King Henry VIII claimed
the title "Supreme Head of the English Church",
and so brought about a breach with Rome. Its
doctrinal position is expressed in the Thirty-
nine articles; the English Bible and Book of
Common Prayer gave the Church of England a distinct identity.[62] The Primate of the Church of
England is the Archbishop of Canterbury. The
Church has 27,200,000 members, 17,460 congregations, 44 dioceses, 13,953 parishes and 18,376
clergy.[63]

RESPONSE.

The Church of England in the general introduction to its response to BEM, points out that it
is important when giving a response to an ecumenical text to bear in mind the claim made for
its achievement by those responsible for the
production of the text. It observed that the Lima
text is not a comprehensive formulation on the
three subjects covered. Rather, it deals mainly
with particular points of misunderstanding and
disagreements which have led to division. Further
it acknowledges that the text has made a significant achievement in the movement towards visible
unity, yet it has not attained a consensus. It
gave the indication that its response is con-

---

62. cf. van der Bent A.J., op. cit., p.185.
63. ibid.

sidered in relation to each of the four questions
asked by Faith and Order Commission. The response
is presented now following the order in its original presentation.[64]

THE BIBLICAL BASIS OF THE EUCHARIST.

The response welcomes the biblical basis of
the eucharist as it was firmly stated in the
eucharistic text and the emphasis as well that
the eucharist is the gift of God. The Trinitarian
presentation of the eucharist set forth in its
meaning as thanksgiving to the Father, as memorial of Christ, and as invocation of the Spirit,
is appreciated, with the remark that "this particular structure provides a welcome balance and
harmony to eucharistic theology."

EUCHARIST AND WORD.

The assertion of the Lima text that the eucharist "always includes both word and sacrament"
E3, is welcome to the Anglicans and they add that
the reading of scriptures and preaching are part
of this proclamation. The response bore testimony
to the statement that the eucharist is the central act of the church's worship,and the recommendation for its weekly celebration on the

---

64. The official response to BEM of the Church
    of England is found in: Thurian M., (ed.),
    Churches respond to BEM Vol III, Geneva, WCC,
    1987, pp.42-49

Lord's Day. For "Anglicans, in whose life the
eucharist has not always played this central
role, are in a position to testify to the enrich-
ment which has resulted from the renewal of the
eucharistic life."

EUCHARIST AND SACRIFICE.

The response gives assent to the description
of the eucharist as the "great sacrifice of
praise." E4. It accepts that the Christian sacrifice of praise is made possible "only through
Christ, with him and in him." E4. It also accepts
the statement that the eucharist is the "living
and effective sign of his sacrifice, accomplished
once for all on the cross and still operative on
behalf of all humankind." E5. It affirms as well
the emphatic statement that the sacrifice of
Christ was once for all, but finds it less emphatic as in the Final Report of ARCIC, where it was
said that the once for all sacrifice of Christ is
made present and effectual in the whole eucharistic celebration; in each case the response saw
the two statements leaning upon the biblical
concept of anamnesis to explain the making present of Christ's once for all sacrifice.

The response approves as useful the use of the
biblical concept of anamnesis whose language
shows "that more than a simple recalling to mind
of a past event is meant when in the sacrament of
the eucharist the sacrifice of Calvary is recalled." The response nevertheless notes down
some misgivings of the concept, anamnesis. It
declares: "However, anamnesis on its own cannot
take all the weight in healing past division on

the eucharist and sacrifice. Indeed some discussions of anamnesis appear to suggest either that Calvary is repeated, or that we ourselves in the act of remembering make effective those benefits of Christ's sacrifice." It shows preference to the use of anamnesis in the ARCIC which reads: "The Commission believes that the traditional understanding of sacramental reality, in which the once for all event of salvation becomes effective in the present through the action of the Holy Spirit, is well expressed by the word 'anamnesis'."[65] This also attracts a cmomment: "The christological and pneumatological settings of eucharistic theology need carefull correlation; and sections B and C of the Lima Text need to be read together."[66]

In its ongoing appraisal of anamnesis the response submits that what is recollected in the eucharist, through the power of the Spirit, is not only the sacrifice of Calvary but the total Christ-event from the creation by the Logos to the consumation of the kingdom. The recall of this salvation history in the opinion of the Anglican Church, gives the church its Christian identity. Hence it welcomes the emphasis on the eucharistic text, which unites the past, present and future of God's act of salvation. "This action brings into the present the once for all offering of Christ on Calvary and is also an anticipatory realization of the future fulfilment of the kingdom."[67] The response affirms the use

---

65. op. cit., p.43. cf. also The Final Report, Elucidation no. 5.
66. ibid.
67. ibid. p.44.

of the concept of anamnesis to bridge two oppo-
sing views, namely: "allowing us to use confidently the language of sacrifice in a context of
recital of all the mighty acts of God in Christ
while relying on the power of the Holy Spirit to
make efficacious the sacrifice offered once and
for all on the cross."[68]

The response further observes that the biblical notion of sacrifice is exceedingly wide. It
cites an example from the Final Report of ARCIC,
to substantiate the wide range notion of sacrifice in the Old Testament: "For the Hebrew sacrifice was a traditional means of communication
with God. The Passover, for example, was a
communal meal; the Day of Atonement was expiatory; and the convenant established communion
between God and man."[69] The same is applicable to
the New Testament as is evident from the writers:
"So Paul, in Romans 3, talks of 'expiation' and
the effects of Christ's death as comparable to
expiatory sacrifice; Hebrews 13 points rather to
the Day of Atonement, likening the sacrifice of
Christ to the sacrificial animal rather than the
scapegoat; the Gospel of John uses the idea of
the Passover sacrifice to elucidate the death of
Christ on the Cross."[70] As the Lima text does not
draw out these various views of sacrifice, the
response wonders whether every view can equally
appropriately be used to reflect on the sacrifice
of Christ when it is called to mind in the eucharist. But the response holds that a breadth of

---

68. ibid.
69. cf. ARCIC, Final Report, no.5.
70. Thurian M., op. cit., Vol III, p.45.

meaning is possible and that the benefit of
Christ's death, although comparable to, surpass
the benefits of the whole of the Old Testament
sacrificial system. Citing commentary E8, the
response concludes by calling for a renewed grasp
of the meaning of sacrifice and the richness of
the concept as applied to the eucharistic
scrifice.

EUCHARIST AND THE HOLY SPIRIT.

The response affirms the way in which the
convergence text develops the pneumatological
aspect of the eucharist as invocation of the
Spirit. It maintains that it is correct that the
Spirit is invoked both upon the community and
upon the elements of bread and wine. The statement: "The whole action of the eucharist has an
'epikletic' character because it depends upon the
work of the Holy Spirit" E16, attracts this submission: "This is an important balance bringing
together the emphases of east and west and avoiding the presence of Christ being concentrated
too narrowly upon the moment of consecration."[71]

EUCHARIST AND PRESENCE.

Concerning the presence of Christ in the eucharist, the response points out that it is only
within the context of the presence of the crucified and risen Christ in the whole celebration
that the relation between the elements of bread

---

71. idem.

and wine and that presence is discussed. It expresses its happiness that the Lima eucharistic
text does not formulate any theory of change. The
response admits that the Final Report of ARCIC
goes beyond the Lima text in affirming the real
presence of Christ, as the former's statement
shows: "Communion with Christ in the eucharist
presupposes his true presence, effectually signified by the bread and wine which, in this
mystery, become his body and blood."[72] This comparison led the response then to say: "It would
seem sufficient and faithful to the belief of the
Church through the ages to uphold the real presence of Christ in the eucharist and his body and
blood truly received in the bread and wine without demanding further agreement on the mode of
that presence in the elements."[73]

RESERVATION.

The response acknowledges that differences
exist within the Church of England itself as well
as between the Churches on the issue of reservation. It goes on to say that some Churches reserve the elements primarily for their distribution to the sick, while others consume the elements in the act of communion. Then it declares:
"Reservation it seems is acceptable because it is
seen as the extension of the eucharist itself."
It calls for respect for the piety and practice
of others but recommends the practice of con-

72. ARCIC, The Final Report, Elucidation, no.6.
73. Thurian M., op. cit., p.46.

suming any of the eucharistic elements not required for communion.

EUCHARIST AND THE KINGDOM.

The response observes with interest, the
statement of the Lima text which says that the
world is incorporated into the eucharistic
action, from the standpoint of creation, E3,4,
redemption E8, and mission E17, 20,21, and all
this gives support to the statement that: "The
eucharist is the feast where the Church may recognize the signs of renewal already at work in
the world, where, united with Christ in a special
way, it prays for the world. It considers this
concern for the world as an integral part of our
common belief on the eucharist, and for those who
participate in its celebration, it entails a new
ethical stance. This is so because "the finality
of Christ's mission in the reconciliation of all
things determines the life and conduct of the
Church and of the individual believer." The response maintains that while we await with hope for
the manifestation of God's new creation, our
motivation should strive for the realization of
God's will in all aspects of life. It goes on to
support the statement which condemns all kinds of
injustice, racism and division, for the eucharist
shows us that our behaviour is inconsistent in
the face of the reconciling presence of God in
human history. This inconsistency in our behaviour demands penitence before approaching the
eucharist.

EUCHARIST AND THE CHURCH.

The response affirms the statement on the
relation between the eucharist and the nature of
the church as it is expressed in the convergence
text on the eucharist. It hopes that a future
work would build upon the emerging ecclesiology,
and declares: "We welcome the emphasis that 'eucharistic celebrations have always to do with the
whole Church, and the whole Church is involved in
each local eucharistic celebration' E19." It
pleads for hard work for the purpose of christian
unity in one eucharistic fellowship on the basis
of the converging theological agreement.

6.4.3 EVANGELICAL LUTHERAN CHURCH IN BAVARIA.

The Evangelical Lutheran Church in Bavaria,
Federal Republic of Germany, was firmly founded
in 1803. The Church is divided into six
districts, namely: Ansbach, Augsburg, Beyreuth,
Munich, Nuremberg and Regensburg. It has a totoal
number of 2,560,000 members, 73 deaneries, 1,514
parishes, 6 regional bishops and 2,032 pastors.[74]

RESPONSE.

In its introduction to the response[75] to BEM,
the Evangelical Lutheran Church in Bavaria,

---

74. cf. can der Bent A.J., op. cit., p.142.
75. This response is found in: Thurian M., (ed.),
    Churches respond to BEM Vol. IV, Geneva, WCC,
    1987, pp.21-41; eucharist section, pp.31-33.

outlined its attitude in making the response in
relation to other churches. Though it does not
close its mind to other traditions and churches,
it treats the response "as an up-to-date and
responsible answer to the judgements and questions
of the convergence documents on the basis of our
confession."[76] This church sees the convergence
text as opening up to it the wealth of theological knowledge and the variety of worship of
other churches.

The response was presented under three major
headings that correspond with the headings in the
convergence text itself, followed by points of
agreement and then reservations and suggestions.
This method is followed in this presentation.

INSTITUTION OF THE EUCHARIST.
AGREEMENT.

The Church accepts the fact that the statement
on the institution of the eucharist took into
account in a balanced way, the findings of modern
exegetics, and the historical institution of the
eucharist by Jesus which formed the focus. The
response agrees as well with the manner in which
the meals of Jesus before and after the resurrection was related to the eucharist and with the
emphasis on the eucharist as a gift. Again it
agrees with the eucharist being considered as
feast of the new Covenant in reference to the
passover and with its eschatological character.

---

76. op. cit., p.24.

The response points out that the word eucharist, is unexplained, and that it is alien to its tradition, which speaks of the holy supper. It is not satisfied with the use of the word to designate the whole service of worship which includes the procalamtion of the word and the administration of the sacrament. Consequent upon this objection, it suggests that in the choice of language, it be made clear that word and sacrament stand with equal rank alongside each other and constantly relate to each other. The response insists that for them, word and sacrament are the central content of worship.

MEANING OF THE EUCHARIST.
AGREEMENT.

The Church affirms the understanding of the eucharist as donation and gift of God and as a visible sign of his mercy. It accepts the following statements: that the eucharist grants community with Christ; is the promise of forgiveness of sins and a pledge of eternal life. The response assents to the trinitarian foundation and evolution of the eucharist, which sets the eucharistic event into the whole action of God in creation, reconciliation and perfection, which in turn expresses the reconciliatory act in Christ in its significance for the entire creation. It appreciates the description of the role of the Holy Spirit which it says was done unequivocally. This it maintains helps to make the role of the church clearer as the one that entreats the presence of God not as the one who controls the gift

of the sacrament. In its opinion the role of the
Holy Spirit wards off a magical understanding of
pronouncing the words of institution. It affirms
as well the emphasis on the real presence of
Christ.

The church accepts as challenge and supports
the "restoration of Sunday worship including
sermon and holy communion." On this ground it
pleads that the ranking of the sermon be preserved and strenghtened, that holy communion retain
its character as offer, and not be interpreted as
a statutory demand. It considers it correct to
associate oral confession with holy communion. On
the ethical implications of the eucharist, the
response is of the opinion that no pressure for
action should come from the Lord's Supper, rather
its effect is to set the christians in motion.

RESERVATION AND SUGGESTION.

The response points out that the eucharistic
text does not properly differentiate the function
of Christ as the Subject in relation to the
Church and the Church in action. It calls for the
strenghtening of E29, where the action of Christ
is outlined. It points out that the text does not
develop the aspect of the eucharist on the forgiveness of sins and maintains that holy communion is inconceivable for us without the element
of personal dedication to the forgiveness of
sins.

The response came up with a bold statement on
the atoning effect of the eucharist: "We believe
that Christ's sacrifice on the cross realized in

the eucharist has atoning significance"; and
rejected what it called "the idea of an additional atoning effect of the memorial of the
victim Christ through the Church." The response
maintains that the real presence of Christ is
inseparably bound to the elements in the celebration of the eucharist. It finds helpful, the
considerations on the epiclesis, in understanding
Christ's presence as a gift, which makes us aware
that in the real presence of Christ, renewal of
life occurs, community is endowed and the power
to active love grows out of experienced reconciliation

CELEBRATION OF THE EUCHARIST.

The response points out that the components of
the eucharistic liturgy mentioned in E27, agree
largely with the tradition of its church. This is
also true in the case of epiclesis and anamnesis.
In connection with the celebration of the eucharist, the response made this statement: "Under no
circumstances may the prayer of thanksgiving, the
words of institution, the elements of bread and
wine and the words of administration be dispensed
with."[77] On the issue of reservation of the sacrament it also said: "In accoradance with our
own tradition of faith and our trust in the promise of Jesus Christ to be present in bread and
wine, a reverent handling of the elements is
necessary."[78]

---

77. op. cit. p.33.
78. ibid.

6.4.4 NETHERLANDS REFORMED CHURCH AND REFORMED
CHURCHES IN THE NETHERLANDS.

The Reformed Churches in the netherlands came
into existence in 1886 separating itself from the
Netherlands Reformed Church. Two denominations
which emanated from the conflict united in 1892
to form the Reformed Churches in the Netherlands.[79] The Reformed Churches of Netherland have
844,427 members, 823 congregations, 1,168
pastors.

The Netherlands Reformed Church had its origin
in the Reformation which stirred the church in
Europe in the 16th century. It bore Calvin's
imprint. The Church has 2,700,000 members, 1,800
parishes, 1,775 pastors.[80] The two Reformed Churches worked together to present a response to the
BEM document. The response gave a hint that in
the Netherlands there has been an ongoing discussion on the eucharist and that the end result is
similar to BEM.

RESPONSE.

The response declared that the Lima eucharist
text rests on six scriptural/theological pillars
which converge to fundamental starting points of
the Reformed tradition, namely:
- the supper is placed in a wide framework to
  include other meals that the Lord shared with his
  followers

---

79. van der Bent, A.J., op. cit., p.164.
80. op. cit., p.162.

- word and sacrament are indivisibly joined
  together.
- the uniqueness and unrepeatable nature of
  Christ's saving work clearly emerge.
- during the celebration, the anamnesis joins
  believers with the salvation brought about in
  Jesus Christ.
- it is through the Spirit that we share in the
  saving gifts of the Lord present at the
  celebration of the eucharist.
- the Lord's Supper is placed within the
  perspective of the kingdom of God.

In addition to these six points are the uniqueness of Christ's saving work; the unrepeatable
nature of his offer; and the role of the Holy
Spirit in the sacrament. On account of the description of the role of the Holy Spirit, the
response maintains that preoccupation with the
moment and manner in which Christ reveals his
presence in the gifts of bread and wine is over-
taken.

The response is not in total agreement with
the statement that the eucharist is both word and
sacrament. It poses two questions namely: whether
the word does not go into the making of the sacrament; and whether the word does not precede
the celebration of the sacrament? The reason for
asking these questions is that "in our tradition
many people do not really see the sacrament as an
instrument of salvation that feeds our faith and
enriches life."[82] The response identifies in this

---

81. Source of the response: Thurian M., (ed.),
    Churches respond to BEM Vol IV, Geneva, WCC,
    1987, pp.100-109.
82. op. cit., p.106.

matter obvious differences between Reformed,
Roman Catholic and Orthodox spirituality, but
maintains that these differences are no stumbling
blocks to communion. Another area of difference
with the Reformed tradition identified in the
convergence text is what the response called the
cosmic interpretation that the Lima text gives to
the celebration of the Lord's Supper, namely:
that the eucharist is called the supreme thanksgiving to the Father for all that he has done in
creation, redemption, and salvation...E3; that
the eucharist is the supreme offer of thanks
spoken by the church on behalf of the whole of
creation. It concludes that "Reformed Christians
cannot easily express themselves in such a way
about the celebration of the Lord's supper."[83]
This difference it maintains will not prevent
communion at the table of the Lord. Finally the
response remarks that the section of the Lima
text which agrees with its theological assump-
tions would make a good basis for the renewal of
communion in the Lord's supper on the way to
ecclesiastical unity.

6.4.5 AMERICAN BAPTIST CHURCHES IN THE USA.

The American Baptist Churches in the USA is a
covenanted fellowship of churches, united by a
common confession of Jesus Christ as Lord and
Saviour according to the scriptures. For the
American Baptist churches, the Bible is the sole

---

83. ibid.

rule of faith and practice, the Holy Spirit the
guide and interpreter. The church has 1,616,992
members, 5,814 congregations in USA, 8,618 congregations overseas, 6,780 pastors in USA and
12,493 church workers overseas.[84]

RESPONSE.

In the introduction to the response, the
church expressed gratitude for the opportunity
offered it to participate with other churches to
make a response to the BEM document. It stated
that their answers are given using the scripture
as the standard, rather than the faith of the
church through the ages. The church does not
regard baptism, eucharist and ministry as sacraments but as rites which necessarily follow on a
prior and inward response to divine initiative or
grace.

The Baptists prefer to use "The Lord's Supper"
as the common designation of what other christians call the eucharist. The reason for this
preference in terminology is to show that the
table does not belong to the church but to the
Lord. The Baptists recognize the biblical validity of understanding the Lord's Supper as
thanksgiving. Following Jesus words at the institution "Do this in remembrance of me", the Baptists accept the central role of anmnesis in
understanding the eucharistic celebration as the
Lima text presented it.

---

84. cf. Thurian M., (ed.), Churches respond to
    BEM Vol. III, Geneva, WCC, 1987, p.257.

The response points out that anamnesis has
been a central aspect of Baptist understanding of
the Lord's Supper, and it affirms its central
place in the eucharist text of Lima. It admits
that the use of the word anamnesis offers the
Baptists the opportunity for a deeper understanding of the notion, to the extent that they
appreciate anew the way in which this memorial
draws them into a deeper communion with God and
as the occasion for Christ to be present.

The response found as challenging, the expression for the meaning of the eucharist as: "thanksgiving, invocation of the Spirit, communion of
the faithful and as meal of the kingdom. While
these are found to illuminate their faith, other
expressions are said to be items for further
study. The Baptists appreciate the manner in
which the eucharist as sacrifice is handled but
at the same time maintaned that "as Baptists, we
stress the sole sufficiency of Christ's sacrifice, and we affirm the manner in which this
section lifts up the Supper as a 'proclamation
and celebration of the work of God'."[85]

The response expresses reservations on the
following statements: that christians receive
'the gift of salvation' through communion; that
the eucharist 'transforms christians into the
image of Christ'. The Baptists see in these
statements the suggestion that sacraments or
rites may be occasions and means of grace, though
not of salvation. Hence they would prefer to say:
"a sacrament dose not transform us, but the grace
of God does."

---

85. op. cit., p.260.

The response affirms that in the Lord's Supper the whole people of God is made manifest; that the Lord's Supper is a sign of God's rule, therefore eschatological, which nourishes the church for its mission. It deplores the division that exists among Christians at the Lord's table. The American Baptists practice open communion and they extend their invitation to all who believe in Christ. Their experience shows that this gesture hardly finds reciprocity from other churches.

The Baptists confess that the presentation of the eucharistic celebration in the text, offers them much from other traditions, which will be of significant value to them. They ackowledge that most of the elements outlined in E27 are found in their worship services, but they would like to avoid standardized forms for fear of the celebration turning out to be a routine. The Baptist welcome the recommendation for frequent celebration of the eucharist, which for them does not mean weekly celebration. It pointed out differences that exist within the Baptists themselves in this matter. While some would prepare themselves properly for Sunday eucharistic celebration by confessing of sins and prayer service; others regard the eucharist either as an 'ad on' or marginal part of the church's life.

6.4.6 EVANGELICAL CHURCH OF WESTPHALIA.

The Evangelical Church of Westphalia in the Federal Republic of Germany, is made up to Evangelical Lutheran Church, Evangelical Reformed

Church and Evangelical United Church. This Church
has 3,600,000 members, 1,676 congregations and
1,600 pastors.[86]

RESPONSE.

The introduction to the response identifies
the BEM document as thought-provoking, which can
help to enliven their worship services and liturgy.
The Church bases its response on the biblical
witness, fundamental concern of the Reformation
confessions and on the latter's historical im-
pact. The response was presented in this order
which we shall follow: criteria for the statement, points of agreement, questions the text
posed on the church and counter questions and
reservations.

The response is found in the official response
of the churches to BEM.[87]

CRITERIA.

This church bases its response on the following
criteria: Its understanding of the eucharist as
contained in the words of institution: Mk.14:22-
24 and parallels as well as 1Cor.11:23-25. The
result of Arnoldshain Theses of 1957 and the
Leuenberg Agreement of 1973. On these basis they

---

86. cf. Thurian M., (ed.), Churches respond to
    BEM Vol. IV, Geneva, WCC, 1987, p.137.
87. op. cit., pp. 137-153. Eucharist section, pp.
    141-144.

could witness together: "In the Lord's Supper
(celebrated in conformity with the words of institution) the risen Christ imparts himself in
his body and blood, given up for all, through his
word of promise with bread and wine. He thereby
grants us forgiveness of sins, and sets us free
for a new life of faith. He enables us to experience anew that we are members of his body. He
strengthens us for all services to all men."[88]
From the Leuenberg agreement they as well witness
together that 'in the celebration of the eucharist we proclaim the death of Christ; we proclaim
the presence of the risen Lord in our midst and
await his future coming in glory.' That the assurance of the forgiveness of sins is received at
the eucharist. Frequent celebration of the eucharist ordained by the church, with confession of
sin as the proper spiritual preparation. That the
eucharist is first and foremost God's action
which is decisive and not the Church's.

POINTS OF AGREEMENT.

The Church of Westphalia agrees with the Lima
eucharist text on the following statements that
Christ in the eucharistic communion:
- stands at the heart of the celebration E13;
- grants communion with himself E2;
- invites to the meal and presides at it E29;
- grants the forgiveness of sins E2, and thus
  fulfilling the promise contained in the words
  of institution.

---

88. op. cit., p.141.

- liberates us for witness and to a new ethics
  E24f;
- unites to 'communion within the body of
  Christ' and thus of the whole church E19;
- guarantees the final coming of the kingdom of
  God E22.

The response accepts as well the arrangement
in which the liturgy of the word precedes the
eucharistic liturgy and appreciates the recommendation for frequent communion. It accepts the
desire for eucharistic hospitality based on mutual understanding which grows from common faith.

QUESTIONS THAT THE CONVERGENCE TEXT POSED ON
THEM.

1. The linking of the eucharist with the meals
   which Jesus shared with his followers during
   his earthly ministry, and the Trinitarian
   role at the eucharist, are accepted as
   deepening and broadening scriptually their
   understanding of the eucharist.
2. The expression of the eucharist by the text as
   thanksgiving to the Father, which points as
   well to the universal aspect of the eucharist
   provokes these words of thanks: "We gratefully
   accept the idea of the universal scope of the
   eucharist, of already being able to join in
   the eternal song of praise of the world renewed by God."[89]

---

89. op. cit., p.143.

3. The clarification of the anamnesis or memorial of Christ by the text to refer to Christ's ministerial offices, E8.

4. The epiclesis which refers to the whole action of the eucharist, is taken to offer the possibility of overcoming the moment of consecration problematic in western christianity, and fixation on the eucharistic elements.

5. The statement that 'the eucharist embraces all aspects of life' E20, and what E21 said on 'solidarity in the eucharistic communion'. enjoy full support from the church.

6. The role of the Triune God as emphasized by the text in the eucharistic liturgy is another aspect which the church desires to comply with in its celebration of the eucharist.

7. Another statement that challenges the Evangelical Church of Westphalia is that of E19, "It is in the eucharist that the community of God's people is fully manifest." Hence the response comes out openly to say: "We must critically ask ourselves whether all of the expressions of life in our church are thus related to the worship service and vice versa, (1Cor.10:16)."

COUNTER-QUESTIONS AND RESERVATIONS.

The response does not accept the exclusive use of the term "eucharist", for fear of its conveying the impression that the church rather than Christ acts. It suggests other expressions: the breaking of bread; the Lord's Supper and comm-

union. It points out that the words "given and
shed for you for the forgiveness of sins", are
the main part of the sacrament, and called for a
separate section in the text on "the eucharist as
meal of forgiveness."

It points out that the statement which holds
that the celebration of the eucharist 'continues
as the central act of the Church's worship' E1,
requires interpretation through E12, because the
preached word and the eucharistic meal are intimately related. The reason being that Jesus gives
himself in both preaching and communion. It
further questions whether E15, does not place in
doubt the proclamation character of the words of
institution, and ascribe to the elements a permanent sacramental character? Then it declares:
"since Christ's presence is central to communion,
in our understanding any independent significance
of the elements of bread and wine is
impossible."[90]

The refusal to admit others to communion is
judged by the response as a denial of the unity of
the body of Christ. It suggests that commentary
E19, ought to have given differentiated information concerning the reasons for any refusal to
admit others to communion. It further argues that
the Lima text is not consistent with the statement
that the whole action of the eucharist has an
epikletic character since it does not go beyond
the division of the epiklesis into an epiklesis
for the elements and an epiklesis for the people.
It considers this to be problematic that the text
presupposes an epiklesis for the elements, and
concentrates too much on the transformation of the
elements.

---

90. ibid, p.144.

6.4.7   THE ROMAN CATHOLIC CHURCH.

The Roman Catholic Church is not a member of the World Council of Churches. It designates officially twelve Catholic members to the Commission on Faith and Order who participate by personal title, as full voting members in the Commission. It is enough to recall that the schism of 1054 A.D. was between the Orthodox Church and the Roman Catholic Church; and that the Reformation Churches in the 16th century severed themselves from the Roman Catholic Church.

In the introduction to its response[91] to BEM, the Roman Catholic Church states that it appreciates the work done by Faith and Order Commission and sees in BEM a significant result of the ecumenical movement. It recommends areas in which dialogue has to be continued namely: ecclesiology, sacrament and sacramentality, the precise nature of apostolic tradition, and the nature of authority in the church.

RESPONSE.

The response was arranged under two major phases: the general appreciation and particular comments. The comments are arranged according to the three main divisions in the eucharistic text itself, that is to say: the institution, meaning and celebration of the eucharist. We follow the same pattern in this presentation.

---

91. My Source of the response is in: SPCU: IS: 65 (1987) 121-139; eucharist section; pp.128-132.

GENERAL APPRECIATION.

   Here it is remarked that Catholics can recognize in the statement on the eucharist much
that corresponds to the understanding and practice of the apostolic faith, especially in the
underlisted points:

a. The sources employed for the interpretation of
   the meaning of the eucharist and the form of
   celebration are Scripture and Tradition.

b. The eucharist is described as pertaining to the
   content of faith. This presents a strong christological dimension, identifying the mystery
   of the eucharist in various ways with the real
   presence of the risen Lord and his sacrifice
   on the cross.

c. The structure and ordering of the basic
   aspects of the eucharistic text, as well as
   their relation to one another, conforms with
   Catholic teaching, especially in the following
   areas:

   - The presentation of the mystery of the eu-
     charist follows the flow of classical eucha-
     ristic liturgies, with the eucharistic theo-
     logy drawing heavily on the content of the
     traditional prayer and symbolic actions of
     these liturgies. The text draws on patristic
     sources for additional explication of the
     mystery of the eucharist.

   - The strong emphasis on the Trinitarian di-
     mension; the source and goal of the eucha-
     rist is identified as the Trinity.

   - The context of the act of the church in the
     eucharistic prayer includes basic elements
     required by Catholic teaching namely:

thanksgiving to the Father; memorial of the
institution of the eucharist and the sacrifice of the cross; intercession made in
union with Christ for the world; invocation
of the Spirit on the bread and wine that it
may become the body and blood of Christ and
on the community that it be sanctified; and
the meal of the New Covenant.

d. The response identifies a strong eschatological dimension in the text, for the eucharist
is viewed as a foretaste of Christ's parousia
and of the final kingdom E6, and given through
the Spirit. It opens up the vision of the
kingdom E22, and the renewal of the world E23.

e. The eucharist is presented as the central act
of the church's worship and the consequent
recommendation of frequent celebration.

f. Finally the text has important ecclesiological
dimension E8, and implications for mission.

PARTICULAR COMMENTS.
THE INSTITUTION OF THE EUCHARIST.

The response appreciates the explanation of
the institution of the eucharist accounts for its
historical grounding in the life and death of
Jesus of Nazareth and also relates it to the
risen Lord. This makes it clear that the eucharistic memorial is not a subjective past event, but
an effective saving mystery of Christ in the
present life of the Church. Hence the risen Lord,
present through the words of institution and the
power of the Holy Spirit is the host and meal of
the Church.

The response notes that the text highlights the link between the Last Supper and the eucharist, and identifies certain descriptions of the eucharist in the text, which the Catholic Church teaches as well namely: the eucharist as 'a gift from the Lord', 'a sacramental meal', given to the Church as a means 'to remember and encounter him', and 'a sacramental meal which by visible signs communicates to us God's love in Jesus Christ.'

THE MEANING OF THE EUCHARIST.

The response finds the defintion of the eucharist as "sacrament of the gift which God makes to us in Christ through the power of the Spirit", as combining two aspects of the mystery of the eucharist, namely: the real presence of Christ and the gift it signified. This gift is identified as "salvation" and is received through communion in the body and blood of Christ. It suggests that instead of saying "...in eating and drinking the bread and wine, Christ grants communion with himself", the unambiguous biblical language, E2 which speaks of participation of the body and blood...in reference to (1Cor.10:16; 16:52-56), should be used.

The response justifies its stand by saying that the section of the convergence eucharistic text it cited points out as well that the true host of the meal and the giver of the gift is Christ.

On the issue of receiving forgiveness of sins in the eucharist which is grounded on Mt.26:28, the response reacts thus: "But the 'assurance of the forgiveness of sins' through the eucharist is preconditioned by the state of reconciliation with God in the Church." It identifies this as pointing to the need for previous reconciliation of sinners, which would take place through the sacrament of penance.

The response makes a remark on the section which deals with "the eucharist as thanksgiving to the Father", by saying that the description of the breadth and depth of the thanksgiving, given in the eucharistic prayer, reflects faithfully the riches of the classical liturgical tradition. It expresses reservation in seeking a connection between the eucharistic prayer and the Jewish prayer (berakah), and asked whether it is appropriate to classify the eucharist as berakah or even to explain it as E3 and E27 do, maintaining that it is derived from the Jewish tradition of the berakah?

The statement "This sacrifice of praise is possible only through Christ, with him and in him" E4, is understood by the response as an affirmation that the eucharistic prayer is first and foremost the thanksgiving of Jesus to the Father. This understanding led to the wish that the relation between the act of the Church and the act of Christ could be more clearly expressed by stating that the Church receives the thanksgiving of Jesus Christ in the eucharist and associates herself with it as bride of Christ in order to express the acceptable thanksgiving for all God's benefits. The guiding principle here is that the thanksgiving of the Church is grounded on the one High Priest. It declares: "In the

Catholic understanding, the eucharist as thanksgiving signifies above all the thanksgiving of
Jesus Christ to the Father, with the offering of
his body and blood for the remission of sins and
the salvation of the world." The response holds
it necessary to clearly say that the gifts of
bread and wine, visible expression of what is
being celebrated here and now, are the sacramental signs of Christ's presence, while speaking
about the bread and wine as a locus for the presence of the world at the eucharist presented to
the Father in faith and thanksgiving.

The response is satisfied with the presentation of the eucharist as anamnesis or memorial of
Christ, and finds acceptable, the analogy between
the memorial celebration of Israel and the eucharist. It goes further to say: "The connection
established between the sacrifice of the cross
and the eucharist corresponds to Catholic understanding. The sacrifice of the eucharist is one
in which the sacrifice of the cross is represented to the end that its saving power be
applied here and now for the salvation of the
world." It goes on to say that the present efficacy of the sacrifice of the cross in the eucharist in reference to E6, is grounded on the presence of the risen Lord who cannot be separated
from his saving work. Christ is present in the
anmnesis as one coming from the future to grant
communion with himself as "a foretaste of the
parousia and of the final kingdom." This points
out again the traditional belief that Christ is
both host as well as gift of the meal.

The response appreciates, how in E7, the intimate relation between the mystery content of

the eucharist and the activity of the Church is
succinctly formulated, which recalls the Catholic
theology's presentation of the threefold dimension of sacramental celebrations. It identifies
the ecclesiological dimension of the eucharistic
doctrine in the text's theology of intercession
in E8. The Church is here seen to be united spiritually and sacramentally to the commemorative
active presence of the sacrifice of Christ. It
refers to two statements, followed by a comment:
in her intercession, the Church makes her own the
very intercession of Christ himself (commentary
8); It is in the eucharist that the community of
God's people is fully manifested. Eucharistic
celebrations always have to do with the whole
Church and the whole Church is involved in each
local eucharistic celebration" E19; and now its
conclusion: This statement implies an understanding of the mystery of Church and eucharist which
corresponds to the traditional eucharistic ecclesiology of the Catholic Church." Analysing
further E8, the response says that the eucharist
embodies the movement of the Church in Christ to
the Father. Hence the value of the thanksgiving
and intercession of the Church is affirmed on the
basis of its inclusion in the intercession of
Christ. This is accepted for its relation to the
teaching of the Catholic Church which expresses
the belief that the eucharist is an offering made
to the Father by the whole Christ, head and body,
in the power of the Holy Spirit.

The notion of intercession as it is used in
commentary 8, E8 and E9, is found to be insuffi-
cient to explain the sacrificial nature of the
eucharist in the Catholic sense. The response

explains that the link between the historical
event of the cross and the present efficacy of
that event is the crucified and risen Lord, who
is also the High Priest and Intercessor. From
this perspective, Christ's historical events
including his unique sacrifice cannot be repeated
or prolonged. However, it argued that since the
High Priest is the crucified and risen Lord, his
offering of self on the cross can be said to be
"made eternal." Therefore to describe the continuity of Christ's saving work only in terms of
simple intercession does not seem to do justice
to the reality of Christ's sacrifice, it concludes. It goes on to suggest that the Church's
activity in the eucharist described as thanksgiving and intercession needs to be filled out by
some reference to the self-offering of the participants of the eucharist, made in union with the
eternal self-offering of Christ.

Referring to commentary 8 once more, which
suggests that Catholic doctrine's reference to the
eucharist as propitiatory sacrifice be understood
in terms of intercession, the response points out
the insufficiency of the statement with the remark that Catholics would ask: "Is it sufficient
to describe the role of Christ, in the "application of the propitiatory effects of the cross",
as "Intercessor"?

The traditional anamnesis prayer expresses the
idea that there is an offering of the one acceptable sacrifice made by the Church in union with
Christ. To this the response adds that for Catholics, this prayer would express the belief that
through the eucharist we are enabled to associate
ourselves with the passover of Christ to his

Father. Then it expresses satisfaction with the statement that relates the preaching of the word to the eucharistic celebration and points out that the statement does not confound the preaching of the word with the eucharist rather it affirms the intimate relation between the two.

The response expresses satisfaction with the passages in the convergence eucharist text that deal with the real presence of Christ, because they appeal not only to the witness of scripture but also to the epiklesis of the liturgy, which asks for the coming of the Spirit on the elements. It maintains that if epiclesis of the Spirit is interpreted here as found in patristic teaching, then the presentation satisfies the requirements of Catholic belief, and submits that Catholic tradition and practice, lay emphasis on the importance of the words of institution within the eucharistic celebration.

The response approves the statement about the mode of Christ's unique presence in the eucharist which "does not depend on the faith of the individual", E13, but remarks that the Catholic faith links the sacrificial aspect of the eucharist to the sacrament of the body and blood more closely than is done in the text. It further explains that according to the New Testament, the statement "This is my body given for you", "this is my blood shed for many...", means that Christ offered himself sacramentally to the Father in the eucharist, in a sacrifice that actualizes the redemption of humanity. It argues then that if Christ now offers himself as a means of sacramental communion to the faithful, it is to allow them to associate themselves with his offering to the Father. Consequently, only insofar as Christ offers himself to the Father in the sacrificial action of the Church's liturgy, do the elements become sacrament of his self-offering to the communicants. It concludes with an observation that despite the use of sacrificial language in E5, and E8, the text "does not say unambiguously that the eucharist is in itself a real sacrifice, the memorial of the sacrifice of Christ on the cross."

Reacting towards commentary 13, the response welcomes the convergence that is taking place and points out that for Catholic doctrine, the conversion of the elements is a matter of faith and is only open to possible new theological explanations as to the "how" of the intrinsic change. With reference to the term transubstantiation, it explains that it is a central mystery of faith for the Catholics, and that Catholics cannot accept ambiguous expressions of that term. It rounds off with the statement that the differences as explained in commentary 13, cannot be accomodated within the convergence text, and recommended further work on this.

The response affirms the section that deals on the eucharist as invocation of the Spirit for its emphasis on the intimate relation between the mystery of the eucharist and the mystery of the Triune God, in a way that conforms with Catholic teaching. The statement which says that the whole action of the eucharist has an epicletic character E16, because of its dependence on the work of the Holy Spirit is decribed as appropriate, for it points to the fact that the eucharist is a holy work from the outset.

The statement of E15, that the bread and wine
become the sacramental signs of Christ's body and
blood, in virtue of the words of Christ and the
power of the Spirit, is accepted as corresponding
to the Catholic teaching, which also refers to
the bread and wine as sacramental signs, (sacramentum tantum), i.e. insofar as they signify.
This section attracts further explanation which
reads: "But the thought that they become sacramental signs is linked to the intrinsic change
which takes place, whereby unity of being is
realized between the signifying reality and the
reality signified." The response understands E15
as referring to the direction of intrinsic change
but remarks that the text is open to the idea
that the gifts undergo a change in meaning, which
does not go beyond the establishment of an
extrinsic relation between the thing signifying
and the thing signified. It finds this inadequate
and calls for further explanation.

The commentary 15, attracts this reaction:
"Our faith in the real presence implies that we
believe that the bread and wine become really the
body and blood of Christ. The phrase "consider it
necessary to assert" is not adequate to express
this. Consider it necessary to confess would be
more appropriate."

E19 of the text, which speaks about "the eucharist as communion of the faithful, is identified by the response as embodying important
ecclesiological points, drawing out ethical implications of participation in the eucharist, and
centres on the need to face and overcome division
within the church and the world. Its reply to
commentary 19, is that an adequate answer could

be given, when the issues raised are situated within an ecclesiology.

The explanation of "the eucharist as a meal of the kingdom" attracts this commentary on the link between baptism and eucharist: "Through baptism one is justified, incorporated into Christ and ordered to the eucharist, which is the representation of the saving mystery of Christ under the aspect of the sharing in the eschatological meal of joy with Christ and the kingdom, unto the glory of the Father." Further, it explains that the links between eucharist and mission is integral to the Catholic explication of the connection between eucharist and life. Hence it says that Christian ethics has a sacramental basis, supporting it with the statement that "through the eucharist the Church not only receives its name (body of Christ), but also its mission to extend Christ's salvation to the world."

CELEBRATION OF THE EUCHARIST.

The description of the elements of the classical liturgical celebration is found adequate. The response considers inadequate the phrase "declaration of pardon", rather it prefers to have a phrase which indicates more precisely the element of true forgiveness of sin in the life of the Christian. It observes that it is important to express the Church's intention to offer the sacrifice, but asks whether it is implied under the anamnesis or memorial. It finds the statement to be weak which says: "eating and drinking in communion with Christ and with each member of the

Church" E2, because it does not sufficiently express the distinction between sacramental participation of the body and blood of Christ and communion with Christ through communion with those who are in Christ.

On the problem of changeable and unchangeable elements of the eucharistic celebration mentioned in commentary 28, the response says it is correctly referred to the responsibility of the Church, who has the assurance of the guidance of the Spirit. It approves the description of the activity of Christ in the eucharist in E29, but remarked that the issue of the president of the eucharist could be better handled in the text on ministry, and laid bay the Catholic position which is that the president of the eucharist must be a priest sacramentally ordained within the apostolic succession.

On the issue of continued presence of Christ in the consecrated elements, E32, the response declares that while it agrees with the first position and with what is positively said about the second position, it only disagrees with those who deny the duration of the real presence after the celebration. It called for a clearer indication of the deeper ecclesiological, sacramental and eschatological grounds for the ancient practice of reservation of the consecrated elements. The response approves the various forms of eucharistic worship properly done as legitimate and praiseworthy ways of acknowledging the continuing presence of Christ in the eucharist.

On the issue of eucharistic sharing, E33, the response points out that the issue has an ecclesial dimension and cannot be resolved in isola-

tion from an understanding of the mystery of the
Church as well as the ministry. What constitutes
the ecclesial communion for the Catholics is
unity in the profession of faith, which is the
very nature of eucharistic celebration. Therefore
unity of faith is the condition for eucharistic
sharing.

6.4.8 EVALUATION.

We selected the response of only seven Churches out of the many responses. As we indicated
previously, the official responses from the Churches have been published in four bands and the
fith and the sixth bands are expected to be produced. In our selection the major Reformation
Churches are represented and of course the Orthodox and the Roman Catholic Churches. The selection of the Evangelical Church of Westphalia was
to serve the purpose of exposing the response of
a united church.

The response made by the Churches reveals that
each confession makes her response to the Lima
Eucharistic text from her stand-point. This is a
relapse to the comparative-ecclesiology-method
which prevailed at the first two World Conferences
of Faith and Order. This method gave way to the
Christocentric-ecclesiology-method since the
Conference at Lund in 1952. This method aimed at
emphasizing those facts which unite the churches
in Christ. It entails a return to the common
sources: the Scriptures, tradition, patristics as
well as to the Councils and Synods of the one
united Church, while producing a report on a topic

discussed by the Commission. This method was used
to produce the BEM document. It became fruitful
that in the echaristic text the Trinitarian method
was used. The method was effective to the extent
that the document on Baptism, Eucharist and
Ministry, (BEM), was unanimously adopted at the
plenary meeting of the Faith and Order Commission
at Lima in 1982. Hence the outstanding remark in
favour of the BEM document that, for the first
time in ecumenical movement theologians of varied
backgrounds from around the world have spoken so
harmoniously on fundamental matters of doctrine.

The Churches in making their response should
have applied this method in order to accelerate
the reception process of the Eucharistic
convergence text. Since the contrary was the case,
the Faith and Order Commission hat to make from
the responses a convergence of convergences. If
the process continues in this manner the question
is, when do we arrive at the consensus.

This relapse into comparative ecclesiology is
not entirely the fault of the churches. The Churches were already conditioned to resort to this
method by the questions posed by the Faith and
Order Commission as a guideline to the response.
The important difference to note is that the
churches this time are giving their opinion from
the highest level of authority over a document
which they contributed in no small way in its
production through their own nominated members who
worked in the Commission.

Let us now put the facts together to see
whether the churches in their responses are
closing ranks as far as the controversial points
are concerned. We shall look at the institution

of the eucharist, the eucharist as sacrifice, the
real presence, reservation and eucharistic hospitality.

THE INSTITUTION OF THE EUCHARIST.

   All the churches under our selection have no
problem in acknowledging the institution of the
eucharist by Jesus Christ at the Last Supper as
was recorded in the scriptures, namely by the
Synoptic writers and by St. Paul. In turn the
Lima text was praised for taking into account the
findings of modern exegetics, and for linking the
eucharist with the earthly meals of Christ as a
sign of the kingdom. All accept the expression
that the eucharist is a sacrament of the gift of
the Lord, the anamnesis of his death and resurrection.
   Objections are registered by the Lutherans and
the Reformed churches over the statement that the
celebration of the eucharist continues as the
central act of the church's worship. This indicated that they are still in difficulty with the
relationship between word and sacrament. They
give the impression that the sacrament is much
more emphasized than the word. However, this
should not have arisen. The Lima text struck a
balance with the statement: "the eucharist includes both word and sacrament; it is a proclamation
and celebration of the work of God." E3. The
Anglican church in its response explained the
statement further saying that reading and preaching are part of the proclamation of the word.
The statement from the Catholic Church's response

goes a long way to help solve the problem: the formulation of the relation of the preaching of the word to the celebration of the eucharist is correct; it does not confound the preaching of the word with the eucharist; at the same time, it affirms the intimate relation between the two."[92]

The next issue that was resisted was the name eucharist. The Lutherans as well as the Baptists fear that the word eucharist conveys the suggestion that the church rather than Christ acts. But the Lima text explained the eucharist under various notions: as anmnesis or memorial of the death and resurrection of Christ; as thanksgiving to the Father; as a sacrifice of praise etc. It gave alternative names for the eucharist namely: the Lord's Supper, the breaking of bread, the Mass, the divine liturgy. The action of Christ and that of the church was specified. Besides E29 outlines the acts of Christ as the one who gathers, teaches and nourishes the church as well as the one who invites and presides over the meal.

EUCHARIST AS SACRIFICE.

The various responses appreciate the introduction of the biblical notion of anamnesis in the Lima text which helps to understand the sacrificial character of the eucharist. Already in the section on the institution of the eucharist, the Lima text declares that Christians see the eucharist prefigured in the Passover memorial of

---

92. IS: 65 (1987), p.130.

Israel's deliverance and calls it the new paschal
meal of the Church. As we have shown earlier in
the exkurs on anamnesis that anamnesis in the Old
Testament is understood as a sacrifice with three
dimensional memorials: the past, the present and
the future; so also was the Lima document faithful to this understanding. This was clearly expressed in E7: "The anamnesis in which Christ
acts through the joyful celebration of his Church
is thus both representation and anticipation. It
is not only a calling to mind of what is past and
of its significance. It is the Church's effective
proclamation of God's mighty acts and promises."
On this biblical understanding and expression,
eucharist is a sacrifice. The Lima text rightly
then in the light of anamnesis established a
connection between the sacrifice of the cross and
the eucharist. E5. And the response from the
Catholic Church while praising the statement of
E5, drives this point home saying: "The sacrifice
of the eucharist is one in which the sacrifice of
the cross is represented to the end that its
saving power be applied here and now for the
salvation of the world."[93]

All agree that the sacrifice of Christ on the
cross is unique and can neither be repeated nor
prolonged. The statement about the eucharist and
sacrifice are as well accepted: the eucharist is
the great sacrifice of praise, E4; the eucharist
is the memorial of the crucified and risen
Christ, i.e., the living and effective sign of
his sacrifice, accomplished once and for all on

---

93. IS: 65 (1987), p. 129

the cross and still operative on behalf of humankind. E5.

The Anglican Church approved the biblical
concept of anamnesis as the recalling of the
sacrifice of Calvary in the eucharistic celebration, but had a misgiving that some discussion of
anamnesis appear to suggest either that Calvary
is repeated or that in the act of remembering the
congregation makes effective those benefits of
Christ's sacrifice. It did not indicate precisely
where such statements were made. The biblical
concept of anamnesis as we pointed out in the
exkurs in the previous chapter, by its definition
rules out the subjective sense of the word. It is
an objective act because something happens in the
cult which does not depend on human person as its
subject. Hence anamnesis is also called a
mysterium. The Lima document itself shows that
the congregation effects nothing by itself alone,
and E4 is a typical example: "This sacrifice of
praise is possible only through Christ, with him
and in him." The Anglicans made a positive statement at the close by calling for a renewed grasp
of the meaning of sacrifice and the richness of
the concept as applied in the eucharist text.

There is a sign of bridging the gap registered
by the Evangelical Lutheran Church in Bavaria. It
urged that holy communion should retain its
character as offer and submitted that Christ's
sacrifice on the cross realized in the eucharist
has atoning significance.

The Roman Catholic Church appreciates the
sacrificial language employed in the text especially in E5 and E8, but pointed out that the
text did not call the eucharist a sacrifice sim-

pliciter. It maintains that the historical events
of Christ including his unique sacrifice cannot
be repeated or prolonged. But it argued that
since the High Priest is the same as the crucified and risen Lord, who is the link between the
historical sacrifice and the present efficacy of
that event, his sacrifice could be said to be
made eternal. This reasoning would do justice to
the continuity of Christ's saving work and the
reality of his sacrifice in the eucharist.

THE REAL PRESENCE OF CHRIST.

The Churches affirmed the real presence of
Christ in the eucharist. Christ's presence in the
eucharist is linked to the elements of bread and
wine by these churches. The Baptists made no
mention of real presence in their response, perhaps it belongs to the issues they assigned for
further study to themselves. In general the churches praise the expressions of the concept of
epiclesis in connection with the real presence of
Christ in the eucharist.

The treatment of the eucharist as invocation of
the Holy Spirit attracted many positive reactions. The one sees it as striking a balance
between east and west and thereby solves the
problem of the moment of consecration, (Anglican). The other sees it as removing the magical
impression of the recitation of the word of institution, (Evangelical Lutheran Church in Bavaria). The Catholic Church says that it welcomes
the passages on epiclesis if they are understood
in the light of the patristic teaching, but

points out as well that she lays emphasis on the
words of institution within the celebration of
the eucharist. The Lutheran Church as well as the
Baptists lay emphasis on the words of institution. The Orthodox response did not mention words
of institution but said that it accepted as element of covergence the statement of E13, that the
eucharist is a sacrament of Christ's body and
blood by the invocation and work of the Holy
Spirit.

But the statement of the Lima text seems to
have struck a balance: "It is in the virtue of
the living word of Christ and by the power of the
Holy Spirit that bread and wine become sacramental signs of Christ's body and blood." E15.

The Catholic and Orthodox Churches have no
problem in talking about the conversion or change
of the elements into the body and blood of
Christ. While the Anglicans affirm the real presence of Christ they are satisfied that the Lima
document does not develop any theory of change of
the elements, and concluded with a statement: "It
would seem sufficient and faithful to the belief
of the church through the ages to uphold the real
presence of Christ in the eucharist and his body
and blood truly received in the bread and wine
without demanding further agreement on the mode
of the presence in the elements."

The Catholics, while welcoming the convergence
taking place on the issue of the real presence of
Christ, points out that the conversion of the
elements is for them a matter of faith and what
is open to discussion is the "how" of the change.

RESERVATION.

The issue at stake here is the affirmation of
Christ's real presence on the elements that remained after the celebration of the eucharist.
The Church of England points this out when she
says: "What is believed about the relationship of
the presence of Christ in the eucharistic elements finds its outward expression in reservation." Thereafter it submits that "reservation it
seems is acceptable because it is seen as the
extension of the eucharist itself." With this
statement the Church of England has come closer
to the Roman Catholics' position in this issue.

The Roman Catholics believe in the duration of
Christ's real presence in the elements after the
celebration, and reserve the sacrament primarily
for the communion of the sick and encourage as
well eucharistic worship properly done, which is
also a way of acknowledging the continuing presence of Christ in the eucharist.

The Evangelical Lutheran Church in Bavaria did
not specifically mention reservation in her response, but recommends a reverent handling of the
elements on account of Christ's presence.

Eucharistic worship was not mentioned by the
churches except the Roman Catholic Church which
practices it. The Anglican Church called for
respect of the piety of others. Eucharistic worship is a custom that developed gradually in the
Catholic Church. The practice is directed toward
sacramental and spiritual communion. While it is
good to uphold the custom, it should not be made
to constitute any obstacle to eucharistic communion with others who do not practice it. The

essential thing is belief in the duration of the real presence of Christ in the elements after the celebration, whether they serve for the communion of the sick or for eucharistic worship.

The issue of the president of the eucharist was commented upon by the Orthodox and Roman Catholic Churches. The Orthodox response regards as equivocal the designation of the priest-president as 'sign' of Christ, and maintained that the scriptures show that the eucharist depends upon the charismatic and sacramental state of the celebrant. The Catholic Church points out that the recognized president of the eucharist is a priest sacramentally ordained within the apostolic succession. The Lima text in E29 shows that there are differences in the practice of the churches on the issue of the presidency. It did not say that the president must be an ordained minister. This issue remains to be precisely clarified by the Faith and Order Commission in order to reach a consensus.

Communion at the table of the Lord is the aim of the discussion on the eucharist and the whole of ecumenical movement. The Orthodox and the Roman Catholic Churches maintain that communion is possible only where unity of faith exists, and therefore rejected the idea of eucharistc hospitality. They underline the importance of the relationship between the mystery of the church and the eucharist.

The Evangelical Church of Westphalia welcomes eucharistic hospitality based on mutual understanding which grows from common faith, and is of the opinion that refusal to admit others to communion abets disunity of the church.

We have concentrated on the controversial
points. The other expressions on the eucharist by
the text which were praised by various responses
include the role of the Triune God in the eucharist, who is identified as the source and goal of
the eucharist. Others are the eucharist as the
meal of the kingdom, which brought out the eschatological dimension of the eucharist; the relation between the eucharist and the church, and
the ethical implications of the eucharist. Although a consensus has not been reached, the
differences are no longer sharp as before.

CONCLUSION.

A flash back at the statement of Bishop
Charles Brent, the initiator of the Faith and Order
Movement, at the close of the World Missionary
Conference at Edinburgh in 1910, will help in
the appraisal of the long journey made by Faith
and Order Commission before arriving at Lima with
the production of the convergence document, BEM
in 1982. The bishop who was perplexed at the
exclusion of discussions on matters concerning
faith and order in the Edinburgh Missionary Conference made a prophetic statement at the close
of the conference. He said inter alia: "During
these days a new vision has been unfolded to us.
But whenever God gives a vision He also points to
some new responsibility, and you and I, when we
leave this assembly, will go away with some fresh
duties to perform, and perhaps as we have thought
of the new responsibilities that this conference
has suggested to us, we have been somewhat
troubled, because already our load is heavy."[1]
   The new responsibility was assumed by the
Faith and Order Commission, which is to steer the
churches towards visible unity by discussing
those matters of faith and order with the intention of reaching agreement on the controverted
issues. The first World Conference on Faith and
Order kicked off at Lausanne in 1927, and from
then on the eucharist featured as one of the
major topics in the agenda. In 1948, the World

---

1. World Missionary Conference, vol. 9, 1910,
   p.330.

Council of Churches was formed with Faith and
Order as a component part. In 1965 the study
project on the eucharist took off at Grandchamp
in Neuchatel. It moved on to Bristol, Louvain and
Accra, continued through Bangalore to Lima. Lima
saw the convergence text of three sacraments
including the eucharist. It was a 55 year long
and arduous journey.

The aim of the W.C.C. as well as the Faith and
Order Commission is "to call the Churches to the
goal of visible unity and in one eucharistic
fellowship expressed in worship and in common
life in Christ, and to advance towards that unity
in order that the world may believe."[2] The Lima
convergence eucharistc text is one of the efforts
in this direction to lead the churches in one
eucharistic fellowship, and the Lima liturgy the
corresponding expression of common worship. The
ongoing response of the churches to the Lima
Document is a necessary follow-up to advance
towards that unity that the world may believe.

The study of the Lima eucharistic text shows
that the Faith and Order Commission handled the
eucharist under the following aspects:

1. The eucharist is the memorial of the life,
   suffering, death and resurrection of Christ;
   what Christ accomplished for us in history, is
   represented in the liturgical celebration of
   the eucharist.

2. The eucharist is a thanksgiving sacrifice and
   intercession, through which we offer our
   praises to God and in turn ask him to make all

---

2. Constitution and Rules of the WCC, in: Gill
   D., (ed.), Gathered for life, Geneva, Wm. B.
   Eerdmans, 1983, p.324.

humankind benefit from his gift of salvation.

3. The eucharist is the work of the Holy Spirit, who at the invocation of the church, makes bread and wine into the signs of the body and blood of the crucified and risen Lord.

4. The eucharist is the real presence of Christ, who gives himself as food, so that our faith may grow and our membership in his body, the church, may become strengthened.

5. The eucharist is a gift from the Lord, which always includes both word and sacrament. Its celebration should take place at least every Sunday.

These agreements were reached by the Faith and Order Commission complimented by the results of the bilateral dialogues on the same subject matter. In the light of these the churches could say in common:

a. In the eucharist, the sacrifice of Christ on the cross becomes present and effective. The purpose for the celebration is not to repeat or perfect the unique sacrifice of Christ, rather to make it actual for us in its effects. Because the eucharist is a memorial in the biblical sense of the word, we are allowed to experience once again the unique event of the cross. It becomes possible for us to offer ourselves with Christ to the Father. The eucharist is not only the sacrament of the redemption of the humankind, which Christ accomplished, it is also a sacrifice of praise and thanksgiving to God for the work of creation and redemption.

b. In the eucharist, the living Christ is really
   present. The response of the Churches attests
   to this common faith in the real presence. As
   the eucharistic text put it: in virtue of the
   living word of Christ and by the power of the
   Holy Spirit, bread and wine become the sacramental body and blood of Christ. Bread and
   wine become the body and blood of Christ, who
   is linked to these visible signs. In this way
   the presence of Christ in the eucharist is par
   excellence and cannot be thought of in another
   form. In the eucharist, the consecrated bread
   and wine are no longer ordinary food and
   drink; but in the deepest truth, their meaning,
   their signification and their substance are
   changed to become the body and blood of
   Christ.

c. Our Christian faith tells us that the eucharist, fruit of the word of Christ and the Holy
   Spirit, continues to build up the church, the
   fellowship of believers, fills it with new
   life, recreates the world and proclaims the
   kingdom of God. The eucharist and the church
   form one reality in God. That is why the
   church alone can celebrate the eucharist, i.e.
   the community which is organically united with
   Christ and the apostles, the basis and funda-
   ment of its existence. In this context, it is
   necessary to point out that the eucharist and
   the apostolic ministry are closely related.

Throughout the Lima text on the eucharist,
convergence statements were recorded on the controversial issues. One of the problems that still
confronts the Faith and Order Commission on the

eucharistic discussion is none other than the
president of the eucharist; in other words the
relation between the eucharist and the ordained
ministry has got to be precisely explained. The
true situations are stated in the bilateral dialogues. From the Lutheran/Roman Catholic Joint
Commission conversations, we noticed that although the episcopal churches accept that an
ordained minister is the legitimate president of
the eucharist, they all do not agree that ordination is a sacrament.[3] The non-episcopal churches
although they may accept that it is not the community which produces and authorizes the office but
the living Christ who bestows it on the community
and incorporates this office into its life,[4]
allows their pastors to be commissioned by a
group of pastors from the church.[5] A full discussion on the ministry is beyond the scope of this
work. The topic has its own problems whose outcome is bound to affect the consensus in the
eucharistic discussion either positively or nega-
tively as the case may be.

The Lima eucharistc text was not precise on
the matter. But if the statement of E29 is to be
taken seriously: "The minister of the eucharist
is the ambassador who represents the divine initiative and expresses the connection of the local
community with other local communities in the
universal church", then it has to be none other

---

3. cf. The Eucharist, LutheranRoman Catholic
   Joint Commission, No. 7.
4. cf. Reformed/Roman Catholic Conversations, The
   Presence of Christ in the World, no. 98.
5. cf. Thurian, M., Wie steht es mit der
   Ökumene?, in: ÖR 32 (1983), p.413.

than an ordained minister in organic union with
the apostles. It is only then that he can represent this divine initiative and be capable of
being a connection between the local church and
the universal church.

The document of BEM is certainly one of the
most significant events in the life of the churches in this ecumenical time. Its importance
stems partly from the convergences with the results of the bilaterals. The coupling of the two
may generate the potential for enriching the
conciliar movement at local levels. The problems
facing the churches now as they are making their
responses to the BEM document, with the eucharistic text in mind is that of the will not of the
mind.

What would be the attitude of a church or
confession towards an aspect of the convergence
statement on the eucharist which challenges its
conviction? Is this church in question going to
stick to its conviction or is it going to be
consequential vis-à-vis the challenges? Should it
not leave vindicating its own truth but agree to
be challenged and if necessary be converted by
the spirit of the truth? The price to pay for the
unity we are seeking for in the eucharistic
communion is to follow the will of God like a star.

Communion at the Table of the Lord will not be
possible when differences in confession of faith
exist. Since the eucharist is a symbol of unity,
unity of faith is indispensable for eucharistic
fellowship. The result of the study project:
"Towards the common expression of the Apostolic
faith today", organized by the Faith and Order
Commission will have to play a decisive role

towards achieving eucharistic communion among the
churches. The Lima eucharistic text, I believe
has not said the last word over the controverisal
issues. Infact this was implied in the preface to
the BEM document, since the Faith and Order
Commission promised to compare and analyze the
implications of the replies of the churches and
to publish them. What we should expect from such
exercise, in my opinion is a convergence of convergences.

There are other factors that militate against
reaching consensus in the matter. The Lima eucharistic text itemized them in E20, where it said:
"The eucharist shows us that our behaviour is
inconsistent in face of the reconciling presence
of God in human history: we are placed under
continual judgment by the persistence of unjust
relationships of all kinds in our society, the
manifold divisions on account of human pride,
material interest and power politics and, above
all, the obstinacy of unjustifiable confessional
oppositions within the body of Christ." The churches must adopt the correct christian approach
and dispositions. An example will go a long way
to clarify this matter further.

Addressing His Holiness Pope John Paul II,
Metropolitan Chrysostomos of Myra, on the occasion of his visit as a Delegate of the Ecumenical
Patriarchate, Dimitrios I, said inter alia: "Your
Holiness, this day will surely come. But our
Churches must prepare and hasten its coming in
full concord, in profound reciprocal understanding, in a spirit of humility and of penitence, not in useless discourses, but by means
of a true dialogue taking the path of reconcilia-

tion, of comprehension, of love, of their convergence and of their union in a single Lord..."[6]
Only in such spirit can we advance towards unity
set in motion by the convergence agreement on the
eucharistic text of Lima and in the bilateral
texts. Let the attitude of the churches be like
that of John the Baptist in reference to Christ,
when he said: "He must grow greater, I must grow
smaller."[7] Applying this principle in the spirit
of humility, conversion and renewal, in truth,
fidelity and love to the will of God, can the
confessionalism and division of the church submer-
ge so that the one, holy, catholic and apostolic
church may emerge. Then the prayer of Christ that
all may be one would have been realized. This is
the gift we await from God the Father, through His
Son in the Holy Spirit.

---

6. cf. SPCU IS 64, II (1987), p.64.
7. Jn. 3:30.

BIBLIOGRAPHY

THE FUNDAMENTAL SOURCES: BOOKS

ABENDMAHLS, Gespräch der EKD, 1947-1957, Verlag
    des Amtsblattes der EKD, 1958
ABBOT W.A., (ed.), The Documents of Vatican II,
    London, Geoffrey Chapman, 1966
BAILLIE D., Marsh T., (eds.) Intercommunion,
    London, SCM., 1952
BAPTISM, Eucherist and Ministry, Geneva, WCC.,
    1982 (FO no. 111).
BATE, H.N., (ed.), Faith and Order Proceedings of
    the World Conference Lausanne, August 3-21,
    1927, Garden City, New York, 1928
BATE, H.N., Brown R.W., Convictions: A selection
    from the Responses of the Churches to the
    report of the World Conference on Faith and
    Order, Lausanne 1927, London, SCM., 1934
BEST, T.F. (ed.) Faith and Renewal, Stavanger
    1985, Geneva W.C.C., 1986.
BISTUMSKOMMISSION für ökumenische Fragen, Münster,
    (Hrsg.) Die Eucharistie im Gespräch der
    Konfessionen, Kevelaer, Butzon & Bercker, 1986
BIRMELE A., Ruster T., Vereint im Glauben getrennt
    am Tisch des Herrn?, Würzburg, Echter, 1987.
CHARLEY J.W., The Anglican Roman Catholic Agreement
    on the Eucharist, Bramcote, Notts, Grove Books,
    1972.
COMMISION on Faith and Order, Sharing in one Hope
    Bangalore 1978, Lausanne, Imprimerie La
    concorde, 1978.
DALY R.J., Christian Sacrifice, Washington D.C.,
    The Catholic University of America Press, 1978.
DAVIES T.G., (ed.) A dictionary of Liturgy &
    Worship, London, SCM., 1972.
EDWARD P., Haymann E., Maxwell W.D., Ways of
    Worship, London, SCM., 1951.
EPTING K.C., Ein Gespräch beginnt, Zürich,
    Theologischer Verlag,1972.
FAITH and Order Louvain, Geneva, W.C.C., 1971 (FO
    No. 59).
FAITH and Order Pamphlets No. 33.
FAHEY M.A., (ed.) Catholic Perspectives on
    Baptism, Eucharist and Ministry, Lanham, New
    York, UPA Press, 1986.
FO/64:25, Vischer L., Thoughts on a Study of the
    Eucharist.
FO/65:33, J.J. von Allmen, Notes on the Lord's
    Supper.
FO/65:85, Report of the Consultation at
    Grandchamp.
FRIELING R., Die Bewegung für Glauben und
    Kirchenverfassung 1910-1937, Göttingen,
    Vandenhoeck & Ruprecht, 1970.

FRIES H., Ein Glaube, eine Taufe, getrennt beim
Abendmahl?, Wien,Köln, Styria, 1971.
Ökumene statt Konfessionen?, Frankfurt, Knecht,
1977.
GAINES D.P., The World Council of churches. A
study of its background and history,
Peterborough, Richard R. Smith, 1966.
GAUGHAM P., (translated), Group of Les Doubes,
Towards a Common Eucharistic Faith, Agreement
between Roman Catholics and Protestants, 1973.
GEMEINSAME Synode der Bistümer in der
Bundesrepublik Deutschland, Freiburg, Basel,
Wien, Herder, 1976.
GERKEN A., Theologie der Eucharistie, München,
Kösel, 1973.
- Jesus unter uns. Was geschieht in der
Eucharistiefeier?, Münster, 1977.
GILL D., (ed.) Gathered for Life, Official Report,
Geneva, Wm. B. Eerdmans, 1983.
HODGSON L., (ed.) The Second World Conference on
Faith and Order, 1937, London, SCM., 1938.
HOWELL C., (Translated), General Instruction on
the Roman Missal, London, C.T.S., 1973.
HUGH M., Edinburgh 1937, The story of the second
world conference on Faith and Order held in
Edinburgh, London, SCM., 1938
JUNGMAN J., The Mass. Collegeville, Minnesota, The
Liturgical Press, 1976.
JURGENS A.W., The Faith of the Early Fathers Vol.
one, Collegeville, Minnesota, The Liturgical
Press, 1970.
KASPAR W., Taufe, Eucharistie und Amt in der
gegenwärtigen ökumenische Diskussion.
Bemerkungen zum Lima-Papier, in: Lothar L.,
(Hrsg.), Praesentia Christi, Düsseldorf,
(Patmos, 1984) 293-308.
KIMME A., Luthertum, Der Inhalt der Arnoldshainer
Abendmahlsthesen, Berlin, Lutherisches
Verlagshaus, 1960.
KINNAMON M., (ed.) Towards visible unity, Vol. I,
Minutes and Addresses, Geneva, W.C.C., 1982.
KIRCHE und Welt in ökumenischer Sicht. Bericht der
Weltkirchenkonferenz von Oxford über Kirche,
Volk und Staat, (Hrsg.) von Forderungsabteilung
des ökumenischen Rates für Praktisches
Christentum, Schweiz, Hüber & Co., 1938.
KONFESSIONSKUNDLICHES Institut, (Hrsg.), Kommentar
zu den Lima-Erklärungen über Taufe, Eucharistie
und Amt, Göttingen, Vandenhoeck & Ruprecht,
1983.
KRÜGER H., (Hrsg.) Ökumene Lexikon, Frankfurt,
Otto Lembeck, Josef Knecht, 1983.
LAZARETH W.H., Growing together in Baptism,
Eucharist and Ministry, A study guide, Geneva,
W.C.C., 1982.

LEHMANN K., Schlink E., (Hrsg.) Das Opfer Jesu
    Christi und seine Gegenwart in der Kirche,
    Freiburg, Göttingen, Herder, Vandenhoeck &
    Ruprecht, 1983.
LENGELING E.J., Die neue Ordnung der
    Eucharistiefeier, Münster, Verlag Regenberg,
    1970.
LENGSFELD P., (Hrsg.) Ökumenische Theologie,
    Stuttgart, Berlin etc., Verlag W. Kohlhammer,
    1980.
LIMOUNIS G., Vaporis N.M., (eds.), Orthodox
    Perspectives on Baptism, Eucharist and
    Ministry, Brookline, Massachusetts, Holy Cross
    Orthodox Press, 1985.
LÖSER W., (Hrsg.), Die Kirchen der Welt: Die
    Römisch-katholische Kirche, Frankfurt, EWV, 1986.
MARTINI H., Sens M., Orientierung Ökumene, Berlin,
    Evangelische Verlagsanstalt, 1972.
MEYER H., Vischer L., eds. Growth in Agreement,
    New York, Ramsey, Geneva, Punlist Press, 1984.
MEYER H., Pfnür V., The Presence of Christ in the
    Eucharist in: The Eucharist, Lutheran/Roman
    Catholic Joint Commission, Geneva, L.W.F.,
    1980.
Minutes of the Meeting of the Commission and
    Working Commitee, 1964, Aarhus, Denmark, FO No.
    44.
Minutes of the Meeting of the Standing Commission
    1979, Taize FO Nr. 98.
Minutes of the meeting of the Standing Commission
    1981, Annecy, FO No. 106.
Modern Eucharistic Agreement, London, S.P.C.K.,
    1973.
MODEROW H.M., Sens M., Orientierung Ökumene,
    Berlin, EV, 1979.
New Directions in Faith and Order, Bristol 1967,
    Geneva, W.C.C., 1968, (FO No. 50).
NIEMEIER G., (Hrsg.), Lehrgespräch über das
    heilige Abendmahl, München, Chr. Kaiser Verlag,
    1961.
One Baptism, One Eucharist and a mutually
    recognized Ministry, Geneva, W.C.C., 1975,
    (FO No. 73).
PATON D.M., (ed.) Breaking Barriers Nairobi, 1975,
    London, SPCK., 1975.
PAUL VI., Mysterium Fidei, AAS 57 (1965) 753-774.
    English: London, C.T.S., 1965.
PIUS XII. Encyclical Mediator Dei, AAS: 39 (1947),
    521-595.
    Encyclical Mystici Corporis, AAS: 35 (1943)
    193-248.

PLANK P., Die Eucharistieversammlung als Kirche,
    Würzburg, Augustiunus Verlag, 1980.
RAHNER K., Die Gegenwart Christi im Sakrament des
    Herrenmahls, in: Schriften zur Theologie IV,
RAHNER K., (ed.) The Teaching of the Catholic
    Church, New York, Abba House, 1967.
RATZINGER J., Kirche. Ökumene und Politik,
    Einsiedeln, Johannes-Verlag, 1987.
RAUCH A., Imhof P., (Hrsg.), Die Eucharistie der
    einen Kirche, München, Kaffke, 1983.
REGIMINI Ecclesiae universae AAS 59 (1967).
RITTNER R., (Hrsg.), Lima und das reformatische
    Proprium, Hannover, Lutherisches Verlagshaus,
    1984.
RODGER P.C., Vischer L. (eds.), The Fourth World
    Conference on Faith and Order. The Report from
    Montreal 1963, London, SCM., 1964.
RORDORF W. and others, (eds.), The Eucharist of
    the Early Christians, New York, Pueblo
    Publisting Co., 1978
ROUSE R., and Neill S.C., (eds.), A History of the
    Emmenical Movement 1517-1948, London, S.P.C.K.,
    1954.
Sacred Congregation of Rites, Eucharisticum
    Mysterium, (Englisch translation) Boston, St.
    Paul's editions, 1967
SARTORY T., (Hrsg.) Die Eucharistie im Verständnis
    der Konfessionen, Recklinghausen, Paulus
    Verlag, 1961
SASSE H., Die Weltkonferenz für Glauben und
    Kirchenverfassung, Lausanne, 3-21 August 1927,
    Berlin, Furche-Verlag, 1929.
Sekretariat der Deutschen Bischofskonferenz,
    (Hrsg.), Schreiben der deutschen Bischöfe an
    alle, die von der Kirche mit der
    Glaubensverkündung beauftragt sind, Trier,
    Paulinus Verlag, 1967.
SCHILDENBERGER J., Der Gedächtnischarakter des
    alt- und neutestamentlichen Pascha, in:
    Neunheuser B., Hrsg., Opfer Christi und Opfer
    der Kirche, Düsseldorf, Patmos, 1960.
SCHILLEBEECKX E., Die Eucharistische Gegenwart zur
    Diskussion über die Realpräsenz, Düsseldorf,
    Patmos, 1967.
STRANKY T.F., and Sheerin J.B., (eds.), Doing the
    Truth in Charity, New York, Ramsey, Paulist
    Press, 1982.
SCHMAUS M., Dogma 5, The Church as Sacrament,
    London, Sheed and Ward, 1975
    Der Glaube der Kirche, Band 2, München, Max
    Hueber Verlag, 1970.
SCHULZ H.J., Die Beziehungen zu den Orthodoxen
    Kirchen, in: Löser W., (Hrsg.), Die Kirchen der
    Welt Band XX, Die Römisch-Katholische Kirche,
    Frankfurt, EVW, 1986.

SCHULZ F., Die Lima-Liturgie, Kassel, Stauda, 1983.

SUPERNO Dei nuti: AAS 52 (1960)

The Eucharist, Lutheran/Roman Catholic Joint Commission, Geneva, The Lutheran World Federation, 1980.

The Jerusalem Bible, Standard Version, London, Darton, Longman & Todd, 1966.

The New Catholic Encyclopedia, Vol. V., Mc Graw-Hill, New York, London, Sydney, Jack Heraty & Associates, Inc. 1981.

TOMKINS O.S., (ed.), The Third World Conference on Faith and Order Lund 1952, London, SCM., 1953.

THURIAN M., Eucharistie, Stuttgart-Mainz, Kreuz Verlag, etc., 1963.
(ed.), Ecumenical Perspectives on BEM, Geneva, WCC, 1983.

THURIAN M., Wainwright G., (eds.) Baptism and Eucharist Ecumenical convergence in celebration, Geneva, ... B. Erdmans, 1984.

THURIAN M., The Mystery of the Eucharist, London, Oxford, Mowbray, 1981.

THURIAN M., (ed.) Churches respond to BEM vol I-IV, Geneva, W.C.C., 1987.

VISCHER G.H., Apostolischer Dienst, Frankfurt, Otto Lembeck, 1982.

VOSS G., (Hrsg.), Wachsende Übereinstimmung in Taufe, Eucharistie und Amt, Paderborn, Bonifatius Verlag, 1984.

VISSER'T Hooft W.A., The Genesis and Formation of the World Council of Churches, Geneva, W.C.C., 1982.
(ed.) The First Assembly of the World Council of Churches, The Official Report, London, S.C.M., 1949.

WARNACH V., (Hrsg.), Odo Casel, Das Christliche Opfermysterium, Wien, Köln, Styria, 1968.

World Missionary Conference Vol. 9, London, Edinburgh, Oliphant, Anderson & Fessier, 1910.

Zur Lehre vom Heiligen Abendmahl. Bericht über das Abendmahlgespräch der EKD 1945-1957, München, Chr. Kaiser Verlag, 1958.

514

PERIODICALS:

ARNOLDSHAIN Theses in: Scotish Journal of Theology
  Vol. 15. (1962) 1-3.
BEISSER F., Thesen zur Konvergenzerklärung über
  "Taufe, Eucharistie und Amt", in: KUD 31 (1985)
  22-31.
BEINERT W., Die Enzyklika "Mysterium Fidei" und
  neuere Auffassungen über die Eucharistie, in:
  ThQT, 147: 2 (1967) 159-175.
BERGER T., Taufe, Eucharistie, Amt: Eine
  liturgiewissenschaftliche Wertung des Lima-
  Dokuments, in: Liturgisches Jahrbuch 35 (1985)
  237-246.
BERTALOT R., Verständigung mit der evangelischen
  Abendmahlslehre?, in: Concilium 3 (1967) 295-
  297.
BUCHRUCKER A.E., Die Realpräsentation des Opfers
  Christi im Abendmahl in der gegenwärtigen
  katholischen Theologie, in: KuD 4 (1967) 273-
  296.
DANTINE J., Zur Konvergenerklärung über Taufe,
  Eucharistie und Amt (Lima 1982) in: ÖR 32
  (1983) 12-26.
GÄDE G., "Das Herrenmahl" und die eucharistische
  Realpräsenz. Theologische Untersuchung zum
  ökumenischen Konsens im katholisch/lutherischen
  Dokument "Das Herrenmahl", in: Catholica, 35
  (1981) 287-317.
GASSMAN G., The Relation between bilateral and
  multilateral dialogues, in: Journal of
  Ecumenical Studies 23:3 (1986)
  - Taufe, Eucharistie und Amt, 1982-1985, in:
  ÖR: 34 (1985) 121-129
  - Die Rezeption der Dialoge, in: ÖR: 33 (1984),
  357-368.
GERKEN A., Kann sich die Eucharistielehre
  ändern?, in: ZK Th 97 (1975) 414-429.
GRONBACH R., Klein L., Überlegungen zur Lima-
  Liturgie, in: ÖR 32 (1983) 27-40.
GUTWENGER E., Pascha-Mysterium und Eucharistie,
  in: ZKTh 89 (1967) 338-346
- Substanz und Akzidens in der Eucharistielehre,
  in: ZKTh 83 (1961) 257-306.
HANS C., Schmidt L., Die Bedeutung der "Lima-
  Liturgie" für die Ökumenische Bewegung, in:
  Liturgisches Jahrbuch 35 (1985) 131-147.
Herder Korrespondenz: Die Eucharistie im
  katholischen und ökumenischen Disput, in:
  Herder Korrespondenz: 22 (1968) 125-130
  Fragen der Theologie und des religiösen Lebens:
  19 (1964-65) 517-520.

HINTZEN G., Transsignifikation und
   Transfinalisation. Überlegungen zur Eignung
   dieser Begriffe für das ökumenische Gespräch,
   in: Catholica, 39 (1985) 193-216
- Gedanken zu einem personalen Verständnis der
   eucharistischen Realpräsenz, in: Catholica, 39
   (1985) 279-310.
HOPKO T., The Lima statement and the Orthodox, in:
   Journal of Ecumenical Studies, 21 (1984) 55-63.
HORVATH T., Who presided at Eucharist? A comment
   on BEM, in: Journal of Ecumenical Studies, 22
   (1985) 604-607.
JUNGMAN J.A., Oblatio und Sacrificium in der
   Geschichte des Eucharistieverständnisses, in:
   ZKTh 92 (1970) 343-350.
- Von der "Eucharistia" zur Messe, in: ZKTh 89.
   (1967)29-40.
KAUFMAN P.E., Intercommuniun and Union, in:
   Journal of Ecumenical Studies,226 (1985) 594-
   603.
LARENTZAKIS G., Die Konvergenerklärung über Taufe,
   Eucharistie und Amt der Kommission für Glauben
   und Kirchenverfassung als Ansporn zur
   intensiveren ökumenischen Arbeit der Kirchen,
   in: ÖR 34 (1965) 428-443.
LAZARETH W., Baptism, Eucharist and Ministry
   Update, in Journal of Ecumenical Studies 21
   (1984) 10-21.
LIES L., Ökumenische Erwägungen zu Abendmahl,
   Priesterweihe und Messopfer, in: ZKTh 104
   (1982) 385-410.
LORENZ W., Die Lima-Erklärung über Taufe und
   Eucharistie und Amt in:ÖR 34 (1985) 26-41.
LÖSER W., Die Konvergenzerklärung von Lima, in:
   ThPh 60 (1985) 481-4985.
MEYENDORFF J., Zum Eucharistieverständnis der
   orthodoxen Kirchen, in: Concilium 3 (1967) 291-
   294.
MEYER B., Calvin's Eucharistic Doctrine: 1336-39,
   in Journal of Ecumenical Studies, 4 (1967).
NELSON J.R., The Holy Eucharist as considered in
   bilateral conversations, in: Journal of
   Ecumenical Studies, 23:3 (1986) 449-471.
NIKOLAOU T., Zum Eucharistie-Text der Lima-
   Dokumente aus orthodoxer Sicht, in: Catholica,
   38 (1984) 307-316
NISSIOTIS N.A., Glauben und Kirchenverfassung -
   eine theologische Konsensus-Gemeinschaft im
   Lichte des Textes "Taufe, Eucharistie und Amt",
   in: ÖR 33 (1984) 322-338.
POWERS J.M., Mysterium Fidei and the theology of
   the Eucharist, in: Worship 40:1 (1966) 17-35.
RATZINGER J., Das Problem der Transsubstantiation
   und die Frage nach dem Sinn der Eucharistie,
   in: ThQT, 147:2 (1967) 129-158
   "Ist die Eucharistie ein Opfer?", in: Concilium
   3 (1967) 239-304

516

"Der Dialog der Wahrheit", Ein Gespräch, in:
KNA-Öki, Information Nr. 30, 21. Juli 1982,
pp 11-14.

SALACHAS D., Der theologische Dialog zwischen der
Römisch-Katholischen und der Orthodoxen Kirche,
in: Catholica 37 (1983) 140-161.

SCHILLEBEECKX E., Transubstantiation,
Transfinalisation, Transfiguration, in: Worship
40:6 (1966) 324-338.

SCHOENMAECKERS E., Die Katholische Kirche der
Niederlande in der Krise der Gegenwart, in:
Orientierung 28 (1964) 19-22.

SCHOONENBERG P., Inwieweit ist die Lehre von der
Transsubstantiation historisch bestimmt?, in:
Concilium 3 (1967) 305-311.

SLENCZKA R., Die Konvergenerklärungen zu Taufe,
Eucharistie, Amt und ihre Konsequenzen für
Lehre und Gottesdienst, in: KuD 31 (1985) 2-19.

SCHULZ H.J., Die Lima-Liturgie, Ausdruck
entscheidender Glaubensgemeinsamkeit, in:
Gottesdienst 18, 1 (1984) 1-4.

SCHULZ H.J., "Wandlung" im ostkirchlich-
liturgischen Verständnis. Eine Orientierung im
Disput um Transsubstantiation und
Transsignifikation, in: Catholica:40 (1986)
270-286.

SCHÜTT R., Eucharistie und Ökologie, in: ÖR 36
(1987) 1-16.

S.P.C.U. Documents:
The Position of the Catholioc Church Concerning
a common Eucharist between Christians of
different confessions, in: S.P.C.U. IS 91 (1970)
21-23.
The Eucharist: Roman Catholic/Evangelical
Lutheran Joint Commission, in:S.P.C.U. IS 39:2
(1979) 23-35

S.P.C.U. Documents:
The Ecumenical Directory (Part one), in:
S.P.C.U. IS 10:2 (1967) 5-12
The Ecumenical Directory (Part Two). in:
S.P.C.U. IS 10:2 (1970) 3-12
Instruction concerning cases when other
Christians May be Admitted to Eucharistic
Communion in the Catholic Church, S.P.C.U. IS
18 (1972) 3-8

S.P.C.U. Documents:
  Catholic/Orthodox Joint Commission 1980, in
  IS:44:4 (1980)
  IS:45:1 (1981)
  IS :46:2 (1981)
  The Mystery of the Church and of the Eucharist
  in the light of the Mystery of the Holy
  Trinity, Munich, Juli 1982, in: IS :49:3
  (1982).
  IS:33:1 (1971)
S.P.C.U. JS:65:III-IV (1987) 121-139
  Catholic Response to "Baptism, Eucharist and
  Ministry"
STANLEY D., Ökumenisch bedeutsame Aspekte der
  neutestamentlichen Lehre von der Eucharistie,
  in: Concilium 3 (1967) 287-290.
TAVARD G.H., The Function of the Minister in the
  eucharistic celebration: An ecumenical approach,
  in Journal of Ecumenical Studies, 4 (1967)
TIMIADIIS E., Einige Bemerkungen zur Enzyklika
  "Mysterium Fidei", in: Conciclium 2 (1966)
  314-317.
THURIAN M., Die Eucharistische Liturgie von Lima,
  in: Liturgisches Jahrsbuch 34 (1984) 21-31
  - "Wie steht es mit der Ökumene?", in: ÖR: 32
  (1983) 399-416
TORRANCE T.F., The Arnoldshain Theses on Holy
  Communion, in: Scotish Journal of Theology Vol.
  15. (1962) 4-35
VAGAGGIUN C., Observations on the Catholic-
  Lutheran Commission's Document on the
  Eucharist, in: S.P.C.U. IS 39:2 (1979) 36-40
VAJTA V., Einige Bemerkungen zur Enzyklika
  "Mysterium Fidei", in: Concilium 2 (1966) 308-
  313.
VOGEL C.J., Die Eucharistielehre Heute, in: ZKTh
  97 (1975) 389-414
VOLK E., Mahl des Herrn oder Mahl der Kirche.
  Theologische Anmerkungen zu einem ökumenischen
  Dokument, in: KuD 31 (1985) 32-64
VOSS G., Das Lima-Dokument "Taufe, Eucharistie und
  Amt" - in katholischer Sicht, in: Catholica, 36
  (1982) 181-214
WALTER K., Auf dem Weg zur Einheit: Erklärung zum
  Thema Lima-Liturgie, in: Gottesdinest 19, 12
  (1985) 89-90
WOHLMUTH J., Eucharistie nach dem Lima-Text, in:
  ÖR 32 (1983) 493-498
- Noch einmal: Transsubstantiation oder
  Transsignifikation, in: ZKTh 97 (1975) 431-440
ZAPHINIS C., Der Theologische Dialog zwischen der
  Orthodoxen und der Römisch-katholischen Kirche,
  in: ÖR 32 (1983) 57-72

518

FURTHER READING PERIODICALS

ALLMEN J.J., Die Abendmahlgemeinschaft aus
    reformierter Sicht, in: Concilium 5 (1969) 250-
    254.
ANSONS G.H., Intercommunion in anticipation of
    greater unity, in: Journal of Ecumenical
    Studies, 11 (1974) 315-321
BAUM G., Communicatio in sacris in the Decree on
    Ecumenisum, in: One in Christ 3:4 (1967) 417-
    428
BARROIS G.A., Closed Communion, open Communion,
    intercommunion?, in: St. Vladimir's Ideological
    Quarterly 12 (1968) 142-150
- Ecumenical Consensus on the eucharist?, in
    op.cit, 15 (1971) 81-84
BASSETT W.W., Intercommunion now?, in: Commonweal
    96:19 (1972) 450-453
BEINERT W., Amt und Eucharistiegemeinschaft, in:
    Catholica 26:2 (1972) 154-171
BERTALOT R., Understanding Protestant teaching on
    the Lord's Supper, in: Concilium 24 (1966) 59-
    65
BÖCKLE F., Intercommunion, in: Stimmen der Zeit,
    185: (1970) 309-320
EVDOKINOV P.N., Communicatio in Sacris: A
    Possibility?, in: Diakonia 2:4 (1967) 352-358
FLANAGAN D., The eucharist in ecumenical
    discussion, in: Irish Theological Querterly, 36
    (1969) 230-244
FLEW R.N., The Nature of the Church, London, SCM,
    1952
FRIES H., Pannenberg W,. Abendmahl und
    Abendmahlgemeinschaft, in: Una Sancta 26 (1971)
    68-88
GALITIS G., Das Problem der Interkommunion in
    Orthodoxer Sicht, in:ÖR 16: (1967) 265-285
GERKEN A., Dogmengeschichtliche Reflexion über die
    heutige Wende in der Eucharistielehre, in ZKTh
    94 (1972)
GERKEN A., Gemeinsames und Trennendes im
    katholischen und evangelischen
    Abendmahlsverständnis, in: Catholica, 27 (1973)
    312-328
- Offener Eucharistiefeier?., in: Theologie der
    Gegenwart 18 (1975) 71-79
GUTWENGER E., Das Geheimnis der Gegenwart Christi
    in der Eucharistie, in: ZKTh 88 (1966) 185-197
HAMER J., Stages on the road to unity. The
    problem of intercommunion, in: One in Christ 4
    (1968) 235-249
HASTINGS A., Is there room today for reciprocal
    intercommunion between Catholics and
    Anglicans?, in: One in Christ 96 (1973) 337-353
HOTCHKIN, J.F. Bilaterals - Phasing into Unity?
    in: Journal of Ecumenical studies 23:3 (1986)
    404-411

HUGUES J.J., Eucharistic sacrifice transcending
the reformation deadlock, in: Worship 43 (1969)
532-544

ISERLOH E., Die Abendmahlslehre der Confessio
Augustana, ihrer Confutatio und ihrer Apologie,
in: Catholica, 34 (1980) 15-35

JANSSEN H., Die Abensmahlslehre Johannes Calvius,
in: Una Sancta 2 (1960) 125-138

JERSILD P., Lutheran view of the real presence in
Roman Catholic theology today,in: Dialog 12
(1973) 134-140

JONG J.P., Die Eucharistie als Symbolwirklichkeit,
Regensburg, Friedrich Pustet, 1969

KANTZENBACH F.W., Einheitsbestrebungen im Wandel
der Kirchengeschichte, Gütersloh, Gerd Mohn,
1979

KAREL J.L., The Lord's unifying gift: the holy
Eucharist, in: Currents in Theology and Mission
6 (1979) 293-299

KEK - Konsultationen zu den Lima-Dokumenten: ÖR 35
(1986) 198-205

KEHL M., Eucharistie und Auferstehung zur Deutung
der Ostererscheinungen beim Mahl, in: Geist und
Leben 43 (1970) 90-125

KERTELGE K., Die soteriologische Aussagen in der
urchristlichen Abendmahlsüberlieferung und ihre
Beziehung zum geschichtlichen Jesus, in:
Trierer Theol. Zeitschrift 81 (1972) 193-202

KILMARTIN E.J., Reception in History: An
ecclesiological phenomenon and its
significance, in: Journal of Ecumenical
Studies, 21 (1984) 34-54

KINNAMON M., Bilaterals and the uniting and
united Churches, in: Journal of Ecumenical
Studies 23:3 (1986) 377-385

KRAFT S., Die eucharistische Epiklese als
ökumenisches Problem, in: Una Sancta, 40:3
(1985)

KORTRIGHT D., Bilateral Dialogue and
Contextualization; in: Journal of Ecumenical
Studies 23:3 (1986) 388-389

KÜHN U., Das Abendmahl - Eucharistie der Gemeinde
Jesu. Zum ekklesiologischen Ansatz des
Abendmahlverständnisses, in: KuD 25 (1979) 289-
302

LOOSKY N., The Eucharistic life: the Church as a
eucharistic community at the local level, in: The
Ecumenical Review, 31 (1979) 69-71

MC DONALD M., Brian J., The Eucharist as witness
to the kingdom of God and experience of God's
reign, in: International review of mission, 69
(1980) 143-150

OBRONCZA J., Die Eucharistie in neuerem
protestantischen Publikationen, in: Theol. der
Gegenwart 19 (1976) 199-205

520

ODUYOYE M.A., The eucharist as witness, in:
   International Review of Mission, 72 (1983) 222-
   228
PANNENBERG W., Die Arbeit von Faith and Order in
   Kontext der Ökumenisches Dialog heute, in: ÖR
   31 (1982) 47-59
SALA G.B., Transsubstantiation oder
   Transsignifikation?, in: ZKTh 92 (1970) 1-34
SCHEELE P.W., Auf dem Weg zum Leben, Vancouver 83
   in katholischer Sicht, in: ÖR 33 (1984) 116-129
SCHLINK E., Problem of communion between the
   Evangelicial Lutheran and the Roman Catholic
   Church, in: The Ecumenical Review, 24 (1972) 1-
   25.
SCHNEIDER TH., Das Opfer der Messe als
   Selbsthingabe Christi und der Kirche, in: Geist
   und Leben 41 (1968) 90-106
- Opfer Jesu Christi und der Kirche, Zum
   Verständnis der Aussagen des Konzils von
   Trient, in: Catholica 31 (1987) 51-65
- Das Opfer der Kirche nach der dogmatischen
   Konstitution "Lumen Gentium" des Vaticanum II,
   in: Wissenschaft und Weisheit 41 (1978) 19-31
TILLARD J.M.R., The Ecclesiological Implications
   of bilateral dialogne, in: Journal of
   Ecumenical Studies, 23:3 (1986) 412-423
WAINWRIGHT G., Eucharist as an ecumenical
   sacrament of reconciliation and renewal, in:
   Studia liturgia, 11 (1976) 1-18
WAINWRIGHT G., Reception of "Baptism, Eucharist
   and Ministry" and the apostolic Faith Study, in:
   Journal of Ecumenical Studies, 21 (1984) 71-82

FURTHER READING BOOKS

AVERBECK W., Der Opfercharakter des Abendmahls in
der neueren evangelischen Theologie, Paderborn,
1966.
AUER J., Ratzinger J., Kleine katholische
Dogmatik, Das Mysterium der Eucharistie VI,
Regensburg, Friedrich Pustet, 1980
BALTHASAR von, H.U., Die Messe ein Opfer der
Kirche?, in: ders. Spiritus Creator Skizzen zur
Theologie III, (Einsiedeln 1967) 166-217
BETZ J., Die Eucharistie in der Zeit der
griechischen Väter, Bd. II, 1. Die Realpräsenz
des Leibes und Blutes Jesu im Abendmahl nach
dem Neuen Testament, Freiburg, 1961.
- Der Opfercharakter des Abendmahls im
interkonfessionellen Dialog, in: Theologie im
Wandel. FS der Kath.Theol. Fakultät Tübingen
(München 1967) 469-491
BLANK J., Was hindert uns? Das Gemeinsame
Herrenmahl der Christen, Pustet, 1987
BLÄSER P., (Hrsg.) Amt und Eucharistie, Paderborn,
Bonifatius-Druckerei, 1973
BOECKLER R., (Hrsg.) Interkommunion,
Konziliarität. Zwei Studien im Auftrag des
Deutschen Ökumenischen Studienausschusses,
Stuttgart, EMV, 1974.
BOUYER L., Eucharist, Theology and Spirituality of
the Eucharistic Prayer, London, University of
Notre Dame Press, 1978
BURNS J.P., Fagin G.M., The Holy Spirit, Message
of the Fathers of the Church, Wilmington,
Delaware, Michael Glazier Inc., 1984
BUXTON R.F., Eucharist and institution narrative.
A Study in the Roman and Anglicam traditions of
the consecration of the Eucharist from eighth
to the twentieth centuries, Great Wakering,
Mayhew-Mc Crimmon, 1976
CLARK F., Eucharistic Sacrifice and the
Reformation, Devon Augustine Publishing Co.,
1980
COVENTRY J., The Eucharist and the sacrifice of
Christ, in: One in Christ, 11 (1975) 330-341
- Intercommunion: a Roman Catholic view, in:
Theology today 71 (1968) 208-213
EDWALL P.-, Hayman E., Maxwell W.D., (ed.) Ways of
Worship, London, SCM, 1951
FAHRENHOLZ G.M., (ed.), And do not hinder them:
An ecumenical plea for the admission of
children to the eucharist, Geneva, W.C.C. 1982
(FO No. 109).

FELD H., Das Verständnis des Abendmahls. Erträge
der Forschung 50, Darmstadt, 1976.
FENEBERG R., Christliche Paschafeier und
Abendmahl, München, 1971
FINCH M., Reardon R., (eds.) Sharing Communion: an
appeal to the churches from interchurch
families, London, Collins, 1983
FLEW R.N., (ed.) The Nature of the Church, London,
SCM, 1952
GOTTSCHALK J., Die Gegenwart Christi im Abendmahl,
Essen, Ludgerus Verlag, 1966
GUEMBE, M.M.G., Rohls J., Wenz G., Mahl des Herrn,
Ökumenische Studien, Frankfurt, Paderborn,
Lembeck-Bonifatius, 1988
HAHN F., Der urchristliche Gottesdienst,
Stuttgart, 1970
- Abendmahl, in :Otto G. (Hrsg.), Praktisch
Theologisches Handbuch (1975) 32-64
HINTZEN G., Die neuere Diskussion über die
eucharistische Wandlung. Darstellung, kritische
Würdigung, Weiterführung, Bern/Frankfurt, 1976
JEREMIAS J., Die Abendmahlsworte Jesu, Göttingen,
1959
KAHLEFELD H., Das Abschiedsmahl Jesu und die
Eucharistie der Kirche, Frankfurt, 1980
KARLSTRÖM N., Ökumene in Mission und Kirche,
München, Claudius Verlag, 1962
KENT J. (ed.) Intercommunion and Church
membership, London, Darton, Longmann and Todd,
1973
KIRCHGÄSSNER A., Interkommunion in Diskussion und
Praxis. Eine Dokumentation, Düsseldorf, Patmos,
1971
KLOPPENBURG B., Ecclesiology of Vatican II
(Translated by O'Connell Matthew), Chicago,
Illinois, Franciscan Herold Press, 1974
KREMS G., MUMM R., Evangelisch-katholische
Abendmahlsgemeinschaft?, Regensburg, Friedrich
Pustet, 1971
LASH N., A Study of eucharistic Worship and
theology, London, Sheed & Ward, 1968
LOTZ W., Das Mahl der Gemeinschaft. Zur
ökumenischen Praxis der Eucharistie, Kassel,
Stauda, 1977
LUBAC H. de, Corpus Mysticum. Eucharistie und
Kirche im Mittelalter, Einsiedeln, 1969
MC SORBEY H.J, Unprecedented Agreement on the
Eucharist, in the Ecumenist 8 (1970) 89-93
MEINHOLD P., Iserloh E., Abendmahl und Opfer,
Stuttgart, Schwabenverlag, 1960
MINEAR S. (ed.) The Nature of the unity we seek,
St. Louis, Bethany Press, 1958

MOLL H., Die Lehre von der Eucharistie als Opfer. Eine dogmengeschichtliche Untersuchung von NT bis Irenäus von Lyon, Köln/Bonn 1975.

NEUNHEUSER B., (Hrsg.) Opfer Christi und Opfer der Kirche, Düsseldorf, Patmos, 1960

NEUNER P., Klein Handbuch der Ökumene, Düsseldorf, Patmos, 1984

PALMER P..F., (ed.) Sacraments and Worship, Westminster, Maryland, The Newman Press, 1955

PASCHER J., Eucharistia. Gestalt und Vollzug, Münster/München, 1947

PATHIL K., Models in Ecumenical dialogne, India, Dharmaram Publications, 1981

PATSCH H., Abendmahl und historischer Jesus, Stuttgart, 1972

PESCH R., Wie Jesus das Abendmahl hielt. Der Grund der Eucharistie. Freiburg 1977.

PITTENGER N., Life as Eucharist, Michingan, G. Rapdis, W.B. Eerdman, 1973

POWERS J., Eucharistie in neuer Sicht, Freiburg, 1969

PRATZNER F., Messe und Kreuzesopfer. Die Krise der Sakramentalen Ideee bei Luther in der mittelalterlichen Scholastik. Wien, 1970

QUASTEN J., Patrology Vol. I-III, Westminster, Maryland, Christian Classics Inc. 1984

RAHNER K., Lengeling E.J., Thüssing W., Eucharistiefeier und Sonntagspflicht des Christen, in: A. Exeler (Hrsg.) Fragen der Kirche heute, (Würzburg 1971) 35-49

RAHNER K., Häußling A., Die vielen Messen und das eine Opfer, Freiburg 1966

REUSS J.M., Opfermahl, Mitte des Christseins. Eine pastoraltheologische Untersuchung zur Meßfeier. Mainz, 1960

SEIDENSTICKER Ph., Lebendiges Opfer (Röm 12,1). Ein Beitrag zur Theologie des hl. Paulus, Münster, 1954

SCHEFFCZYK L., Die Heilszeichen von Brot und Wein. Eucharistie als Mitte des christlichen Lebens. München, 1973

SCHLINK E., Das Herrenmahl, in his: ökumenische Dogmatik, Göttingen, Vandenhoeck & Ruprecht, 1983 (490-512)

SCHNEIDER Th., Deinen Tod verkünden wir. Gesammelte Studien zum erneuerten Eucharistieverständnis, Düsseldorf, 1980

SCHNEIDER Th., Zeichen der Nähe Gottes, Mainz, Matthias-Grünewald Verlag, 1984

SCHULTE R., Die Messe als Opfer der Kirche. Die Lehre frühmittelalterlicher Autoren über das Opfer, Münster, 1959

SCHÜTTE H., Ziel: Kirchengemeinschaft, Paderborn, Bonifatius-Verlag, 1985

SCHWAGER R., Geht die Eucharistie auf Jesus zurück?, in: Orientierung 39 (1975) 220-223

SIMONSON C., The Christology of the Faith and

Order Movement, Leiden/Köln, E.J. Brill, 1977

SKOGLUND J.E., Nelson J.R. Fifty Years of Faith and Order, St. Louis, Bethany Press, 1963

STROMBERG J., (ed.), Sharing one bread, Sharing one mission: The eucharist as missionary event, Geneva, W.C.C., 1983

SUTTNER E.C., (Hrsg.), Eucharistie Zeichen der Einheit, Regensburg, Friedrich Pustet, 1970

TRÜTSCH J., Taufe - Sakrament der Einheit: Eucharisite, Sakrament der Trennung?, Zürich, Benziger, 1980

URBAN H.J., (Hrsg.), Handbuch der Ökumenik, Band I-III, Paderborn, Bonifatius Verlag, 1985

VAN DER BENT A.J., Vital Ecumenical concerns, Geneva, WCC, 1986

VISCHER L., The Epiclesis: Sign of unity and renewal, in Studia Liturgia, 6:4 (1969) 30-39

VISCHER L., Die Einheit der Kirche, München, Kaiser Verlag, 1965

WALTER E., Eucharistie Band 2, Freiburg, Basel, Wien, Herder, 1974

WARE K., Communion and intercommunion, Minneapolis, Light and Life, Pub. Co. 1980

WIEDERKEHR D., Das Sakrament der Eucharistie, Freiburg/Schweiz, 1976

Anton Grabner-Haider

Strukturen des Mythos
Theorie einer Lebenswelt

Frankfurt/M., Bern, New York, Paris, 1989. 511 S.
Europäische Hochschulschriften: Reihe 20, Philosophie. Bd. 273
ISBN 3-631-40773-4   br./lam. sFr. 78,--

Mythische Weltdeutung rückt heute stark in unser Interesse, wir erwarten uns davon Impulse für die eigene Lebensorientierung. Doch muß die herkömmliche Mythosforschung durch neue wissenschaftliche Disziplinen ergänzt werden. Hier werden Methoden der Kulturanthropologie, der Sozialwissenschaft, der Kommunikationsforschung, der Sozialpsychologie und der Sprachanalyse angewandt. Zugleich wird ein Überblick über die wichtigsten Mythen aus allen Kulturen geboten, es werden Weltdeutungen, Menschenbilder, Lebenswerte, Lebensformen und Sprachstrukturen analysiert. Und es wird nach dem Stellenwert des Mythos in einer wissenschaftlichen Lebenswelt gefragt.

Aus dem Inhalt: Lebenswelt des Mythos und der Religion - Mythosdeutungen - Göttliche und dämonische Wesen - Menschenbilder und Personstrukturen - Sprache des Mythos - Mythos und Vernunft - Stammesreligionen und Volksreligionen - Universale Religionen - Mythos und Esoterik - Humanisierung des Mythos.

Verlag Peter Lang Frankfurt a.M. · Bern · New York · Paris
Auslieferung: Verlag Peter Lang AG, Jupiterstr. 15, CH-3000 Bern 15
Telefon (004131) 321122, Telex pela ch 912 651, Telefax (004131) 321131

Edmund Weber (Hrsg.)

Christentum zwischen Volkskirche und Ketzerei

Frankfurt/M., Bern, New York, 1985. 109 S.
Studia Irenica. Bd. 28
Herausgegeben von Prof. Dr. Edmund Weber und Dr. Axel Swinne
ISBN 3-8204-8891-X   br. sFr. 26,--

Volkskirche und Ketzerei bilden elementare Tangenten der Wirklichkeit des Christentums. Unter Bezugnahme auf Kirchensoziologie, Sozialgeschichte und wissenschaftliche Irenik werden beide Aspekte der Ekklesiologie in Geschichte und Gegenwart exemplarisch beleuchtet.

Aus dem Inhalt: Soziologie der Volkskirche - Pietismus in Hessen - Schleiermacher - Katharer und Freigeister - Die andere Kirche.

Verlag Peter Lang Frankfurt a.M. · Bern · New York · Paris
Auslieferung: Verlag Peter Lang AG, Jupiterstr. 15, CH-3000 Bern 15
Telefon (004131) 321122, Telex pela ch 912 651, Telefax (004131) 321131

Joseph Overath

Kirchengeschichte
Orientierungshilfen, Standpunkte, Impulse für heute

Frankfurt/M., Bern, New York, 1987. 234 S.
Europäische Hochschulschriften. Reihe 23, Theologie. Bd. 294
ISBN 3-8204-9697-1   br./lam. sFr. 50,--

Die elf Beiträge verstehen sich als Orientierungshilfen und Impulse
für heute. Sie versuchen die Gegenwart der Kirche im Lichte der Ver-
gangenheit zu deuten, fordern auch zu einer Stellungnahme heraus.
Kirchengeschichte als theologische Disziplin leistet damit einen Beitrag zur Klärung des Verhältnisses von Tradition und Fortschritt in der
Kirche.

Aus dem Inhalt: Sentire ecclesiam - Weichenstellungen im 19. Jahr-
hundert - Gegenwart aus der Kirchengeschichte verstehen.

Verlag Peter Lang Frankfurt a.M. · Bern · New York · Paris
Auslieferung: Verlag Peter Lang AG, Jupiterstr. 15, CH-3000 Bern 15
Telefon (004131) 321122, Telex pela ch 912 651, Telefax (004131) 321131

Markus Eham

Gemeinschaft im Sakrament?
Die Frage nach der Möglichkeit sakramentaler Gemeinschaft
zwischen katholischen und nichtkatholischen Christen.
Zur ekklesiologischen Dimension der ökumenischen Frage. - 2 Teile

Frankfurt/M., Bern, New York, 1986. XXVIII, 851 S.
Europäische Hochschulschriften: Reihe 23, Theologie. Bd. 293
ISBN 3-8204-8846-4   br./lam. sFr. 150,--

Ausgehend von der Beobachtung gegenwärtiger «Lähmungserscheinungen» im
ökumenischen Gespräch versucht der Autor von einer geschichtlichen Profilierung
des sakramentalen Kirchengedankens her, diesen als eine katholisch-ekklesiolo-
gische Grundoption auszuweisen, die - in kritischer und heuristischer Funktion - als
innerer Verknotungspunkt der ökumenisch brisanten Detailfragen (Eucharistieverständnis, kirchliches Amt, apostolische Sukzession) ausgemacht werden kann.

Helmut Echternach

Dogmatik I
Ökumenischer Glaube - heute
Spiritus Sanktus non est skeptikus
Luther

Frankfurt/M., Bern, 1983. 251 S.
Europäische Hochschulschriften: Reihe 23, Theologie. Bd. 189
ISBN 3-8204-7200-2   br. sFr. 63,--

«Was heißt glauben»? Es wird versucht, diesen ebenso fundamentalen wie kom-
plexen Begriff in seinen vielfachen Bedeutungen zu umschreiben: als Antwort und
damit als urliturgisches Geschehen; als transzendierenden Existenzvollzug; als
Gegenwart des Zukünftigen; als -immer angefochtene- Gewißheit: Während alle
Wissenschaft ihrem Wesen nach möglichst bedingungslose Erkenntnis anstreben
muß und darum nur relative Gewißheit erreichen kann, sind Glaubenssätze Aussagen
von bedingter Gewißheit - bedingt durch göttliches Handeln und auch durch
spezifisches menschliches Verhalten - und darum in dieser Bedingtheit von absoluter
Gewißheit. Darum ist Glaube nicht nur eine Fülle von Bewußtseinsakten, sondern ein
reales Geschehen in den ontologischen Tiefendimensionen.

Verlag Peter Lang Frankfurt a.M. · Bern · New York · Paris
Auslieferung: Verlag Peter Lang AG, Jupiterstr. 15, CH-3000 Bern 15
Telefon (004131) 321122, Telex pela ch 912 651, Telefax (004131) 321131